A PLEDGE WITH PURPOSE

A Pledge with Purpose

Black Sororities and Fraternities and the Fight for Equality

Gregory S. Parks

Matthew W. Hughey

NEW YORK UNIVERSITY PRESS

New York

NEW YORK UNIVERSITY PRESS
New York
www.nyupress.org

References to Internet websites (URLs) were accurate at the time of writing. Neither the author nor New York University Press is responsible for URLs that may have expired or changed since the manuscript was prepared.

Library of Congress Cataloging-in-Publication Data
Names: Parks, Gregory, 1974- author. | Hughey, Matthew W. (Matthew Windust), author.
Title: A Pledge with Purpose : Black Sororities and Fraternities and the Fight for Equality / Gregory S. Parks, Matthew W. Hughey.
Description: New York : New York University Press, 2020. | Includes bibliographical references and index. | Summary: "A Pledge with Purpose" explores Black sororities and fraternities and the role(s) that they play in the fight for equality"—Provided by publisher.
Identifiers: LCCN 2019029137 | ISBN 9781479823277 (cloth) | ISBN 9781479817283 (ebook) | ISBN 9781479859634 (ebook)
Subjects: LCSH: African American Greek letter societies—History—20th century. | Civil rights movements—United States—History—20th century. | African American student movements—History—20th century. | African American college students—Political activity—History—20th century.
Classification: LCC LC2781.7 .P37 2020 | DDC 378.1/982996073—dc23
LC record available at https://lccn.loc.gov/2019029137

New York University Press books are printed on acid-free paper, and their binding materials are chosen for strength and durability. We strive to use environmentally responsible suppliers and materials to the greatest extent possible in publishing our books.

Manufactured in the United States of America

10 9 8 7 6 5 4 3 2 1

Also available as an ebook

To our Big Brothers:

. . . for guiding the 4 Suns of the Nile and so many others:
Dean of Pledges Rob Byrd, "Southern Comfort"
Assistant Dean of Pledges Kirby Parker, "Quarter Pfunck"

. . . for forging Blue Genesis II: Σ. S. B. and more under the
Crescent Moon:
Dean of Pledges Frantz France Dautruche, "Smiley"
Assistant Dean of Pledges Terrence Morrow, "Dr. Seuss"

CONTENTS

Introduction

Black Greek "Racial Uplift"

In the popular imagination, black fraternities and sororities are caught between—to reference the ancient Greek mythology of Odysseus—the monster of Scylla and the whirlpool of Charybdis. On the one hand, the films of *Animal House* (1978), *School Daze* (1988), *Stomp the Yard* (2007), and *Burning Sands* (2017) all contextualized and popularized historically black Greek-letter organizations (BGLOs). Throughout televisual mediums, BGLOs are characterized as color-struck groups that embrace little more than identity politics and public "step show" performances. Romanticized and exoticized, BGLOs seem to exist as little more than caricatures to be laughed at or as colorful entertainers for whites who know little of Greek life on the other side of the color line.

On the other hand, the past few years of actual news coverage of these organizations have not been kind. Every handful of months, so it seems, a hazing-related injury or death is reported. The Alpha Phi Alpha fraternity had two deaths in 2018, one at the University of California, Riverside and the other at Lincoln University, Missouri; the Northwestern University chapter of Alpha Kappa Alpha sorority saw one pledge, suffering with anxiety and depression, commit suicide in 2017. In 2019 a pledge of Kappa Alpha Psi fraternity at Delaware State University died after crashing his car due to alleged sleep deprivation from hazing. In 2019 Omega Psi Phi fraternity ultimately halted all social and "pledge" activities in the wake of the collapse and death of a student who was a Division I football player at Georgia Tech. For many, death and violence are what define BGLOs.

However, these groups have a long and rich history of service, advocacy, resistance, and racial uplift. This story is the third way between that proverbial rock and hard place. The knowledge of what these organizations have done—and continue to do—charts a path not to myth and mist, but toward the facts and functions of BGLOs. Consider that this story is now well over a century old. In October 2005, the National Pan-Hellenic Council hosted its national convention in Chicago. In doing so, the body that is the umbrella organization for the nine major BGLOs celebrated its seventy-fifth anniversary. The event overlapped with another anniversary celebration that took place on November 19, 2005, at Cornell University. On that date, the first of these BGLOs began its centennial celebration at the place of its founding in 1906. Alpha Phi Alpha fraternity—brotherhood to the likes of Martin Luther King, Cornel West, Thurgood Marshall, Paul Robeson, and many others—began its yearlong celebration, featuring the publication of several in-house books, a traveling museum exhibit, and a PBS documentary. It also showcased the groundbreaking of the one-hundred-twenty million dollar Martin Luther King Jr. Memorial on the Mall in Washington, D.C., which was spearheaded by Alpha Phi Alpha. These events culminated in a centennial anniversary convention in July 2006 in Washington. In 2008, 2011, 2013, and 2014, Alpha Kappa Alpha sorority, Kappa Alpha Psi fraternity, Omega Psi Phi fraternity, Delta Sigma Theta sorority, and Phi Beta Sigma fraternity, respectively, celebrated their centennials.

It is no accident that many of the best and brightest African American leaders of yesteryear and today have come from the ranks of these organizations—also known as the Divine Nine (fraternities—Alpha Phi Alpha, Kappa Alpha Psi, Omega Psi Phi, Phi Beta Sigma, and Iota Phi Theta; sororities—Alpha Kappa Alpha, Delta Sigma Theta, Zeta Phi Beta, and Sigma Gamma Rho). BGLO members such as Garrett Morgan (inventor of the traffic light) and Dr. Mae Jemison (engineer and astronaut) charted new courses in science. Men and women like Earl B. Dickerson and Dorothy Height left an indelible mark on the areas of racial uplift and women's rights. Visionaries such as Mary McLeod Bethune (founder of Bethune-Cookman College) and Dr. Charles Wesley (historian and college president) were towering figures in education.

Born at the dawn of the twentieth century, BGLOs not only served to solidify bonds between African American college students but also had (and continue to have) a vision and sense of purpose: civic action, community service, philanthropy, and high scholasticism. BGLOs were an integral part of what W. E. B. Du Bois of Alpha Phi Alpha termed "the talented tenth"—the top 10 percent of African Americans, who would serve as a cadre of educated, upper-class, motivated individuals and would acquire the professional credentials, skills, and economic (as well cultural) capital to assist the remaining 90 percent of the race with attaining socioeconomic equality. The founding impetus for BGLOs is intertwined with the history of collegiate literary societies, white college fraternities and sororities, black benevolent and secret societies, the black church, and the broader racial milieu that Phi Beta Sigma member Alain Leroy Locke coined as the "New Negro" ethos. Together, BGLOs' collective history bespeaks fidelity to the overarching principles of racial uplift.

BGLOs have been influential in the African American community both historically and contemporarily. Unlike their white counterparts, BGLO members remain committed to and active in these organizations long after their college years. As such, BGLOs have served as civic as much as fraternal organizations. After a century, however, and despite being almost three million members strong, the public knows little about BGLOs beyond their high-energy step shows and periodic wrangling with hazing incidents.

And in just the past few years, scholars have begun to explore the role that black fraternal organizations have played in African Americans' quest for civil rights and social equality. Yet, there has yet to emerge a narrative that takes on BGLOs' racial uplift strategies and their lasting legacy of community service, civil rights, policy agendas, and philanthropic service. Accordingly, we have written *A Pledge with Purpose* to both fill this gap and compare these organizations not only with one another, but in relation to their own variations over time, as each of these organizations shifted tact toward differing racial uplift ends with variegated strategies. One of the challenges to doing this work, as we admit up front, is that the archives from which we have drawn our research are uneven across BGLOs. Some organizations have robust records, particularly when it comes to organizational periodicals. Others have limited archives in that regard. Also, even though each BGLO has a national history book, those texts are not even in their coverage of their respective organizations' racial uplift work. Hence, treatment within this book is not necessarily even across organizations.

Uplifting the Race: Through the Years

BGLOs are unique, important, and relevant social institutions, grounded in both the African and the American social and cultural exigencies. Even more, they and their members have served as significant forces in the struggle for social equality of people of African descent. In this book we explore the complexity of this racial uplift activism and agenda. *A Pledge with Purpose* charts the arc of African American experiences through the lens of BGLOs. Specifically, we advance a historical narrative that uncovers how BGLOs were shaped by, and labored to transform, the changing social, political, and cultural landscape of black America. By moving through varied historical eras toward the present, we center our analysis on the first eight BGLOs' signature social uplift programs and the variations across these black fraternities and sororities. BGLOs and their attendant national programs changed in their pace and intensity both over the years and in relation to one another. For example, BGLOs' early focus (1906–1929) was on promoting black access to higher education and strategies for success once students were enrolled. However, these programs manifested differently from organization to organization. While fraternities like Alpha Phi Alpha and Omega Psi Phi concentrated their energies on the reeducation and social ties of the black already elite in the northeastern United States, Phi Beta Sigma and Zeta Phi Beta expanded south to draw their membership from and institute their educational programs amid a decidedly black working and middle class. Similarly, Delta Sigma Theta recruited black women from the U.S. South to move to the West (particularly California) to gain employment as teachers. Comparatively, when the civil rights era began (1941–1963), BGLOs were at the forefront of the battle for de jure equality. Yet each organization had a slightly different picture of how de facto equality would be achieved. While some organizations centered their energies on lawsuits and accompanying social science evidence to sway the courts, others labored to engage in voter registration, in the establishment of international chapters in Africa and the

West Indies that were intimately connected with decolonization, or in local cooperative programs with doctors and civil rights organizations to eliminate health disparities in areas like the Mississippi Delta.

What Is Racial Uplift?

In the following chapters we examine how each of the first eight BGLOs engaged in "racial uplift" praxis in six separate yet sometimes overlapping areas:

1. Civil activism (civil and human rights litigation)
2. Civic education (informing African Americans about their civil duties, responsibilities, and rights, especially as pertaining to enfranchisement and public office)
3. Public policy (largely federal and state-level prodding to produce or practice civil and human rights procedures and legal prosecution)
4. Philanthropy (fund-raising for scholarships and/or specific people/ areas in need)
5. Community service (mentoring and informal teaching)
6. Community organizing (recruiting for direct action, e.g., boycotting or civil disobedience)

A Pledge with Purpose thereby serves as a critical barometer for, and reflection of, both the collective African American racial uplift struggle and the heterogeneous, highly variable, and sometimes antagonistic strategies of black Americans in their great (and unfinished) march toward freedom.

In so doing, we reveal some important insights. For instance, not all organizations were equally engaged in all these areas at the same time. And many of these organizations' commitment to one or more of the above six areas certainly waxed and waned over time. Moreover, members of some groups took up areas of racial uplift when their organizations went in differing directions. These insights all gesture toward important organizational questions: Why did organizations change or keep their tact? Why did certain organizational ideals appeal in certain practices? Did members work with and/or against their organizations' foci? And finally, to what extent did BGLOs structure their members' racial uplift activism in relation to the larger racial zeitgeist? On top of these, some unpleasant questions (especially for members and/or fans of BGLOs) are raised: Did "racial uplift" exclude those not in the middle or upper classes of black life? Did black fraternities traffic in or at least fail to confront much of the sexism and patriarchy that pushed their sorority colleagues to the margins of racial uplift activism? These questions and more are explored in the following chapters.

1

The Preconditions for Uplift (1865–1905)

In 1865 the Civil War ended, and with it what was called the "peculiar institution"[1]—the institution of legal chattel slavery. During that year, state by state, nearly four million African Americans were released from slavery. The famed African American educator Booker T. Washington recalled the day he was told of the end of slavery. He was nine years old, living in Virginia:

> As the great day drew nearer, there was more singing in the slave quarters than usual. It was bolder, had more ring, and lasted later into the night. Most of the verses of the plantation songs had some reference to free-dom. . . . Some man who seemed to be a stranger (a United States officer, I presume) made a little speech and then read a rather long paper—the Emancipation Proclamation, I think. After the reading we were told that we were all free, and could go when and where we pleased. My mother, who was standing by my side, leaned over and kissed her children, while tears of joy ran down her cheeks. She explained to us what it all meant, that this was the day for which she had been so long praying, but fearing that she would never live to see.[2]

In short succession, the U.S. Congress passed the Thirteenth, Fourteenth, and Fifteenth Amendments—known as the Reconstruction Amendments—which were meant to provide some constitutional basis for black legal, and ostensibly social, equality.[3] Subsequently, blacks witnessed an almost immediate rise in political and economic agency and power.[4]

However, within a decade after the end of the Civil War, southern white Democrats began to implement strategies that worked to reverse these gains. By 1877 the disputed presidential election of Republican Rutherford B. Hayes was resolved by a backroom deal in which Democrats conditioned the inauguration on federal troop withdrawal from the South and the implicit agreement that the federal government would not interfere in southern politics.[5] That year marked the end of Reconstruction, and legal racial segregation—what would be known as "Jim Crow"—began to spread, state to state, throughout the nation.[6]

The following decades would be referred by race and racism scholars as the Nadir—the time period that scholars consider the lowest point of American race relations (1877–1923). During this period, blacks witnessed a spike in lynchings and disenfranchisement.[7] And some fail to realize that the Ku Klux Klan and the practice of lynching originated *after* slavery.

In this milieu, blacks and their allies of other racial groups helped create a host of institutions out of the necessity to resist racial intimidation, exploitation, and oppression.[8] For example, some white northern industrialists suggested that it would be the top 10 percent of the black race that should be educated to lead the other 90 percent of blacks toward social and economic parity with whites. As Henry Lyman Morehouse (for whom Morehouse College was named) stated in 1896, "In the discussion concerning Negro education we should not forget the talented tenth man. An ordinary education may answer for the nine men of mediocrity; but if this is all we offer the talented tenth man, we make a prodigious mistake.... The tenth man, with superior natural endowment, symmetrically trained and highly developed, may become a mightier influence, a greater inspiration to others than all the other nine, or nine times nine like them."[9] However, it would be the noted sociologist W. E. B. Du Bois who would popularize the term "talented tenth" as the cadre of blacks with academic training and resources who should uplift African Americans.[10] Accordingly, in 1905, he and more than two dozen other activists met during the Niagara Conference—the precursor to the National Association for the Advancement of Colored People (NAACP)—to search for approaches to black freedom.[11] It was within this cultural environment that academic institutions, such as Cornell University and Howard University, played a role in influencing how the black fraternal movement would unfold over the years—birthing the first collegiate black fraternity in 1906 (Alpha Phi Alpha at Cornell) and third black fraternity in 1911 (Omega Psi Phi at Howard).[12]

But these events and institutions did not suddenly spring out of the ether. Rather, there were key activities, ideologies, and practical strategies at play long before 1906, and even long before emancipation in 1865.

That is, it was not only the racial zeitgeist of the early twentieth century and the accompanying campus environments that informed black Greek-letter organizations' (hereafter BGLOs) founders of the type of organizations to create, but these men and women were also inspired by their engagement with a host of other types of organizations—the black church, black secret societies, collegiate literary societies, and white collegiate fraternities.[13]

The Black Church

The early black church arose in the 1770s out of the conditions of slavery and, ultimately, racial segregation.[14] In fact, "whenever these [religious] societies were organized, they began to protest against White prejudice and neglect, and with the objective of providing not only for religious needs, but for social service, mutual aid and solidarity among people of African descent."[15] The black church served as the center of social and cultural life in black communities and influenced BGLOs by providing their founders with guiding principles.[16] In fact, a predominant number of BGLO members were active parishioners of local black churches and viewed BGLO membership as supplemental to their spiritual life.[17] Additionally, black churches lent BGLOs the ideals of brotherhood/sisterhood, community service, and civic action.[18]

Black Secret Societies

Black secret societies evolved as blacks sought ways to deepen personal ties, embrace ritualized processes, and deal with their exclusion from white secret societies.[19] These organizations, such as the Masons and Elks (quasi-secretive mutual aid societies), offered spiritual, psychological, and material uplift.[20] By providing educational opportunities, purchasing property, and caring for the sick, widows, and orphans,[21] these fraternal groups sought to build a community, while also combating the effects of systemic oppression.[22] Moreover, the formal organization of black secret societies provided a level of power, particularly the power of group solidarity, to which they previously did not have access.[23] Utilizing this power allowed black secret societies a larger public voice on political issues.

The first of these societies emerged in response to the oppression blacks experienced during the American Revolution.[24] Most notably, in 1775, Prince Hall founded a version of black Freemasonry (now known as Prince Hall Freemasonry).[25] Throughout the nineteenth century, over sixty other black secret societies were founded.[26] The first of these societies emerged in response to the oppression blacks experienced during the American Revolution.[27] Among these societies were the Grand United Order of Odd Fellows (1843), the Knights of Pythias (1864), and the Improved Benevolent Protective Order of the Elks of the World (1898).[28] By 1915, roughly two-thirds of prominent blacks were members of multiple black secret societies.[29] Freemasonry's inherent link to Christianity and emphasis on truth, charity, brotherhood, and community building made it the model of early black secret societies.[30] Indeed, early black secret societies, including Prince Hall Freemasonry, encouraged members to "respect and help each other, work to end slavery, and show love to all humanity."[31]

Black secret societies played three major roles in the development of black fraternities. First, just as black secret societies were created to give members "a sense of social relationship and responsibility to one another"[32] under the theme of racial uplift, black fraternities were created in response to racial hostility experienced by black members of colleges and universities.[33] Second, black secret societies provided black fraternities with an effective organizational structure to carry out their mandates.[34] Finally, black fraternities were organized under the same multidimensional purpose of providing mutual support to members and the greater black community.[35] The role that black secret societies played in the development of black fraternities can be attributed to the fact that many black fraternity founders either were members of black secret societies or were connected to black secret societies through their already established family relationships.[36]

Created in response to the oppression experienced by free blacks in the late eighteenth and nineteenth centuries, black secret societies were trailblazers in social change and social reform.[37] Although black benevolent societies and churches provided various levels of support and community, black secret societies also included an organizational structure that unified local chapters, regional areas, and the national body.[38] This organizational structure allowed for the perpetuation of black secret societies and provided a framework for leadership training. Additionally, and unlike other black fraternal groups or churches, black secret societies had restrictive membership and secret rituals that made them, for later years, a nearly perfect model for the clandestine operation of BGLOs under the nose of Jim Crow.[39]

In addition to these influences, the 1903 formation of Sigma Pi Phi (known as the "Boule," which means "a council of noblemen") in Philadelphia was inspirational to the soon-to-be-founders of collegiate-based organizations. The most successful (and now oldest) African American Greek-lettered organization, Sigma Pi Phi, was founded because black professionals were not offered membership in most of the mainstream professional and cultural associations because of their leadership by whites and the climate of the day. The Boule's founders, including black professionals such as physicians, dentists, and pharmacists (Robert J. Abele, Edwin C. Howard, Eugene T. Hinson, Algernon B. Jackson, Henry McKee Minton, and Richard J. Warrick), quickly prevented undergraduate students from joining and never founded any college chapters. Minton wrote that members would not be "selected on the basis of brains alone but in addition to congeniality, culture and good fellowship; that they shall have behind them [at initiation] a record of accomplishment, not merely be men of promise and good education" and that Sigma Pi Phi would contain the "best of Skull and Bones of Yale and of Phi Beta Kappa."[40] Despite this extreme exclusivity, as a Greek-lettered organization it provided an early template to the eight organizations that would be founded over the next two decades.

Collegiate Literary Societies

Literary societies were founded at colleges and universities between 1760 and 1860 in response to the restrictive nature of the American collegiate curriculum.[41] They filled the void left in the restrictive curriculum by feeding students' desires to develop debating, writing, and public speaking skills.[42] Literary societies were on the decline decades before the first black fraternity was created, yet they indirectly influenced black fraternities because of their influence on white fraternities, which was a source of inspiration for BGLOs.[43] Literary societies existed at black colleges as early as the mid- to late nineteenth century.[44] They also uniquely contributed to black fraternities by providing them with a template for a broad sense of intellectualism.[45] Finally, literary societies contributed to the structure of black fraternities through their use of secret initiation rites, mottoes, and badges to distinguish members.[46]

White College Fraternalism

Though literary societies ultimately lost traction due to declining interest, students who sought to obtain more rights, correct the perceived wrongs of college administrations, and facilitate social outlets, developed college fraternities.[47] The first white college fraternity, Phi Beta Kappa, was founded at the College of William and Mary in 1776, and by the 1820s the Greek-letter fraternity movement had become firmly established at colleges and universities across New York and Virginia.[48] Early fraternities contributed to student life by affording students a social network and engaging them in social activities.[49] In addition to setting goals for individual members, including high academic standards and the pursuit of excellence, fraternities also provided social escapes for students through drinking, card playing, smoking, and womanizing.[50] White fraternities served as the framework for the creation of their black counterparts.[51] Just as white fraternities provided a social escape for white students, black fraternities "filled a niche in the college experience" for black students.[52]

The Seeds of Black Greek-Letter Organizations

The germinating synthesis of ideals and practices common in the black church, black secret societies, collegiate literary societies, and white collegiate fraternities began to take root in the institutional spaces of places like Cornell University and Howard University. These spaces began to nourish practices that would become the form and function of BGLOs founded on those campuses in the following years.[53]

For example, prior to the founding of Howard University in 1867, few blacks had access to a formal education.[54] The school grew to symbolize the growing racial consciousness and desires for equality among the black populace.[55] Freed slaves sought outlets for increasing their education, whether through self-teaching or unrecognized (both formal and informal) academic programs.[56] At its founding, Howard was one of the few integrated universities to admit comparable numbers of black and white students.[57] Howard would go on to excel at mobilizing black students to become involved in racial uplift activism during college and after graduation.[58] As the university shared values of education and social justice, expectations for moral high mindedness set the tone for the fraternities and sororities established at Howard.[59]

The scenario was different at predominately white colleges and universities. In 1865, Cornell University was founded to make education more applicable to the workforce and to "develop the individual man . . . as a being intellectual, moral, and religious; and to bring the force of the individual to bear on society."[60] According to Cornell's great seal, written by founder Ezra Cornell and refined by Andrew Dickson White, the university's first president, "I would found an institution where any person can find instruction in any study."[61] Prior to 1900, however, fewer than a dozen black students were enrolled at Cornell.[62] But by 1918, less than two decades later, forty-three black students were attending the university, with their numbers continuing to increase in each successive year.[63] Yet despite increased black enrollment rates at Cornell, many of these students left records describing their isolation from the larger, white student population.[64]

To fully understand this environment, we must first understand the increasing black student population in the early 1900s in the context of U.S. Supreme Court's 1896 *Plessy v. Ferguson* decision.[65] Again, this was the period of the Nadir. One of the central debates of the day was how African Americans could and should be uplifted, bookended by ideologies of Booker T. Washington on one hand and W. E. B. Du Bois on the other. Black students at Cornell, and their families, were concerned with these issues for both academic and pragmatic ends.

For example, Alpha Phi Alpha founder Henry Arthur Callis's grandfather was born into slavery but was eventually liberated by Union soldiers; Callis was ultimately educated at the Hampton Institute (now Hampton University) and went on to become a successful pastor within the African Methodist Episcopal Zion Church.[66] The status of his relatives as former slaves was a significant influence on Callis's perspective on the "Negro" experience in the United States. His father was stolen from slavery at a young age by Union troops, and his mother was stolen from Maryland with her child in her arms.[67] On the subject of his relatives' status as slaves, Callis once remarked, "Was not that enough to found Alpha with its fundamental purposes of education and unfettered citizenship?"[68] Indeed, Callis himself had been deeply influenced by Du Bois,[69] and it could be said that Du Bois had an effect on the founding of Alpha Phi Alpha. Du Bois's early writings (e.g., *The Philadelphia Negro* [1899] and *The Souls of Black Folk* [1903]) had been the topic of discussion in the Social Study Club (the literary society that served as the direct precursor to Alpha Phi Alpha's formation).[70] That relationship would continue to prove influential as in 1909 the Epsilon Chapter of Alpha Phi Alpha at the University of Michigan would initiate Du Bois as an honorary member.[71]

After his graduation from high school and before beginning at Cornell University, Callis spent some time in Boston, where some of his relatives lived. Callis stated that during his time there he met several other Ivy League students of African descent, yet felt that they were still not accepted as equals in society, despite their high academic pedigree.[72] During this period after Reconstruction, many African Americans began to seek higher education, and Cornell University began accepting some such students.[73] Some of these students lived in the Ithaca, New York, community, which had a history of action in the Civil War and civil rights movement, with a stop on the Underground Railroad and appearances by famous African American activists.[74] The African American students quickly began socializing with each other as they were ostracized from white students outside of the classroom.[75]

It was among these students that Callis began his studies at Cornell in the fall of 1905, striving to become a physician. Though there were other African American students enrolled at the university, retention rates were low and many of the few African American students did not return for the next year.[76] The majority of the blacks on campus worked their way through school, often in the houses of established fraternities.[77] Exposure to these organizations, coupled with the isolating experience of being a minority at a predominately white institution, instilled a desire in African American male students to form a fraternal order of their own.[78] While at Cornell, Callis remarked in 1906 (the year in which Alpha Phi Alpha was founded) that "discrimination and the stigma of segregation were large in one-third of our nation. In the remaining two-thirds, discrimination was overtly supported and habitually practiced."[79]

Given their collective understanding of discrimination and the need to organize to combat the effects of Jim Crow, a small group of African American students began having weekly social study club meetings at each other's residences.[80] The first group of men included Callis, Charles Henry Chapman, George Biddle Kelly, Nathaniel Allison Murray, Robert Harold Ogle, Morgan T. Phillips, Charles Cardoza ("C.C.") Poindexter, Vertner Woodson Tandy, and George Tompkins.[81]

Late in the fall 1905 semester, with Poindexter as their president, these students formed the Social Study Club, holding informal meetings throughout the academic year.[82] The chief focus of the organization was its members' social and academic pursuits; however, the group was also concerned with African Americans' struggle for racial equality.[83] While the Social Study Club flourished during the 1905–6 academic year, the idea of forming a fraternity soon gained traction among a number of the members.[84]

BGLOs on predominately white campuses provided black undergraduate students a sense of community and might in the face of exclusion and ostracism.[85] These organizations provided support for scholarship, service, and socializing.[86] Though the aims remained the same, BGLOs on predominately black campuses differed slightly in their impetus. Like white fraternities—which differed along the lines of class, status, and pedigree—BGLOs also felt those same divisions.[87] In fact, it was in response to the exclusivity and "snobbishness toward the darker students and those not from prominent families" by the Alpha Phi Alpha Chapter at Howard University that Omega Psi Phi would be founded in 1911.[88]

2

The Genesis of Black Greek-Letter Organizations (1906–1922)

In this chapter we proceed with an organization-by-organization review of the context of the founding of each fraternity and sorority, focusing on how the leaders applied their worldview on uplift to both the principles and programming of each organization, with attention to their attitudes toward and engagement with racial uplift praxis. Moreover, given that their respective founding years run from 1906 to 1922, we offer some insights into the early years of uplift work of each of the first seven organizations, as the others came into existence. These early years highlight the various ways in which the respective organizations sought to actualize their missions beyond themselves.

Alpha Phi Alpha Fraternity

As introduced in the previous chapter, members of the Cornell University Literary Society met in March 1906.[1] Led by Callis, the other members—Chapman, Kelly, Murray, Ogle, Phillips, Poindexter, Tandy, and Tompkins—decided that the Literary Society should be renamed Alpha Phi Alpha.[2] By the May 23, 1906, meeting, the new name was formally approved. In the fall semester of the following academic year, the minutes from the October 27, 1906, meeting show that the members again voted on the name Alpha Phi Alpha, this time acknowledging a more fraternal influence by stating, "Henceforth the group [will] be known by these three Greek letters."[3] Three days later, October 30, three men were initiated into the society—Eugene Kinckle Jones, Lemuel Graves, and Gordon Jones.[4]

However, at the organization's November 6, 1906, meeting, the fraternity idea was again raised but went unresolved. Poindexter was reported to have said that he knew of no "historical background" on which African Americans could base a fraternity.[5] Realizing the inevitability of the society's move toward a fraternal orientation, Poindexter failed to attend the group's next meeting on December 4, tendering his letter of resignation, which was read by Callis. At this meeting, the majority voted for the organization to formally become a fraternity. The seven founders, designated "Jewels" by the organization, were Callis, Chapman, Jones, Kelley, Murray, Ogle, and Tandy.[6]

Callis encapsulated the thrust of the fledgling fraternity, in part, when noting the following: "Society offered us narrowly circumscribed opportunity and no security; out of our need, our fraternity brought social purpose and social action."[7] Elsewhere, he noted that "Alpha Phi Alpha was born in the shadows of slavery and on the lap of disenfranchisement. We proposed to . . . bring leadership and vision to the social problems of our communities and the nation; to fight with courage and self-sacrifice every bar to the democratic way of life."[8] Indeed, the aim of Alpha Phi Alpha was to "destroy all prejudices," and the desire to join in the cause arose on other campuses and in other communities.[9] Not unlike its white counterparts, Alpha Phi Alpha expanded, chartering its second chapter at Howard University (Beta Chapter) in 1907.[10]

The fraternity quickly grew and matured. It held its Third General Convention in Philadelphia from December 27 to December 30, 1910.[11] The *Howard University Journal* stated that this convention marked the moment when the fraternity "passed from the formative and constructive stage into an organization based on fundamental ideas and universal truths."[12]

Members of Alpha Phi Alpha would embody the fraternity's focus. For example, founded in 1910, the National Urban League was one of the chief civil rights organizations, and many of its early leaders would be drawn from the ranks of Alpha Phi Alpha. Its first executive secretary, Brother George Edmund Haynes, an Alpha Phi Alpha brother and trained sociologist, played a key role in getting the organization, then titled the Committee on Urban Conditions Among Negroes, off the ground.[13] Under his leadership, the National Urban League addressed issues facing the great numbers of African Americans who moved into the urban centers of America in the early decades of the twentieth century.

In the following year of 1911, the fraternity established Alumni chapters, the first of them in Louisville, Kentucky (Alpha Lambda), to allow those men who were not enrolled in a university or whose university did not have a chapter of the fraternity an opportunity to participate in the brotherhood.[14] In recruiting new members, the focus of the Alpha Phi Alpha brothers was to rush members of "scholarship, fellowship, and devotion to the cause."[15]

At the Sixth General Convention, from December 29 to December 31, 1913,[16] the fraternity journal, the *Sphinx*, was established.[17] It was made to be a quarterly journal with a subscription cost of fifty cents[18] and intended to contain fraternity news and editorials.[19] It would serve as a major chronicle of the fraternity's history and vision. In the inaugural issue of the *Sphinx*, in March 1914, it chronicled that brothers from different chapters came together at the General Convention for "the general uplifting and bettering of an organization which stands for the uplifting of the Race." Looking beyond the fraternity, George William Cook, secretary of Howard University, called for Alpha Phi Alpha members to "assist the NAACP in its noble work of curbing prejudice against the race."[20] Heeding Cook's call, every member pledged support for the NAACP.[21] This commitment should have been of little surprise because in reflecting on the purpose of the fraternity, it was noted that Alpha Phi Alpha's purpose was to "labor for the greatest purpose that can animate the conscience of man . . . to try to lessen the painful achings of the souls of black folk—discriminative prejudice."[22] The founding brothers sought "to accomplish the great and imperative need of humanity—equal justice."[23] In January 1914, chapters of the fraternity underscored this vision by sending letters of thanks to Oswald G. Villard, a founding member of the NAACP, for his efforts on behalf of colored people.[24]

In July 1914, when World War I arose, many African Americans hoped that the war would bring about the demise of racial inequality in America. Large numbers of African American men had served in the armed forces throughout the war, and Alpha Phi Alpha successfully lobbied for a government military camp to train African American officers.[25] The training camp was in Iowa. Despite the success of the training camp, the military remained segregated and unequal.[26]

In the June 1915 issue of the *Sphinx*, Roscoe Conkling Giles, a member of one of the first groups of initiates into Alpha Phi Alpha and the first African American graduate of Cornell Medical School, wrote about the state of the race during that period. He noted that progress had been made regarding race relations and vis-à-vis the conflict between the

North and South. However, he noted that northerners had become less active in vindicating African Americans' rights and indifferent in defending them from the "assaults of the enemy."[27] Giles then challenged the men of Alpha Phi Alpha to actively fight against prejudice and discrimination.[28] During the same period, Zeta Chapter (Yale University) initiate William M. Ashby published a book, *Redder Blood*, offering solutions to the race question and "refut[ing] the many superficial and unsatisfactory solutions that law-makers would impose upon us."[29]

While the organization was growing, in its first ten years (1906–1916) the fraternity had failed to develop an official program for racial uplift. However, an article by Frederick H. Miller in the April 1916 issue of the *Sphinx*, titled "To Alumni," articulated his belief that one of the fraternity's goals should be to recruit intelligent community leaders as undergraduates so that they can later attempt "to fully emancipate the downtrodden millions and lead the twenty millions of tomorrow to an abiding place in the history."[30] He argued that the Alpha Phi Alpha spirit was what was needed to break African Americans' obeisance to whites; he went on to add that in this struggle, no organization was greater for "the future of the American Negro" than Alpha Phi Alpha.[31]

Organized racial uplift work began in earnest that year. Most of the growth of chapters had occurred in the North and Midwest, and in 1916 the fraternity began to contemplate establishing a chapter at a southern university, to, in their words, "do the race a great good."[32] In Connecticut, Zeta Chapter reported that it had been involved in the new movement in the country to uplift African Americans, specifically by being engaged in social service work.[33] In the Midwest, members of Epsilon Chapter (University of Michigan) were active in organizing a local branch of the NAACP.[34] In Philadelphia, members of Rho Chapter—the first citywide chapter—developed a Racial Welfare Committee dedicated to offering a series of lectures in large churches to discuss issues pertaining to racial conditions and developments.[35]

Despite these efforts, there remained debate among the membership as to the fraternity's purpose. In his article titled "The Aim of Alpha Phi Alpha Fraternity," which appeared in the December 1916 issue of the *Sphinx*, Alpha brother Numa P. G. Adams proposed that the fraternity's purpose be to work for "the higher education of the Negro," which would entail providing education where lacking or encouraging it where extant.[36] On the other hand, the fraternity could devote itself to social work. Adams believed that the focus should be on higher education because African Americans needed more educated individuals to lead the race.[37]

These debates spread through the fraternity. Back on the campus of Cornell University, in 1917 members of the founding chapter held debates on subjects "concerning the present day Negro."[38] They hoped to broaden this dialogue to the wider public in hopes that it would be an educational opportunity for them.[39] Later that spring semester the Cornell chapter created a weekly public forum in which African Americans could hear and discuss issues their race was facing.[40] During the same period, Zeta Chapter went beyond their regular "smokers" (named after social get-togethers in which attendees smoked and socialized) for African American Yale students for the "benefits of association and solidarity" and their musical and literary club.[41] They also helped New Haven high school students plans for college.[42]

Only one year into what became known as the Great Migration (1916–70) of African Americans from the South to the North and West, Harvard University chapter members attempted to solidify the "proper racial and social consciousness" among the members of the fraternity by having regular discussions on topics such as the "Migration of the Negroes."[43] In Philadelphia (Rho Chapter), members planned a series of lectures and public meetings in an effort to increase their work for good among all people of color.[44] At the University of Pittsburgh (Omicron Chapter), alumnus and attorney R. L. Vann was "instrumental in securing employment for about two hundred and fifty colored men" in Pittsburgh.[45] More generally, chapters on the East Coast distributed information to boys in YMCAs in an effort to dispel beliefs that college would be too expensive and thus unattainable.[46]

The year 1917 saw Alpha Phi Alpha, particularly through issues of the *Sphinx*, debating the ambit of its racial uplift vision—advocating broadening it in various directions or narrowing and sharpening its focus. For instance, in one 1917 article titled "Ideals for Which Alpha Phi Alpha Stands," J. M. Sampson argued that the fraternity operated on the idea that knowledge is the most effective means of combating prejudice.[47] The aforementioned Numa P. G. Adams wrote "The Place of Fraternity Life in Negro College Life," and stated that fraternities aid students in larger universities to escape a feeling of isolation and social ostracism. Students organize into fraternities "for their own protection and for social advantage."[48] He went on to state that these fraternities form "a strong bond of union among the Negro college men who are destined to become the leaders of tomorrow."[49] However, the most definitive assessment came from one of the founding "Jewels," George Biddle Kelley. In his "The History and Purpose of Alpha Phi Alpha," Kelley made it plain; Alpha Phi Alpha was founded, in part, to show that African American college men were "united for race uplift."[50]

With the United States reaching a critical point in its conflict with Germany in World War I, Alpha Phi Alpha began its initial movement to obtain positions of leadership in military service. After the United States declared a state of war on April 6, 1917, Beta Chapter (Howard University) successfully lobbied for the establishment of an Officers Training Camp.[51] With the backing of Howard University, Beta Chapter undertook the project of interviewing government officials in order to convince them that African American troops were fit to serve as officers.[52] On June 15, 1917, a training camp was established in Des Moines, Iowa.[53] In total, fifty-eight Alpha Phi Alpha members joined the camp.[54] The Fort Des Moines "Roll of Honor" at the completion of the training camp saw thirty-two members commissioned, with five commissioned members receiving a captaincy.[55] Of the remaining group of thirty-two, 90 percent were commissioned as first lieutenants.[56] Alpha brothers also made impacts in the Medical Officers Training Camp at Fort Des Moines, as fifteen brothers were selected as medical officers. Additionally, three Alpha brothers were chosen as dental officers.[57] At the close of the training camp, General President William Pollard issued a statement commending the organizing efforts of Beta Chapter. All told, the training camp saw nearly six hundred colored men receive commissions from the hands of the U.S. government. Considering this achievement, General President Pollard noted, "If for another ten years, we should do no more than continue as before to furnish to the various communities strong, influential men, we may yet consider that we have accomplished this year a feat sufficient to justify the existence and claims of the Fraternity. In this one accomplishment, we have rendered to our race a service that shall mark an epoch in its history."[58] Alpha Phi Alpha men were also engaged in direct action against racial discrimination. For example, in

1918 Alpha brother Daniel David Fowler wrote a letter detailing the rising occurrences of prejudice and discrimination in the state of Ohio.[59] He also requested help from the fraternity's general president, noting that white colleges in Ohio—i.e., Western Reserve, Case School of Applied Science, Oberlin, Ohio State University, and Wittenberg College—refused to accept African American students. Fowler suggested that an Alpha Phi Alpha delegation meet an Ohio representative to investigate and resolve the discriminatory acts.[60]

In response, Alpha brother W. H. Hughes sent a letter to all white college presidents in Ohio. He argued that there existed no reason why African Americans should not be admitted into any college having the Student Army Training Corps (SATC). Dr. Thwing, of Western Reserve University, replied that African Americans may be admitted when it is the usual custom of the institution.[61] Captain Francis M. Root, of Oberlin College, replied that without any orders from Washington he would take no notice of their communications and that while he intended no discrimination, he was to carry out the Army's orders that African American and white troops segregate.[62]

However, later that year the U.S. War Department ruled that students should be admitted regardless of race if they measure up to the standards of the corps, which did not include skin color, with "no segregation, no discrimination."[63] As a slow and small integration took place, white attitudes toward African American corps members were less than positive. Xi Chapter (Wilberforce University in Ohio) expressed regret over negative attitudes toward the inclusion of African Americans in the SATC organizations and advocated using the fraternity's influence to confront those attitudes throughout Ohio.[64]

By the conclusion of World War I in late 1918, Alpha Phi Alpha members found themselves transitioning to leadership positions due in part to the national change in focus—from wartime to peacetime activities—which would include a redoubling of efforts to achieve social equality in the civil sphere. For instance, the head of the National Urban League, Alpha brother George Haynes, stepped down to take a position in President Woodrow Wilson's administration as director of the newly established Division of Negro Economics.[65] In his place at the National Urban League, Haynes was succeeded by one of Alpha Phi Alpha's founders,

Eugene Kinckle Jones,[66] who would direct the organization until his retirement in 1941.[67]

Members of Beta Chapter published an article in an October 1919 issue of the *Sphinx*, noting how recently returned veterans were desirous of their "full portion of rights and privileges as any other class of people."[68] Acknowledging the racial intimidation and maltreatment of black veterans now returned to the United States, the members of Beta Chapter fell short of advocating the taking of the law into one's own hand, but they urged members to take every opportunity to "further the cause of freedom" that passed by them.[69] Furthermore, in the same October 1919 issue of the *Sphinx*, the fraternity highlighted the paradox of the U.S. government fighting to secure liberty abroad but flouting it with regard to a group of its own citizenry. A very pointed cartoon included among the last pages depicted a lynching with the caption, "The Records of History will show that the United States of America in 1918 fought valiantly for—Democracy IN EUROPE."[70] These words and images would prove prophetic in the summer of 1919—what would be called the "Red Summer" due to the blood spilled from the hundreds of deaths and casualties across the United States as a result of race riots that were most often characterized by white mobs attacking African Americans[71]—when Alpha Phi Alpha president Daniel Fowler urged the members to act in unanimity and "step in and strike a blow that will advance the interests of our race or prevent the occurrence of some dastardly outrage that may tend to depress our advancement."[72]

By the close of 1919, at the fraternity's Twelfth General Convention, the delegates discussed the current racial climate and issued "an appeal to the college men of the country to take the lead in the fight for equal citizenship."[73] At the fraternity convention, Emmett J. Scott spoke to a public audience about racial progress and urged "the stamping out of lynching, higher wages and improved labor condition," along with equal voting rights and adequate education facilities.[74] The fraternity's vice-president, Lucius Lee McGhee, harshly denounced the individuals (both within and outside of the fraternity) who advocated the doctrine of submission or meekness as embodied in a spirit of "this is good enough for us, and this is all we can expect" and went on to state that "we are in a battle for human rights."[75]

At the convention, Alpha brother Roscoe Giles asked that the Executive Committee of respective chapters should act as a Vigilance Committee.[76] In that capacity, they would work with social service agencies to safeguard the constitutional rights of African Americans. The purpose was intended to offer sound advice to the race in crises, to fight Negro-baiting propaganda in the press, to demand equal opportunity, and to keep the chapters informed of new developments.[77] Drawing upon his own professional expertise as a physician, Giles also suggested that members aid in collecting reliable health statistics on the Negro population to combat "medical" racism.[78]

Debates over the direction of the fraternity would not be easily settled, but the fraternity found somewhat of a compromise position at the General Convention of 1919 by turning toward efforts that encouraged young African Americans to pursue education. At the convention, the fraternity created the Commission on Graduate Work and Public Affairs.[79] The commission was tasked with the following duties:

> To (1) conduct the work of the Fraternity in aiding graduate brothers in all matters affecting the welfare of such brothers in their lives and their own personal advancement, (2) to meet at some place to be decided upon by the committee at a time prior to each convention and to recommend the action, if any, which the convention should take toward specific public questions affecting the Fraternity or any particular chapter, or the Negro people generally or any part of the same, and (3) to send out immediately a form of questionnaire to every Alpha Phi Alpha man whose address could be obtained ascertaining the name, address, occupation or profession, his standing, influence and connection in the community.[80]

During the discussion of the duties of the commission, Alpha brothers Simeon S. Booker and A. E. Robinson—along with other brothers— made remarks about an educational movement sponsored by Alpha Phi Alpha. The movement's initiative was toward "influencing colored students of the country to go to high school and college."[81] With the backing of the delegates of Pi Chapter (Case Western Reserve University), the Go-to-High-School, Go-to-College movement began. The program was intended to, as the name suggests, help young African American men matriculate through high school and college. Simply put, the program assumed that education would improve the state of the race.[82] The General Convention set aside the first week of June as "Go to College and Go to High School Week," during which chapters would distribute informative materials and send speakers to local schools and churches urging parents to put their children through higher education by showing the advantages of doing so.[83]

By the early 1920s, the Go-to-High-School, Go-to-College program took center stage in the fraternity's national movement. The aspirations of the campaign's committee were for the message to reach every high school and as many communities as possible either by personal contact or through distribution of educational leaflets, letters to pastors, meetings, conferences, and interviews.[84] General President McGee pushed the movement by sending letters that urged the following: "Each chapter is hereby called on to function in this movement. In this effort, we must not shoot in the air, but accomplish results. No feeble effort will be effective, but each chapter must put its part of the program over with interest and drive."[85] The results of the movement were immediately successful, as nearly all chapters responded. At the Thirteenth General Convention, held in Kansas City in 1920, attendees decided that the national Go-to-High-School, Go-to-College movement would continue for the next five years, with maximum efforts devoted to the campaign.[86] Additionally, each individual chapter was to carry on a campaign in its area that was best suited to local conditions.[87]

For example, for the second annual Go-to-High-School, Go-to-College campaign, the Commission of Graduate Work and Public Affairs sent out a letter with a slogan stating "We Must Reach One Million Pupils."[88] In addition, the commission distributed a folder with inspirational images and quotes, along with informational tables that showed the difference in wages between those who stayed in school and those who left school. Furthermore, General President Booker issued a statement that backed the slogan and set forth another goal: "We are on the verge of our great educational drive. The signal has been given, the slogan adopted, get your grip and with a united, steady dead pull, win. One hundred thousand homes must be reached and one million youth must be inspired to stay in school. The opportunity is at hand."[89] The movement again received national attention, that of President Warren G. Harding. In a letter penned to Brother Norman L. McGhee, Harding wrote that the results of the campaign of 1920 seemed to justify the repetition of the efforts and that there was still a great need to reduce illiteracy among African Americans.[90] All said, Alpha Phi Alpha's message reached far and wide, as Go-to-High-School, Go-to-College messages were found in schools, churches, newspapers, and public assemblies; on placards in stores and on street cars; and at individual conferences with parents and students.[91] The fraternity saw education directly connected to economics, which in turn was related to racial equality. For example, Sigma Chapter (Harvard University), worked toward community uplift in and around Boston by "furnishing the various social working organizations and churches with speakers for different occasions."[92] In addition to becoming involved with sponsoring forums, they also hoped to stimulate interest in business among African American men, as they believed that "inter-racial relations between the Negro and the white man will improve in proportion as the Negroes' economic condition is advanced."[93]

By 1921, General President Simeon S. Booker had pushed to advance the fraternity's ideals in three ways. First, he called for a renewed loyalty to the fraternity and its chapters on the part of members.[94] Second, given new fraternity policies, there became an increased focus on selecting the best men in every community for membership.[95] Third, with the burgeoning success of the Go-to-High-School, Go-to-College program, Booker called for members to grow the program and to offer twenty-five collegiate scholarships.[96]

That same year, abolitionist Frederick Douglass (who was a relative of one of the founders of Alpha Phi Alpha, Henry Arthur Callis) was posthumously inducted as an honorary member of the fraternity.[97] President Booker gave a speech regarding the inspiration and lessons Douglass could offer to fraternity members.[98] The following year, 1922, Alpha Phi Alpha members traveled to Douglass's home as a sort of pilgrimage.[99] Whether intended or not, Douglass' honorary membership served as a backdrop for the fraternity's racial uplift thrust. For example, one article in the February 1922 issue of the *Sphinx*, called for the black fraternities and sororities to meet once every four years to discuss things such as academics and racial policy.[100]

With the success of the Go-to-High-School, Go-to-College movement (in 1922 it was estimated that the forty-two chapters reached over two million children with its message),[101] and just before the fraternity convention in 1922, President Booker called for programs to expand beyond education to concentrate on the civic and economic affairs of all people.[102] In response, the 1922 December issue of the *Sphinx* called for the formation of an African American national bank in Harlem.[103] Members such as Benjamin T. Johnson began to more explicitly articulate a view of racial progress through the lens of economic uplift, noting that African Americans' growth as a community was directly correlated with African American business success.[104] Johnson predicted that fifty years in the future the development of the race would be led by African American businessmen, namely, bankers, brokers, manufacturers, and economists.[105]

These early years highlight that, first, race consciousness was central to the identity of Alpha Phi Alpha and, likely by extension, its members. Such race consciousness was evident in the ideals espoused and vision articulated in such places as the fraternity's national journal—the *Sphinx*. This race consciousness was intentional and concrete; however, the fraternity manifested it in an evolving fashion. Early in its history, this organizational race consciousness was exemplified by community service and philanthropy in educational endeavors. However, as the organizations grew and proliferated across the nation, the racial uplift work on the part of the fraternity and its members was evinced in economic endeavors and civic activism to shape public policy.

Alpha Kappa Alpha Sorority

The formation of Alpha Phi Alpha's Beta Chapter at Howard University, by founders Jones and Murray on December 20, 1907, saw the induction of charter members Welford W. Wilson, C. Edmund Smith, A. Peyton Cook, John A. McMurray, George A. Lyle, Carl A. Young, J. Oliver Morrison, Moses Alvin Morrison, James R. Chase, Cornelius S. Cowan, J. Russel Hunt, William D. Giles, Robert E. Giles, Daniel W. Bowles, Morris S. Walton, Junius W. Jones, and James E. Hayes.[106]

High school sweethearts, and later husband and wife, George A. Lyle and Ethel Hedgeman played crucial roles in expanding black "Greekdom" at the time.[107] Hedgeman entered Howard University in 1904, however she fell and was injured in her second year and had to take a break from her studies. Nevertheless, she stayed engaged with Howard

University life, especially the choir, the nearby YWCA, and Christian activities at the university. While at Howard, Hedgeman was inspired by the accounts of Tremaine Robinson, a faculty member at Howard who shared her sorority experiences from her time at the Women's College at Brown University in Providence, Rhode Island.

Based on these conversations, and with the support of Alpha founder George A. Lyle, Ethel Hedgeman began discussing with her friends and classmates the idea of creating a black Greek-letter sorority.[108] These colleagues—Beulah Burke, Lillie Burke, Margaret Flagg Holmes, Marjorie Hill, Lucy Slowe, Marie Woolfolk Taylor, Anna Easter Brown, and Lavinia Norman—are credited with creating Alpha Kappa Alpha in accordance with Hedgeman's vision on January 15, 1908.[109]

During their first organizational meeting, the students elected Hedgeman as temporary chairwoman, and organized committees to draft a constitution and determine nomenclature and symbols.[110] Two faculty members, Ethel T. Robinson and Elizabeth Appo Cook-Robinson, agreed to serve as informal advisors during the sorority's development.[111] The sorority sent Hedgeman and Woolfolk to meet with Howard's president and deans, and the group was granted permission to proceed with quick approval.[112]

The sorority decided to proceed under the name "Alpha Kappa Alpha" because those were the first Greek letters of the words contained in the sorority's motto "by culture and by merit."[113] The sorority's symbol was designated as the ivy leaf, and the sisters chose the colors of salmon pink and apple green, which symbolized "abundance of life, womanliness, fidelity, and love."[114]

Although Hedgeman was credited with envisioning Alpha Kappa Alpha, the newly adopted constitution required that the organization's president be a senior, so Slowe (who would in 1917 become the first black woman athletic champion after winning the women's singles title at the first American Tennis Association national championships)[115] was elected as the sorority's first president.[116] To ensure the sorority's continuity, the group invited seven honor student sophomores to join Alpha Kappa Alpha without initiation: Joanna Berry, Norma Boyd, Ethel Jones, Sarah Meriweather, Alice Murray, Carrie Snowden, and Harriet Terry.[117] Alpha Kappa Alpha began formal initiations the following year.[118]

Working in the context of patriarchal assumptions about the role of women—and uniquely, the place of educated black women at the time— the first few years of Alpha Kappa Alpha proceeded slowly and with some controversy. For instance, during the academic year of 1911–12 there were more than twenty active members of the sorority and the organization became an influential part of student life at Howard.[119] By the spring of 1912, however, founder Nellie Quander learned that several other newly initiated members of the sorority planned to change the colors, letters, and constitution of the sorority and to make it more active outside of Howard. On January 13, 1913, the entire twenty-two-member undergraduate chapter voted to transform the original Alpha Kappa Alpha into Delta Sigma Theta sorority (which we will discuss later in this chapter). Regardless, Quander and early initiates maintained the identity of Alpha Kappa Alpha and set up a three-person committee that successfully petitioned to incorporate the sorority as a perpetual entity: Alpha Kappa Alpha was nationally incorporated on January 29, 1913.

In its first few years the sorority helped to support fellow members by providing scholarship funds for both domestic and foreign studies. Moreover, members of the sorority encouraged and promoted black artists and social justice advocates, such as director and actor Nathaniel Guy, whose Washington, D.C., company performed African American playwright Angelina Weld Grimké's anti-lynching play *Rachel* in 1916. For the first production of the play the program read, "This is the first attempt to use that stage for race propaganda in order to enlighten the American people relating to the lamentable condition of ten millions of colored citizens in this free republic."[120]

In 1913 members of the sorority voted to extend their first honorary membership—the highest honor that the sorority can pay—to sociologist Jane Addams, the legendary founder of Chicago's Hull House and a pioneer in professionalizing social work as a discipline. That same year their second chapter was chartered at the University of Chicago, and the following year the third chapter (Gamma Chapter at the University of Illinois at Urbana-Champaign) was established.

By 1917 the sorority turned its attention to African American migrants from the Deep South by making toys for needy children at Freedman's Hospital in Washington, D.C., while the few chapters were instructed to offer programs in African American history, literature, music and art to promote and increase race consciousness at their respective college campuses.[121]

In the first ten years of existence, the sorority grew to a total of two hundred members and held its first national convention at Howard University in 1918. The convention was attended by less than a quarter of the membership,[122] but those present agreed to formalize the sorority even more. By 1920 the pledge was written and adopted, and members had become active in lobbying for anti-lynching legislation.[123] Also that year the Kappa Chapter (the seventh chapter at the time) was chartered on the campus of Butler University in Indiana.

A year later, in 1921, at the convention at the YWCA Recreation Center of Indianapolis, the sorority's crest was designed by Kappa Chapter member Phyllis Wheatley Waters and the official organ of the sorority, the *Ivy Leaf*, was established. The *Ivy Leaf* not only would serve as a medium of exchange for news and information about members and their activities but also would encourage members' creative writing efforts.[124]

The 1921 convention was arguably the sorority's most important to date, as the first action program to be implemented on a national scale was adopted. The sorority decided that "Founders Week" would be a set-aside period each January to commemorate the sorority's founding with a program of African American history, literature, and music or art to promote and increase race consciousness. The first issue of the *Ivy Leaf* was introduced that year.

In 1922 the sorority chapter at Temple University (Mu Chapter) held its first educational meeting with the objective to inspire young people to go on to high school and college and to raise money for the scholarship fund. Attendees raised thirty-three thousand dollars for the fund.[125] And the chapter at Ohio State University (Theta) held a charity ball with the presence of the "Anti-Lynching Crusade Girls." The Crusade Girls, who were all members of the sorority, netted the newly formed woman's league against lynching benefits both in cash and in publicity. The proceeds of the charity ball went to the filling of Christmas baskets for the worthy poor of the city.[126] In December of that year the same chapter hosted a Progressive Whist Dinner Party and gave the money earned to the fostering of Negro art and culture. They also offered a scholarship to the high school girl who at graduation had the best four-year record.[127]

Despite these early shudders of the organization, a review of the first years of the sorority reveals that members displayed a sincere interest in the philosophy of academic achievement and urged each other to dovetail attention to scholarship with sisterhood, race consciousness, and organizational commitment.

Kappa Alpha Psi Fraternity

In 1903, at Indiana University, there was an African American fraternal organization known as Alpha Kappa Nu Greek Society. While little is known about this organization, some speculate that too few black students could keep the organization running, as attendance was already sparse, and many of the black students at Indiana had to withdraw from school for economic reasons. Some historians have found that the organization had a membership of ten, which was the entire black population of Indiana University.[128]

Others speculate that former members and/or the reputation of Alpha Kappa Nu reached the ears of two of the soon-to-be founders of Kappa Alpha Psi—Elder Watson Diggs and Byron K. Armstrong, who had matriculated at Indiana University after having been students at Howard. They were already familiar with the Beta Chapter of Alpha Phi Alpha fraternity and the Alpha Chapter of Alpha Kappa Alpha sorority.

Regardless, when Diggs and Armstrong transferred to Indiana University, they immediately faced racial hostility and ostracism. The state of Indiana had fostered an atmosphere of resentment and violence toward people of color. Noted historian Howard Peckham observed of Indiana that "Hoosiers were not racially tolerant: they didn't like Indians and they didn't like Negroes. They had largely ousted Indians from the area, and had, by stipulations in the new constitution, forbidden Negros to enter the state."[129] Furthermore, journalist John Bartlow Martin covered the preponderance of "sundown towns" prior to World War I in Indiana, noting that many Indiana roadside signs read, "Nigger, Don't Let the Sun Set on You Here."[130]

According to fraternity historian William L. Crump in *The Story of Kappa Alpha Psi*, Diggs and Armstrong were routinely denied the use of entertainment and recreational facilities at Indiana and quickly became resolved to alleviate their treatment. Accordingly, they, along with seven other African American male students, began laying the ground-work for a fraternal organization and temporarily organized themselves under the name Alpha Omega. After research regarding the contours of a Greek-letter society, the nine men, plus one additional student, met to establish the fraternity.[131] On January 5, 1911, ten founding members came together to form Kappa Alpha Nu: Elder Watson Diggs, Ezra D. Alexander, Byron K. Armstrong, Henry T. Asher, Paul Caine, Guy L. Grant, Edward G. Irvin, John M. Lee, Marcus P. Blakemore, and George Edmonds.[132]

From the onset the fraternity would be based on Christian ideals and a fundamental purpose of achievement—as seen in the fraternity motto, "Achievement in every field of human endeavor—seeking to push Black youths to achieving accomplishments beyond even their own dreams or realities."[133] Diggs pushed for authenticity and uniqueness within the fraternity's rituals and organization, with such commitment to this ideal that he took a course on Greek heraldry while Armstrong studied Greek mythology. And while the fraternity organized itself around Christian ideals and achievement, another important element was inclusivity—not extending membership based solely on wealth or status.[134] The frater-nity was expected to become a national organization, and by the end of the 1910–11 school year the founding members had filed their applica-tion for incorporation.

The fledgling fraternity faced an uphill battle for recognition on the campus of Indiana University and in Bloomington. While the organiza-tion may have been officially incorporated in Indiana, the university's administration refused to grant the fraternity a charter; accordingly, the group went unrecognized on campus. Additionally, fraternity members were unable to obtain meeting spaces on campus and encountered simi-lar obstacles when trying to secure a fraternity house. Unrelenting per-sistence and fortitude eventually afforded the fraternity marginal access to rights and privileges enjoyed by their white counterparts and rental of a small house.[135] These victories at Indiana were matched by the charter-ing of three chapters in the Midwest. By 1914 the fraternity was expand-ing in numbers and impact, both on the college campuses home to its chapters and in the larger black community.[136]

In December 1914, during the fraternity's national convention, leg-islation was proposed to change the name from "Kappa Alpha Nu" to

"Kappa Alpha Psi." This decision partially grew out of a desire to incorporate a Greek character into the alphabetical designation, but the presence of an overt Greek letter was a "secondary concern." What seemed primary was white racism on Indiana's campus. While Elder Watson Diggs was observing a young fraternity initiate named Frank Summers compete in a track meet, he overheard fans referring to the member as a "Kappa Alpha Nig," after which he began a campaign to rename the fraternity.[137] The resolution to rename the group was adopted in December 1914, and fraternity records show that "the name acquired a distinctive Greek letter symbol and KAPPA ALPHA PSI thereby became a Greek letter Fraternity in every sense of the designation." Grand Polemarch Elder W. Diggs confirmed the name change, using a national proclamation, and the fraternity has been known as Kappa Alpha Psi since April 15, 1915.[138]

The fraternity grew slowly but consistently. By 1913, the group had expanded with a second undergraduate chapter at the University of Illinois (Beta Chapter) and a third at the University of Iowa (Gamma Chapter). After expansion to three predominantly white universities, Kappa Alpha Psi chartered undergraduate chapters on the campuses of historically black colleges and universities (HBCUs): Wilberforce University (Delta Chapter) and Lincoln University (Epsilon Chapter). By 1920 Xi Chapter was chartered at Howard University, and the fraternity entered the Ivy League with the founding of Omicron Chapter at Columbia University and the South with a chapter at Morehouse College in 1921.

It would not be until 1922 that the fraternity began to formally discuss racial uplift politics. Prior to then, fraternity endeavors had concentrated on self-preservation for black students—especially those on white campuses. It was in that year that Leon Wop Stewart conceived of Kappa Alpha Psi's first national program, titled "Guide Right," which would consist of educational and occupational guidance of youth in high school and college, primarily inspirational and informational in character.

Omega Psi Phi Fraternity

On November 17, 1911, Omega Psi Phi became the first BGLO founded at a historically black university.[139] Three Howard University juniors, Edgar A. Love, Oscar J. Cooper, and Frank Coleman—affectionately known as the "three musketeers" due to their friendship and devotion to one another—along with Dr. Ernest E. Just, a faculty advisor, founded the organization based on scholarship, manhood, perseverance, and uplift.[140] The motto they chose, "Friendship is essential to the soul," was reflective of the close bond held between Love, Cooper, and Coleman.[141]

Although Alpha Phi Alpha and Alpha Kappa Alpha chapters at Howard University existed before Omega Psi Phi's founding,[142] Omega's founders faced an uphill battle as secret fraternal college-based organizations were viewed with trepidation. Faculty questioned the effect of such organizations, particularly with respect to the moral development of young college men.[143] In preparation for the founding of Omega, Love, Cooper, and Coleman conducted research on fraternities and fraternity critiques—particularly concerns of faculty and administration. Fully aware of the potential concerns of the university and opposition they may face, the soon-to-be founders committed themselves formally to establishing the fraternity. Immediately thereafter, the three undergraduate founders went about identifying potential charter members. After careful consideration, they selected ten men "who were considered to be worthy from the point of view of scholarship, ability to fraternize, courage, and the other cardinal principles already agreed upon."

The founders and charter members then drafted their organization's constitution and presented it to the university administration for approval, but the university council rejected it. The founders and charter members were not dissuaded, however, and continued to discuss the matter with the council. Faculty approval was slow going and the brothers were impatient to receive what they believed would be inevitable— university approval—so as a result, they went on to announce the fraternity themselves. By posting placards measuring three and a half by six inches around campus listing the fraternity's name and the names of the founders and charter members, the men announced their existence. The next day, Howard University president Dr. Wilbur P. Thirkeild addressed the campus regarding the young men's actions by declaring that Omega Psi Phi did not exist at Howard University.

With their commitment and belief in the fraternity unflagging, the brothers of Omega Psi Phi began lobbying faculty to approve the budding organization. The Howard administration remained slow to respond to the brothers' request for recognition, and the brothers—being men of action—continued to move forward by voting in another class of members. After much deliberation, the faculty was prepared to recognize the fraternity, but only as a *local* organization and with recommendations for changes to its constitution. Though the founders were amenable to addressing the faculty's recommendations for changes to the constitution, they had always maintained national aspirations and would not bend on this point.[144] They submitted a revised constitution, but the administration persisted with its caveat that the fraternity remain local. Despite the many recommendations from faculty to maintain a local-only organization, the brothers were insistent on maintaining a national scope, and their dogged persistence eventually paid off. Omega Psi Phi became recognized as a national organization and approved by the university council.[145]

Delta Sigma Theta Sorority

In 1912 many of the members of Alpha Kappa Alpha sorority felt uneasy in their organization. In particular, twenty-two members felt as though a change was needed. Seemingly frustrated by the lack of attention to social issues beyond the affairs of campus society at Howard and wishing to reorganize, sorority members moved to change the sorority's name and symbols as well as to be more politically oriented.[146] Moreover, they felt that Alpha Kappa Alpha was solely a female derivative of the Beta Chapter of Alpha Phi Alpha fraternity, with no individual meaning and no "Greek distinctive" letters.[147] Moreover, according to Delta Sigma Theta's historian Paula Giddings, the twenty-two women were concerned that since Alpha Kappa Alpha was not incorporated, there was no "legal entity." Since there was no charter, there was no authority to form other chapters, thus limiting their ability to enlarge the scope of activity.[148]

This endeavor had momentum from the beginning, as seven of the twenty-two were elected officers of Alpha Kappa Alpha: Myra Davis Hemmings, president; Ethel Cuff black, vice-president; Edith Motte Young, secretary; Jessie McGuire Dent, corresponding secretary; Winona Cargile Alexander, custodian; Frederica Chase Dodd, sergeant-at-arms; and Pauline Oberdorfer Minor, treasurer. In December 1912 these twenty-two undergraduates voted to change the organization's name to "Delta Sigma Theta," which was to reflect the change in the direction and philosophical underpinnings of the organization.[149]

Yet, this push to change the name, colors, direction, and overall identity of the organization caused a conflict between the twenty-two members and the one alumna member Nellie Quander, who wished to keep the previous name and functional status quo. Quander issued an ultimatum and deadline to stop the efforts to reorganize the sorority.[150] The twenty-two declined and unanimously voted to reorganize, even prior to Delta Sigma Theta being approved by the Howard University administration.[151] Hence, Delta Sigma Theta was founded on January 13, 1913, by twenty-two young women who broke away from Alpha Kappa Alpha's chapter at Howard University.[152] The new sorority was officially incorporated on February 18, 1913, making Delta the first sorority composed of undergraduate African American women to apply to the trustees of any university for the right to become an incorporated body.

From the onset, members of Delta Sigma Theta seemed less confined by the social conventions of the day. While BGLOs share similar values and goals for advancing civil rights, "the women of Delta Sigma Theta sometimes put themselves at risk and have engaged in the most direct forms of activism of any of the BGLOs."[153] In fact, Delta Sigma Theta's identity as an organization harkens back to women like Coralie Franklin Cook, many of whom would later become Delta Sigma Theta members and who served as pillars of black women's involvement in the suffrage movement. For example, less than three months after their founding, Delta Sigma Theta was one of the key African American organizations to participate in the Women's Suffrage March on March 3, 1913.

Since its inception Delta Sigma Theta has maintained a constant focus on using its position in society to promote higher standards in human treatment and to improve race and gender relations.[154] Two months after the formation of Delta Sigma Theta, the new members participated in what would be their first public effort for civil rights. On March 3, 1913, Osceola Adams led the new Delta Sigma Theta members—along with five to ten thousand other women—down Pennsylvania Avenue in support of women's voting rights. Over the next decade and a half, Delta Sigma Theta quietly continued its involvement in civil rights. It wished to remain a viable organization, but its outward support of such controversial topics would potentially disrupt its ability to operate.[155] Delta Sigma Theta members found ways of being actively involved with and supportive of civil rights organizations by strategically engaging in both indirect and direct action.

Delta Sigma Theta also promoted its public policy goals by extending honorary membership offers to prominent African American leaders. Mary Church Terrell and Coralie Franklin Cook—two women active in the Washington Women's Colored League—were some of the first honorary members. Terrell eventually became president of the National Association of Colored Women's Clubs, chairman of the Coordinating Committee for the Enforcement of the District of Columbia Anti-Discrimination Laws, and the first African American woman elected to the United States Congress of Women. Terrell remained a strong voice for Delta Sigma Theta throughout her life by giving speeches on behalf of the sorority and lending her name to most of the group's endeavors. Nannie H. Burroughs, another honorary member, was the founder of the National Training School for Girls in Washington, D.C. Hallie Quinn Brown, a renowned professor and dean at Allen University in South Carolina and ultimately Wilberforce University in Ohio, became another honorary member. Brown was well known for her traveling presentations and her leadership in a wide variety of organizations in Ohio. One of the most important honorary members was Mary McLeod Bethune, founder of Bethune-Cookman College in Florida and of the National Council for Negro Women, a cabinet position under Franklin Delano Roosevelt. Bethune also proved to be instrumental in promoting the goals and policies of Delta Sigma Theta throughout her lifetime as an honorary member.[156]

More broadly, public policy has served as an important interest to Delta Sigma Theta since its inception. The sorority's Five-Point Program focused on education, employment, housing, and race and intercultural relations. These initiatives continued to drive the sorority's community service and policy work. The organization's involvement in the political sphere has taken a wide variety of forms, from lobbying efforts, voter registration, and supporting members running for public office to sending members as representative delegates to conferences, political events, and international excursions.[157]

In December 1913, the sorority sent M. Frances Gunner to the Intercollegiate Socialist Society conference in New York. Though Gunner was the only African American student present at the conference, her voice was heard over the three days. Her presence established a strong foundation in public policy that Delta Sigma Theta built upon for years to come. Perhaps the group's most significant endeavor during this time of activity was its leading role in urging the United States to remove its forces from Haiti. Delta Sigma Theta lobbied hard for President Wilson to leave Haiti. When Wilson's administration decided to use a commission to determine the best course, Delta Sigma Theta worked to get two members on that commission, Mary Church Terrell and Alpha Phi Alpha member Rayford Logan. Neither were appointed, but Delta Sigma Theta's work was not in vain; the president of the Tuskegee Institute, Dr. Robert Russa Moton, served as an advisor in the process that ultimately resulted in U.S. withdrawal from Haiti in 1934.[158]

Phi Beta Sigma Fraternity

One of the three founders of Phi Beta Sigma fraternity was Abram Langston Taylor. Born in Summerville, Tennessee, on January 19, 1890, he was known for his above average height and lanky composure. "His eyes were set deep in a brown skin face that showed a square chin and prominent ears."[159] Yet his physical charisma was only an accoutrement to his mentally keen and emotionally balanced persona, as his most distinguished characteristic was his slow and methodical style of speech and movement.[160] "He walked slowly, talked slowly, in a low monotone. But underneath his deliberate speech, thought and movement was an inner urge that drove him on to the completion of any task to which he once set his mind."[161] Founder Taylor was rumored to be undefeatable in debate and argumentation. Consequently, he commanded the respect of his peers for his unwavering loyalty and devotion to both his moral principles and nurturing of friendships.[162]

In 1909, Taylor graduated from the Howe Institute (now LeMoyne-Owen College) in Memphis, Tennessee. It was in Memphis during the summer of 1910 that Taylor met a young alumnus of Howard University who recounted his appraisal of Greek-letter fraternities at Howard. At that time, Taylor was already accepted as a student at Howard and was scheduled to matriculate at the university in the fall of 1910.[163] Taylor's

talk with the young man germinated the idea for Phi Beta Sigma fraternity. Taylor wrote,

> If we are to be precise about it, the idea of the Fraternity had its origin
> not at Howard University, as might be expected, but in my hometown of
> Memphis, Tennessee. . . . One dull summer day in 1910, I was on my way
> home from downtown and paused for a while at Bumper Beale Street
> Grocery Store to pick up the latest news from the Squash Center, which
> usually held afternoon sessions there. I engaged in a conversation with a
> young man recently graduated from Howard University, and since I had
> decided to go to Howard, I was very much interested in what he had to
> say about the University. He dwelt at the length on the activities of Greek
> Letter fraternities. His talk gave me an idea, and from that day on, Phi
> Beta Sigma was in the making.[164]

Taylor entered Howard University on November 23, 1910, and began
almost immediately to lay the plans to begin a new fraternity

Creating a fraternity was an ambitious task, but Taylor was determined to see his vision come to fruition, and in the fall of 1913, after
three long years of diligent and arduous groundwork, Taylor approached
Leonard F. Morse, his former school roommate, with the idea of forming a new fraternity.[165] Morse was a prodigy—the first to graduate from
Howard in three years with both associate's and bachelor's degrees.[166]
Also while a student, Morse was the YMCA's director of social service
from 1913 to 1914, president of the Young Men's Progressive Club from
1914 to 1915, and tutor of languages and history.[167] Extremely educated,
Morse went on from Howard to obtain bachelor of divinity degrees from
Wilberforce University and the Payne School of Divinity, a master's from
Northwestern, and both a doctor of philosophy and a doctor of psychol-
ogy from the College of Metaphysics in Indianapolis. He received an
honorary doctor of divinity from Allen University in Columbia, South
Carolina, and an honorary law degree from Edward Waters College in
Jacksonville, Florida.[168]

After careful discussion, Taylor and Morse chose one of their mutual
friends, Charles I. Brown, to be the third founder. Born in Topeka, Kansas, in 1890 to Rev. John M. Brown and Maggie M. Brown, Charles was

said to be "of average size, brown skin and princely in his manners. In dress, in movement, in speech Brother Brown was the 'perfect gentleman.'"[169] "This is to say, he had that gracious courtesy that is commonly associated with the Eighteenth Century ideal type; never hurried, never flustered, reticent and affable."[170] Brown finished at Howard Academy in 1910, was class chaplain in 1913, was a member and president of Chaplain Classical Club in 1912 and 1913, respectively, was president of the Classical Club in 1914, and wished to pursue postgraduate work in Latin. In addition, he was selected as "The Most To Be Admired" for the class of 1914.[171] Accordingly, Brown was very popular with both the student body and the Howard University administration. The 1914 Howard University yearbook, under the "Personals and Applied Quotations" section, documents Brown's words: "No legacy is so rich as honesty."[172]

Taylor recorded for posterity the events that led to the fraternity's formation after this fateful encounter: "The first meeting of the organizing committee was held at my home in the 1900 block of 'S' Street, Northwest, Sunday November, 2nd. The second meeting was held the next Tuesday at Morse's rooming place in the 1900 block of 3rd Street, Northwest."[173] A few short days later, on November 13, 1913, Taylor, Morse, and Brown met with nine of their undergraduate colleagues from Howard University (S. P. Massie, J. A. Franklin, J. E. Jones, B. A. Matthews, W. F. Vincent, T. L. Alston, W. E. Tibbs, J. H. Howard, and I. L. Scruggs) about forming the new fraternity.[174] Taylor wrote, "During the remainder of November and December, meetings were held on the 'Hill' (Howard University) during which time nine students were accepted for membership and plans for the fraternity were discussed and developed."[175]

Just a few months later in the Bowen Room of the Twelfth Street Branch YMCA in Washington, D.C., on a Friday evening (January 9, 1914), the three founders and nine initial members officially organized the fraternity around the three principles of brotherhood, scholarship, and service. Founder A. L. Taylor recounts that meeting: "As chairman of the organizing committee, I reported how I had conceived the idea of the founding of the Fraternity and the three years of unrelenting toil I had given to the development of the plans. I closed the report by recommending that we form a permanent organization to be known as Phi Beta Sigma Fraternity. Upon a motion made by Charles I. Brown, seconded by William F. Vincent, the recommendation was accepted and

Phi Beta Sigma became a national fraternity in fact as well as in our dreams."[176] The Board of Deans at Howard University recognized the new fraternity on April 15, 1914, and the April 24 issue of the *Howard University Journal* (the student publication at Howard University at the time) made public the organization by stating, "The Fraternity is the result of the efforts of Messrs. A. L. Taylor, L. F. Morse and C. I. Brown; and promises to be a vital force in the moral, social and intellectual life of the University."[177]

Just weeks later, on May 4, 1914, at 2226 Sixth Street Northwest, fourteen additional members were added to the three founders and nine original members. Together, the twenty-six members of Phi Beta Sigma then organized the first chapter within the new fraternity: Alpha Chapter.

Phi Beta Sigma was founded as an organization that viewed itself as "a part of" the general community rather than "apart from" society. In this sense, the fraternity was formed to exist as part of a greater brotherhood that would be devoted to the "inclusive we" rather than the "exclusive we." Taylor, Francis, and Morris believed that each potential member should be judged by his own merits rather than his family background or affluence: without regard of race, nationality, socioeconomic background, skin tone, or texture of hair.

For instance, in the fraternity history book, *Our Cause Speeds On* (1955), editors W. Sherman Savage and Lawrence D. Reddick recount the uncharacteristic intraracial black diversity of the early members of Sigma:

I. L. Scruggs. Short and dumpy with an enthusiasm that burned so brightly that today . . . he is still unsurpassed in ardor and zeal. W. E. Tibbs . . . Brown skin, slight of build . . . he talked fast, moved fast and thought with lightning speed. . . . Jacob E. Jones can best be described as a handsome black boy. Six feet tall, well-proportioned, "Jake" Jones was a tailor's model. . . . J. R. Howard. A smooth, round-faced boy, he always appeared for classes trim and neat as a pin. . . . S. P. Massie . . . the tallest of all the charter members. He was dark-skinned with large feet. He spoke in a soft, quiet tone and always wore an infectious smile. . . . Vincent was unassuming yet brilliant . . . W. F. Vincent was tall, fair-skinned with bushy, straight brown hair. . . . T. L. Alston was light brown and a little freckled with reddish hair.[178]

Leonard F. Morse summed up the entire group: "Each one was different in temperament, in ability, in appearance; but that was why they were chosen by the three Founders. We felt that a fraternity composed of men who were all alike in habits, interests and abilities would be a pretty dull organization."[179]

From its inception, Taylor, Francis, and Morse also thought of the fraternity as a vehicle to deliver services to the general community rather than as a mechanism for nepotism or self-congratulatory betterment. In this sense, the founders attempted to build a radically democratic organization, predicated upon the respect of individual rights while privileging a noncoercive, consensus-building discourse in which participants would overcome egotistical or class-based agendas in favor of spiritually and rationally evenhanded agreement. For the founders, a significant tenet for African American self-determinism and autonomy was the implementation of critical self-reflection and discourse that would facilitate emancipation from myopic dogma and blind tradition.

Therefore, instead of following in the steps of what was becoming a "talented tenth"[180] cadre of separatist elitism among many black organizations at the time, the founders felt that both the fraternity and society would be best served by pursuing more democratically inclusive methods of association. Rather than using the fraternity as a vehicle for the attainment of knowledge and skills to be utilized exclusively for themselves, the founders held a deep conviction that they should return their knowledge and ideas to the communities from which they came.

Hence, the founders did not wish for the iconography of Greek letters to supersede the actions of the members who wore those letters. Further, the principles of brotherhood, scholarship, and service that were laid down by the founders were meant to be at the forefront of all fraternal activities. Accordingly, the philosophy of the fraternity was crystallized in

> service, service not only for the Fraternity, but for the general welfare of the society in which we live. Sigma believes further that symbols have no real meaning or function until they are put into everyday practice according to the meanings assigned them by the Fraternity. Symbols do not make the man, but are meaningful only when the interpretation of these become dynamic factors in determining everyday behavior. There is much that can be written and said about the philosophy of Phi Beta

Sigma Fraternity, but nothing said or done will be of any real meaning or consequence unless the practice of that philosophy can be seen in terms of Brotherhood, Service and Scholarship in the daily living of its members.[181]

During the summer of 1914 (only 150 days after the organization's charter was granted) the efforts of I. L. Scruggs led to the fraternity's procurement of a house. The three-story brick house at 1907 Third Street Northwest amazed the campus community partially because of the rapidity of its acquisition as well as the fact that it was the largest facility of any of the existing fraternal organizations at Howard.[182] Securing a house was crucial to the fraternity's operations. The house not only served as headquarters for its members, but its library and art gallery were open to the public as well. The house would later serve as the location for Phi Beta Sigma's inaugural convention.[183]

Sigma was soon expanding its reach across campus. A. M. Walker, the first initiate of the fourteen-person pledge class, was elected associate editor of the *Howard University Journal* and founder A. L. Taylor was made circulation editor. Other brothers soon held notable positions: W. F. Vincent was president of the debating society, W. H. Foster was president of the college YMCA, J. Berry was president of the Political Science Club, J. Camper became captain of the Howard football team and E. Lawson was president of the Athletic Association.[184]

Seeking to further the fraternity's intellectual pool, several affluent African American scholars were inducted as honorary members: Dr. Edward Porter Davis, former dean of liberal arts at Howard University; Thomas M. Gregory, noted orator, playwright, and theater director; Dr. Alain Leroy Locke, the first black Rhodes Scholar; and Dr. Thomas W. Turner, a nationally known botanist. Davis, Gregory, Locke, and Turner were the first graduate members of Phi Beta Sigma. The securing of these honorary members not only ensured support from the faculty but also increased the intellectual vigor of the organization.[185]

The fraternity also aimed its expansion toward the racially divided south. On March 5, 1915, professor Herbert L. Stevens from Wiley College in Marshall, Texas, was admitted as a graduate member by a special decree of the Fraternity General Board. Later that year on November 13, Stevens helped found the second chapter, Beta, at Wiley College.[186]

It was at this time that the fraternity had another unique opportunity to expand. The group received a letter dated December 11, 1915, from Kappa Alpha Psi founder and grand polemarch Elder W. Diggs. The letter, on official stationery, offered to merge Kappa Alpha Psi with Phi Beta Sigma. At the time Kappa was establishing itself in the Midwest while Sigma was expanding in the East and South. The fraternity's General Board considered the proposal but turned it down in its reply to Diggs, written by Taylor, dated December 18, 1915.[187]

Throughout its history, especially in its beginning, Phi Beta Sigma boasted the membership of many great individual proponents of African American civil rights. In 1916, at Phi Beta Sigma's first annual Conclave, Phi Beta Sigma member L. M. Hershaw received recognition for his work as one of the nine founders of the Niagara Movement—a forerunner to the NAACP.[188] Hershaw delivered the Conclave's opening address amid applause for his civil rights work.[189] In 1916 a major civil rights struggle began that would not be truly resolved until World War II was brewing. The First World War had just begun, and Phi Beta Sigma members, particularly Phi Beta Sigma member T. Montgomery Gregory, joined in the fight to allow African Americans to hold officer positions in the U.S. military.[190] The students and faculty of Howard University created a committee to coordinate efforts to end Jim Crow in the military and allow African Americans to assume leadership roles. Gregory was made the chairman of this committee and within days began to broaden the committee to include other colleges.[191] This group eventually came to be known as the Central Committee of Negro College Men,[192] and it succeeded in its goal because some three hundred congressmen and senators pledged their support. Approximately fifteen hundred African Americans with college degrees were selected by the committee as potential candidates for an African American officer training program. Because of the efforts of the Central Committee of Negro College Men, the War Department reluctantly agreed to establish an officer-training program for African Americans.[193] The program accepted 1,250 new members, was called the Seventeenth Provisional Training Regiment,[194] and was housed at Fort Des Moines, Iowa.[195]

While the fraternity grew in its first three years (from December 27 to 30, 1916, Sigma held its first national convention in Washington, D.C.), by 1917 the group's chapters were beginning to be depleted due to the

U.S. government's "call to arms" to serve in World War I (1914–1918). By this time, only Alpha Chapter showed signs of activity and "only one new chapter had been added. That same year, 1917, was sadly memorable for the death of one of the most ardent and useful of the original twelve chartermen—W. F. Vincent. Brother A. Langston Taylor recalled the last words he heard from Brother Vincent . . . : 'Taylor, carry on for Sigma, until we meet again.'"[196] Founder Taylor called on the National Board to fill the vacancies created by the "call to arms." By June 1919, the General Board reorganized itself, moved the Washington, D.C., fraternity house to a new location at 325 T Street Northwest, and reactivated all but one of its chapters. It was largely through the efforts of Taylor and a few select others that the fraternity was able to continue to operate while numerous Sigma men served on the European battlefront.[197] Due to their efforts the fraternity was also incorporated in Washington, D.C., on April 29, 1920, and the first issue of the *Phi Beta Sigma Journal* was printed in November 1921.[198] With Sigma regrouping due to the dedication of its founders, the next Conclave was held in Atlanta (December 27–31, 1921) at Morris Brown College, home of the Zeta Chapter of the fraternity. This meeting was also the first ever inter-fraternity Conclave (with Omega Psi Phi fraternity). As a result, a plan was set in motion to hold an Inter-Fraternity Conference, which occurred the following year (April 24–26, 1922) in Washington, D.C.[199]

Through these programs and other facets of the fraternity structure, the founders' agenda and ideology spread to other influential members within the group. Notable Sigma brother James Weldon Johnson wrote "The Negro National Anthem," known as "Lift Ev'ry Voice and Sing," A. Philip Randolph organized the Brotherhood of Sleeping Car Porters, and Howard University professor of philosophy Alain Leroy Locke wrote *The New Negro*, in which he described the emergence in the 1920s of a new zeitgeist, an innovative spirit that did not rely on older models but, rather, embraced a "new psychology" and "new sprit" toward social transformation.

Other dramatic social changes were also taking place. While Johnson, Randolph, and Locke were key thinkers in the Harlem Renaissance, there was a concurrent rebirth of white nationalism that led to the popular passage of stringent anti-immigration laws, especially the Immigration Act of 1924. In 1920 the Volstead Act became effective, starting Prohibition, and on August 18 of the same year Tennessee delivered the crucial thirty-sixth ratification necessary for the final adoption of the Nineteenth Amendment, finally giving women the right to vote. With such changes taking place in all aspects of social life, many felt it appropriate for a change regarding options for black sororities. At the 1919 Conclave, the brotherhood appointed founder A. L. Taylor and new brother Charles Robert Samuel Taylor to pursue the search for a worthy sister organization. From the memoirs of Taylor comes a glimpse of the seed of what was to become Zeta Phi Beta sorority:

> As though moved by some pulling power, I recall how I thought of a sincere and enthusiastic young woman, who for me was the embodiment of our brotherhood in the sisterhood of which I dreamed. She had character and gifts. She had a beautiful spirit and intellectual effectiveness. She had appeal in her personality and in her words. I knew that if I won her, she would not give up until she had perfected a nucleus of a sisterhood for Phi Beta Sigma. Arizona Leedonia Cleaver was the chief builder and she asked fourteen others to join her. I shall never forget the first meetings held in the dormitory rooms of Miner Hall.[200]

Thus in 1920 Phi Beta Sigma helped to establish its sister organization: Zeta Phi Beta sorority.

Zeta Phi Beta Sorority

Zeta Phi Beta sorority was founded in 1920 at—like its black sororal predecessors—Howard University.[201] In 1919, Phi Beta Sigma fraternity founder Charles Robert Samuel Taylor encouraged his girlfriend, Arizona Cleaver, to create a sorority. Despite some advances, the Roaring Twenties were characterized by an entrenched system of de jure and de facto sexism and racism. Fifteen young women heeded the call for a new sorority to aid in the endeavors of African American women's social transformation. From the very beginning these women tried to set a new course, to set a higher standard. Unfortunately, the general Howard University campus community was not very kind to the idealistic young women, as some branded them the "praying band" because of their religious character.[202]

One by one, the group of fifteen dwindled until only five women remained: Cleaver, Pearl Anna Neal, Myrtle Tyler Faithful, Viola Tyler Goings, and Fannie Pettie Watts. They became the five founders (known as the "Pearls") of Zeta Phi Beta. With the help of Phi Beta Sigma founder Abram L. Taylor (with the assistance of Sigma brother Charles Robert Samuel Taylor), Zeta Phi Beta Sorority, Inc. was established on January 16, 1920, at Howard University. Zeta Phi Beta's first formal introduction to the Washington community was held at the Whitelaw Hotel, followed by a formal welcome to the campus by the sisters of the Alpha Chapter of Alpha Kappa Alpha and Alpha Chapter of Delta Sigma Theta in the Assembly Hall of the Miner Building on campus.[203]

After gaining permission from the Howard University administration, the five founders of Zeta Phi Beta held their first Boulé (convention) with their Sigma brothers in 1920 (an occurrence repeated in 1936, 1957, and 1991),[204] and the chapter began to grow. Many women expressed interest in becoming members of Zeta Phi Beta. However, due to apprehension over the required high academic standards, an inability to afford initiation fees (that today would appear quite nominal), concern over a white and/or male backlash to black female empowerment, and uncertainty about a sorority that seemingly eschewed elitism and separatism, many did not follow through on their intentions. However, there were soon twenty-five women eager to join the Zeta movement. Yet out of this group only four aspirants (Gladys Warrington, Harriet Dorsey, Pauline Philips, and Nellie Singfield) obtained membership. This small cadre, influenced by the distinctive ideology of the sorority, labored to accelerate Zeta's growth.

Almost immediately they began to lay the groundwork for the establishment of chapters all over the United States. While many of the other BGLOs focused on establishing chapters at predominately white educational institutions, Zeta (like her brother Sigma) directed attention to HBCUs to make inroads into the communities that would most benefit from their services. Therefore, instead of establishing chapters in urban Chicago, New York and Detroit, they focused on the deeply racially divided states in the South including Alabama, Missouri, and North Carolina. Zeta's first two chapters after Howard University were established at historically black universities (Morris Brown College and Morgan State College), followed by a citywide chapter in San Antonio, Texas.

Sigma Gamma Rho Sorority

The economic conditions and social ostracism at predominantly white colleges and universities in the early part of the twentieth century resulted in close companionship among black students, who saw a need for black sororities and fraternities.[205] Sociologist Marcia D. Hernandez concluded that most black women likely joined sororities and maintained their ties to the group because of opportunities to engage in sisterhood, community service, philanthropy, and professional development.[206] In fact, in many ways black sorority women borrowed a set of ideals and continued a tradition established by Mary Church Terrell and the National Association of Colored Women, which had adopted a progressive agenda that focused on child care, employment training, wage equity, and living the motto "Lifting as We Climb."[207]

Sigma Gamma Rho was founded in 1922, at what is now Butler University in Indiana.[208] Its seven founders included Mary Lou Allison Gardner Little, Dorothy Hanley Whiteside, Vivian Irene White Marbury, Nannie Mae Gahn Johnson, Hattie Mae Annette Dulin Redford, Bessie Mae Downey Rhoades Martin, and Cubena McClure. Sigma Gamma Rho was organized at a time when the Ku Klux Klan (KKK) membership included one-third of native-born white males in Indiana.[209] In fact, the grand dragon of the Indiana KKK, D. C. Stephenson, later resided near Butler University.[210]

Conclusion

In this chapter we covered the founding years of the eight BGLOs between 1906 (Alpha Phi Alpha fraternity) and 1922 (Sigma Gamma Rho sorority). While the latter groups' coverage was truncated, we see some notable trends. These organizations' early years reflect an effort to gain some footing in the world. Beyond their founding as a means for racial security and solidarity at predominantly white institutions and a sense of elitism at Howard University, the early twentieth century was also a time of expansion for these organizations. Moreover, it was a time of self-discovery. In addition to the more insular reasons for founding and expanding, BGLOs spent the first two decades of the first century after slavery's abolition developing nascent ideas about what college-age and college-educated African American men and women could do for the race. What was most critical during these years was not so much the specific actions taken but rather their collective worldviews that were taking form.

3

Finding Their Way

Black and Greek in the Midst of the Harlem Renaissance, the Roaring Twenties, and the Adolescence of Jim Crow (1923–1929)

The years directly following the founding of the last of the original eight organizations (Sigma Gamma Rho sorority in 1922), in the wake of the African American Nadir, and as the United States settled into both Jim Crow segregation and the unequal prosperity of the Roaring Twenties, BGLOs grappled with the direction of their organizations. The 1920s also witnessed an explosion of black creative and intellectual thought in what has been called the Harlem Renaissance. While this period has been well documented, few scholars have examined the extent to which BGLO members were at the forefront of the Harlem Renaissance—from Phi Beta Sigma member Alain Leroy Locke and Omega Psi Phi member Langston Hughes to Zora Neale Hurston of Zeta Phi Beta and Gwendolyn Bennett of Delta Sigma Theta. This was a time of cautious optimism, excitement, and debate, which would sharpen the focus of these organizations by the time the country moved into the Great Depression in the 1930s.

Self-Determination through Educational Attainment

Many organizations evidenced a multifaceted approach, which was decidedly uneven in its development and application. In the early 1920s, for instance, due to perhaps Kappa Alpha Psi's ideals, the zeitgeist of the time, or both, the group's members began to push against the bulwark of white supremacy with diverse foci. Noted educator and member of Kappa Alpha Psi fraternity Henley L. Cox penned an article in the *Kappa Alpha Psi Journal* about the broader freedom movement being taken up among African American college students.[1] In his piece, Cox wrote about the National Federation of Negro Students movement—a movement among African American students aimed at creating a state of racial consciousness to better achieve social progress. Mirroring that organization, members of Kappa Alpha Psi helped to form the American Federation of Negro Students (AFNS), which comprised college students from all regions of the nation. The first conference of the AFNS was held April 6 to 9, 1923, at Howard University. This conference developed a five point program: "1. The promotion of co-operation, 2. The stimulation of race pride, 3. Encouragement of education, 4. Promotion of higher racial culture, [and] 5. Giving of intelligent consideration to race relations."[2] Committees were formed around each of the points and proposed the following national-scale drives: "1. A drive for economic co-operation, beginning the first week in December 1923, 2. [a] drive to instill race pride, beginning the fourth week in March, 1924, [and] 3. [a] drive for better and more universal education, beginning in June, 1924."[3] Members, often overlapping with membership in both Kappa Alpha Psi and AFNS, implemented these drives by dividing the United States into five zones, then selling the National Federation of Negro Students' programs to their respective constituencies.

This early emphasis on education was shared by other organizations such as Delta Sigma Theta sorority. Beginning in the 1920s, each spring saw May Week, which became a staple of the sorority's service. It was implemented by Delta Sigma Theta's first national president, Sadie Alexander, a civil rights activist and outspoken critic of racial discrimination, segregation, and employment inequality. Alexander created May Week as an outreach initiative to inform elementary schoolchildren and their parents of the benefits of higher education.[4] Every year for one week in May, each chapter reached out to the local community through a series of presentations and activities to demonstrate the importance of higher education to young students. Not long after the initial implementation, May Week programs expanded to create study groups for high school students and college freshmen led by the local Delta Sigma Theta chapter.[5]

Beginning in 1922, Delta Sigma Theta sorority created the Scholarship Award Fund and the College Tuition Fund for both promising and needy students, funded each year by chapters and members. The first scholarship assisted young women to afford college; the latter funded graduate-level work.[6] The most common and celebrated educational philanthropy of Delta Sigma Theta is the Jabberwock. Created in 1925 by the Iota Chapter in Boston, the Jabberwock is a variety show put on to raise money for the sorority's scholarship funds. A typical Jabberwock requires countless hours of rehearsal and production by numerous competing teams. In the end, the audience decides the best team, and all the money raised goes toward benefiting women believed to hold the most promise for uplifting the race and advancing women's rights. Since its inception, almost all chapters have adopted some form of the Jabberwock as a staple of Delta Sigma Theta life.[7]

A couple years later, in 1924, Alpha Phi Alpha began to emphasize its successful Go-to-High-School, Go-to-College campaign. As one author penned in the *Sphinx*, African Americans had been in contact with Europeans for four and a half centuries and had not been permitted to develop the higher qualities of other races.[8] Since their arrival on American soil, African Americans' condition had not changed. However, they had patiently begun to ascend the road of education. Starting with participation in the Civil War, proving their ability as soldiers and loyalty as patriots, African Americans had begun to accumulate property, build schools and churches, enter into white schools, and ultimately prove that they were of merit.[9] It was noted that distinction in higher education was also a growing area for African Americans—producing scholars in nearly every field.[10] Accordingly, the underlying message of the Go-to-High-School, Go-to-College movement was to urge colored youth to take advantage of educational opportunities for the making of a better people; the future of the African American race was in their own hands, no longer those of the white philanthropist.[11] As the campaign gained momentum, the fraternity pushed to extend the program's scope. The goal was to reach the masses in a push aided by the increased infrastructure offered by the national campaign.[12]

Again, almost all fraternity chapters' reports in the *Sphinx* noted an increased effort in regard to reach and the potency of their individual executions of the campaign.[13] For example, the chapters in Atlanta (Eta Lambda, Alpha Rho, and Alpha Pi) created an essay contest with the topic "Why Go to College" and engaged all senior English teachers in the area to have their students participate.[14] Upsilon Chapter sent over fifty letters to editors in the states of Oklahoma and Kansas for publicity about the Go-to-High-School, Go-to-College movement. They also asked their alumni to hold meetings and give lectures to students in their areas. Furthermore, they wrote handwritten letters to high school graduates encouraging them to attend college.[15]

Phi Beta Sigma fraternity also engaged in racial uplift programs focused on educational attainment and educational philanthropy. The largest and most continuous philanthropy detailed in the fraternity history book, *Our Cause Speeds On*, is the Douglass Scholarship (later renamed as the Phi Beta Sigma Scholarship Fund), named after the great champion of African American civil rights Frederick Douglass and created to assist students deemed worthy.[16] The Douglass Scholarship has a complicated history and has helped many young scholars in need of financial support to graduate from college. The Douglass Scholarship's inception occurred at the 1920 Washington, D.C., convention, just six years after the fraternity itself had been born.[17] However, due to the fraternity's youth, the Douglass Scholarship was not awarded for several years. At the 1921 Atlanta Conclave, the desire to implement the Douglass Scholarship was reemphasized.[18] Phi Beta Sigma founder A. L. Taylor, in a general letter to the brotherhood, declared that a tax on graduate members would be earmarked specifically for scholarships. As J. S. Hughson wrote in an article in the *Crescent*, "This commendable and important function should not lag or cease for lack of funds and cooperative interest on our part. Let such good work go on."[19]

From its early years onward, Phi Beta Sigma viewed education as essential for improving African Americans' standards of living. In the spring 1925 issue of the *Crescent*, an article on the eleventh annual Conclave features several excerpts from Phi Beta Sigma member Dr. I. Garland Penn's address regarding education in the South. In one such excerpt, Dr. Penn asserted, "Our twenty millions [*sic*] of dollars of property had been established by Northern philanthropists, to help stem the tide of ignorance of our group in the South. . . . Our gratitude must be expressed by the carry-on spirit and not by mere empty expressions of praise and thanks."[20] Dr. Penn emphasized the role of the "college man" in maintaining high standards of education in "institutions of learning."[21] Phi Beta Sigma's emphasis on education was also demonstrated when some of the Conclave delegates visited the grave of Mrs. Fannie Jackson Coppin, described as a "pioneer in Negro education, being the founder of founder of Cheney Institute in Philadelphia."[22] The national president of Phi Beta Sigma at the time, Arthur W. Mitchell, stated, "I know of nothing more appropriate than the brief address of our great General Pershing, who before the tomb of Lafayette, said, 'Lafayette, we are here.' In these same words we may say to this distinguished lady who blazed the way in a new and untried field of educating Negroes, Fannie Jackson Coppin, we are here."[23] These educational efforts were mirrored by activities of Alpha Kappa Alpha sorority. For instance, in 1924 the Xi Chapter (Detroit) organized an Ivy Leaf Club to get high school girls interested in college. They invited fifty girls to a program at the YWCA, in which several women spoke about college life and then asked the girls if they wanted to join the Ivy Leaf Club as "younger sisters." Younger sisters were expected to participate in sorority programs, raise money, host an essay contest, and engage in community service.[24] Similarly, in the mid-1920s, the Zeta Omega Chapter raised money for a hundred-dollar scholarship given to the most qualified (in terms of academics and cocurriculars) young woman at Howard High School in Wilmington, Delaware. The money was raised through a play given by a group of high school students, a bake sale at the public market, and a candy sale by members of the chapter.[25] By 1926 members of the Alpha Beta Chapter contributed to the Endowment Fund for Atlanta University.[26]

Blending Education with the Pursuit of Human and Civil Rights

Due to their early success, BGLO educational programs were recognized by many BGLOs as potential avenues for civil rights pursuits. For instance, the Kappa Alpha Psi fraternity saw the racial uplift programs of civil rights litigation and educational initiatives as mutually supportive. By 1922, Kappa Alpha Psi's oldest and longest-running service program—Guide Right—was reenvisioned and would later be heralded as the fraternity's most noteworthy achievement.[27] The program was designed to assist high school seniors to choose and pursue careers consistent with the fraternity purpose of "achievement."[28] Guide Right was created by Leon W. Steward in St. Louis and incorporated under the administration of the fourth grand polemarch, W. Ellis Stewart. J. Jerome Peters, chairman of the local committee at the time and future eighth grand polemarch, helped to ensure that Guide Right was adopted as the fraternity's national service program,[29] later writing that the program's purpose was "probably as old as man's consciousness of his obligation to aid in the endeavors of his fellowmen."[30] The legislation to enact the program nationwide was passed at the Twelfth Grand Chapter Session of the fraternity Conclave. Initially, the program was emphasized over a seven-day period called Concentration Week, but by 1923 Guide Right had become a year-round effort.[31]

By 1924, May 18 to 25 was designated as National Guide Right Week, with the edict that it was a simple plan in which every chapter could engage.[32] The plan was simply to conduct the greatest amount of service as possible.[33] Throughout the week, meetings, interviews, and conferences took place among young men and women from all over the country. The Upsilon Chapter of Kappa Alpha Psi initiated the Guide Right Movement locally in Los Angeles, California as a means of encouraging high school boys and young college men to become interested in and continue their interest in the importance of promoting education. Their campaign paralleled the YMCA "Find Yourself" Campaign in helping these young men find their vocations.[34]

Kappa Alpha Psi instituted the Guide Right Movement to help guide and encourage youth toward school and educational attainment. To promote and assist the Guide Right Movement, the grand polemarch broadcasted the aims and goals of the movement over the radio in the spring of 1924 to reach out to other individuals to become involved. In the wake of the radio broadcast, statistics derived from ten chapters of Kappa Alpha Psi show that 2,500 individuals attended various fraternity meetings and 1,286 high school students participated in the fraternity-led activities.[35] At Guide Right committee meetings, representatives from various employment sectors expressed the opportunities and requirements necessary to enter their vocations, and boys were given self-analysis surveys to be completed by the next day, after which they were to meet with an interviewer who would provide them with guidance and advice.

In that same year, Kappa Alpha Psi began to engage more fully with social justice activities. The 1924 Grand Chapter Meeting (Kappa Alpha Psi's annual meeting) provided a platform for members to discuss and devise strategic plans on how to secure civil rights through litigation and direct action with other social justice organizations. For instance, in early February 1924, the Negro Sanhedrin (or All-Race Conference) took place in which trade unions, civic groups, and fraternal organizations met.[36] Its purpose was to devise action plans for how to protest for the legal and human rights of black tenant farmers and wage workers, as well as how to expand the larger goals of civil rights.[37] Out of this conference several goals were agreed upon, all related to the development of Negro youth, Negroes' contributions to civilization, and voter engagement.[38]

In 1924 Kappa Alpha Psi members Elisha Scott and R. M. Van Dyne litigated *Thurman-Watts v. Board of Education* up to the Kansas Supreme Court.[39] In the case, a prelude to the U.S. Supreme Court's *Brown v. Board of Education* decision,[40] Scott and Van Dyne represented an African American student who was denied admission to Roosevelt Junior High in Coffeyville, Kansas.[41] The city built a new Roosevelt Junior High School, a measure that African Americans had voted for, supported, and helped fund through their taxes.[42] Despite this, African American youth were turned away when they attempted to register along with white youth. The Kansas Supreme Court stated that the school was a high school (ninth through twelfth grade), and, according to the state law of Kansas, neither the superintendent of schools nor the board of education possessed the authority to separate white and colored pupils unless that power was expressly given by another statute.[43] Scott and Van Dyne prevailed, claiming that the ninth grade was part of high school and separate high school education was not allowed except in Kansas City, Kansas.[44]

By 1926 the Grand Chapter of Kappa Alpha Psi took a stand in Washington, D.C., when it adopted a resolution that brought attention to the inequality of educational opportunities afforded to young African Americans in the South versus those available to whites. At this time southern states were spending four to five times more on white than on African American youth education.[45] Such inequality was built on the argument that white southern men paid most of the public taxes, so their children were entitled to a better education. However, this was untrue, as African Americans paid just as much public taxes; therefore, their children were entitled to the same education as white children. This resolution highlighted the inequality forced on African American children by a system controlled by white southern men, who disproportionately allocated public funds in favor of their own children as opposed to the benefit of all.[46]

Other organizations followed suit. Some members of Alpha Kappa Alpha began to occasionally confront racial discrimination. For example, members of the Lambda Omega Chapter approached a local clothing store to interview the manager to ascertain his reasoning for terminating all negro girl employees.[47] It is unclear if such confrontations resulted in any rectifications of such discrimination.

Alpha Kappa Alpha's slight attention to social justice was also magnified by other organizations. For instance, Phi Beta Sigma fraternity made an interesting move at the 1926 Greensboro (North Carolina) Conclave. The delegates appointed a commission of brothers to investigate the economic, social, and health conditions in Haiti during the U.S. occupation, which lasted from 1915 to 1934.[48] They were also tasked with visiting the Virgin Islands in order to "make a thorough study and investigation of the conditions which are alleged to exist there and upon returning to the States, make a report of their findings along with recommendations to the proper authorities."[49] The proposed commission was apparently "actuated by an earnest desire to see our great Fraternity step out into broader fields of service."[50]

The focus on social justice seemed to spread among the BGLOs. In December 1923, the Sixteenth General Convention of Alpha Phi Alpha fraternity pledged financial support to the NAACP for "its determined fight for the passage of the Dyer Anti-Lynching Bill."[51] Within the following months, the fraternity decided to participate in the Negro Sanhedrin conference on February 11, 1924, by pledging to send ten delegates to the convention.[52] At the conference, the fraternity wished to address racial inequality and how unequal relations across racial groups related to religious, political, educational, industrial, economic, and other social aspects of society.[53] One fraternity member said of the conference, "The time has now come when the Negro must think for himself and speak for himself in terms of his own understanding of his own condition."[54]

By 1925 it was clear that BGLOs where merging educational philanthropies, programs, and civil rights agendas—all toward the purpose of a racial consciousness and uplift. For instance, Alpha Phi Alpha member V. E. Daniels, dean of Wiley College, wrote in the *Sphinx* on the need for such consciousness raising.[55] Daniels emphasized that facts often take time to become established and accepted. Hence, most people's reactions to the world are based on their subjective opinion of that world.

Specifically related to African Americans, Daniels continued, they are a nation within a nation, and the black nation is heterogenous and alienated from former cultures and tribes.[56] Daniels thus concluded that the major problem facing the African American freedom struggle was how to make individual African Americans racially conscious. Retracing the history of this effort, he noted how individuals such as David Walker and Frederick Douglass spread their writings and speeches to increase race consciousness.[57] Looking to other institutions, Daniels identified the African American church as central to shaping race consciousness and thought that the church could, along with the African American press, be instrumental in a new push for racial consciousness in the 1920s.[58] Discourse about racial consciousness raising within the fraternity varied. The June 1925 issue of the *Sphinx* contained an essay by one member who detailed the importance of athletics for consciousness raising not only among blacks, but across the color line: the article explained how white students, who often do not know how to engage African American students, can learn through sports.[59] Another article detailed how crucial opposition to harmful racial caricatures (such as African American mammy imagery) was for racial consciousness raising and called for memorials to the services rendered by African Americans to be built in the Washington, D.C., area.[60]

Individual fraternity chapters remained diligent in this agenda. For example, Epsilon Chapter (Ann Arbor, Mich.) had Alpha member W. E. B. Du Bois speak on "Africa and America."[61] Delta Lambda Chapter (Baltimore) cooperated with different civic organizations, including National Negro Health Week, the NAACP, and the National Urban League.[62] In the Midwest, Theta Lambda Chapter (Dayton, Ohio) joined with other organizations in the city to protest racial segregation in public schools.[63] Similarly, the Go-to-High-School, Go-to-College campaign had success in Evanston and Chicago, with Alpha members going into schools and churches to speak about the importance of racial equality and black pride. Furthermore, many newspapers "gave news items and editorials" on the matter. Many leading ministries in the communities offered their support.[64]

At the close of 1925, the message coming out of the General Convention in Detroit was that education, hard work, and mindful association with others would be the keys to African American uplift.[65] The idea of the "first African American to do . . ." had been hailed as the hero of the race, the example to aspire to.[66] However, in order for members of the race to move past being confined to themselves, they had to "accept nothing but the world's best" as the standard, because otherwise complacency and lack of desire would spawn a lack of innovation and stall forward momentum.[67] Hence, by 1927 Alpha Phi Alpha began offering a Life Insurance and Endowment Plan to help more people with their education and provide a safety net for their families.[68] Locally, chapters like Beta (Howard University) received cooperation from the Board of Education for their Go-to-High-School, Go-to-College work.[69]

Economic Development and Community Service

The early 1920s saw BGLOs focus not only on civil rights and education but also on the development of economic opportunity. For instance, the conclusion of Phi Beta Sigma fraternity's first decade (1914–24) saw the formation of their first official national program: Bigger and Better Business. One of the first nine initiates of the fraternity, I. L. Scruggs, wrote,

> Philadelphia, 1924, Phi Beta Sigma Fraternity "arrived." We had a mob of people at this Conclave. There were representatives from twenty-eight chapters and all the trimmings. The introduction of the Bigger and Better Negro Business idea was made by way of an exhibit devoted to this topic. The Bigger and Better Negro Business idea was first tested in 1924 with an imposing exhibition in Philadelphia. This was held in connection with the Conclave. Twenty-five leading Negro Businesses sent statements and over fifty sent exhibits. . . . The response was so great that the 1925 Conclave in Richmond, Virginia voted unanimously to make Bigger and Better Negro Business the public program of the Fraternity, and it has been so ever since. Phi Beta Sigma believes that the improvement and economic conditions of minorities is a major factor in the improvement of the general welfare of society.[70]

Phi Beta Sigma's public policy initiatives of the time were numerous. Significant overlap existed between the fraternity's public policy programs and programs for civil rights, philanthropy, and community service. Specifically, these Phi Beta Sigma public policy programs concentrated on African American economic and educational status and were designed to aid African Americans and other disadvantaged groups throughout the Northern Hemisphere. While Phi Beta Sigma undoubtedly valued education, the star of the group's public policy initiatives, however, designed to better African American and other disenfranchised groups' quality of life, was the Program for Bigger and Better Business.[71]

The brothers of Phi Beta Sigma created one of their first public policy directives geared toward African Americans at the 1923 Nashville Conclave, under the leadership of national president John W. Woodhouse.[72] The northern movement of African Americans and the prospects of African American businesses were the major issues discussed, and the fraternity decided to appoint a commission to study the northern migration of African Americans during the early twentieth century.

Around the summer of 1924, fraternity founder A. L. Taylor spearheaded a conference on the problems and outlook of African Americans in business and economic progress given the early stages of the Great Migration. This conference would spark one of Phi Beta Sigma's greatest and most successful fraternity programs—Bigger and Better Business. Soon after Taylor's visionary conference, the December 1924 issue of the *Crescent* contained a report detailing the "South-North Negro Migration."[73] The report estimated that approximately half a million African Americans had moved north between 1916 and 1924 and detailed some of the reasons for this migration, namely economic opportunity and escape from legal and racial discrimination in the South. It also discussed some of the social ramifications, including difficulties adjusting to northern urban centers for new arrivals. At the next Conclave, held in Philadelphia in 1924, there was a discussion of "Bigger and Better Race Business"—a proposal to advance the causes of both black capitalism and civil rights—and an educational conference on the similar subject of "The Young College Man's Part in the Development of Business."[74] The fraternity's Bigger and Better Business Program was evaluated and passed with flying colors at the Philadelphia Conclave. About forty independent African American businessmen sent in statements about business strategies, and fifty contributed exhibits showing their unique strategies. Due to the enormous success of the program in Philadelphia,

conference attendees unanimously voted to make the Bigger and Better Business Program the fraternity's official public program at the 1925
Richmond Conclave.

In 1926 Phi Beta Sigma fraternity launched a long-range campaign to educate African Americans about the economic potential of
black America, to promote business education, and to encourage African Americans to support African American businesses. As part of
this long-term campaign, the national fraternity body and local chapters would host Bigger and Better Business Weeks at the beginning of
April. During these weeks, African American businessmen would tell
audiences about their personal formulas for success and their unique
business strategies.[75] The description in the *Crescent* of the 1927 Bigger
and Better Business Week clearly explains the nature of the program:
"Chapters, both graduate and undergraduate, make special preparation
and render public programs in connection with schools and churches
in the interest of Negro Business. Outstanding speakers are sent to the
large centers of Negro population and address mass meetings on some
practical business subject."[76] One of these outstanding speakers was the
national president of the fraternity, who visited numerous cities during 1926, including Buffalo, Atlanta, Raleigh, and St. Louis. In addition
to mentioning the activities of the fraternity's president, the *Crescent*
includes a description of the specific program in Buffalo, during which
"all the pastors of colored churches cooperated in having one large mass
meeting at which assembled more than a thousand colored people."[77]
The program itself consisted of "music, short addresses by local businessmen, an essay contest by high school pupils (essays on subjects relative to Negro business and calculated to arouse interest in the study of
business)."[78] This type of program was held not only in Buffalo but in
"scores of other cities where Sigma has active chapters."[79]

By 1926, Alpha Phi Alpha fraternity's Go-to-High-School, Go-to-
College program was thriving, but the needs of the African American
community were growing.[80] The fraternity was not only grappling with
its duty to mankind but also looking for new ways to support the community, including providing scholarships for those who had trouble
paying for their education.[81] In fact, in reflecting on the need for this
initiative, it was noted that Greek-letter fraternities became common
among African American students for the same reason they were among

other races: these organizations were one of the only vehicles by which they could carry out a cooperative and intertwined agenda of economic, educational, and social uplift. These endeavors highlighted the founding visions of BGLOs; consider Alpha Phi Alpha's founding question: "What can we do to make our people rise?"[82]

By the end of 1926, the *Sphinx* included some early contemplation about working across organizational lines for the betterment of the African American community. For example, the December issue included an editorial from Alpha Kappa Alpha sorority concerning their desire to have a pan-fraternal convention to discuss a service project that might be executed across multiple different Negro Greek organizations.[83] In the same issue, brother John E. Oakes, Alpha Pi Chapter (Atlanta University), wrote about the need to focus on economics in the African American community.[84] In the article, he wrote that economic prosperity is what causes a race or a nation to be respected by other races and nations.[85] Economic prosperity is intimately intertwined in nearly all areas of social life: it keeps the "wolf" of poverty away, allowing other talents to develop.[86] In his assessment, African Americans would accomplish more when the race had achieved a state of economic prosperity. He went on to note that a large part of the suffering economic condition of African Americans resulted from the type of instruction that was given in African American schools.[87] As such, he called for African American teachers to not only address illiteracy but also focus on commerce and finance in order to produce more businessmen.[88] According to Oakes, the race needed lawyers in the courtroom and dentists and doctors to safeguard health, but it would be through businessmen that the race as a whole would make real strides.[89]

Community service may arguably be the area in which Delta Sigma Theta's efforts have been the most felt throughout its history. The organization's commitment to communities through empowerment, sisterhood, and leadership has not wavered since its inception. Many of the founding members could be found at the local Freedmen's Hospital at Howard University providing cheer to sick children and making nightgowns for adult patients.[90] Leadership through service and sisterhood are common themes that bind black sororities. Delta Sigma Theta members have not only engaged in passive activism but also been proactively and passionately at the forefront of movements for equality and social justice as membership expanded beyond college campuses.

Several Alpha Kappa Alpha chapters also engaged in community service in the 1920s—especially in volunteerism with the indigent and needy. For instance, in 1924, members of Lambda Omega Chapter made dresses for needy children as well as volunteered at the Colored Orphan's Home by conducting game and storytelling days as well as giving out apples to hungry children. Moved by many of their activities, Phillis Waters, a member of the chapter, adopted an orphaned child that year.[91] In April 1925, the Lambda Chapter held a Vocational Guidance Week in which they put on a literary and art contest to stimulate and encourage high school girls and to arouse interest in the national and local vocational guidance program.[92] In 1926, members of the sorority in Newport News, Virginia, hosted the Huntington High School senior girls during Vocational Guidance Week by putting on a musical and literary program. Through short talks with the girls they were able to impress the value of vocational guidance.[93] That same year Kappa Chapter (Butler College) gave a Christmas party at the orphan's home[94] and joined an Inter-racial Club at the college that sought to develop appreciation and a finer relationship between black and white college women.[95] On December 18, 1927, members of the Beta Omega Chapter visited Leed's Farm, a correctional institution for city prisoners, and put on a short program for the female inmates. They sang Christmas corals, read, and gave other remarks. At the end of the program each inmate was given a Christmas package of "goodies" (generally inclusive of small toys and candy).[96]

Community service is a major tenet of Phi Beta Sigma, as can be seen in the fraternity's motto: "Culture for Service, Service for Humanity." Starting in 1914, the fraternity maintained a Sunday school and was able to convince many brothers and non-brothers who had never gone to church to become regular church attendants.[97] In its early days the fraternity also started a library and an art gallery in the fraternity house that were open to the public. Fraternity members also founded the Benjamin Banneker Research Society and the Washington Art Club.[98] During World War I the fraternity shied away from community service but picked it back up once the fraternity had reclaimed enough members returning from war to be a healthy organization.

In 1923, Phi Beta Sigma began its first national public program, called the Clean Speech Movement, initiated by the Mu Chapter at Lincoln University.[99] The objective of this program was to curb the use of swear words among young African Americans, "to serve as a check on the use of slang and vulgar expressions, and to promote better speech in general."[100] It included a Clean Speech Week during which brothers in individual chapters of the fraternity pledged not to use swear words, and which was to include a daily address delivered by one of its members or a member of a different national fraternity. Furthermore, Clean Speech Week concluded on Sunday with a public meeting with a graduate or honorary member of Phi Beta Sigma acting as principal speaker and "musical selections" by members of the fraternity and its sister sorority, Zeta Phi Beta.[101] Unfortunately for the well-meaning brothers of the time, the Clean Speech Movement was not well received and made little headway.[102] The fraternity's future community service programs would be more successful.

The Phi Beta Sigma fraternity developed various charitable programs, some with more success than others. Greensboro, North Carolina, was the host city of the 1926 Conclave, and the fraternity voted to donate funds toward the construction of a hospital there.[103] At this Conclave the fraternity also voted and paid for a lifetime membership in the Association for the Study of Negro Life and History and later voted to contribute funds to Dr. Carter G. Woodson, the association's founder and director. On a more international note, in the March 1927 edition of the Crescent, the fraternity published an editorial imploring their brothers to donate money to the Haitian Commission, which was investigating the conduct of the occupying U.S. Marines in Haiti.[104] The fraternal leadership set an ambitious goal of fund-raising, and while they were unable to meet this goal, they still raised a fair amount for the cause. The second 1927 issue of the Crescent made further attempts to rouse members to contribute money to the Haiti Commission and solicited donations for the Clean Speech Movement.[105]

Working closely with its constitutionally bound brother organization, Phi Beta Sigma fraternity, Zeta Phi Beta sorority was focused on community service early on—especially in the southern states. In 1923 (just three years after its founding), Theta Chapter was established in Marshall, Texas, at Wiley College (where Phi Beta Sigma's Beta Chapter

was founded), making it the first chapter of any black sorority to organize a collegiate chapter in Texas. Even after chartering chapters in more
racially integrated cities, Zeta Phi Beta continued to make a concerted
effort to develop chapters at the nation's historically black colleges and
universities and in other areas of the South.[106] Because of the vision of
the founders of Zeta Phi Beta Sorority, Inc. (A. L. C. Stemons, M. T.
Faithful, V. T. Goings, F. P. Watts, and P. A. Neal), such grand endeavors
were begun, and it was because of the founders' continued work that the
sorority's goals reached fruition.

In those early years, members understood the necessity of ensuring the permanence of the organization. Accordingly, founder Myrtle
Tyler (Faithful) and four other Zeta sisters, Gladys Warrington, Joanna
Houston, Josephine Johnson, and O. Goldia Smith, first incorporated
the sorority on March 30, 1923, in Washington, D.C. (The sorority was
also incorporated in the state of Illinois in 1939.)[107] Based on the simple
belief (shared with their brother fraternity Phi Beta Sigma) that Greek-
letter elitism and socializing should not overshadow the real mission
for progressive organizations—to address societal mores, ills, prejudices,
poverty, and health concerns of the day—the founders departed from
the predominant models for elite black female coalitions. Instead they
sought to establish a new organization predicated on the precepts of
"scholarship, service, sisterly love, and finer womanhood" that were to
be the animating core of all sororal activities.

A Larger Vision: Toward Raising Racial Consciousness

Toward the end of the 1920s, many of the leaders of BGLOs saw the need
to not only encourage formal education and pursue civil and human
rights legislation and social activism, but also gain support for their
missions through racial consciousness raising. For instance, Omega Psi
Phi instituted the annual celebration of National Achievement Week, an
event meant to celebrate and inform communities about African American history and life in a way that inspires pride for the African American
community,[108] and to imbue self-respect among African Americans and
motivating African Americans to accomplish "worthy . . . contributions
to civilization."[109] Originally presented to the fraternity by Dr. Carter G.
Woodson (the second African American after W. E. B. Du Bois to earn

a PhD from Harvard) in 1920, National Achievement Week began as Negro History and Literature Week—which was the original precursor to what we now know as Black History Month. The Grand Conclave encouraged all chapters to celebrate by preparing displays of notable African Americans, donations of black-authored books, and discussions at local schools, churches, and other public spaces in their respective communities.[110] In 1925, the celebration was renamed National Negro Achievement Week and reorganized to better reflect the significant accomplishments of blacks that might otherwise go unnoticed by the general public, particularly for young people.[111]

The first national director of Negro National Achievement Week, Linwood G. Koger, guided chapters' individual celebrations by advising each to achieve certain goals: appoint a director responsible for planning and executing the community's celebration, design programs with wide appeal, organize speakers and essay contests to involve the community, and prepare or acquire appropriate literature to advertise and supplement the celebration's offerings.[112] The annual essay contest not only provided a means of community involvement but also functioned as an opportunity to encourage the study of African American history and life. In addition to the essay contest, the celebration involved recognition and awards for outstanding achievement. Each chapter awarded Achievement Scrolls to the member "who has made the most significant contribution to any area of human endeavor above and beyond the call of duty or who has exhibited eminent achievement in the face of great odds."[113]

By the mid-1920s, Alpha Phi Alpha members became more adamant that the fraternity must raise black racial consciousness. Individual members took it upon themselves to give speeches to urge people to get in the fight by joining the fraternal organizations and related organizations with which they worked. For example, Jesse E. Moorland, a prominent worker at the YMCA, was the first African American to speak before the University of Michigan since Booker T. Washington. Moorland's speech was titled "Our Greatest Challenge"—by which he meant facing racial inequality.[114] Zeta Chapter's I. N. Porter lectured at the Masonic Club about "Racial Impressions."[115] At Tau Chapter (University of Illinois), a series of articles were published in the *Daily Illini* regarding racial equality. The articles were sources of campus debate and were often the talk of campus. The first article discussed the importance of education for African American students and how it could increase their social standing. The article pointed out that people are a product of how they are raised and to what they are exposed. Responding to this article, a Mr. Sabin wrote about why social equality across the races was a bad idea, and why equality should, and would, not occur. A response to Mr. Sabin by Alpha Phi Alpha members detailed his ignorance in all things related to African Americans and highlighted how such opinions lack intelligence but were not wanting in prejudice.[116]

By 1927 Alpha Phi Alpha fraternity leadership and members were calling for greater engagement around issues of race. General president Raymond W. Cannon called for all like organizations to consider themselves in one union for the purpose of uplifting the race and developing the ability to serve.[117] Noted historian and Alpha Phi Alpha brother Rayford W. Logan urged fraternity members to annually observe Negro History Week to show that "Alpha Phi Alpha realizes the necessity for such study and officially endorses the annual effort to stimulate, foster, and perhaps revive enthusiasm for this praiseworthy endeavor."[118] In the June 1927 issue of the *Sphinx*, Logan noted that brother W. E. B. Du Bois advocated for a pan-African meeting to discuss race relations. As such, Alpha Phi Alpha planned to send delegates to the next Pan-African Congress meeting, to help bring more awareness to racial issues in America.[119]

The *Sphinx* was also used to bring other issues of race to the consciousness of Alpha Phi Alpha members during this period. In one article, an editorial originally published in the *Chicago Defender* in response to the Annual Formal of the Theta Chapter, the author claimed that there was a growing tendency on the part of African American men and women toward self-segregation, manifested in "college activities and social functions."[120] The author speculated that the separation was based on a self-conscious attitude, stemming from an inferiority complex that makes people of color uncomfortable in relationships with the white race. He went on that there was no sane argument against the intermingling of the races in school and college activities and social functions because the races will forever have to coexist and depend upon one another. The only way to meet the uncomfortable feeling was to mingle with the people who cause the uncomfortable feeling.[121]

By the end of the 1920s, Alpha had begun to collect its history in order to reflect on what worked and what lay ahead. Fraternity member and noted historian Charles H. Wesley produced the first history book of the Alpha Phi Alpha fraternity in 1929. In collecting and organizing the information about the fraternity, it was clear that its agenda was necessary and wanted: Alpha Phi Alpha had established eighty-five chapters and had over three thousand members.[122]

Likewise, Delta Sigma Theta issued its first public statement regarding race relations, stating, "We feel deeply the need for protest against the growing prejudice of all kinds in the United States of America. The time has come when we feel called upon to give voice for the first time to the strong feelings that have possessed us."[123] By 1929, under the direction of Ethel LaMay Calimese, Delta Sigma Theta engaged in one of its largest public-policy-related endeavors, the Vigilance Committee. Layle Lane and Sarah Speaks created the Vigilance Committee—which later became the Public Affairs Committee—at the 1929 National Convention to maintain meaningful and sustained connections with the political goals of the sorority. Soon after its creation, the Vigilance Committee began its work by sending a questionnaire to all chapters requesting their views on anti-lynching laws, reorganization of the courts, education funding, military expenditures, and unemployment protections.[124] These questionnaires shaped Delta Sigma Theta policies for the following decade. The Vigilance Committee worked in various ways to bring attention to and rectify a wide range of acts of injustice.

As the Great Depression suddenly gripped the country beginning in October 1929, Delta Sigma Theta members quickly mobilized to help the most vulnerable in society. Throughout the country, Delta Sigma Theta chapters presented money to charitable organizations, gave food baskets to those in need, provided aid to the elderly, donated clothes, purchased playground equipment, and paid nursery workers' salaries.[125] During this time Delta Sigma Theta members also spent much of their funds on supporting children—providing milk, toys, and various picnics and parties for underprivileged children.[126] One of the most common projects was furnishing African American hospitals with beds, linens, and hospital machinery, as well as painting the facilities and providing other necessities.[127]

Combined with the varied pursuits of educational attainment, philanthropy, economic attainment, community service, civil and human rights, and, later, racial consciousness raising, BGLOs were positioned in a unique place in black America to address the sudden socioeconomic crisis of the depression at the dawn of 1930s—which not only hit African Americans much harder than whites, but also provided conditions for a white backlash against black progress, which was often interpreted as a threat to white progress in a time of pinched resources. Particularly because of this context, in 1930 BGLOs united to form the National Pan-Hellenic Council—which we will examine to begin the next chapter.

Conclusion

In the years just after the founding of the first eight BGLOs, as a collective they were still searching for an identity beyond themselves. While their respective founders articulated a general vision in regard to racial uplift—more or less—what it meant in tangible terms remained to be seen. In the midst of the Harlem Renaissance, Roaring Twenties, and Jim Crow era, these college-educated men and women understandably turned toward the role of education, in and of itself, as a key to racial progress. In addition, BGLOs began to see education as foundational to the pursuit of human and civil rights. Moreover, their work in the areas of economic development, community service, and consciousness raising became foundational. These efforts would serve as a precursor to a more robust civic activism and effort to shape public policy that would begin to emerge in the 1930s.

4

Black Greek-Letter Organizations as Social Welfare Nets (1930–1939)

W. E. B. Du Bois joined Alpha Phi Alpha fraternity and cofounded the NAACP in 1909. The following year, Du Bois would become the NAACP director of publicity and research and in that role would, over the next two decades, serve as editor of the *Crisis* even as he was an active member and supporter of the fraternity. For Du Bois, these interests often merged. He wrote articles for the fraternity journal the *Sphinx*, which advertised and asked for fraternity cooperation with NAACP initiatives, while in the pages of the *Crisis*, every achievement and growth of Alpha Phi Alpha (as well as other BGLOs) was celebrated.[1] However, it was during this time that ideological divides would grow within the NAACP as well as in other black organizations like fraternities and sororities.

Du Bois was, early on, the public face of both the *Crisis* and the NAACP. Especially during the Roaring Twenties, the *Crisis* generated revenue that kept Du Bois and much of the association rather flush. Walter White became president of the NAACP in 1931 and was known as a staunch advocate of legal strategies toward integration, whereby Du Bois was becoming convinced that racial equality could best be attained by protest and agitation and in conjunction with the dismantling of imperialist and colonial capitalism around the world. The relationship between Du Bois and White was becoming quarrelsome. In addition, by 1931 both subscription numbers and income at the *Crisis* were dropping fast, which, as historian Patricia Sullivan put it, "made Du Bois increasingly dependent upon the financial support of the association, allowing White to push for more oversight. Du Bois insisted that the future of the *Crisis* and the association were inextricably bound. Hardly any board members shared that assessment. Du Bois's old supporter, Mary White Ovington, was quite matter of fact in telling him that the association had eclipsed the *Crisis* in importance and advised that 'it cannot belong to you as it has in the past.'"[2] By late 1931, the NAACP was on the edge of bankruptcy. Economic pressure and ideological debates were at a head. White suggested cutting organizational salaries by 5 to 10 percent and putting the *Crisis* under his own, rather than Du Bois's, oversight. Du Bois responded with an open letter to the NAACP board, accusing White of lying: "Unless Mr. White is going to be more honest and straight-forward with his colleagues, more truthful in his statement of facts, more conscientious in his expenditures of money . . . the chief question before this organization is how long he can remain in his present position and keep the NAACP from utter disaster."[3]

The association was audited, finding that White spent rather extravagantly on social events and tended to treat branch offices as mere sources of revenue, while Du Bois used the pages of the *Crisis* to dig into how black Americans viewed the Communist Party, sponsoring a symposium published in a two-part series in April and May of 1932. As the presidential election geared up, the NAACP put many of these internal debates on the back burner, but they were not resolved. In fact, White pointed the NAACP in the direction of using legal challenges to discrimination and the pursuit of racial integration, while Du Bois openly advocated that the association should be a clearinghouse of local initiatives, whereby authority and power would be decentralized into branch offices as "living cells of activity and ideals."[4]

In 1933, Franklin D. Roosevelt took office as president and acted swiftly to stabilize the economy via his New Deal. Yet to the dismay of the NAACP and White, Roosevelt would not pursue civil rights. Still, White attempted to change FDR's mind, even fostering a close relationship with Eleanor Roosevelt. Perhaps reading the writing on the wall, Du Bois resigned as director of publicity and research and returned to his professorship at Atlanta University. And by the next year Du Bois's rift with the NAACP was made complete when he penned a sarcastic letter, albeit based in pragmatism, that broke with the association's promotion of racial integration: "I know that this article will forthwith be interpreted by certain illiterate 'nitwits' as a plea for segregated Negro schools. It is not. It is saying in plain English that a separate Negro school where children are treated like human beings, trained by teachers of their own race, who know what it means to be black, is infinitely better than making our boys and girls doormats to be spit and trampled upon and lied to by ignorant social climbers whose sole claim to superiority is the ability to kick niggers when they are down."[5] The NAACP asked Du Bois to retract his statement and change his position. Du Bois refused and resigned completely from the association.

These same ideological debates (integration or nationalism, social change through legal maneuvering or direct action, and economic or political initiatives) were beginning to rage within the headquarters and chapters of BGLOs. The diversity of "New Negro" ideas from the Harlem Renaissance, the promise of a new world of labor under the banner of "Marxism," and the burgeoning first wave of white feminism that was being both adopted and challenged by black feminism qua "womanism" were manifest in sundry debates about how best to uplift the race. These questions were all the more pressing in the midst of the Great Depression.

The economic downturn hit nearly all Americans, but African Americans were particularly affected; by 1932, nearly 50 percent of all African Americans were out of work.[6] On top of that, both the social perceptions and realities of the intersection of race and labor compounded these difficulties. In many northern cities, whites called for African Americans to be fired from their jobs as long as there were (or believed to be) large swaths of out-of-work whites. And in the South, the price of cotton declined while inflation increased, which economically pinched the wages and profits from King Cotton. Southern whites interpreted economic hardship as a form of anti-white conflict whereby African American laborers were undercutting their efforts—hence lynchings in the South dramatically increased throughout the 1930s. The United States averaged seventeen reported lynchings per year during the 1920s, but the Great Depression brought that number to twenty-one in 1930, to twenty-eight in 1933, and then to twenty in 1935.[7] This increase inspired BGLO leaders to work with the NAACP (as individual members who were dual members of both organizations and through official fraternal and sororal cooperation with the NAACP) to pressure Congress, again, to pass anti-lynching legislation.

Political changes were also afoot. While African Americans had supported the Republican Party as the party of Lincoln, the election and presidency of Franklin D. Roosevelt softened the racial edge of the Democratic Party and began to lure voters away from the GOP. President Roosevelt accomplished this by entertaining black visitors at the White House, maintaining an unofficial "Black Cabinet," and occasionally broaching racial issues in a sympathetic tone during his "fireside chats." Despite FDR's turn away from civil rights in his New Deal platform, historian John Hope Franklin stated that FDR ushered in a "sense of belonging [African Americans] had never experienced before."[8] Nonetheless, discrimination was rampant in the New Deal housing and employment projects that began in the 1930s, and FDR backed away from much of the racial equality legislation that he had previously promised African American voters.

This context provided the conditions for BGLOs to band together, not only continuing their social uplift engagements from the previous decade, but also debating, cooperating on, and emphasizing various social welfare programs to stem the tide of economic and social maladies. For example, the National Pan-Hellenic Council (NPHC) was established on May 10, 1930 at Howard University, with Matthew W. Bullock (a distinguished racial activist, scholar, and member of Omega Psi Phi)[9] as the active chairman and B. Beatrix Scott (fifth international president of Alpha Kappa Alpha) as vice-chairman. NPHC was established with the following purpose and mission: "Unanimity of thought and action as far as possible in the conduct of Greek letter collegiate fraternities and sororities, and to consider problems of mutual interest to its member organizations."[10] The founding members of the NPHC were Kappa Alpha Psi and Omega Psi Phi fraternities, along with Alpha Kappa Alpha, Delta Sigma Theta, and Zeta Phi Beta sororities. The council's membership expanded as Alpha Phi Alpha and Phi Beta Sigma fraternities joined in 1931 and Sigma Gamma Rho sorority joined in 1937.

From the onset, the NPHC was a loose-knit body. It could not afford to hold all the BGLOs together with a narrow ideological agenda. Rather, it would serve as a clearinghouse of information and a regular meeting ground to coordinate member organization activities. Given that the NPHC was to "consider questions and problems of mutual interest to its members," the early national activities of the umbrella organization centered on racial discrimination on white campuses and economic recovery, particularly through participation in FDR's Joint Committee of the National Recovery Administration[11]—an agency designed to eliminate "cut-throat competition" by bringing industry, labor, and government together to create codes of "fair practices" and set prices (however, by 1935, the U.S. Supreme Court declared the agency unconstitutional). On local college campuses, NPHC chapters began popping up in consort with the founding of more BGLO chapters. For example, at Howard University BGLO members agreed that the NPHC's purpose "was to unite the Greek letter fraternities and sororities into one cooperative body dedicated to benefitting the campus as a whole. The aim of the Council is to promote the Greek-letter ideas of scholarship and character, and to develop those ideals through concerted effort, friendly rivalry, and a full-orbed recognition of over-all, fundamental purposes to which each of the organizations is individually committed."[12] The implementation of this purpose varied from locale to locale. But in broad strokes, most BGLO activity—through the NPHC—came in line with White's vision of the NAACP: to promote legal challenges to discrimination, to pursue education, to engender fellowship, and to promote what might be called the "respectability" of the race. For example, a January 1936 edition of the *New York Amsterdam News* (a preeminent black newspaper of its day) reported on a black sorority meeting whereby "two sorors gave a report on the activity of the Pan-Hellenic Council and later the group pledged its unanimous cooperation to foster among fraternities and sororities interest in and support of the N.A.A.C.P."[13] And in 1938 the same paper reported a meeting of Iota Phi Lambda sorority (founded in 1920 as the first African American Greek-lettered business sorority, in which dual membership with the sorority and NPHC sororities was allowed), whereby the "program was opened by the signing of the Negro National Anthem . . . and by Mr. Charles Collins who greeted the body on behalf of the Pan Hellenic Council. . . . the following recommendations and resolutions of national importance were adopted. . . . Commendation to Walter White, national Executive Secretary of the N.A.A.C.P."[14] By 1939, the NPHC seemed to be slowly turning inward, toward orchestrating uniformity and promoting education: "It has as its general purpose to bring about a closer inter-fraternal relationship between Negro fraternities and sororities, the standardization of membership requirements and encouragement of high scholarship."[15]

The story of how BGLOs—both independently and under the auspices of the NPHC—labored to grow and engage in racial uplift in the most economically depressed time of the nation's history, within the context of Jim Crow, is complex. There was no one overarching agenda, goal, or method. As there were debates within the NAACP, so there were debates within and across these fraternities and sororities. Accordingly, in this chapter we dive into that historical density through an examination of how these national groups and local chapters addressed the challenges of the 1930s through the promotion of their own organizations as social welfare "safety nets," and by advocating public policy reform, lynching legislation, legal challenges to segregation, community organizing, and civic education.

Black Greek-Letter Organizations as Safety Nets

Throughout the 1930s, many BGLOs engaged in various philanthropy programs in an effort to fill the gap between abject poverty and a basic level of human dignity. From the available information, we note a gender difference in how sororities and fraternities engaged in charity and philanthropy. First, sororities engaged in much more charity work than their fraternal counterparts. Second, sororities concentrated more on local fund raising events, donations of material goods, health and well-being programs, and the well-being of children, whereas fraternity endeavors to function as safety nets largely constituted job placement programs and collegiate scholarships. Together, this reflects some of the gender politics and expectations of gendered roles predominant in the era. However, as Deborah Whaley makes clear in *Disciplining Women,*

> Black sororities are sister organizations to women's clubs and other civil rights organizations of the nineteenth and twentieth centuries. In the nineteenth and twentieth centuries, women's clubs provided a gender-exclusive arena for self-actualization through involvement in political and social reform. These groups emerged at a critical historical moment when White women and women of color began to organize for enfranchisement and create social reform movements to address issues such as health care for poor and working-class families, child welfare, temperance, and literacy . . . to prove that education and political work were neither trivial nor impractical for women.[16]

Hence, we view sorority activities not only as the result of somewhat restrictive gendered roles, but as rather radical politics that situated black sororities on the cutting edge of these new social reform issues.

There are some substantial differences between sorority and fraternity engagement with charity and philanthropy. For instance, black sorority understandings of charitable and philanthropic activities were often defined by the extent to which general improvement in black women's lives could be realized, especially in the field of education. Sorority activities were often focused on education for varied reasons. First, teaching was a feminized occupation; it was often perceived as a professional form of mothering, for which black women were well suited; the role of "'othermothering' routinely done by African American women for their students and between generations of educators is salient to our research linking black sororities and the profession of teaching."[17] Second, demographic trends supported this avenue for charitable work: "Black Greek-letter sororities, instead of fraternities . . . [were] well positioned to play a role in recruitment and retention of schoolteachers as 'the largest share of members is employed in the field of education, followed by law, business, medicine, and social service professions.'"[18] Third, black sororities saw the development and support of black schoolteachers as both gender and race work, which would result in both "feminist gains as well as race-directed respect."[19] Fourth, the promotion of black women into the teaching profession meant their continued uplifting of the race, especially in a context in which "'getting an education' for African Americans meant that individual accomplishments often translated into benefits for one's community."[20] Not ironically then, many of the founders of the four black Greek-letter sororities were schoolteachers.

> Since their establishment, black sororities have focused on education as doorway to economic and community advancement. . . . They have solidified this endeavor by creating foundations that offer scholarships and fellowships. Since these organizations were created, they have raised millions of dollars in scholarship funds for African Americans as well as other racial and ethnic minorities. Sigma Gamma Rho championed chapter-based scholarships shortly before the Great Depression. . . . Likewise, during their 1937 national convening, the women of Delta Sigma Theta launched a nationwide library project. Their efforts addressed an urgent need in black communities, including many rural areas, for literature education. Of the 9 million African Americans residing in the rural south, two thirds were without library services and, as such had

very little exposure to books. . . . Some of the rural towns continued the
sorority's efforts by creating permanent library collections. . . . The Deltas were also instrumental in lobbying state legislatures in the South for
library funds and when none were allotted, they provided bookmobiles
with librarians.[21]

While there was some overlap with fraternities in the realm of education, particularly in awarding scholarships, a significant difference
resulted from the exclusion of women from much of the formal business
world, whereby black fraternity men became more directly involved in
legal and business activites than their sorority member counterparts.[22]

For example, raising funds and awarding scholarships to deserving
youths was a priority for Sigma Gamma Rho throughout the 1930s. By
the advent of World War I, national, regional, and even local scholarships were routinely awarded to promote and reward high ethical standards and scholastic achievement.[23] In 1935, Sigma Gamma Rho's Tenth
Boulé (national convention) foreshadowed the sorority's later community service and philanthropy. Under the direction of Bertha Black
Rhoda (international grand basileus from 1934 to 1944), the sorority un-
veiled its Vocational Guidance program. This program took members
on tours of industrial plants and compiled a list of appropriate books
for youths so that members could better educate young adults. Sigma
Gamma Rho also honored the NAACP via commendation for its service in advocating for African Americans living in the southern United
States. Sigma Gamma Rho's Thirteenth Boulé's (in 1935) theme, "How
Does Your Sorority Meet the Needs of Your Community?," showed that
personal achievement was not the only concern of Sigma Gamma Rho.
At that Boulé, Sigma Gamma Rho member Francis Moss Mann created
the Employment Aid Bureau, which was not a traditional employment
aid bureau but instead took the individual experience and background
of each member into consideration and placed that member in a position where she could not only help her community but also personally
thrive.[24]

Since the sorority was young (founded in 1922), the Employment Aid
Bureau was created to aid Sigma Gamma Rho members only; however,
its structure reflected the sorority's community service efforts of later
years. The Fourteenth National Boulé continued Sigma Gamma Rho's

trend toward multibenefit project programs. In 1939, that Boulé created the African Book Shower and the Circulating Library on Wheels.[25] The former project sent books to Wilberforce Institute in Cape Town, South Africa, while the latter provided Florida youths with a traveling library. Both programs extended Sigma Gamma Rho's ideals of education and youth service.

Zeta Phi Beta also engaged in several philanthropic activities with an emphasis on those struggling in the economic crunch of the Depression. However, the precise contours of that support would be the subject of much debate in the sorority throughout the 1930s. For instance, at the sorority's 1935 Boulé—under the administration of Violette N. Anderson (international grand basileus from 1933 to 1937)—it was suggested that the sorority sponsor a recreation project.[26] Initially, Zeta Phi Beta member Anita Turpeau Anderson presented a recreation plan for a rural southern district. However, after conferences with Dr. Ambrose Caliver of the Department of the Interior, it was decided that Coatesville, Pennsylvania, would be the project's location. The Coatesville Project began on July 28, 1935, to focus on the creative aspects of leisure time,[27] and chairman Gertrude Hamm encouraged participants (women, girls, and small boys) to realize the value of such time and how to use it.[28]

This program indicates the financially privileged position of the members. Soon, however, members felt that attention to leisure time, while important to battle mental distress and depression, was not enough. Most African Americans were hit too hard by the Great Depression to engage in leisure time activities, and the members turned their privileges toward other ends. As the Depression lingered during the administration of Nellie B. Rogers (international grand basileus from 1937 to 1939), the St. Louis chapter of Zeta Phi Beta joined an interracial effort to help needy children.[29] Similarly, in 1939, the administration of Edith Lyons (international grand basileus from 1939 to 1940) and the Nu Alpha Chapter sponsored several scholarships, donated toiletries to the Delinquent Youth Council, and sponsored the Trojan Club. An article in their sorority organ, the *Archon*, reported that they purchased a building for a youth center, financed a summer school, and monetarily supported efforts to provide art and music education to children from four to fourteen years of age.[30] Educators and church members—black and white—volunteered as staff.[31]

Chapters of the sorority also began to diversity their philanthropic programs. For example, Knoxville's Nu Zeta Chapter sponsored several service programs in 1938–39. The chapter awarded its first scholarship to a senior at Knoxville College with plans to make the scholarship a yearly award. In December, Nu Zeta worked with Delta Sigma Theta and Alpha Kappa Alpha chapters to cosponsor its annual Phillips Schuyler Baby Contest to raise two hundred dollars. Finally, in February the chapter donated between seventy-five and a hundred magazines to the children at the Deaf and Dumb School as a part of its Finer Womanhood Week. Zeta member H. C. Edmonds and her husband were both the supervisors of the school.[32] And in 1939, Beta Zeta Chapter of Zeta Phi Beta donated a shack to a YWCA camp.[33]

Near the end of the decade, debate had coalesced into three prongs of philanthropic support. Sister Dorothy M. Hendricks from New York City gave a speech at a 1939 regional conference on the three "fields" where she believed Zeta Phi Beta's members should focus their philanthropic efforts. The first was the "field of guidance," in which sisters should work with young people to help them find their talents and give them opportunities to use them.[34] In the "field of inspiration," Hendricks said that the sisters should "consider ourselves first and the young people about us second" so as to serve as better role models.[35] Finally, the third field Hendricks noted was "trail-blazing," the intention of working hard to forge a path for young people to have more opportunities as they grow up.[36] The sorority largely followed suit with individual chapters taking the lead—especially in the South.

For instance, the theme of Zeta Phi Beta's May 1939 Southern Regional Conference was "Greek Letter Organizations as Assets to Racial Betterment." The sorority awarded three scholarships at the conference. It also donated eighty dollars to nurse A. S. B. Miller from the Fort Worth Public School's Health Department to go toward ZPB's project, Fitting Indigent School Children with Glasses.[37]

Also in 1939, members of the Nu Alpha Chapter in Houston gave a "soap shower" and donated toiletries to the Delinquent Youth Council, an organization that worked with underprivileged children in the area. The sisters also created several scrapbooks with Christmas cards to give to patients at various hospitals around Houston.[38] The Nu Chapter in Atlanta held an Our Finer Womanhood Week in 1939 that consisted of several service programs. The sisters presented a Literary and Musical Cheer Up Program for residents at the Afro Old Folks Home and held a nursery shower for children attending the West End Nursery School. The chapter also held a brides' contest to raise three hundred dollars for a student at the Maggie Walker High School with no arms and legs to purchase artificial limbs.[39] Psi Zeta Chapter from Fort Worth, Texas, held its second annual Zeta Blue Revue in 1939 with over eight hundred guests to raise money to purchase glasses for children in need. Chapter members also held a shower for one of the sister's infants to present the child with ten dollars, the first payment of her college entrance fee.[40]

As early as the 1930s, Delta Sigma Theta supported organizations such as the National Urban League, the NAACP, the Association for the Study of Negro Life and History, and the National Youth Administration. BGLOs were beginning to expand and connect with other civil rights organizations and solidify relationships that would last for decades. It was during this time, particularly during national president Vivian Osborne Marsh's administration, that Delta Sigma Theta began working with Alpha Kappa Alpha on two of its initiatives, the Mississippi Health Project and the National Non-Partisan Council.[41] The Mississippi Health Project helped provide medical care and immunizations to those living in rural Mississippi, and the National Non-Partisan Council worked with the NAACP to promote its future goals.[42] While Alpha Kappa Alpha took the lead on the projects, Delta Sigma Theta contributed regularly to promoting these endeavors.[43] Delta Sigma Theta members continued their work with the NAACP on the Fund for Freedom project, to which members annually contributed money and support.[44] These efforts would reverberate for decades; by the 1970s, 87 percent of the chapters pledged life membership to the NAACP, while 67 percent of the chapters annually contributed to other civil rights organizations.[45]

Alpha Kappa Alpha directed most of its organizational activities into the philanthropic dimensions of racial uplift in the 1930s. Local chapters were especially active in these endeavors. Throughout 1931, chapters engaged in relief work among the neediest, such as sorority chapters sponsoring Bundle Showers (bundles of cast-off clothing and solicitations) at local YWCAs.[46] Alpha Tau Omega Chapter engaged by participating in a carnival presented by the Woman's Club at the recreation center, in which they donated funds to the Orphan's Home Drive.[47] And the Alpha Rho Chapter hosted a cabaret party for the benefit of their local scholarship fund.[48]

In 1932 the Nu Chapter helped the community by feeding milk to children in the model school and feeding needy families at a local community center.[49] At the same time the Alpha Omega chapter held a bake sale for the benefit of the scholarship fund,[50] and the *Ivy Leaf* covered the activities of Alpha Beta Omega Chapter: "Realizing the necessity of practical service at this time, we have bent our efforts toward alleviating the suffering of the unfortunates of community. To this end we distributed baskets of food to the needy families of the city during the Thanksgiving and Christmas season."[51] During that same year, the Alpha Chi Omega Chapter from Tulsa, Oklahoma, donated twenty-five dollars to the Relief Program of the local Community Chest Fund to assist the struggling in their community and began to discuss the plans "to give a local scholarship of $25.00 to some deserving girl." And the Epsilon Chapter in Massachusetts worked with the Women's Service Club by "filling the baskets for poor families." By December 1932, taking notice of the financial crisis of the country, Epsilon decided that instead of throwing a party for children, they would "undertake the support of a needy family of four, with two minor children for the next twelve months." Around Christmas 1932, the chapter set aside money to provide the family with "food, clothing, and fuel" for the next year. They also "provided a well-stocked market basket containing Christmas delicacies, toys for the children, and much-needed clothing."[52]

By 1933, the sorority made a special contribution to St. Paul's African Methodist Episcopal (AME) church and dovetailed those events with the sorority's Founder's Day, when they held a service with a series of speakers that discussed the sorority's programs to contribute to and positively impact the local community.[53] The Alpha Rho Chapter of Alpha Kappa Alpha from Wichita, Kansas, collected and distributed "old clothing to the less fortunate on Thanksgiving" and again during Christmas. In addition to this, they also had guests for a party bring food as their admission. The food was then used to create baskets for the needy during Christmas.[54] And by December 1933, Mu Omega Chapter established a health committee that visualized and planned a program that met the needs of establishing better health habits in schoolchildren from the first through twelfth grades.[55]

In 1934, Eta Omega Chapter donated "fifteen baskets to needy families" around Christmas in Louisville, Kentucky. Kappa Omega donated money to the Penny Fund in Atlanta. Alpha Chi Omega donated clothing to the less fortunate in Tulsa. Sister Althea Findley "assisted in the compilation of statistics gathered during the Negro Health Survey." Alpha Sigma "used the proceeds of its rummage sale" to make baskets for the needy in Phoenix. The basket program was popular among Alpha Kappa Alpha chapters, who donated money toward various charities and sheets to hospitals.[56] And several members traveled to Mississippi to continue to support the Institute for Colored Teachers.

Throughout 1934 and 1935, the sorority began to direct more attention to health initiatives. The Mu Omega Chapter of Indianapolis established a health club program for elementary schools. The clubs met about every two weeks and garnered over two hundred members. The same committee also furnished and maintained a room at Douglass Hospital, in which they held a regular reading and book review group of over five hundred.[57] By December 1935, these endeavors coalesced into Alpha Kappa Alpha's National Health Project.[58] The "purpose of the health project is to disseminate information as to what has been done for the less fortunate, and to encourage the undertaking of similar projects be persons or organizations interested in the promotion of health and educational opportunities for children living in less progressive communities."[59] By 1939, Alpha Kappa Alpha's Health Project had provided health services for over five years, including but not limited to immunization services, dental services, and prenatal exams.[60] Chapters, such as Nu Chapter (at West Collegiate Institute—now West Virginia State University), continued to support the endeavor at the time with frequent monetary donations to the Health Project and sponsorship of the "inoculation of pre-school children."[61]

The sorority's attention to health disparities inspired related initiatives. Many members of Alpha Kappa Alpha also worked with Delta Sigma Theta members on the Mississippi Health Project and took up their own endeavors. Led by Alpha Kappa Alpha member and doctor Dorothy Boulding Ferebee, the sorority opened a free clinic in Mississippi that gave smallpox and diphtheria vaccinations and treated malaria for two weeks; the clinic served about thirty-five hundred youths and adults.[62] Alpha Kappa Alpha also used the Mississippi Health Project to send out a social survey and then planned a supplemental project that reflected the needs of the community as seen in the collected socioeconomic data.[63] Also, Alpha Kappa Alpha member Mary Williams merged sorority initiatives with work on health care for African Americans. For example, Williams was responsible for greatly reducing typhoid fever near the Tuskegee Institute and was the only "colored person" in 1924 to receive a scholarship from the American Child Health Association. That same year, Williams spoke to the American Public Health Association about "Future Possibilities of an All-Around Public Health Program That Would Benefit the Rural Child." During this meeting she was given a gold medal for her accomplishments. In 1927 she helped organize "one of the first Programs of Public Health Work for Negroes in the Mississippi Flood Area." In 1929 Williams received a scholarship to take a postgraduate course at Harvard. In 1930 "she was appointed a member of the White House Conference," and discussed "Rural Children and Their Disadvantages in the Public Health Program." She also assisted the Medical Direction of AKA's Health Project. In addition to all of this, she was the home service worker for Tuskegee Institute's Chapter of the American Red Cross, the only chapter not run by a white person, and Williams was on the American Red Cross National Committee on Flood and Relief Problems. By 1938 Williams turned much of her attention to the eradication and prevention of syphilis in the Deep South. In 1938 she met with first lady Eleanor Roosevelt (who became an honorary member of Alpha Kappa Alpha) to discuss "National Problems That Confront the Negro Women and Children of Today." And while in residence at the Tuskegee Institute, Williams assisted with the John A. Andrew Clinic—the purpose of which was to promote public health in the African American community.[64]

Throughout the latter half of the 1930s, the sorority expanded philanthropic activities in sundry ways—mainly relying on the initiatives of individual chapters, who themselves partnered with local organizations. For instance, the Alpha Alpha Omega Chapter of Pittsburgh participated with the YWCA, Community Fund, Pittsburg Unity of the National Negro Health Movement, and several other charities and donated books to help rebuild a library damaged by a fire.[65] The Beta Delta

Chapter of St. Louis held a booth for "the May Day Celebration of the Orphans Home," and the Beta Kappa Omega Chapter organized a Negro History contest for middle schoolers in Kansas and hosted a breakfast in order to raise funds for their NAACP project. And various members of the sorority in the greater New York City area worked on the "campaign to revive the New York Branch of the Association for the Study of Negro Life and History."[66]

In 1937 chapters continued to focus on supplying basic necessities to families suffering under the Great Depression. The Phi Omega Chapter of Winston-Salem, North Carolina, raised enough money to add a full-time African American nurse to the City Health Department and launched a library drive to encourage interest in the Moses Horton Branch Library among African Americans.[67] The Beta Epsilon Omega Chapter of Memphis organized a Thanksgiving project to bring coal and food to twelve families.[68] The Alpha Kappa Omega Chapter of Houston provided a quart of milk every day for a year to five needy children who were registered with the Houston Tubercular League.[69] Additionally, the Alpha Kappa Omega Chapter also raised four hundred dollars to purchase furniture for the Crippled Children's Ward in the new hospital designated especially "for Negroes."[70]

In 1938 the sorority sent representatives to the Conference on the Participation of Negro Women and Children in Federal Welfare Programs,[71] where women and children gathered to express their "eagerness to cooperate with the women of America to achieve together the bright goals of democracy and human welfare."[72] The sorority reported that "Negro women and children do not participate in federal welfare progress to any extent in proportion to their need" and "that this condition is the direct result of . . . virtual exclusion from . . . federal departments and bureaus."[73] Alpha Kappa Alpha thereby recommended that "representative leadership among Negroes in various administrative posts" should be immediate.[74]

And in 1939 the sorority stepped up its financial donations to like-minded organizations and people in need. For example, Alpha Alpha Omega Chapter contributed to the NAACP,[75] while the headquarters of Alpha Kappa Alpha gave a five-hundred-dollar donation to the NAACP,[76] and Beta Beta Delta Chapter sponsored a ward at Jackson Negro Hospital in Mississippi and took up financially supporting an im-

poverished rural school.[77] Meanwhile the Alpha Iota Chapter continued
to support Deep South sharecroppers with money and clothing.[78]

The previous pages have concentrated on sororities' philanthropic
and charity work, which dwarfs similar initiatives of the fraternities.
Moreover, as noted above, fraternity endeavors to act as safety nets centered largely, albeit not exclusively, on the creation of job placement programs and the provision of scholarships for college. For example, Kappa
Alpha Psi continued its Guide Right program and created the Guide
Right Commission for April 20 to 27, 1930, for the observance of Annual Guidance Week. Due to the high black unemployment rate at the
time, consideration was given to placing workers with lower education
and experience in industrial jobs. The Guide Right Movement inherently realized that, while beneficial to many, a college education was not
the only way to pursue a fulfilling and productive future. Consequen-
tially, Guide Right adjusted its focus to include giving guidance to some
young boys toward opportunities available in myriad vocations, and not
encouraging everyone to pursue a college education without more individual consideration.[79] As a result of this shift, the program was able to
reach even more people. In 1939 the Kappa Alpha Psi organ the *Journal*
noted that nearly all of the eighty-two national chapters participated,
reaching five thousand interested high school senior boys and young
men, and an event called Guide Right Sunday was attended by about
twenty-five thousand people and garnered major news coverage.[80] In
subsequent years, the Guide Right program principles, aims, and definitions would constantly be clarified and modified to address expenditures
and future efforts of the program, reflecting historical trends around the
country with regard to African American communities.

For Omega Psi Phi, the organization struggled early on in its history to offer financial assistance to members and nonmembers alike to
pursue their education. However, between 1923 and 1938, the organization eventually materialized a national scholarship program.[81] The fraternity's Scholarship Commission, formed in 1938, reviewed scholarship
applications and determined to whom and for what amount the fraternity would offer assistance. Assistance offers were generally modest, one
hundred to five hundred dollars annually, and offered on a competitive
basis to undergraduates through scholarships and graduate students
through fellowships.

Alpha Phi Alpha continued its dedication to philanthropy through scholarships and fellowships in pursuit of their goal to further education of the youth. During the Twenty-Fifth General Convention, the director of education, Rayford Logan, reported that the fraternity had awarded a total of $2,400 in scholarships and fellowships.[82] At the end of 1935, the fraternity purchased $993.75 worth of government bonds for the 1934–35 academic year.[83] With careful consideration, the committee split the allotted fellowship in half, awarding $450 to James B. Browning and Joseph Himes for their graduate work at the University of Michigan and Ohio State University, respectively.[84]

The Twenty-Seventh General Convention, held in New York during August 1939, established a Committee on Employment Opportunities under the leadership of B. T. McGraw.[85] With a thousand-dollar budget, the committee drafted three objectives: (1) to study the technique of organizing, directing, and controlling the collective action of African American communities to increase employment opportunities; (2) to unearth and evaluate business investment opportunities for African American funds; and (3) to make known the best available avenues and methods for sound investment of such funds to increase African American employment.[86] Also, Dr. Andrew E. McDonald and Dr. Andrew J. Young volunteered in Louisiana to facilitate the Clinic on Wheels program, which provided dental care to indigent African Americans in rural areas.[87] Alpha Chi Chapter urged other chapters to follow in its footsteps in awarding annual undergraduate scholarships to students at their respective universities.[88] Alpha Zeta Chapter (West Virginia State College) initiated an annual award to be given to the freshman student with the highest academic performance for the year.[89] In an address in Chicago, Alpha Phi Alpha member and executive secretary of the Wabash Avenue YMCA George R. Arthur encouraged his fraternity brothers to be concerned about the state of Negro youth and consider appointing a national committee on the "preservation of Negro Youth" designed to address problems facing this group, particularly those surrounding incarceration and criminalization.[90]

The fraternity also awarded scholarships to promising members, such as John Hope Franklin, the future historian of Fisk University. In addition, the fraternity gave a scholarship to Ewart Gladstone Guinier, a Jamaican migrant to the United States who left Harvard because of racial discrimination and attended (with help from Alpha Phi Alpha) City College of New York.[91] Guinier would go on to become, in 1969, the first chairman of the Afro-American Studies Department, with an honorary doctorate degree and tenure, at Harvard University.[92] Logan revealed the motivation behind the scholarship foundation: "I would say that the purposes of the Alpha Phi Alpha Foundation are to promote scholarship by encouraging Negroes to continue their education and by aiding worthy brothers to do so; to educate Negroes in their rights and obligations as citizens, in the benefits that they can derive from the exercise of these rights; and to devise ways to overcome obstacles that prevent them from exercising those rights and finally to contribute our share of intelligent leadership in helping Negroes to obtain as much economic security as is possible at the present time."[93] As revealed in Logan's understanding of the scholarship, the fraternity was turning more and more of its attention away from philanthropy and toward the attainment of economic security.

Challenging Jim Crow through Public Policy Reform

Delta Sigma Theta engaged in a letter-writing campaign to address various Jim Crow issues and policies that would adversely affect African Americans. When the Smoot-Hawley Tariff Act of 1930 was up for review before Congress, Delta Sigma Theta urged Congress not to pass the bill, which would have imposed the highest tariffs on imports in American history and would have had an increased negative effect on African Americans living under Jim Crow. Delta Sigma Theta viewed the tariff as counterproductive to economic growth and African American economic vitality.[94] Also in 1930 the Hoover administration sent mothers overseas to view their slain sons lost at war; however, African American mothers were given inferior accommodations on the trip to France. Delta Sigma Theta spoke out to protest such treatment and demanded the administration rectify the problem. Similarly, the Hoover administration would not allow an African American football player from Ohio State University to play in a game against the U.S. Naval Academy. Delta Sigma Theta chapters around the nation wrote letters to the administration to protest the unfair treatment. Delta Sigma Theta also wrote to President Hoover to urge his support of disarmament with other nations at the London Naval Conference.

Delta Sigma Theta did not limit its lobbying to the government either, as the sorority appealed to many other institutions, including predominantly white colleges and universities. Delta Sigma Theta pressured the University of Michigan and Ohio State University to end discriminatory practices. Through Delta Sigma Theta's work, both universities made concessions that ultimately led to more equal treatment for African American students. At the University of Illinois, Delta Sigma Theta president Ethel Calimese wrote letters to the dean of women, held numerous meetings with her, and ultimately convinced her to openly acknowledge and address campus climate issues impacting African American students.[95] Delta Sigma Theta members expanded their policy proposals beyond traditional civil rights issues.

During the 1930s, Delta Sigma Theta members assisted individuals unfairly targeted for their civil rights work. For example, Louise Thompson was a member of Delta Sigma Theta and of the International Workers Order (IWO), a socialist organization working to promote a more socialist agenda. The IWO was founded in 1930 to provide workers with affordable life insurance; it was unique among fraternal groups as membership included "more than fifteen different nationalities, organized in their own national sections, plus native born black and white workers."[96] The IWO was one of the most "leftwing of all fraternal organizations and the most successful Communist-led mass organizations . . . by the mid-1930s it was one of the fastest growing fraternal organizations."[97] In 1934, Louise Thompson was arrested in Birmingham, Alabama, in conjunction with her support of a strike by a racially integrated union, the International Union of Mine, Mill and Smelter Workers (informally known as the "Nigger Union" by many locals). When her arrest became national news in 1934, Delta Sigma Theta members immediately stepped forward to facilitate her release. Although the sorority's efforts did not seem to directly impact Thompson's case, Delta Sigma Theta's open support cemented its place among radical social activist organizations and demonstrated a high level of commitment to social justice among its members.

Many Delta Sigma Theta members were committed to achieving economic justice and actively supported public policy initiatives to address employment inequality. In 1930, members wrote to the Secretary of Labor, urging him to create a long-range public works program. In conjunction with this endeavor, Delta Sigma Theta enlisted the help of Oscar De Priest, the first African American elected to Congress from a northern state.[98] When the Roosevelt administration created the Joint Committee on National Recovery during the Great Depression, Delta Sigma Theta sent Esther Popel Shaw to represent its interests before the committee and contributed significant funds to projects sponsored by the Joint Committee on National Recovery to ensure its success.[99] Another common endeavor for Delta Sigma Theta was promoting education via legislation. In 1937 Congress was on the verge of passing the Harrison-Black-Fletcher Bill for federal aid to education. Although the bill increased funding, it made no allocations to African American institutions. In response, hundreds of Delta Sigma Theta members sent letters to their congressional representatives and staged protests to the bill, which ultimately failed.[100] Delta Sigma Theta also became active in supporting Congressman Arthur W. Mitchell, who regularly introduced bills that worked to eliminate discrimination and segregation.[101]

While most members of Alpha Kappa Alpha were engaged in philanthropic endeavors, several also engaged in public policy reform. In 1933 Member Idabelle Lindsay persuaded the sorority leadership in St. Louis to send telegrams protesting the acquittal of men charged with a lynching in St. Joseph, Missouri.[102] In 1934 member Pearl Mitchell, who worked as a Juvenile Court probation officer in Ohio and was president of the Cleveland NAACP, made several speeches about how to successfully block segregation legislation and presented a talk titled "A Front Against Lynching."[103] By 1936 members of the Tau Omega Chapter regularly participated in the Joint Conference Against Discriminatory Practices. This group worked to get rid of all types of discrimination in city departments of education, health, home and work relief, and WPA employment. These chapter members were also active in a campaign "to open all municipal hospitals in New York City to Negro physicians and nurses for training and practices."[104] In 1930 the Beta Gamma Omega Chapter collected two hundred signatures for a petition in support of a Federal Anti-Lynching Bill.[105] Additionally, several members worked on the Our Lobby Project, which recommended legislation to support Howard University's Department of Commerce and Finance and the Youth Congress.[106] Last, Ellie Alma Walls, of Alpha Kappa Omega Chapter, became the secretary of the Education Committee of the Texas

Interracial Commission and spearheaded work to pass a bill to provide aid for African Americans traveling out of state for graduate work.[107]

In addition, public policy issues came to the center stage of Phi Beta Sigma at the 1934 Washington, D.C., Conclave. The fraternity voted to create a committee dedicated solely to public policy matters.[108] The Public Policy Committee did not hesitate to start doing their job. Soon after the 1934 Conclave, the Public Policy Committee urged the fraternity to come forth with a broad-based program that would address the problems of "the great masses of the African American people."[109] This started the fraternity along its course toward the great Social Action Plan. Per the Social Action Plan, local chapters were encouraged to sponsor forums and roundtable discussions on current political and economic questions. Some members pushed for the fraternity's Bigger and Better Business Program to be meshed with the National Negro Business League, but eventually the fraternity decided against this idea. In the March 1935 issue of the *Crescent*, James Jackson suggested that African Americans "buy black," meaning that they should give first preference to African American merchants when buying goods or services and second preference to merchants who employed African Americans.[110]

The second 1935 issue of the *Crescent* was particularly important because it expanded upon the rationale behind Phi Beta Sigma's public policy initiatives. This issue contained one article about the dangers of communism to the African American, another article that advocated a "cooperative society," and yet another extolling education as the "way out" for African Americans.[111] The idea of cooperatives was nothing new, however, as an article in a 1929 edition of the *Crescent* discussed. The Colored Merchants Association, described therein, was a business cooperative whose practices included "buying in large quantities, maintaining uniform service, and advertising cooperatively."[112] This enabled them to "sell with profit at greatly reduced prices."[113] Interestingly, the southern, slightly more conservative brothers had yet another theory that they explained in the July 1937 issue of the *Crescent*. They believed that the best way to build bigger and better business among African Americans, and thus increase their quality of life, was through "consumer and credit cooperative movement."[114] During this time there was no consensus among the brothers as to what public policy approach was the best suited to better African Americans' quality of life.

A Business Men's Luncheon was held at the 1938 Winston-Salem Conclave. During the luncheon, local leaders talked about the African American problems and opportunities in the business world.[115] At the same Conclave, the Resolutions Committee came up with several resolutions; the most important was that a pamphlet be prepared by the fraternity on the business methods and achievements of African American businessmen.[116]

In an initiative, presumably approved at the previous 1936 New York City Conclave by the Resolutions Committee, Phi Beta Sigma member Emmet May and newly elected national fraternity president James Weldon Johnson signed into action a program to send letters to President Franklin D. Roosevelt supporting the Black-Connery Wages and Hours Bill,[117] and to Senators Robert F. Wagner and Royal S. Copeland supporting the Wagner-Van Nuys Anti-Lynch Bill.[118] They sent another letter to President Roosevelt opposing Hugo L. Black's elevation to the U.S. Supreme Court because of his "social background, affiliation with un-American Organizations, and prejudice towards Jews, Catholics and [African Americans]."[119]

Civil rights issues took center stage at the 1937 Detroit Phi Beta Sigma Conclave. The fraternity's national officers announced that "a protest had been lodged with the World Almanac for not listing [African American] Greek-letter organizations." Likewise, they announced that "a protest was lodged with the national news-gathering agencies for not covering [African American] collegiate sports contests." During the same Conclave, the Program for Social Action was given the objective of equalizing educational opportunities for African Americans, including equalizing teacher salaries. This specific area was picked because

> the salaries of black teachers during the 1930s were far below those of whites. The monthly salary of black teachers in the South in 1930 was about 60 percent of the white average, $73 for blacks and $118 for whites, with the yearly school term in white schools about two months longer, which added to the salary gap. Poorly paid teachers are not necessarily poorly trained or unable to educate their students, but the meager wages of black teachers in the 1930s did not lure the most promising college graduates into rural Jim Crow schools. Horace Mann Bond, a noted black educator, administered the Stanford Achievement Test to a large

group of black teachers in Alabama schools in 1931. He discovered that their average score was below that of the national level of ninth-grade students. Almost half of the black teachers had not mastered the material that eighth-graders were expected to know. And many of these teachers were assigned to teach students in grades above their own level of knowledge.[120]

In addition, the Phi Beta Sigma Conclave delegates voted to support the NAACP, the National Bar Association, the NPHC, and the National Urban League. It appears the delegates believed these organizations were the most effective advocates of African American civil rights at that time. In fact, Phi Beta Sigma, or at least many of the individual brothers, had established the value of the NAACP's efforts toward achieving legal and social equality for African Americans. In a 1929 editorial in the *Crescent* titled "The Negro's Best Champion," Phi Beta Sigma member James Weldon Johnson stated that "the importance of the National Association for the Advancement of Colored People . . . lies in its being the first successful effort to organize the minority sentiment on race relations for effective concerted action. . . . It has gone into the fundamental structure of the law. Five victories before the Supreme Court stand to its credit."[121] A decade later at the 1939 Washington, D.C., Conclave, newly elected national fraternity president George W. Lawrence gave a stirring speech in which he pledged that the brotherhood would continue to work with like-minded groups in the fight for equality, but would not compromise or let cooperation with other groups delay Phi Beta Sigma from their mission, saying, "We care not what others may do. We cannot detour. We will not retreat!"[122]

Likewise, Kappa Alpha Psi began to challenge racial inequality via public policy endeavors. For instance, in December 1936, at the Twenty-Sixth Grand Chapter Meeting in Washington, D.C., the fraternity ratified a plan to change the requirement that photographs be submitted with civil service applications.[123] Previously, applicants were required to submit their photographs, which led to African Americans being identified, discriminated against, and bypassed.[124] The Twenty-Sixth Grand Chapter Meeting also went on record criticizing the Lynch Law and endorsed the NAACP in their mission to admit African Americans into state-owned higher education institutions for courses not offered at black colleges.[125]

Lynching Legislation

Jim Crow, especially in the time of the Depression, had a system of racial etiquette in place that

> displayed and reinforced racial hierarchy. In Natchez, Mississippi, in the 1930s, black people could not enter or leave a white's house by the front door. So strong was this ceremonial rule, researchers observed, that whites would lock the back door, but not the front, when leaving home. Blacks had to address whites by titles: "Boss," "Sir," "Mister," or "Missus"; whites would address blacks by first names only. White people required titles because they had to be treated as representatives of the entire white race, whatever their personal worth; they were symbols as well as individuals. The use of a title also avoided any claim to familiarity, thus protecting the "ideal sphere" of honor around every white person. Whites denied blacks this sphere of honor, privacy, and protected space.[126]

The greatest penalty for breaking these rules of racial etiquette was lynching. While the high point for lynchings was 1892 and lynchings overall were on the decline, the 1930s saw a rise in their numbers.[127] While a lynching is generally defined as "an extra-legal execution, by a group of perpetrators, of one or more persons alleged to have committed a crime or violated important informal norms,"[128] there were many so-called "legal lynchings" in which a "speedy trial" was a less-than-subtle euphemism for charging, arresting, and sentencing people of color to death on trumped-up or overblown allegations. In this sense, both "legal" and illegal lynchings were also symbolic and meant to function as a form of social control à la terrorism. There were variations to this terrorism, such as "[1] 'mass mobs' involving a large part of the white community and displaying the ritual characteristics . . . ; [2] 'terrorist mobs,' more secretive killings by small groups of 'whitecappers' or other white organizations; [3] 'private mobs,' usually involving only a few participants and operating in secret; and [4] 'posse' lynchings, in which the victim was killed while being pursued by legal, or at least quasi-legal, authorities."[129] Throughout the 1930s many BGLOs engaged federal and state legislatures to produce civil and human rights policies, procedures, and legislation. For instance, through the 1930s Sigma

Gamma Rho officially supported the Costigan-Wagner Anti-Lynch Bill by encouraging each member to write a letter to her representative asking him or her to support the bill. Beginning in 1930, Delta Sigma Theta worked closely with the NPHC to promote projects to better African American lives.[130] Together, Delta Sigma Theta and the NPHC began to more overtly challenge state and federal civil codes of Jim Crow, which governed most of everyday life for African Americans. In the early 1930s many of the review dates for these codes neared, and Delta Sigma Theta members all over the country mailed in letters protesting the codes and advocating for change.[131] For instance, in 1930 there was a vicious lynching in Sherman, Texas, which prompted the Vigilance Committee to send a written condemnation to the city's mayor for his actions during and after the incident.

At the Twenty-Seventh Grand Chapter Meeting in December 1937, "reports revealed . . . active campaigning for the passage of anti-lynching legislation; [and] Fraternity representation at the National Negro Congress and the National Negro Business League."[132] Resolutions passed during the annual Conclave of Kappa Alpha Psi urged the fraternity to undertake the following measures: (1) petition both President Roosevelt and Congress to pass the Anti-Lynching Bill; (2) fight to have the photo requirement for civil service exams abolished; (3) encourage African Americans to become members on policy-making government bodies; and (4) help create a bureau in Washington to look after the interests of African Americans.[133] At the following Grand Chapter Meeting, Kappa Alpha Psi affirmed allegiance to the U.S. Constitution and pledged support of movements working for universal civil rights.[134]

Also in 1937, President Roosevelt was supposed to fight for antilynching legislation.[135] The passage of such a law would be largely symbolic, as it represented the eradication of one of the most heinous forms of violence against African Americans. Kappa Alpha Psi encouraged members to write their congressmen and senators to ensure they too would back the passage of this bill and work for legislation that would make life safer and easier for African Americans in the United States.[136] Despite these labors—and even with the activism of Ida B. Wells, Mary Burnette Talbert, Angelina Grimké, and Juanita Jackson Mitchell—no federal anti-lynching legislation was ever passed (nearly two hundred anti-lynching bills had been introduced between 1892 and 1968).

Legal Challenges to Segregation

After facing major setbacks in advancing federal anti-lynching legislation, many BGLOs and their members turned toward promoting those civil rights through litigation under established law. One particular area of focus was desegregation efforts, particularly in schools. The context in which they were operating was stark. As public policy scholar Jeffrey A. Raffel notes:

> By 1930, it was clear that the *Plessy* decision stood as a major obstacle to achieving better schools for negroes. While the Court had propounded a principle of separate but equal, the emphasis was on separate, not on equal. For example, in South Carolina, per-pupil expenditures for white students were ten times that for colored students and in Florida, Georgia, Mississippi, and Alabama, the ratio was five to one. Dual systems had become the rule in the South. School boards were running two sets of schools, one for colored children and one for white. (In Delaware, even this was not good enough; the state also had a system for Moors and a system for Indians.) The colored systems were under-funded, under-maintained, and under-performing.[137]

To address these inequalities, for example, Sigma Gamma Rho raised funds to assist legal teams who fought court cases to eradicate inequality and injustice.[138] This funding program was overseen by the Education Commission, composed of members Edith Malone Ward, Ida Laws, and Ethel Garner.[139] Additionally, in 1937 the Alpha Kappa Alpha Committee on Public Affairs was formalized as a standing committee with power to act on matters of importance. In reference to the "Scottsboro Boys" (nine African American teenagers in Alabama falsely accused of raping two white women on a train in 1931), the committee commended the actions of all groups and individuals who participated in their defense and expressed its gratitude for their untiring, persistent effort and zeal in bringing about the exoneration of four of the defendants.[140]

In 1930 Alpha Phi Alpha increasingly began to raise awareness about racial discrimination against African Americans. For instance, attorney and member Raymond Pace Alexander noted that "the system of American color prejudice was an entirely false and monstrous thing—

something entirely constructed by the white American in order to exploit the Negro."[141] From his perspective, Americans viewed blacks as indolent, lazy, and shiftless and as composing a large percentage of criminals.[142] As a growing number of black activists and leaders had come to believe, Alexander similarly echoed that blacks were treated better in Europe.[143] On other fronts, the general officers of the *Sphinx* asked the readers for help: "We desire to know if any racial discrimination is practiced in your college or university and, if so, the principal forms and their effect."[144] The fraternity was specifically focused on admissions, athletic and scholastic team participation, extracurricular activities, ROTC acceptance, use of communal space, and so forth.[145] This call to action was so the members of Alpha Phi Alpha could thus take action to correct the issues. A clarion call was made—"If we are going to get somewhere as a race, we must not only advance ourselves individually, but we must help those about us in the struggle."[146]

In 1931 Alpha Phi Alpha began to grapple publicly with the role that the major political parties played in propagating racism and discrimination against blacks. One piece in the *Sphinx* noted that racism in the United States had led by 1931 to "a new Negro who knows no party by name but every man by his deeds, regardless of party affiliation."[147] Part of what may have given rise to this was—as indicated in another article in the *Sphinx* titled "What led to Freedom"—the change of the Republican Party from encouraging emancipation to disregarding blacks completely pursuant to its Lily-White Policy.[148]

During the Great Depression the fraternity and its members broadened their respective racial uplift agenda, vision, and strategies. The fraternity established the Committee on Public Policy to focus on national issues that affected African Americans.[149] Among the new approaches was a focus on the emerging concept of civil rights and litigation became a new tactic. In 1932 Charles Hamilton Houston (Alpha Phi Alpha), along with J. Alston Atkins (Omega Psi Phi), Carter W. Wesley, and James M. Nabrit Jr. (Omega Psi Phi), prevailed on behalf of the movants in *Nixon v. Condon*.[150] The case was originally brought in the Western District of Texas in 1929,[151] then was affirmed by the Fifth Circuit in 1931.[152] In *Nixon* the court struck down a Texas statute that prohibited African Americans from participating in the Texas Democratic primary election. The Texas Legislature then repealed the invalidated statute and replaced it with a new one. The new law provided that every political party would henceforth "in its own way determine who shall be qualified to vote or otherwise participate in such political party."[153] The executive committee of the Texas Democratic Party then adopted a resolution stating that "all white democrats who are qualified under the constitution and laws of Texas" would be allowed to vote.[154] In the 1928 Democratic primary, Nixon again tried to vote. He was denied on the ground that the resolution allowed only whites to vote.[155]

Nixon sued the judges of election in Texas to recover damages for their refusal to permit him to cast his vote in a primary election solely because of his race. The District Court dismissed the action,[156] which was affirmed by the U.S. Court of Appeals for the Fifth Circuit.[157] Before the court, appellees argued that there was no state action and therefore no equal protection violation because the Democratic Party was "merely a voluntary association" that had the power to choose its own membership.[158] The court held that because the Texas statute gave the party's executive committee the authority to exclude would-be members of the party, the executive committee was acting under a state grant of power.[159] Because there was state action, the case was controlled by *Nixon v. Herndon*, which prohibited state officials from "discharging their official functions in such a way as to discriminate invidiously between white citizens and black."[160]

During this period many civil rights issues arose in the context of education. This issue was discussed in detail at the Special Convention of 1934, which was called to discuss the purposeful exclusion of African Americans from the universities of Maryland, Virginia, North Carolina, and the District of Columbia and from Catholic University.[161] The fraternity sought to lead the fight against U.S. universities and set the following goals: "(1) admittance of black students on the same basis as other students; (2) larger appropriations for black colleges within the states; or (3) payment of the tuition of black students to schools outside of the non-admitting states."[162] In preparation for this uphill battle, the fraternity selected representatives from the Washington Branch of the NAACP and the New Negro Alliance.[163] After the convention a black student seeking admission to the University of Maryland—Donald Gaines Murray—was deemed a qualified candidate for Alpha's program. Alpha agreed to aid in its first mission led by attorney, Alpha Phi Alpha brothers Belford V. Lawson Jr., Theodore M. Berry, Thurgood Marshall, and Charles Hamilton Houston.[164] At this time Houston was also involved with a campaign to break down educational inequalities at state colleges.[165]

In fact, in 1934 Lawson began to develop a case against the University of Maryland as part of an effort to realize Houston's equalization plan for fighting segregation. He enlisted support from both Alpha Phi Alpha and the Washington, D.C., chapter of the NAACP.[166] In November 1934 Lawson invited Marshall and William Gosnell to a meeting to discuss a strategy for the case against the university.[167] Marshall, whose Baltimore chapter of the NAACP was disgruntled with the inherent temerity in the D.C. chapter's intention to file a civil rights suit in Baltimore, abstained from the meeting.[168] A week after the meeting Lawson found an appropriate plaintiff for his case: Donald Gaines Murray (Kappa Alpha Psi), a recent graduate of Amherst College who came from a notable black family and wished to attend the Maryland School of Law.[169] Soon, Houston heard that Lawson had found the perfect plaintiff for the case against the University of Maryland and decided to intervene.[170] With Marshall as co-counsel, Houston, armed with the resources of the national office of the NAACP, wooed Murray away from Lawson and filed the case himself against the University of Maryland School of Law in 1935.[171]

Ultimately, Marshall and Houston would represent Murray. Having been refused admission to the University of Maryland School of Law because of his race,[172] Murray appealed to the University Board of Regents and was rejected again.[173] Alpha Phi Alpha aided in the litigation. On January 25, 1935, the City Court of Baltimore reviewed Murray's appeal and ordered the university to admit Murray, stating that he could not be excluded based on race.[174] That decision was sent to the Court of Appeals of Maryland, where it was affirmed.[175] Murray was then admitted to Maryland's law school. When it was found that Murray was unable to pay his tuition and textbooks, Alpha Phi Alpha assumed his obligations and paid his expenses. It is important to note that Murray was not a member of Alpha Phi Alpha, demonstrating that members of the fraternity not just were leaders within the fraternity but also served outsiders in their quest to end discrimination practices.[176]

The case went on to become a landmark victory against segregation and began Thurgood Marshall's meteoric rise within the civil rights movement. Lawson was slow to forget this usurpation and, nearly ten years later, threatened to deny Marshall the funding he needed to file a case against the Texas Democratic Party and file a separate suit unless Marshall promised Alpha Phi Alpha some of the credit for the eventual win.[177] Despite any friction caused by Marshall's commandeering of Murray from Lawson and the New Negro Alliance, both men were able to continue to work together to promote civil rights. In 1935, for example, both assisted the state attorney of Maryland in prosecuting a policeman who had maliciously gunned down an innocent black man in Bladensburg, Maryland.[178] Though the policeman was acquitted, merely bringing the case to trial was considered an achievement.[179] In 1935 another discrimination case arose where the University of Missouri School of Law refused to admit Alpha Phi Alpha brother Lloyd L. Gaines on account of his race.[180] Continuing on the Murray momentum, Alpha Phi Alpha Charles Houston and Sidney R. Redmond sued the school. Despite having great representation, the writ of mandamus (an order from a court to a government official instructing them to fulfill their duties) was denied.[181]

Within the fraternity, its 1936 Committee on Public Policy consisted of general president Charles H. Wesley, general secretary Joseph H. B. Evans, and fraternity members Howard H. Long, H. J. Richardson Jr., and Bert Andrew Rose. The committee's first task was to aid Congressman De Priest in addressing segregation in the National Capital Restaurant. The committee worked to coerce other congressmen to support De Priest's efforts to pass the Anti-Lynching Bill and also participated in the activities of the National Recovery Program.[182] The fraternity's activities included efforts to ensure the passage of the Anti-Lynching Bill, which was organized and led by Wesley, Evans, and Long.[183] The following year, in 1937, the fraternity's Committee on Public Opinion focused on equalizing educational opportunities for African Americans via amendment to the Harrison-Black-Fletcher Bill.[184]

Beyond the work of the fraternity, individual members continued to push for civil rights. Thurgood Marshall and Charles Houston, along with Leon A. Ransom (Kappa Alpha Psi) and Edward Lovett (Kappa Alpha Psi), litigated *Williams v. Zimmerman*, a case at the Maryland Court of Appeals. In this case a black girl and her father appealed the dismissal of their petition to compel Catonsville High School, a public school for white children, to admit her. She was refused admission solely because of race. A high school was provided for black children in Baltimore, which offered equal facilities for her education had she qualified. Petitioners contended that the child met the qualifications but that she was considered unqualified based upon a test that was not equally given to white and black children. Further, it was argued that she should have been admitted to the white school because of its convenience and because she had a legal and constitutional right to the educational facilities within the county. The court did not find the qualifying test to be unconstitutional discrimination. While the administration to black and white children had slight differences, they were not enough to justify the court to compel admission to the white school.[185]

Individual members picked up the mantle as well. Charles W. Anderson became the first African American to occupy a seat in the Kentucky legislature and more broadly a southern legislature since Reconstruction. He successfully fought against bills that would allow a physical partition to segregate whites and African Americans in buses and a bill that would allow the installation of a public whipping post for African Americans who had committed misdemeanors. Anderson also successfully fought to repeal Kentucky's public hanging law and introduced the first antidiscrimination law concerning public buildings and public works in a southern legislature.[186] In 1938 Charles Houston and Sidney Redmond successfully litigated the *State of Missouri ex rel. Gaines v. Canada* case.[187] Therein, the registrar of the Law School of the University of Missouri had refused admission to Lloyd Gaines because of his race. At the time there was no law school specifically for blacks within the state. Gaines cited that this refusal violated his Fourteenth Amendment right. The state of Missouri had offered to pay for Gaines's tuition at an adjacent state's law school, which he rejected. Gaines brought this action for mandamus to compel the university to admit him. The writ was denied by the Circuit Court. This decision was affirmed by the Supreme Court of Missouri. The U.S. Supreme Court held that when the state provides legal training, it must provide it to every qualified person to satisfy equal protection. It cannot send them to other states or require sufficient demand from black students for the training. The judgment of the Supreme Court of Missouri was reversed and the case remanded.[188]

Member Thurgood Marshall represented the plaintiff in *Gilbert v. Highfill*.[189] In that case the plaintiff—a black junior high school principal in Brevard County, Florida—sued the County Board for Public Instruction and the county superintendent. Gilbert claimed that the current salary schedule allotted lower salaries to African American teachers than to their white counterparts. He claimed to be a fully qualified teacher who had served eleven years in the public school system. He further alleged that he and other black educators were paid significantly less than white educators in the same county and that these differentials were based solely on race.[190] The court found no law that required the board to establish salary schedules, only to determine the pay of the teachers. Further, the court decided that the board would know better than anyone else what each teacher was worth and how much to pay them. They decided not to question the decisions of the board. Additionally, the plaintiff sought a new salary schedule without seeking to annul the present schedule. On these grounds, the court upheld the decision of the lower court, which ruled in favor of the defendants.[191]

In Maryland, Thurgood Marshall and Charles Houston, along with Leon Ransom (Kappa Alpha Psi) and Edward P. Lovett, litigated *Mills v. Lowndes*.[192] Walter Mills, an African American teacher, filed the action in order to combat the Maryland practice of paying African American teachers in African American schools' salaries lesser than those paid to white teachers in white schools who had the same professional qualifications. The suit argued that this practice was a violation of the Fourteenth Amendment.[193] The defendant moved to dismiss the complaint on the grounds that it did not state a sufficient cause of action to justify the relief sought. The court dismissed the complaint because the defendants were general state officers and not county officials, and the responsibility for the discriminatory acts was with the county officials. The court also stated that the real objective of the injunction was to tie up money from the equalization fund and prevent its distribution to counties as beneficiaries, and that an injunction would be detrimental to elementary school education in counties participating in the fund.[194]

During Omega Psi Phi's first fifty years, members played a significant role in advancing civil rights, especially through litigation and legal support. During the 1930s, Omega Psi Phi brothers made their mark in the area of civil rights. In 1931 Roy Wilkins became involved with the NAACP as an assistant secretary under Walter Francis White.[195] W. E. B. Du Bois would leave the NAACP in 1934,[196] and Wilkins replaced Du Bois as editor of the *Crisis*, the NAACP's flagship publication. His work with the NAACP would set Wilkins on his multi-decade civil rights engagement.[197]

In 1932, after graduating from Morehouse College, Emory O. Jackson went on to join the *Birmingham World*, a publication that shared news largely ignored by the national media, including stories about black achievement and accomplishments. He became managing editor and wrote about *Brown v. Board of Education*, among many other topics. After serving in World War II, Jackson joined Birmingham's NAACP chapter. There he led a successful challenge against Birmingham's discriminatory municipal zoning laws. In response to those civil right victories, however, the Ku Klux Klan began a vicious terrorization of the black community between 1948 and 1957. Still, Jackson tirelessly fought for voting rights and believed that true change would come with voter registration, amassing black power in politics, and working for permanent change in courts and legislatures.[198]

The 1932 presidential election was one of the first U.S. elections in which candidates seriously considered the impact of the black vote. Roosevelt and the New Deal were seen by some BGLO leaders as a potential challenge to Jim Crow and racial inequality. This precipitated a slow shift to the Democratic Party from the party of Lincoln. For instance, Phi Beta Sigma fraternity member Arthur W. Mitchell of Chicago switched from the Republican to the Democratic Party in 1932, and two years later (coinciding with his last year as international president of the fraternity), with the backing of several BGLOs, Mitchell became the first black Democrat elected to Congress. Hence, the power of the black vote and black representation seemed more conspicuous than ever. BGLO members turned toward the legal restrictions from voting and holding office.

For instance, during the 1930s Omega Psi Phi brothers argued several important voting rights cases.[199] In 1932 the Texas Democratic Convention adopted a resolution that effectively barred African Americans from voting in democratic primaries. The Democratic Party resolution, as adopted by their State Convention, stated that "all white citizens of the State of Texas . . . shall be . . . entitled to participate in [the party's] deliberations."[200] In response, Jasper Alston Atkins, former grand basileus, argued *Grovey v. Townsend* before the U.S. Supreme Court.[201] The court considered whether the Constitution or Texas law prohibited the refusal of absentee ballots to African American men in the primary election. Petitioners argued that the Democratic Party's acts constituted a violation of the Fourteenth and Fifteenth Amendments of the Constitution. The court held that no constitutional right was violated because the party's actions could not be construed as a state action. Furthermore, the court cited Texas Supreme Court cases in reasoning that the state cannot interfere with the party's right to organize or determine the qualifications— here, whiteness—of its members. Because the court did not recognize the party's action as an extension of the state, and because private political groups have a right to assemble as they wish, the court reasoned that there were no Fourteenth or Fifteenth Amendment violations.[202]

Six years after *Grovey*, the Supreme Court held that primary elections were an integral part of state elections in *United States v. Classic*.[203] By 1944 the court would change course regarding *Grovey* and *Classic*. Alpha Phi Alpha member and future U.S. Supreme Court justice Thurgood Marshall, along with William H. Hastie, argued another Texas case, *Smith v. Allwright*, before the court.[204] Similar to *Grovey*, *Allwright* involved an African American citizen denied a ballot, or the chance to cast a ballot, in the 1940 Texas Democratic primary election for the Senate, House, and state gubernatorial candidates.[205] The District Court for the Southern District of Texas ruled against the prospective voter, and the Circuit Court of Appeals affirmed the ruling on the grounds of *Grovey*. The Supreme Court granted certiorari to resolve the conflict between *Grovey* and *Classic*. The court reversed by holding that primaries had become such an essential part of candidates' selection that the right to vote was violated when racial discrimination occurred in primary elections. The rationale applied was largely the same as *Classic* in noting that racial discrimination within primaries "adopts and enforces the discrimination against Negroes." This was decided despite objections that Texas primaries were less state funded than those in Louisiana (under *United States v. Classic*), which indicates that it is the selective power within primaries that matters, not the level of direct state involvement in the primary elections.[206]

Hastie litigated numerous other cases to advance social justice for African Americans.[207] In the 1939 *Mills v. Board of Education* case, an

African American teacher sued the Board of Education, alleging that African American teachers were paid less solely because of race, in violation of the Fourteenth Amendment. The Maryland District Court analyzed whether the statutes had a disparate impact on the plaintiff by analyzing whether the difference in salaries occurred because of race. The court found that the disparity stemmed from racial discrimination. The board was subsequently enjoined from discrimination in salaries based on race, but not the practice of applying judgment to determine the respective salary amounts for teachers.[208]

Kappa Alpha Psi also engaged in litigation efforts in the 1930s. In 1935 Kappa Alpha Psi member Donald Gaines Murray fought to desegregate the University of Maryland Law School. Murray was denied admission to the University of Maryland Law School, although he met all its admission standards; he was denied admission solely because he was black. The court noted that the Fourteenth Amendment requires a state to extend to its citizens "substantially equal treatment in facilities it provides from the public funds." Additionally, the court noted that while segregation is lawful, "separation of the races must nevertheless furnish equal treatment."[209] The court held that because Maryland did not offer a separate law school for black students, "if those students are to be offered equal treatment . . . they must, at present, be admitted to the one school provided."[210] Alpha Phi Alpha member Thurgood Marshall had litigated the case, which began his meteoric rise within the civil rights movement.[211]

The year 1938 was fruitful for Kappa Alpha Psi members in the area of social justice. Kappa Alpha Psi member J. W. Holland received praise from the National Problems Advisory Committee at the Cleveland Conclave for his protestation of a local radio station using derogatory terms to describe African Americans.[212] The National Problems Advisory Committee also filed a lawsuit against the Hollenden Hotel under Ohio civil rights laws after the hotel refused accommodations to Kappa Alpha Psi members during their annual convention.[213]

In another case Kappa Alpha Psi member Leon A. Ransom, along with Alpha Phi Alpha member Charles Hamilton Houston, succeeded in having reversed the Kentucky Court of Appeals in the case of *Hale v. Kentucky*.[214] Hale, a twenty-year-old African American man, was charged with murdering a white man who had been molesting African American women in an African American neighborhood. Hale's trial lawyers, from a prestigious white law firm, were unable to convince the trial court judge to address the issue of exclusion of African Americans from the jury panel.[215] As a result, an all-white jury convicted Hale, and he was sentenced to death the day after the trial began in October 1936. As pointed out by Ransom in regard to the case, "It call[ed] the attention of the southern states to the fact that Negroes have got to be tried in keeping with the Constitution, and this ought to serve as a warning to all where this question is concerned."[216] Ransom argued that the jury commissioners excluded African Americans from the jury pool because of their race; therefore, Hale was denied equal protection of the law in violation of the Fourteenth Amendment of the U.S. Constitution.

Ultimately, the U.S. Supreme Court ruled that Hale's civil rights had been violated and noted that, "We are of the opinion that the affidavits, which by the stipulation of the State were to be taken as proof, and were uncontroverted, sufficed to show a systematic and arbitrary exclusion of Negroes from the jury lists solely because of their race or color, constituting a denial of the equal protection of the laws guaranteed to petitioner by the Fourteenth Amendment."[217] Ransom also represented Walter Mills, an African American teacher who claimed that a state statute providing a minimum scale of salaries for white teachers and a lower minimum scale for teachers in black schools was unconstitutional in *Mills v. Board of Education.* The district court ruled the statute resulted in unconstitutional discrimination. The judge stated that the pleadings and testimony clearly established that there was unconstitutional wage discrimination because of race. The judge stated that while the statute on its face was not unconstitutional, the board of education's practice of having different salary scales for white and black teachers was unconstitutional in application.[218]

Similarly, in another of Ransom's civil rights cases, the court in *Bone v. State* (1939) held that it was a violation of the Fourteenth Amendment Equal Protection Clause for a state to systematically exclude those eligible for jury service based solely upon race. The replacement of a few jury members with African American jury members did not cure the error of systematically assigning a full jury, against the Fourteenth Amendment. The court further explained that the error was not in the fact that the jury was composed of all white jurors, but the fact that the jury was based on a system that purposely excluded African American jurors.[219]

In 1939 Indiana University had a practice of denying African American students the right to eat anywhere but one sandwich shop.[220] The discriminatory practice led Kappa Alpha Psi member and law student Samuel L. Patterson to call for a meeting of all African American students at the university in order to overcome the conditions.[221] Around the same time the Washington Alumni Chapter urged Congress to abolish racial discrimination in the army—an endeavor that would soon become very important as the United States would join the fray of World War II.[222]

Community Organizing

Throughout the 1930s one of Belford Lawson's significant achievements was his cofounding of the New Negro Alliance. At a time when the principal civil rights organizations (NAACP and National Urban League) employed a variety of strategies—lobbying, litigation, education, and negotiation—in their fight for civil rights, the social changes of the 1930s created a climate that fostered direct-action economic protests.[223] The Alliance, adopting this new approach, was one of the original organizations to successfully demonstrate grassroots economic protests in the civil rights context.[224] Events from the first third of the twentieth century helped facilitate the evolution from traditional methods of expression to the "Alliance-type" protests, including (1) the Great Depression, which compounded the already-existing economic disparities rooted in racial discrimination; (2) the Great Migration, which saw blacks leave their southern, rural communities for large urban "ghettos" where racial discrimination persisted; (3) the 1920s Black Renaissance, where the "New Negro" ideal of improving the status of blacks through cultural and intellectual achievement infused a race-consciousness in young blacks who rejected the anti-confrontational nature of older, traditional blacks; (4) the increasing use of direct-action techniques among communist and socialist groups; and (5) the passage of the Norris-La Guardia Act on March 23, 1932, which prohibited courts from issuing injunctions against "labor disputes."[225]

The main impetus for the New Negro Alliance protests was the pervasive employment discrimination against blacks throughout the United States and especially in Washington, D.C.[226] Black D.C. residents accounted for 29 percent of the District's total population, yet "black D.C." was regarded by many as a "secret city"—seemingly invisible to whites in the city, which systematically discriminated against blacks on the basis of race.[227] While they were among the best-educated blacks in the nation and constituted a large minority of its residents, they were largely restricted to menial jobs.[228] Despite the availability of a few menial jobs, 40 percent of black residents remained unemployed.[229] Several governmental entities directly discriminated against the black residents. The Civil Works Administration, for example, expressly discriminated against blacks.[230]

The New Negro Alliance took root in the summer of 1933 at Hamburger Grill, a white-owned restaurant located in a black D.C. neighborhood. On August 28 its manager fired three of its black employees and replaced them with three whites, despite the fact that it relied heavily on its black customer base for business.[231] In retaliation, a group led by John Aubrey Davis (another D.C. activist) picketed the restaurant, causing the three terminated employees to be rehired the following day at higher wages and fewer hours.[232] On the heels of the successful rehire at the restaurant, Davis visited Lawson and Franklin Thorne at Lawson's law office to discuss the Alliance's future picketing strategy.[233] With that, the Alliance was formed and the movement to secure black jobs and higher wages began.[234]

A few days after the picket at Hamburger Grill, the Alliance held its first public meeting. Attendees included the Hamburger Grill picketers along with the older, established community leaders whom Davis regarded as overly passive in their approach to fighting discrimination.[235] Lawson persuaded several other young black attorneys to join the fledgling organization, including William Hastie (Omega Psi Phi), Thurman Dodson (Omega Psi Phi), Edward Lovett (Kappa Alpha Psi), Edward Beaubian, and Thelma Ackiss.[236] Additionally, an array of teachers and local businessmen joined the organization.[237] Despite this broad support, there were some early critics, who viewed the Alliance's strategy as antagonizing and risky, carrying the potential to induce a white backlash.[238] The Alliance's strategy was simple: ". . . collision course with retail stores in black neighborhoods. Demanding that blacks be hired in proportion to their patronage, the Alliance conducted surveys to determine the volume of patronage and then confronted store officials with its demands. If store officials took 'no definite action' within a reasonable period, the Alliance began door-to-door distribution of materials that explained the reasons for its next action, picketing. At the same time, it obtained pledges to boycott the store unless and until its demands were met."[239] The Alliance's first project was an easy success. Lawson and Davis met with the personnel administrator of the *Evening Star*, the leading newspaper in D.C., to demand that the paper hire black paperboys, threatening a boycott otherwise.[240] The paper complied within three weeks.[241]

Following its success at Hamburger Grill and with the *Evening Star*, the Alliance shifted its gaze to the Great Atlantic & Pacific Tea Company (A&P) grocery store chain. A&P had recently opened a new store in D.C. but hired only white employees.[242] Following two weeks of futile negotiations with A&P management, the Alliance, inspired by a successful boycott of an A&P in Columbus, Ohio, organized a picket of the D.C. store on September 27, 1933.[243] Two recent college graduates carrying signs reading "Buy Where You Can Work, No Negroes Employed Here" were arrested for violation of a local ordinance that prohibited carrying a sign without a permit.[244] Lawson fought to have the charges dropped, convincing the court that the ordinance applied only to commercial advertising and to broaden its coverage would deprive persons of their constitutional rights.[245] In early October 1933, the Alliance added two more A&P locations in D.C. to its boycott.[246] Following the successful boycott, by December 1933 A&P had hired eighteen black employees, including one manager.[247]

On December 16, 1933, the Alliance published its first issue of its weekly newspaper, *New Negro Opinion*.[248] By early 1934 the Alliance had grown to about a thousand members.[249] The Alliance continued negotiating, but largely stopped picketing after two D.C. stores sought and were awarded injunctions against the Alliance.[250] On December 3, 1934, Lawson argued before the U.S. Court of Appeals for the District of Columbia on behalf of the Alliance.[251] In *New Negro Alliance v. Kaufman*, the plaintiff, Harry Kaufman, Inc., owner and operator of a D.C. department store, filed a complaint against the Alliance for "unlawfully picketing and boycotting the store" and requested that the court issue a permanent injunction against the Alliance's picketers.[252] The district court issued a preliminary injunction and Lawson immediately appealed.[253]

On appeal, Lawson argued that because that dispute between the Alliance and Kaufman was a labor dispute and the Norris-La Guardia Act prohibited courts from granting restraining orders and injunctions against such disputes, the lower court improperly granted the injunction.[254] The Court of Appeals dismissed Lawson's appeal on the grounds that the district court's orders were interlocutory and not appealable.[255] Citing the D.C. Code, the court determined that the preliminary injunction was not a "final order, judgment, or decree," nor was it an interlocutory order "whereby the possession of property is changed or affected."[256] As such, the court dismissed Lawson's premature appeal without prejudice.[257]

While the court refused to examine *Kaufman* on its merits, the following year Lawson found himself fighting another injunction on behalf of the Alliance. There, the Alliance had targeted Sanitary Grocery,[258] another operator of many grocery stores in the D.C. area.[259] In accordance with its picketing plan, the Alliance requested that Sanitary employ African Americans in managerial and sales position in a new store it had recently opened.[260] After Sanitary ignored the request, Alliance picketed.[261] Following *Kaufman's* lead, Sanitary filed suit in federal court seeking a permanent injunction against the Alliance's pickets.[262]

On May 12, 1936, the U.S. District Court for the District of Columbia granted Sanitary's injunction and Alliance appealed. On appeal, Alliance again argued that the Norris-La Guardia Act protected their pickets from court injunction.[263] However, the U.S. Court of Appeals for the D.C. Circuit affirmed the lower court's opinion, holding that the Norris-La Guardia Act did not apply because an employer-employee relationship did not exist between the picketers and Alliance.[264] In its conclusion the court held that despite Alliance's commendable goal of improving black opportunities, it was not justified in "ignoring the rights of the public and the property rights of the owner of the business."[265]

Despite the setback in the *Sanitary Grocery Store* decisions, the Alliance continued to successfully picket elsewhere, using a variety of techniques, including mass mailings, petitions, and negotiations. This success led to greater support from churches, the black-owned *Washington Tribune*, local and national leaders, homemakers, fraternities, and community groups.[266] Between 1937 and 1939, the local D.C. NAACP chapter had its charter revoked after a dispute with the national NAACP;

the Alliance was able to fill that void and increase its membership.[267] The Alliance estimated that by 1936 about seventy-five thousand dollars and three hundred jobs for black clerks had been secured.[268] Furthermore, the Congress of Industrial Organizations and some white organizations began to offer support to the Alliance.[269]

Ultimately, the U.S. Supreme Court granted certiorari in the *Sanitary Grocery Store* case. However, William Hastie, recently appointed to the U.S. District Court for the District of the Virgin Islands in 1937 by President Roosevelt, would be unavailable to argue before the court.[270] Belford Lawson, five years out of law school, served as lead counsel in the case before the court. On brief attorneys for the petitioner were Lawson as well as Thurman L. Dodson (Omega Psi Phi) and Edward P. Lovett (Kappa Alpha Psi). Theodore M. Berry and Thurgood Marshall as well as James M. Nabrit Jr. (Omega Psi Phi) served as of counsel.[271]

Appealing to the U.S. Supreme Court, Lawson argued the *Sanitary* case on March 2, 1938. The court ultimately reversed the Court of Appeals' holding, remanding the case in favor of the Alliance. In its landmark decision the court looked at the language of subsection (a) of section 13 of the Norris-La Guardia Act and held its definitions to plainly embrace the controversy that gave rise to the instant suit and classified it as a labor dispute despite the fact that Alliance was not an employee of Sanitary.[272] In clear contrast to the lower courts, the Supreme Court emphatically stated that the act was intended to cover labor disputes between interested parties and was not limited only to those situations involving an employer and its employee:

> The act does not concern itself with the background or the motives of the dispute. The desire for fair and equitable conditions of employment on the part of persons of any race, color, or persuasion, and the removal of discriminations against them by reason of their race or religious beliefs is quite as important to those concerned as fairness and equity in terms and conditions of employment can be to trade or any form of labor organization or association. Race discrimination by an employer may reasonably be deemed more unfair and less excusable than discrimination against workers on the ground of union affiliation. There is no justification in the apparent purposes or the express terms of the act for limiting its definition of labor disputes and cases arising therefrom by excluding those

which arise with respect to discrimination in terms and conditions of employment based upon differences of race or color.[273]

The court further examined the act's legislative history and determined that its purposes were to prevent fraud, breach of peace, violence, or conduct otherwise unlawful and to allow dissemination of information by those people interested in a labor dispute concerning the terms and conditions of employment.[274] Peaceful and orderly dissemination of information by those defined as persons interested in a labor dispute concerning terms and conditions of employment should be at liberty to advertise and disseminate facts and information as well as peacefully persuade others to concur in their views respecting an employer's practices.[275] *Sanitary* was thus a monumental victory: it established the right to picket by people unaffiliated with labor unions,[276] and it also secured Lawson's name in the annals of history as the first black lawyer to win a case before the U.S. Supreme Court.[277]

Civic Education

Through their Bigger and Better Business program, the Phi Beta Sigma fraternity urged collegiate faculty to adjust their college curriculums to teach courses on business so that African Americans would "warrant and get support and patronage from other races as well as the [African American] race."[278] Bigger and Better Business Week continued to be Phi Beta Sigma's focus in terms of public policy and community outreach; in an issue of the *Crescent* from later in 1931, Phi Beta Sigma member and business specialist with the Department of Commerce James A. "Billboard" Jackson issued the following statement in support of Bigger and Better Business Week: "It has commanded newspaper space, aroused public interest, riveted the friendship of many of the struggling Negro business folk, and arrested the attention of those who think in terms of economics."[279] Jackson's viewpoint on service was clear, as he further stated that the "greatest service to humanity known today is commerce."[280]

The fraternity clearly took the circumstances of the Great Depression into account in its approach to public policy during those years. In his 1931 editorial, "Will the Depression Bring the Negro to His Senses,"

Edward S. Bishop extolled Phi Beta Sigma's potential for improving the standard of living for African Americans and called for a business-focused approach. "As a national fraternity, a group of men with the well-being of the race at heart, Phi Beta Sigma can play a big part in bringing the Negro to his senses by opening his eyes and showing him his predicament; by emphasizing our Bigger and Better Business Week; by encouraging cooperative buying and selling of our merchandise and other commodities; and by members of graduate chapters pooling their savings and investing them in some business that will prove to the race and to the world the value of economic power and racial cooperation."[281] Alpha Phi Alpha's consistent mission was to help "[train] youth for a life of usefulness."[282] In the *Sphinx*, W. A. Robinson highlighted that "Negro schools and Negro children yet suffer severely on account of the discrimination in expenditures for Negro and white schools."[283] In fact by 1930 "[the fraternity's] purpose [was] no longer one of mere internal uplift, the organization ha[d] dedicated itself to the very lofty cause of education."[284] This was accomplished through "essay contests among high school students, banquets to them, oratorical contests, distribution of literature, vocational guidance, and public mass meetings."[285] Indeed, the very nature of the Go-to-High-School, Go-to-College program was emphasized as one of serving "as a medium to get youth to continue their education."[286] By 1930 the U.S. Census indicated that more black children were going to school than in previous years.[287] Further championing the cause of education, the fraternity awarded Miss Estelle Chotella Hill of Atlanta University a scholarship for academic merit as part of their efforts to implore the necessity of education.[288]

Alpha Phi Alpha chapters, both collegiate and alumni, also carried forth the fraternity's mission. Epsilon, Gamma, Alpha Zeta, Alpha Theta, Alpha Rho, and Alpha Sigma chapters all executed successful Go-to-High-School, Go-to-College or similar educational programs.[289] The Go-to-High-School, Go-to-College conference, held by the Alpha Theta Chapter, brought together communities in Cedar Rapids, Davenport, Des Moines, and Sioux City.[290] In doing so the chapter presented talks, held conferences and mass meetings, and distributed literature insisting on the higher education of black youth.[291] Similarly, the Cleveland-area chapters as well as Beta Lambda, Phi Lambda, and

Tau Lambda all pushed forward with the Go-to-High-School, Go-to-College and similar educational programs.[292]

In the summer of 1933, Alpha Phi Alpha members Robert Weaver and John P. Davis formed the Joint Committee on National Recovery (JCNR).[293] The JCNR was made up of several civic, fraternal, sororal, and religious organizations with the common goal of race advancement.[294] The organization was supposed to be a springboard for grassroots protest but was primarily an "information clearinghouse."[295] As the organization grew, it became apparent that the conglomerate was not as well received as the founders had hoped.[296] The Urban League would not affiliate with the JCNR because it wanted its own organization to deal with the economic crisis.[297] The NAACP wanted an organization that it could control, and internal rivalries as well as personal vendettas against members kept the organization from realizing its potential as a change agent.[298]

That same year Alpha Phi Alpha brother Rayford W. Logan started the Education for Citizenship program. This was a voting rights campaign formed as an alternative to the Go-to-High-School, Go-to-College program, which appealed largely to more privileged African Americans.[299] The purpose of the initiative was to prepare blacks to vote in an effort to increase participation by all blacks in their local political processes and to challenge disenfranchisement in the Jim Crow South.[300] A committee was formed in 1933 to spearhead the effort.[301] Lugenia Hope was appointed chairwoman of the committee, and the first "school" was formed in Atlanta at the Butler Street YMCA.[302] Logan took over the school until 1938, when he left for Howard University in Washington, D.C.[303] Students enrolled in the program were to be subjected to the sort of intense questioning that they would likely receive from a registrar when attempting to register.[304] The school started successfully, attracting over a hundred fifty students to the first set of six-week sessions and almost three hundred to subsequent sessions.[305] This process helped to instill confidence in a populace that for decades had been forced through various intimidation tactics to refrain from participation in the political process.[306]

At Alpha Phi Alpha's 1933 General Convention, Rayford Logan was elected director of education.[307] Logan proposed that the fraternity adopt a new, more inclusive community action plan that catered to the needs of all blacks, not just those who were college students or graduates.[308] Accordingly, after the success of the Education for Citizenship flagship school, other schools were started through local chapters of Alpha Phi Alpha.[309] Also at the General Convention, the fraternity authorized the formation of the Committee on Public Policy, created in response to the de facto exclusion of black Americans from the New Deal programs.[310] The committee's objective was to determine "the status of the black population, both as to employees in the New Deal agencies and as to the services rendered, which were affecting its place in American life." The committee took on a large-scale research project on the topic that lasted eighteen months and resulted in a three-part report written by Logan and published in the *Sphinx* between 1935 and 1937.[311] The committee's report shed much light on the situation, effectively reflecting the exclusion of blacks from the benefits of the New Deal programs.[312] The report showed that of fifty-eight thousand appointments to the new agencies, blacks filled fewer than three hundred, and they were the lower grade positions.[313]

Alpha Phi Alpha's social ideals widened in the years following the 1933 General Convention. Although the Great Depression plagued the country with drastic changes in economic conditions, Alpha Phi Alpha members continued to implement programs in service to African Americans.[314] The Alpha Phi Alpha efforts were always created with the foundational purpose of helping the community achieve a higher social, economic, and intellectual status. In December 1933, Alpha Phi Alpha's publication, the *Sphinx*, noted the following issues: (1) industrial unionism, (2) war and fascism, (3) farmer-labor party, (4) National Negro Congress, and (5) the Olympics.[315] Additionally that year, Alpha Phi Alpha brother L. Howard Bennett addressed the larger nature social problems as well as other problems that affected African Americans. In confronting those issues, Bennett had proposed a committee designated to public affairs.[316]

In 1934 the NAACP National Convention backed Alpha Phi Alpha's Education for Citizenship program, and similar drives began to appear around the South. After five years of existence, the program had reached over a hundred thousand blacks.[317] Even more, the fraternity continued to assist and serve the JCNR. In 1934 the fraternity's Committee on

Public Policy launched its investigation of the federal agencies under the New Deal was authorized at that year's Special Convention.[318] That investigation was implemented to determine the New Deal agencies' treatment and relationships with the African American population and took place from September 1934 to January 1935.[319] Alpha Phi Alpha was transparent with these investigation efforts and kept a continuous flow of communication between members, evidenced by the fact that findings were recorded and reported in the *Sphinx* to inform readers.[320]

In 1936 the fraternity's Education for Citizenship program, soon to be named A Voteless People Is a Hopeless People, and the Go-to-High-School, Go-to-College program continued reaching more people.[321] Throughout 1936, significant activities in the fraternity were being conducted across the country. There were mass meetings, radio talks, plays and pageants, displays of placards, and the tagging of individuals. These tags bore the slogan "A Voteless People Is a Hopeless People." The slogan was used with telling effects in many parts of the North and South as brothers in the fraternity worked in the voting campaigns and in the citizenship programs. As part of the campaign there were public meetings, public forums, oratorical contests, and discussions of jury service, the ballot, and representation in state and national affairs. The purpose of this initiative was to organize and advocate so that blacks in the South might exercise the right to vote. Many chapters were interested in the initiative.[322] That same year, Alpha Phi Alpha brother Jesse Owens won four Olympic gold medals for the United States along with other Alpha Phi Alpha brothers who joined him on the podium.[323] They sent a powerful message in response to Hitler's notion of the superiority of the Aryan race.

As had been the case since its inception, the *Sphinx*, at the close of the 1930s, was still being used to raise critical issues about African Americans' racial progress. In one 1938 article titled "Does the Negro Really Care?," African Americans were discussed as trying to imitate the social pleasures that their white counterparts indulge in rather than invest their income in economic planning or African American capitalistic ventures.[324] Instead of concerning themselves with extravagance, according to the author, African Americans should have been using their financial resources to help advance the race.[325] And it was clear that as a fraternity, Alpha Phi Alpha was doing just that. The fraternity had been making financial contributions to other African American organizations, including the Association for the Study of Negro Life and History, the International Committee of African Affairs, the NAACP, the National Urban League, and the Southern Tenant Farmers Union.[326]

The fraternity's director of education, Rayford Logan, called for the development of the Go-to-High-School, Go-to-College movement in areas where it was still needed. He also drew attention to the political achievements of brothers and called for all the fraternity brothers to emulate them to increase the political interest of African Americans. One way this was encouraged was through the emphasis on the debate of the Harrison-Black-Fletcher Bill that each chapter was encouraged to entertain.[327] In many respects, chapters heeded the call. Alpha Rho Lambda Chapter (Columbus, Ohio) began regularly holding public forums on a variety of current event issues that have been very popular. The aim was to show the public that the fraternity chapter was not just a social organization.[328] Alpha Pi Lambda Chapter (Winston-Salem, N.C.) hosted an annual oratorical competition with the theme "The Negro Faces America's Social Problems."[329]

The privileged position of some sorority members was shown throughout each organization's national magazines, for example, Sigma Gamma Rho's the *Aurora*.[330] Members had the money and time to travel, to contribute to scholarships, and to participate in fashion shows; the members were also quite aware of their privilege.[331] During the Great Depression sorority women occupied a rare position. As mentioned, about half of blacks in northern cities were unemployed—a rate double that of whites.[332] In the agricultural South, where most of blacks lived, conditions were worse because the benefits of the New Deal often missed black workers due to racial discrimination.

As Sigma Gamma Rho noted in a 1939 issue of the *Aurora*, the ratio of workers among black women was reported by the Women's Bureau of the U.S. Labor Department to be twice as high as that among white women.[333] Nine-tenths of employed black women worked in farm, domestic, or personal service under substandard working conditions.[334] With the Great Depression lingering until World War II, this number did not include the unemployed.

However, black sorority women had the skills and the means to engage in significant community racial uplift. Many of them joined sororities specifically because they also felt a responsibility to help the less privileged. Sigma Gamma Rho's emphasis on education extended beyond the sorority and to the community through its creation of various African American history projects. First, in 1932, Sigma Gamma Rho member Pearl Schwartz White of Zeta Sigma in St. Louis organized teas, lectures, book reviews, and exhibits for the local community to learn about "Negro History."[335] Further, at Sigma Gamma Rho's Ninth Boulé (national convention), Zeta Sigma chapter presented an exhibit in conjunction with Upsilon titled "Negro Achievements Exhibit." In 1934 its Delta Sigma chapter created and shared an outline that studied African Americans as individuals, citizens, and contributors to American life. Sigma Gamma Rho member Monet Harrison Fowler, of New York City, creatively spread African American history by establishing a school of Creative Negro Art and a chorus that sang songs in African languages.[336]

Also at the Tenth Boulé, Congressman Arthur Mitchell, the only African American representative in Congress at that time, issued a challenge to Sigma Gamma Rho.[337] Congressman Mitchell encouraged the sorority to continue breaking down barriers of racial equality through understanding and education. Sigma Gamma Rho answered by addressing the needs of the times. First, the sorority finalized a research project that culminated in the creation of a literary contest. The initial contest was "designed to answer the need of literature suitable for Negro children of the intermediate grades." Sigma Gamma Rho member Edith Malone Ward was granted an extension to continue the project "as long as it [was] effective." The contest would eventually prove to be not only effective but also versatile, as the theme would change annually to address the pressing issues of that year. Next, Sigma Gamma Rho members at the Tenth Boulé decided to continue the Vocational Guidance Program.[338] The program was a counseling service geared toward skilled labor and one of Sigma Gamma Rho's earliest such projects.

The literary contest was held again in 1936 at the Eleventh Boulé. That year the contest comprised short story entries about African American life.[339] The winner was a short story titled "Let Them Speak for Themselves," written by Sigma Gamma Rho member Annie Weston of New York City. The literary contest would become a staple of Sigma Gamma Rho's efforts to advance education. The contest furthered multiple sorority ideals by encouraging the creation of literature on African American history and fostering scholarship and achievement amongst sorority members. Personal achievement would prove to be a lasting goal of Sigma Gamma Rho. The Eleventh Boulé decided to have each campus chapter present a personal award to one woman from each chapter's affiliated university who displayed "outstanding scholarship" throughout the year. Sigma Gamma Rho's efforts to nurture its members' ambitions proved worthwhile, as Sigma Gamma Rho member Hattie McDaniel became the first African American to receive an "Oscar" for her role as Mammie in *Gone with the Wind*.[340]

Delta Sigma Theta members also fought on the frontlines for social justice during the 1930s, putting them on a trajectory for even greater achievements over the decades. For example, member Amelia Boynton Robinson's early activism began around the 1930s when she met her co-worker and ex-husband Samuel Boynton in Selma, Alabama. Together they cofounded the Dallas County Voters League in 1933, where they advocated for voting, education, and property rights for underprivileged African Americans. Robinson's work continued even decades later when she planned the Selma to Montgomery March on March 7, 1965, with Alpha Phi Alpha member Rev. Dr. Martin Luther King Jr., an event that became known as "Bloody Sunday." Publicity of this event, specifically the beatings of Robinson and other protesters in the streets, prompted a national outcry that led to the signing of the Voting Rights Act on August 6, 1965, by President Lyndon B. Johnson. In her later years Robinson served as the vice-president of the Schiller Institute, where she continued to be an active member in promoting civil and human rights, and in 1990 she was awarded the Martin Luther King Jr. Medal of Freedom.[341]

At the 1930 Conclave in Tuskegee, Alabama, Phi Beta Sigma solidified the requirements of a recipient of the Distinguished Service Key, the award that would come to be recognized as the greatest honor bestowed by Phi Beta Sigma. The reward was created to encourage community service among the brothers, and in order to receive it a brother must have made an "outstanding contribution to the work of the fraternity or to the general welfare" (of African Americans or American citizens in general) on a national scale.[342] Later, in 1932, when the fraternity issued a new revision of its constitution, the Distinguished Service Key would be given only to a brother who had made "remarkable contributions to humanity and to the fraternity."[343] This award was rarely given, and when it was the recipient had rendered a monumental act of community service. For example, brother James W. Johnson was awarded a Distinguished Service Key for giving up a high-paying job and moving to Knoxville, Tennessee, where he led a successful effort to add the eleventh and twelfth grades to African American high schools.[344]

In 1932, the fraternity adopted new bylaws as well as a new constitution. Part of the new bylaws was a community service item titled Sigma Educational Week, which was to be held annually during the first week of November. In later years the Sigma's Social Action Program, seen as a "child of [their] motto," would challenge all brothers to contribute in some way to their common goal of "Full-Fledged Freedom for Every American Citizen," whether through taking on leadership roles, working with existing community activities or creating new groups, or donating time and money to local and national efforts.[345] Additionally, in a somewhat radical departure from their more traditional service activities, the fraternity launched an investigation into the living conditions of the inhabitants of Haiti and the Virgin Islands, intending to facilitate better understanding between U.S. and island residents.[346]

In the early 1930s, Phi Beta Sigma vice-president Zaid D. Lenoir proposed the fraternity augment its scholarship program by having the national body, as well as the local chapters, extend scholarship loans to needy brothers as long as they were in good standing with the fraternity.[347] The Great Depression severely curtailed many of Phi Beta Sigma's projects, but despite the difficulties of this dreary period that lasted until the 1940s, the fraternity continued conducting charitable activities. For example, in 1932 the Great Depression was in full swing, yet the fraternity still earmarked funds from each member's annual tax for the scholarship fund. Also in 1932 the Douglass Scholarship was changed to the Phi Beta Sigma Scholarship Loan Fund. The creation of the fund was the beginning of the fraternity's Scholarship Loan Bank Account. In furtherance of Phi Beta Sigma's scholarship program, a "committee that sought to improve the Frat's program" at the 1933 Chicago Conclave recommended that each chapter establish a local scholarship fund.[348] Further, the delegates at the 1938 Winston-Salem Conclave saw more progress for the fraternity's philanthropic goals, resolving that each fraternity region would grant one or more scholarships in the field of business administration, and they authorized the board to make a contribution to the NAACP.

So in 1933 Omega Psi Phi embarked on the Negro Achievement Project, which was intended "to acquaint Negros with the fact that they have a glorious past, that the present is full of opportunity considering what has been accomplished in the past, and that might be an incentive to have them visualize a more glorious future."[349] The point of the project was to inspire African Americans to engage in racial uplift endeavors. Reflecting the zeitgeist of the times, the program made a distinction between "Negro Renaissance" and the "New Negro Renaissance" (drawing from Phi Beta Sigma member Alain Leroy Locke's 1925 book qua manifesto, *The New Negro: An Interpretation*).

Alpha Kappa Alpha also engaged in civic education programs. To encourage and stimulate effort for higher education among worthy African American women, the sorority offered a foreign fellowship every two years for one thousand dollars, and about forty local scholarships annually, ranging from twenty-five to six hundred dollars.[350] In March 1934, a vocational guidance week was held and gathered several hundred students who were mentored by teachers and citizens engaged in various occupations.[351]

These endeavors were taken up by individual members as well. In March 1934 Alpha Kappa Alpha member and renowned educator Fannie C. Williams addressed a sociology class at the Tuskegee Institute on "The Effect of the Depression on Education." She also addressed the Interracial Committee of Southern Women on "The Need of Nursery School in New Orleans for Negro Children of Pre-School Age."[352] In September of that same year two Alpha Kappa Alpha members delivered addresses at the National Association for Teachers in Colored Schools,[353] and Ida L. Jackson wrote an article, "Summer School for Teachers," about Saints Industrial School in Lexington, Mississippi. Jackson and several others discovered that the school was in an area where the "conditions are much the same amount the mass of Negroes as during the Post Civil War period." Most of the teachers were not trained beyond the seventh grade, and Jackson and her team developed a summer school for teachers in those rural areas.[354]

While BGLOs began the 1930s by forming the cooperative National Pan-Hellenic Council, the end of the decade saw the formation of another organization. In 1938, at the Joint Founders' Day Celebration at Howard University, Alpha Kappa Alpha founder and incorporator

Norma Boyd proposed a cooperative lobbying group between the three Washington sorority chapters.[355] This plan resulted in the National Non-Partisan Lobby on Civil and Democratic Rights (NPC), later renamed the National Non-Partisan Council on Public Affairs. The NPC was the first full-time congressional lobby for promoting African American civil rights. It aimed to improve conditions for African Americans through opportunities in public service, education, and employment.[356] To accomplish this goal the NPC encouraged the African American community to become fully integrated and increase participation in every aspect of democracy.[357] The NPC focused its efforts on keeping African American voters informed by educating them about proposed and pending legislation and encouraging them to communicate with their respective congressmen.[358] NPC also pressed Congress to pass legislative provisions and programs ensuring "the equitable distribution of funds, facilities, and services" in various communities and to provide the supervision necessary to make sure such policies remained enforced.[359]

Howard University graduate and law student William P. Robinson was appointed as the NPC's first legislative representative.[360] Its headquarters were established in Washington, D.C., so that the NPC had great access to both the public and the nation's capital.[361] At the time it was the first national African American women's organization in America with a "full-time office and a full-time staff devoted entirely to public affairs and paid for by the membership of the organization."[362]

The NPC covered four areas: (1) information, (2) contacts, (3) presentations for congressional committees, and (4) patronage endorsements.[363] Its initial objectives included eradicating police brutality in the District of Columbia and establishing home rule.[364] It also pushed to extend the Public Works Program and set a minimum wage for women in the laundry industry.[365] Its office reviewed important bills and sent its findings to Alpha Kappa Alpha chapters and other interested organizations.[366] Norma Boyd intended for Alpha Kappa Alpha chapters to serve as representatives in their local political networks.[367] The chapters' first goal was to strengthen the NPC's capacity for recognition and influence through an effort to register all eligible voters in their communities for the 1940 presidential election.[368]

While the NPC was dissolved in 1948, in its place Alpha Kappa Alpha established the American Council on Human Rights with the help of

Delta Sigma Theta, Zeta Phi Beta, and Sigma Gamma Rho sororities as well as Alpha Phi Alpha, Phi Beta Sigma, and Kappa Alpha Psi fraternities, which we will discuss in the next chapter.

Conclusion

In the midst of the Great Depression, BGLOs responded to the needs of their communities by serving as social safety nets and providing goods and money to those in need. This decade also saw a bourgeoning civic engagement on the part of BGLOs around education of civic responsibility and direct action. More specifically, BGLO members began to employ a new set of tools in their civic engagement—that is, law. On one front they used it to shape public policy. On another they employed it in the courts to change the ways in which access to the polls, for example, was interpreted to fall under the province of the U.S. Constitution.

5

Spreading the Word

Black Greek-Letter Organizations, Democracy, and the Great Migration (1940–1948)

On September 1, 1939, Germany invaded Poland, effectively beginning World War II. Two years later, on December 7, 1941, the United States entered the war as a direct result of the Japanese attack on Pearl Harbor—effectively extinguishing American isolationism and throwing into chaos traditional racial dynamics. Roosevelt's Executive Order 9066 resulted in the placement of more than 110,000 West Coast Japanese Americans into detention camps. The draft and loss of white male workers to the military put people of color and women into jobs previously restricted. The U.S. military itself both reinforced and broke apart racial color lines, using the Tuskegee Airmen and the Navajo Code Talkers, while facing resistance from the Japanese American "No-No Boys" and those opposed to the segregation of the U.S. military, which would remain in effect until Truman signed Executive Order 9981 in 1948.

The latter issue of military racial segregation was one that activists, black Greeks included, had fought against since World War I. As the United States entered World War II, labor leader and Phi Beta Sigma member A. Philip Randolph threatened to organize a march on Washington, D.C., to protest job discrimination in the military and other defense-related activities, in which he would bring "ten, twenty, fifty thousand Negroes to the White House lawn" if need be.[1] In response, President Roosevelt issued Executive Order 8802, stating that "there shall be no discrimination in the employment of workers in defense industries and in Government, because of race, creed, color, or national origin." While the order was the first presidential directive on race since Reconstruction and established the Fair Employment Practices Committee to investigate allegations of discrimination, segregation still prevailed. So, while Randolph's march on Washington was called off, it laid the groundwork for a march that would take place in 1963—the March on Washington for Jobs and Freedom, organized by several BGLO members, including Phi Beta Sigma members John Lewis and A. Philip Randolph, Omega Psi Phi member Roy Wilkins, and Alpha Phi Alpha member Martin Luther King Jr.

The near quarter century between World War II and the 1963 March on Washington was marked by increased racial activism and agitation by black fraternities and sororities, who were, like much of black America, increasingly impatient with the pace toward, and backlashes against, racial equality. It was in the early part of this time frame that the National Non-Partisan Lobby on Civil and Democratic Rights (NPC) began to pick up steam, fueled by the dynamo that was black fraternalism.

From the NPC to the American Council on Human Rights

As mentioned in the last chapter, the NPC was founded in 1938 by Alpha Kappa Alpha as the first full-time congressional lobby for nonwhite, particularly African American, civil rights. The NPC covered four areas: (1) information, (2) contacts, (3) presentations for congressional committees, and (4) patronage endorsements. Its initial objectives included the eradication of police brutality in the District of Columbia and the establishment of home rule. It also pushed for extending the Public Works Program and setting a minimum wage for women in the laundry industry. Its office reviewed important bills and sent its findings to Alpha Kappa Alpha chapters and other interested organizations. One of the founders of Alpha Kappa Alpha, Norma Elizabeth Boyd, intended for Alpha Kappa Alpha chapters to serve as representatives in their local political networks. It was not until 1940 that the chapters set their first goal, which was mainly internal, to strengthen the NPC's capacity for recognition and influence through an effort to register all eligible voters in their communities for upcoming presidential elections.[2]

This work was not simply done in isolation. For example, collaboratively, Alpha Phi Alpha, Kappa Alpha Psi, Omega Psi Phi, and Phi Beta Sigma worked to get African Americans integrated into the national defense. This joint effort sought to redress "discrimination against [African Americans] in the armed forces and industry after the outbreak of World War II." This effort achieved two major feats. First, it led to the drafting of the Hamilton Fish amendment to the Burke-Wadsworth Bill, forbidding racial discrimination in the selection and training of draftees. Second, President Roosevelt issued an order appointing African American reserve officers.[3]

The NPC continued to grow in size and influence following World War II through participation in the passing of antidiscrimination legislation in Congress in 1941 and its support of the National Recruiting Drive for Negro Women for the war program and the Farm Security Administration Act.[4] When the Farm Security Administration was at risk of being abolished, the NPC helped to save it and prevented thousands of African American farmers from becoming "hired hands."[5] The NPC also saw the admission of African American women officers into the Navy in 1944. As one of the sponsors of the National Wartime Conference, the NPC was responsible for bringing in two African American speakers to talk about the lack of opportunities for black women in the Navy. These lobbying efforts were successful and led to the admission of black women into the Women's Army Auxiliary Corps at a time when the Navy was the only service in the armed forces where blacks served on an integrated basis.[6]

The NPC made great strides in influencing the legislature as well as establishing projects to improve the lives of African Americans, and especially women, in the areas of housing, labor, and health care. With regard to housing, the NPC pressured Congress into upholding the promise made when the Sojourner Truth Housing Project was created and ensured that blacks officially retained the right to live in the housing project as originally planned.[7] Regarding the Lucy D. Slowe Housing Project for Defense Workers in Washington, D.C., the NPC was able to get the rent lowered from $8.85 to $7.00 a week, which led to a savings of more than $12,000 a year for black women.[8] In the health care and labor arena, the NPC obtained a nondiscriminatory amendment to the Nurse Training Act, which led to an increase in the funding appropriated for nurse training.[9] This was the first and only antidiscrimination amendment in that session of Congress, and it allowed for black nurses in nonsegregated areas to have access to training in nearby hospitals.[10] To protect labor in general, the NPC successfully opposed the Austin-Wadsworth Bill or Draft Labor Bill because it was unnecessarily aimed at conscripting labor during wartime, which the NPC and other Americans feared would be enforced unfairly.[11]

The NPC made other influential moves vis-à-vis Congress on a range of topics. For example, it supported the Federal Aid to Education Act, which provided a raise in teachers' salaries to "reduce the inequalities of educational opportunities" and to ensure schools remained open.[12] The NPC also successfully lobbied for the passage of the Anti–Poll Tax Act, which prohibited charging a fee of any kind as a requirement for voting as well as an act that devoted $30,000 "for a shrine at the birthplace of George Washington Carver, agricultural scientist, Tuskegee Institute Professor, and member of Phi Beta Sigma fraternity."[13] After aiding in the passage of the Lanham Act, which allotted $300,000 for housing grants and $200,000 for community service, the NPC devoted efforts to a study of the Children's Bureau, which revealed inequities between black and white children. The NPC also called a conference of representatives, organizations, and agencies to discuss the improvement of community services for black children by the Children's Bureau. Also, in the education arena the NPC worked to establish price control for the cost of education and helped with efforts to enact a civil rights bill for the District of Columbia.[14]

The NPC cooperated with local and national organizations and agencies whose goals coincided with its own, such as the NAACP, the Urban League, the Congress of Colored Women's Clubs, the American Federation of Churches, the United Office and Professional Workers of America, the National Association of Graduate Nurses, the Brotherhood of Sleeping Car Porters and Auxiliary, and New York Voter's League.[15] In addition to these collaborations, the NPC's activities included the promotion of legislation, the distribution of publications and information informing sorority members and others of important social issues, and the pursuit of national integration through the Department of State, the United Nations, and the United Nations Educational, Scientific, and Cultural Organization.[16] Along the way the NPC changed structurally. While the NPC was originally a lobbyist group, members would prepare testimony for congressional hearings and report the results back to the larger NPC umbrella group.[17] The NPC presented its final report at the 1948 Boulé in Washington, D.C.[18] While it was successful in forging relationships with other organizations and agencies, especially other Greek organizations, many of the member organizations recognized that the NPC's success overly depended on support from Alpha Kappa Alpha sorority, and that sufficient support for the continuance of the NPC was lacking.[19]

The first few years of the NPC's existence accomplished much, but sporadically. It was soon recognized that while each organization was engaging in various social uplift programs, greater cooperation would be necessary. For instance, by 1945 Alpha Phi Alpha looked to work more formally with other African American fraternities and sororities on racial uplift issues. In the December issue of Alpha Phi Alpha's the *Sphinx*, a member of Omega Psi Phi, J. H. Calhoun Jr., was allowed to pen an article. In his piece, "How Can Negro Greek-Letter Societies Cooperate?," Calhoun argued for capitalizing on the already existing similarity in the structures of each individual organization and that a new pan-Hellenic council should be formed to be a clearinghouse for more mass action across the organizations.[20] Such work was seen on the local level. For example, the Alpha Nu Lambda Chapter of Alpha Phi Alpha fraternity, in conjunction with other Greek-letter organizations, the NAACP, and another local social uplift organization, distributed handbills throughout their area that encouraged African Americans to register to vote at the local courthouse.[21] Though two hundred attempted to register as a result, only twelve succeeded. A lawsuit by the NAACP (with support from Thurgood Marshall) followed, challenging the refusal to allow such numbers of people to vote.[22]

Early in 1946 the National Pan-Hellenic Council announced their program for the year, which included securing better housing, equalizing teaching salaries, and abolishing the poll tax.[23] By the summer of 1946, Alpha Kappa Alpha leaders met in Detroit with other BGLO leaders in the hopes that they could collaborate, thus amplifying their collective resources.[24] By affirmative vote of over two-thirds of the Alpha Kappa Alpha chapters, the sorority, via supreme basileus Edna Over Gray, invited the heads of the other seven BGLOs to attend a meeting in Atlanta in May 1947.[25] To formulate the structural vision for the partnership, Gray invited the national presidents of each organization to participate in a meeting in Baltimore in July 1947.[26]

Between January and March 1948, seven of the BGLOs—Alpha Kappa Alpha, Alpha Phi Alpha, Delta Sigma Theta, Kappa Alpha Psi, Phi Beta Sigma, Sigma Gamma Rho, and Zeta Phi Beta—secured approval from their national conventions to create and join the cooperative program.[27] In March of that year the group held an organizational meeting in Baltimore.[28] The organization was solidified; committees were appointed and Gray was elected the first president of the newly formed American Council on Human Rights (ACHR). The last BGLO group secured approval from its body in December 1948 and joined the ACHR shortly thereafter.[29]

The ACHR's constitution provided for complete equality of representation and financial responsibility by each of the constituent organizations. Per its constitution, the ACHR was to "provide a joint and cooperative non-partisan body through which together the member organizations may (1) study questions of domestic and foreign policy and legislation as they affect civic rights and human relationship. (2) Develop and use procedures and means whereby it may best express its opinion on such questions and seek to have enacted, administered and enforced the law effectuating the same."[30] The board of directors included three delegates from each organization, one who would always be its national president.[31] Program proposals were adopted at the June 1948 meeting. Kappa Alpha Psi member Elmer W. Henderson was appointed executive director in July 1948, and the ACHR's national office opened in Washington, D.C., in August of that year.[32] Yet while the transition of the NPC to the ACHR was under way, the individual BGLOs remained engaged in diverse social uplift activities under their individual direction, as we recount below.

Black Legal Minds: Black Greeks versus Jim Crow, Esquire

As World War II came, so did an increasingly diverse approach for racial uplift from Alpha Phi Alpha and its members. At the Twenty-Eighth General Convention of Alpha Phi Alpha in December 1940, following an incident of discrimination in a Kansas City restaurant, alongside recognition of the high rates of racial segregation in Kansas City,[33] the fraternity's Committee on Discrimination was appointed by general president Charles H. Wesley. Raymond Pace Alexander was appointed chairman, and after his efforts, restaurant authorities assured that no more incidents would occur.[34] The fraternity also established the Committee on Public Opinion, chaired by Howard H. Long. Other members of this committee had been among the leadership in the Coordinating Committee's program for the equalization of educational opportunities for Negroes through the amendment of the Harrison-Black-Fletcher Bill.[35]

Alpha Phi Alpha members also aided in developing the Southern Negro Youth Congress, a program geared toward encouraging youth to take an interest and participate in the political process. This program mainly focused on teaching youth how to navigate and dismantle the disenfranchising voting barriers that African Americans faced, primarily in the South.[36] For example, Alpha member William J. Powell focused his attention on heightening awareness and interest in aviation among blacks. The fraternity believed that breaking into aviation would offer blacks an opportunity to increase their overall economic power, which would decrease racial discrimination in society.[37] In addition, Alpha member Thurgood Marshall represented a black schoolteacher and the Norfolk Teachers' Association on appeal from a decision of the District Court for the Eastern District of Virginia. The District Court had denied the plaintiffs' request for declaratory judgment and injunction against defendants for racially discriminating salary schedules.[38] The schoolteacher was fully qualified with equal education, experience, duties, and services to the state. He was receiving a salary of $921 per month, while white high school teachers were receiving a minimum annual salary of $1,200 per month.[39] The court determined that this was a clear and obvious case of racial discrimination and that the practical application of the presented salary schedule was to pay black teachers and principals of equal qualification, certification, and experience less compensation than their white counterparts solely on account of their race or color. The court held that the plaintiff did indeed have the right to complain of such injustices, even though he had entered into a contract determining his salary.[40] The plaintiff was not asking for additional compensation for the current year but sought injunctive relief for the future. The decision of the district court was reversed, and the case remanded for further proceedings.[41]

By 1940 Kappa Alpha Psi was still building upon the social justice legacy of decades prior. At the Thirtieth Grand Chapter Meeting in Kansas City, the fraternity focused on new resolutions, including the following:

(1) a call upon Kappamen to continue fighting for the placement of a black on the federal Civil Service Commission; . . . (3) a call upon members and chapters to support the National Committee on the Negro in Defense; (4) a call to support the Geyer Anti–Poll Tax Bill; (5) offer of

the Fraternity's services to the United States Commission on Education; (6) endorsement of the effort of Louisville teachers to equalize salaries; . . . (8) decision to study the matter of a Washington lobby in the interest of blacks; (9) decision to use Fraternity influence to insure [*sic*] coverage of domestics, laborers and farm workers under the Social Security Act; . . . (11) endorsement of the federal anti-lynching bill; . . . (14) decision to call upon Congress to pass legislation making it mandatory to select government employees consecutively from civil service lists rather than under the rule of three.[42]

Also in 1940, Earl B. Dickerson litigated *Hansberry v. Lee* all the way to the U.S. Supreme Court. In *Hansberry* the Supreme Court considered whether petitioners were bound by a judgment rendered in earlier litigation to which they were not parties. In that earlier litigation Lee had argued that Hansberry violated a neighborhood agreement not to sell, lease, or permit any blacks to occupy any land within the neighborhood. Even though the agreement stated it would be effective only if 95 percent of occupants signed it—and only 54 percent did—the circuit court held that the issue of performance of the condition precedent to the validity of the agreement was res judicata; thus, the court held for Lee and found the agreement to be effective. The Supreme Court reversed and held that neither of the parties to the previous litigation that validated the agreement represented the interests of Hansberry; therefore, to enforce such an agreement would deprive Hansberry of due process.[43]

Leon A. Ransom also represented four African American defendants who were arrested without warrants and confined in the Florida Broward County Jail. The 1940 case, *Chambers v. Florida*, resulted from police attempts to solve the May 13, 1933, robbery and murder of a white man. The African American men were arrested and subjected to repeated questioning over five days. In that time African American prisoners were often disallowed to see or confer with counsel, friends, or family. After the fifth day of questioning had elicited no confession, police began a concentrated effort against a small number of prisoners in which they were questioned all night—with only short intervals for food and rest—until four of the prisoners confessed to the murder. The state used the confessions in the murder prosecutions, in which the four men were sentenced to death. The Supreme Court reversed the decision and held that the methods used to procure the confessions and their use as the basis for conviction and sentencing constituted a denial of due process because the confessions were obtained by coercion and duress.[44]

In 1941 Alpha Phi Alpha members Sidney Redmond, Charles Houston, and Henry D. Espy, along with John A. Davis, litigated *State ex rel. Bluford v. Canada*.[45] The Supreme Court of Missouri heard the case on appeal from the Circuit Court of Boone County. The appellant filed a petition for a writ of mandamus to compel the registrar of the University of Missouri to admit her as a student in the School of Journalism. She was denied admission based solely upon her race.[46] The circuit court denied the writ. The Supreme Court of Missouri affirmed, stating that it had a duty to maintain segregation if it did not come in conflict with the U.S. Constitution, even though Lincoln University, designated for black students, did not have a journalism program. The court did say that equal facilities had to be offered, but that the Lincoln Board had the discretion to determine whether there was proper demand to furnish new facilities.[47]

That same year Thurgood Marshall represented the plaintiff in *McDaniel v. Board of Public Instruction for Escambia County*.[48] The plaintiff was a black public school principal in Florida. He sued, on behalf of himself and others similarly situated, the school board and sought a declaratory judgment that the policy of the defendants fixing salaries for black teachers and principals of equivalent status to white teachers and principals a lower compensation was unconstitutional under the Fourteenth Amendment. The defendants contended that the plaintiff should not be able to represent any other class than the principal and that regular teachers should not be included in the suit. They also contended that the alleged acts could not violate the Fourteenth Amendment as they were acts of the county school system and not of the state.[49] The plaintiff was as qualified as any white principal, held the same teaching certificate, and performed the same duties. He was receiving a salary of $165 per month, while the minimum salary of a white high school principal was $200 per month. The court determined that this constituted discrimination. They also held that the plaintiff could represent teachers as they were all members of the same profession. Finally, they held that the county school system was acting as an agency of the state and could therefore be subject to Fourteenth Amendment restrictions. The motion of the defendants to dismiss the case was denied.[50]

In 1941, after the Japanese attack on Pearl Harbor, Kappa Alpha Psi urged chapters and members to support and participate with the Office of Civilian Defense and to continue supporting legislation to get rid of the poll tax, lynching, and limitations on the use of franchise.[51] In general, the fraternity called for active seeking of "fuller democracy for all Americans and fuller citizenship rights for Negroes—in the belief that America shall also preserve democracy the world over by widening the base of democracy here at home."[52]

That same year Alpha Phi Alpha members Charles Houston and Thurgood Marshall were fighting the good fight for equality. In one case Dallas F. Nicholas (Omega Psi Phi), Robert P. McGuinn (Omega Psi Phi), and Charles Houston (Alpha Phi Alpha) represented the appellee in *Durkee v. Murphy*.[53] The appeal was heard by the Court of Appeals of Maryland from the Superior Court of Baltimore City. It was an action by D. Arnett Murphy against Frank H. Durkee and others, constituting the Board of Park Commissioners of Baltimore City, for a writ of mandamus (an order from a court to an inferior government official ordering the government official to properly fulfill their official duties) to remove a restriction that segregated black and white golfers and to admit the plaintiff, a black golfer, to the white courses.[54] Defendants appealed the issuance of writ of mandamus and an order refusing to fix a penalty on the appeal bond offered in stay of execution and from the writ issued in accordance with the court's order. The court found that segregation was in the power and discretion of the board and was consistent with the Constitution.[55] Additionally, the court reasoned that the admission of black golfers to the white course was the wrong remedy for the alleged unequal treatment because the board had discretionary power to remove the alleged inequality in several ways. The court reversed the order and remanded the case for a new trial.[56]

In 1942 the courts rendered decisions on two cases litigated by Thurgood Marshall. First, in *Thomas v. Hibbitts*, a black teacher sued the Nashville Board of Education, individual board members, and the superintendent on behalf of himself and all others similarly situated.[57] He claimed that the board fixed salary schedules in such a way to pay black teachers and principals a lower salary than their white counterparts. Though they held the same qualifications and performed the same duties, white teachers were compensated anywhere from twenty-five to fifty-five dollars more per month than their black counterparts, and white principals were paid a hundred fifty dollars more per month than black principals.[58] The defendants claimed that this discrepancy was due to the difference in economic conditions between the two. Black teachers were more numerous than white teachers, their living conditions were less expensive, and they could be employed to work at a lower salary than white teachers. Though he applied for and accepted his job under the conditions of the present salary, it did not prevent him from calling into question the constitutionality of the discriminated salaries. He was not entitled to recover the difference from previous years' salaries. Declaratory judgment and an injunction were issued to prevent the board from fixing salaries in a discriminatory way during the next fiscal year.[59]

Second, in *Smith v. Allwright*, a man was denied permission to vote in the Democratic primary in Texas due to his race. While he was otherwise fully qualified to vote, he asked for a declaration of his right and five thousand dollars in damages.[60] The lower court ruled in favor of the defendants, and the plaintiff appealed. The appeals court had to determine whether the primary was held under provisions of the state statutes, an election to which the Constitution applied, or whether it was merely a party procedure.[61] *Grovey v. Townsend* was controlling in this case, which did not render the primary an election in the constitutional sense. As there was no substantial difference between that case and this one, the judgment of the lower court was affirmed.[62]

Members of other BGLOs were highly active in civil rights litigation. For instance, in the 1942 case of *State ex Rel. Michael v. Witham*, the Tennessee Supreme Court held that racial separation in educational institutions was constitutional, so long as equal educational instruction was available to both races.[63] Kappa Alpha Psi member Leon A. Ransom represented the African American applicants to the University of Tennessee, who claimed that they were denied admission to the school because of their race in violation of the Fourteenth Amendment. The Tennessee Supreme Court found it was the duty of the State Board of Education to ensure equivalent facilities for African Americans. However, the court held that the admission denials were not unconstitutional because the programs that the plaintiffs sought to enroll in were also offered at the Tennessee Agricultural and Industrial State College for Negroes.[64]

Members of Kappa Alpha Psi began broadening their approach to civil rights. For example, resolutions passed in November of 1943 at the Thirty-Third Grand Chapter Meeting of Kappa Alpha Psi in St. Louis included "(1) condemning continued refusal of the United States Navy to accept black women as WAVES [Women Appointed for Voluntary Emergency Service], or to grant commissions to black men; (2) condemning the continued refusal of the armed services to enlist black nurses although the Army needed 60,000 more nurses; (3) deploring continued failure to use black soldiers as combat troops . . . (6) authorizing the Fraternity to take steps to join with other agencies to correct the many grievances suffered by black soldiers, and continued discrimination."[65] The very next year, 1944, black women were allowed to serve in WAVES. Moreover, the fraternity passed a resolution that recommended Congress enact "legislation to provide that every member of the armed forces be subject only to military law for offenses committed or allegedly committed against a state while in the armed forces."[66]

On other fronts in 1943, Alpha Phi Alpha member Thurgood Marshall had been litigating an equal pay case, *Turner v. Keefe*, in Florida.[67] The plaintiff was a black schoolteacher who sought to obtain declaratory judgment to the effect that the policy, usage, and custom of the defendants in maintaining a salary schedule that fixed the salaries of the plaintiff and others at a rate lower than those of white teachers with equal qualifications was a denial of equal protection under the Fourteenth Amendment. Defendants specifically denied discriminatory salary practices based on race or color.[68] They alleged that the salaries paid to all teachers had been controlled by supply and demand laws under which the defendants were required to pay white teachers a higher salary than black teachers. Further, they claimed that white teachers and principals as a group possessed greater qualifications than their black counterparts. However, following the institution of this action, the Board of Public Instruction of Hillsborough County, Florida, adopted a new salary schedule that rated teachers in three classifications based on character, scholarship, and performance. The plaintiff conceded that the new schedule appeared fair upon its face but was applied in a discriminatory manner.[69] The court reviewed the classifications and, allowing room for slight errors considering the newness of the scale, found that it was applied in a nondiscriminatory manner. Further, thirty-five black teachers were interviewed, all claiming to be satisfied with their salaries, though unsatisfied with their new ratings. The court found as fact that the new rating was uniformly applied and that no discrimination based on race or color was evident.[70]

Alpha Phi Alpha members continued their activism. In *James v. Marinship Corporation*, the plaintiff was a black skilled craftsman who sued his employer and a local union chapter.[71] The union prohibited black workers to be members and instead required that they join an auxiliary group. The auxiliary group did not provide the same benefits and privileges as the main union. A closed shop was maintained, requiring all potential employees of Marinship Corporation join the union or auxiliary. Despite the union prohibiting black workers from joining, their membership in its auxiliary group was required if they wished to work. Marinship was required to terminate the employment of any black employee who was not a member of the auxiliary, and they were notified that not doing so was a breach of contract with the union.[72] The trial court issued a preliminary injunction restraining Marinship from this action. The defendants appealed, claiming that business agents of the union chapter acted impartially and without discrimination. The court disagreed and held that maintaining a closed shop (a place of work where membership in a union is a condition for being hired and for continued employment) as well as closed membership were equivalent to barring certain persons from their right to work. Though the defendants argued that these actions were allowed separately, the court maintained that together they constituted discrimination. On these grounds the Supreme Court of California affirmed the lower court judgment.[73]

Thurgood Marshall, with the support of Alpha Phi Alpha, also litigated many other cases that were decided in 1944. In *Morris v. Williams*, the plaintiff was a black schoolteacher in Little Rock, Arkansas, who brought suit against the board of directors and superintendent of schools.[74] She contended the existence of (1) a schedule of salaries, which discriminated against the plaintiff and other black teachers and principals on account of race or color; (2) a policy, custom, or usage to pay black teachers and principals less salary and compensation than their white counterparts; and (3) a constitutional violation under the Fourteenth Amendment.[75] The plaintiff introduced the minutes from a board meeting in which a salary schedule was approved and adopted.

However, this schedule made no indication of race or color. It simply stated the starting salaries for any teacher in the elementary, junior high, and senior high schools. The plaintiff claimed that a fixed salary based on education and years of experience would be ideal to prevent discrimination. The superintendent testified that during his first year, beginning in 1941, he maintained the previous year's salaries because he lacked sufficient information with which to base any changes.[76] The next year, when the suit was filed, he decided to make very few changes, knowing that any change would be interpreted in light of the case. He further testified that upon hiring and salary, he based his decisions on education and experience plus certain other intangible qualities, which determine what value a teacher brings to the school system.[77] The court determined that the plaintiff failed to provide sufficient evidence for her case. There was no constitutional violation because there was no proven salary schedule or custom of salary discrimination. Costs of this action were taxed against the plaintiff.[78]

In *Railway Mail Association v. Corsi*, Edward R. Dudley and Thurgood Marshall, along with Milton R. Konvitz, William H. Hastie (Omega Psi Phi), and Leon A. Ransom (Kappa Alpha Psi), served as amicus curiae for the NAACP Legal Defense Fund. The defendant, the industrial commissioner of the state of New York, attempted to enforce a statute against the Railway Mail Association, which would prevent it from discriminating against its membership because of race or color.[79] The plaintiff, denying its classification as a labor organization, sought to enjoin the defendant from enforcing such an order. The lower court ruled in favor of the plaintiff, and the defendant appealed. The plaintiff argued that it was permitted to perform insurance business within New York and was therefore not a labor organization. The court reviewed the facts to answer the question of whether Railway Mail Association fell within the definition of a labor organization.[80] In the official bulletin of the U.S. Department of Labor, the Railway Mail Association was indeed classified as a labor union. The organization assumed credit for securing beneficial legislation for its members and, by its own acts, had interpreted its charter to include phases of collective bargaining and dealing with the federal government concerning grievances, terms and conditions of employment, and rendering its members mutual aid and protection. It came well within the definition of a labor union.[81] The next question presented to the court was whether the plaintiff violated section 43 of the federal Civil Rights Law. Its constitution restricts membership only to white or Caucasian individuals and Native American Indians. Applicants for membership were required to state their race in writing. The court determined that the insurance features of the plaintiff's power were in addition to and did not alter its status as a labor union. The order and judgment of the lower court was reversed and granted in favor of the defendant.[82]

Along with attorney A. T. Walden, Thurgood Marshall represented the plaintiff in *Davis v. Cook*.[83] Therein the defendants, the Board of Education of Atlanta, asked the court to dismiss the case brought against them by a black schoolteacher. Defendants claimed that the complaint should rightfully be made against the state of Georgia, an indispensable party, and that the court was without jurisdiction. The plaintiff alleged that the board had a policy, custom, and usage to pay black teachers and principals less than their white counterparts.[84] Though they all possessed the same teaching certificate required by the public school system, and perhaps had the same qualifications, experience, and duties, black teachers were consistently paid a lower salary because of their race. This denied them their equal protection of laws. A salary schedule was fixed to pay black teachers less than white teachers and using state funds to do so.[85] The court held that a true controversy between parties did in fact exist and that the school officials were acting under the color of authority of the state of Georgia. Acting with the authority of the state, though their actions may not be authorized by the state, constituted an unconstitutional act under the Fourteenth Amendment. On these grounds, the court denied the motion to dismiss.[86]

Charles Houston litigated *Steele v. Louisville & Nashville Railroad Company*.[87] The suit, brought by William Steele against the Louisville & Nashville Railroad Company, Brotherhood of Locomotive Firemen and Enginemen, and others sought to enjoin enforcement of agreements between the defendants that discriminated against black firemen in favor of white firemen and for other relief.[88] A decree dismissing the bill was affirmed by the Supreme Court of Alabama, stating that while they had jurisdiction, on merits the petitioner's complaint stated no cause of action. It pointed out that the Railway Labor Act placed a mandatory duty on the railroad to treat the Brotherhood as the exclusive representative of the employees in its craft and that the Brotherhood was entitled to enter into agreements.[89] The Supreme Court reversed and remanded the case for further proceedings not inconsistent with its opinion. It stated that the Brotherhood, under the Railway Labor Act, had to represent all members of its craft, the majority and the minority, and had to act for and not against those members.[90]

Finally, in *Smith v. Allwright*, Thurgood Marshall and William Hastie (Omega Psi Phi) represented a black citizen of the state of Texas who was denied the right to vote in a primary election.[91] He sued the Democratic Party, and his petition was denied. He appealed to the U.S. Supreme Court. The defendants argued that primary elections were private, not state, matters. Primary elections were left to the political parties and were, therefore, not a state function. However, the court determined that the right to vote in a primary is an integral part of the election process and is a right secured by the U.S. Constitution.[92] Under the Fourteenth and Fifteenth Amendments, this right cannot be abridged because of race or color. Though previous cases had ruled in favor of the defendants, the court determined that they were not bound by those decisions that they believed to be erroneous. When the plaintiff was prohibited from obtaining and completing a ballot in the primary election, he was denied the right to vote due to his race.[93] The court determined that this act was under the color of authority of the state of Texas and was therefore an unconstitutional act. The defendants argued that, as private citizens, they could discriminate against whomever they so chose. However, political parties were a guaranteed right under the Texas Bill of Rights, making any discriminatory action by their officials a state act. The decision of the lower court was reversed.[94]

Alpha Phi Alpha members brought these first forty years of Alpha Phi Alpha's existence into clarity. Attorney Sidney A. Jones wrote in the June 1945 *National Bar Journal* on the Supreme Court's role in Jim Crow segregated transportation. He discussed the inequality brought about under the guise of "separate but equal" accommodations and the Supreme Court's ability, but refusal to put an end to the injustice.[95] Charles Houston and Thurgood Marshall continued their assault on racial discrimination in the courtroom. In *Thompson v. Gibbs*, Marshall represented a plaintiff who brought action against the school board and superintendent of schools of District No. 1 in Richland County, South

Carolina.[96] He alleged that the school district's discriminatory pay schedule, which favored white teachers over black teachers, violated the Fourteenth Amendment. While the defendants claimed to have a system set up to deal with allegations of discriminatory pay, the court required its own analysis. Teacher salaries in Richland County were withdrawn from both state and county funds. The county funds were distributed within the discretion of the county board. A temporary state act had recently been announced that drew a salary table that allotted pay to teachers based on their classification of experience and performance on an examination. Prior to this act, salary schedules in South Carolina had been blatantly discriminatory. Realizing this, the defendants sought to revamp and make changes to the salaries so that they were fair for all.[97] The court felt that enough of the pay disparity had been reconciled to allow the defendants more time before a final judgment. The evidence showed that the county funds were being assigned in such a way to prove that the board took the action of erasing discriminatory pay seriously. Therefore, the court allowed the school board until April 1, 1946, to show that the pay schedules had been completely rid of discriminatory action.[98]

As 1945 ended, a federal court in Alabama decided yet another case tried by Marshall. In *Mitchell v. Wright* the plaintiff, a black man, sued when he was prohibited from registering to vote in Macon County, Alabama.[99] He alleged that he met all the qualifications required of a registered voter, including the ability to read and write and the ownership of land. He presented himself at the Macon County Court House, filled out his application, produced two persons to vouch for him, and answered such questions as were asked in proof of his qualifications. Unlike the white persons presenting themselves for registration, he was required to provide two references and wait long hours before being permitted to file his application. His application was then denied because of his race. As the officials were acting under the authority of Macon County and Alabama state law, the plaintiff claimed that this action was in violation of his rights under Article I and the Fourteenth, Fifteenth, and Seventeenth Amendments of the U.S. Constitution. He sought a declaratory judgment, a permanent injunction, and five thousand dollars in damages.[100] The defendants, administrative officials of the state of Alabama, filed a motion to dismiss this case as a class action.[101] The court held that a class action must include others similarly situated in an actual, real situation, not merely a possibility. The purpose of such a suit is to determine the rights of a distinct class of individuals by one common final judgment. The plaintiff failed to identify such a class. The court determined that others similarly situated was too broad a definition and must be determined on an individual basis. It was not up to the court to define such a class. Further, the court determined that the plaintiff had not exhausted all administrative remedies before bringing the matter to court.[102] After being denied entrance to the initial parts of the election machinery, the plaintiff sought judicial action and forsook the remaining parts of the machinery that may have granted him relief. However, Alabama law allowed for any person denied registration to appeal his case. The complaint was dismissed on these grounds.[103]

Charles Houston, along with W. A. C. Hughes, litigated *Kerr v. Enoch Free Library of Baltimore City*, heard on appeal by the Fourth Circuit.[104] Kerr, a black woman, complained that she was refused admission to a library training class conducted by the Enoch Pratt Free Library of Baltimore City because of her race. Kerr alleged that this was a violation of the Fourteenth Amendment. The defendants claimed that the plaintiff was not excluded because of her race, that the library was a private corporation, and that it did not perform any public function as a representative of the state.[105] The district judge agreed and dismissed the case. However, the Court of Appeals found that Kerr was excluded from the library because of her race and that the authority of the state was invoked to create the library, so it was not a private corporation. The judgment of the district judge was reversed and the case was remanded.[106]

In another case litigated by Marshall, *Morris v. Williams*, the plaintiff was a black schoolteacher in Little Rock, Arkansas, who sued the board of directors and the superintendent of the public schools of the Little Rock Special Schools District.[107] The teacher claimed that the discriminatory salary practices by the district were in violation of the Fourteenth Amendment of the U.S. Constitution. The defendants denied that there was any policy, custom, or usage that assigned differences in salary to white and black schoolteachers and principals solely based on race. Two questions were presented for the court's determination. First, whether there was a salary schedule that discriminated solely based on race or color. Second, whether there was a policy, custom, or usage to pay black teachers lower salaries than white teachers because of race.[108] The court found no evidence of a salary schedule, discriminatory or otherwise, that existed in the Little Rock Special Schools District. The defense claimed that any difference in teacher salary was due to a difference in qualifications, duty, experience, or an intangible something extra required by a person to be a good teacher. The court found evidence in the board of directors meeting minutes that new black teachers were assigned a salary of $615 a year in elementary schools and $630 in high schools, while white teachers were assigned a salary of $810 in the lower grades and $900 in high school.[109] Additionally, yearly advances in salary were assigned disproportionately between the races, with white teachers always receiving a higher pay raise. The court determined that very substantial inequalities existed and that such inequalities had existed and continued for a period of several years. They also determined that no explanation of these inequalities existed in the records of the board meetings. Inequalities were clearly based solely on race.[110] Therefore, the court reversed the judgment of the lower court and remanded the decision with instructions to enter the declaratory judgment originally sought.[111]

In 1946, fraternity members such as Thurgood Marshall and Alexander Pierre Tureaud continued to wage legal battles throughout the federal courts of appeals. In *Chapman v. King* Marshall and Tureaud, among other attorneys, represented King—a qualified and registered black voter in Muscogee County, Georgia.[112] On the day of the Democratic primary, King was denied the right to vote by executives of the Democratic Party based solely on his race. The District Court judge concluded that this was a violation of the Fourteenth, Fifteenth, and Seventeenth Amendments of the U.S. Constitution because the state of Georgia acts through political parties. Therefore, the state was enforcing a discriminatory act, which was unconstitutional.[113] On appeal, the Fifth Circuit found that because the primary election was an integral part of the election machinery, denying one's right to vote in the primary was tantamount to denying one's right to vote in any election.[114] When racial exclusions of a party were enforced by the state, the action was in violation of the Fifteenth Amendment. The court affirmed the decision of the lower court in King's favor.[115]

Also in the Fifth Circuit, Marshall represented the appellant in *Mitchell v. Wright*.[116] The appellant was a black man who attempted to register to vote in the state of Alabama. He possessed all the qualifications to be a registered voter in the state.[117] He alleged that he properly filled out his voter application, and the defendants refused to register him and others because of their race.[118] The District Court held that this refusal was determined to be an action under state authority, which deprived the right to vote to black individuals. Since voter registration was necessary to participate in the election process, the refusal to register an individual was equivalent to denying him the right to vote.[119] While the defendants claimed that the plaintiff did not exhaust his administrative remedies before pursing legal action, the Fifth Circuit determined that any person in Alabama who was denied registration had the right to appeal to the circuit court.[120] The Fifth Circuit determined that though this law appeared fair upon its face, it was in fact administered in a discriminatory manner as to deny black people the right to vote. Accordingly, the judgment of the lower court was reversed and the case remanded for further proceedings.[121]

Marshall also represented an African American appellant before the U.S. Supreme Court in *Morgan v. Commonwealth of Virginia*.[122] Appellant was a black passenger on a bus traveling from Virginia to Maryland. When the driver requested that she move seats, she refused and was subsequently arrested.[123] A Virginia statute required the separation of white and black passengers on both interstate and intrastate motor carriers.[124] The question for the Supreme Court was whether this statute unlawfully burdened interstate commerce. Given that uniform interstate commerce rules are necessary, the court declared that seating arrangements for different races must follow a single, uniform rule to not burden interstate commerce. The court reversed the decision of the Virginia Supreme Court on the basis that the provision of the Virginia Code, which segregated passengers on interstate buses, created an undue burden on interstate commerce.[125] It also attempted to reach beyond the borders of its own state by governing interstate travel. Because the code could not be enforced by a single, uniform rule, it violated the Commerce Clause of the U.S. Constitution.[126]

On February 26, 1946, a white mob gathered around the Maury County Courthouse in Columbia, Tennessee, while African American citizens and military veterans gathered a block south along the segregated business section known as the Mink Slide.[127] When four highway patrolmen were sent to the Mink Slide to investigate a call, shots were fired that wounded all four officers. The next day a sweep of the Mink Slide resulted in the arrest of over a hundred African Americans—all of whom were denied bail and legal counsel. The NAACP, through Thurgood Marshall, hired Omega Psi Phi members Z. Alexander Looby and Maurice Weaver to represent twenty-five African Americans arrested in connection with the shootings.[128] Looby and his legal defense team ultimately achieved the unthinkable—the acquittal of twenty-three defendants by an all-white jury.[129] While two men were found guilty, they were never retried due to a lack of evidence.[130]

On October 10, 1947, Omega Psi Phi member Grant Reynolds, along with Phi Beta Sigma member A. Phillip Randolph, organized the Committee Against Jim Crow in Military Service and Training.[131] Reynolds became a World War II chaplain for the U.S. Army in 1941. However, he resigned in early 1944 because of the prevalent racism throughout the military. The Committee Against Jim Crow in Military Service and Training successfully lobbied President Truman's Executive Order 9981, signed on July 26, 1948.[132] On that date Truman spoke of equality for all persons in the armed forces and outlined ten legislative objectives for strengthening constitutional rights of minorities.[133]

Around this same time Omega Psi Phi member Lincoln J. Ragsdale was integrating the Army Air Corps.[134] Ragsdale graduated from Tuskegee flying school in Alabama.[135] Although he was unable to fly a military combat mission, he was commissioned as a second lieutenant in the Army Air Corps.[136] He encountered severe racism within the military and went on to become very active in securing civil rights.[137]

In New York in 1947 Thurgood Marshall and Robert Carter litigated *Dorsey v. Stuyvesant Town Corp.*[138] The plaintiffs sued Stuyvesant Town Corporation for racial discrimination. Stuyvesant was building a new housing development in New York City. They did not want to admit black tenants into their area, known at the time as Stuyvesant Town.[139] The question was whether the operators of Stuyvesant Town could select tenants of their own choice and whether they could refuse tenants based on race, color, creed, or religion. Previous decisions settled the matter that a private landlord could exclude tenants of a particular race, color, creed, or religion.[140] Unsuccessful attempts had been made to assert housing as a fundamental civil right. Review of the laws regarding this clearly showed that housing was not a recognized civil right.[141] The plaintiffs also confused Stuyvesant Town as a public project. Stuyvesant Town was not a low-rent housing project for persons of low income. Though they were serving a public purpose by redeveloping and rehabilitating a substandard and unsanitary area, the public purpose was terminated by the end results, which was not for public use. Stuyvesant Town was never a public project, and Stuyvesant was not a public corporation.[142] The court ruled that they could not interfere in the matter of private companies, holding for the defendant.[143]

In Michigan Alpha Phi Alpha members Carter and Marshall represented the defendants—a black man, his white wife, and her white parents—in *Northwest Civic Association v. Sheldon*.[144] Prior to the suit defendants sought to purchase a piece of property in Security Land Company's subdivision. The subdivision consisted of 338 lots restricted to the use of white or Caucasian people. Of these 338 lots, 310 stated that restriction in the chain of title. Inadvertently, the remaining 28 did not contain this statement.[145] The plaintiffs, Mrs. Sheldon and her parents, met with the real estate agent who had the sale of the property in charge. Mr. Sheldon was not present at these meetings. The real estate agent testified that he informed Mrs. Sheldon and her parents of the restriction placed on black residents. However, the deed to their property did not explicitly contain this statement. No black person or family had ever before resided in the subdivision until Mr. Sheldon moved in with his wife, leading to the present case.[146] Defendants claimed that Mr. Sheldon's Fourteenth Amendment rights were violated. However, the court held that it was contrary to neither public policy of the state nor the Constitution for a private landlord to permit and enforce certain restrictions upon the use and occupation of real property. Defendants relied on the fact that this restriction was not stated in the chain of title for their property.[147] The court held that the purchasers were informed of the restriction and had no right to believe otherwise.[148]

In Tennessee, Carter and Marshall lost their case—*Kennedy v. State*—before the Supreme Court of Tennessee. In that case the defendant was a black man convicted of assault with intent to commit murder in the second degree. Though no witnesses saw him firing the shots, he was found in possession of a gun and near a discharged gun after the shooting. He sought review of his case, claiming that the trial court erred in not holding that he was discriminated against by excluding black voters from the jury. However, the Supreme Court of Tennessee found that the jury pool consisted of four black voters, and thus there was no discrimination. The judgment of the lower court was affirmed.[149]

In Louisiana, Alpha Phi Alpha member Alexander Pierre Tureaud—attorney for the New Orleans chapter of the NAACP during the civil rights movement—and colleagues prevailed in *State v. Perkins* before the Supreme Court of Louisiana. The case argued that when an African American defendant faced charges affecting his life or liberty, the Equal Protection Clause required the opportunity to have members of his race serve on grand and petit juries. The Court of Appeals affirmed the sentence given the following statements: "We find no substance in this proposition. In the first place, the evidence shows that the general venire lists complained of were supplemented so that there were five Negros thereon. Moreover, we do not understand that a person charged with crime is entitled to have an exact percentage of persons of his race, in comparison to other races, placed on the general venire. The Consti tution forbids discrimination, it does not deal with percentages."[150]

In *Sipuel v. Board of Regents of the University of Oklahoma*, the plaintiff, Ada Sipuel, was denied admission to the only taxpayer-funded law school in the state of Oklahoma at the time because of her race. Sipuel was fully qualified in prelaw academics and moral character, but nonetheless was denied admission solely based on her race. She petitioned the District Court of Cleveland County, Oklahoma, and the case worked its way to the Oklahoma Supreme Court, which upheld the decision of the lower district court. Carter and Marshall represented the plaintiff in state court. The petitioner sought a writ of mandamus to compel the University of Oklahoma to admit her to its law school, claiming her denial violated her Fourteenth Amendment rights. Separate education had always been the state's policy and had been upheld by voters, taxpayers, educators, and patrons of both races. If the University of Oklahoma had admitted Sipuel, they would have been subject to criminal penalty, as it was a crime in Oklahoma for a school to admit, or an instructor to teach, a student of a different race. This was thought to be for the greater good of both races. The court noted that the petitioner sought not to enjoin the state to establish a law school for black students, rather to admit her to a law school for white students. They also noted that this did not take into fair account the separate school policy of the state. The court concluded that Sipuel's rights were not violated. She had the right to either attend a law school for black students in the state or attend such a school in another state. The laws of Oklahoma stood, and the judgment of the trial court to deny writ of mandamus was affirmed.[151] On appeal, Marshall along with Amos Hall (Omega Psi Phi) and Frank D. Reeves litigated the case before the U.S. Supreme Court. The court reversed, holding for the petitioner.[152]

In South Carolina, Carter and Marshall prevailed in two cases— *Elmore v. Rice* and *Wrighten v. Board of Trustees of the University of South Carolina*, both before the South Carolina federal trial court. In *Elmore v. Rice*, the plaintiff, a fully qualified black voter, sued the Democratic Party. He and certain other qualified black voters entered the polling place on the appropriate date, at the appropriate time. After requesting ballots and permission to vote in the Democratic Primary, they were denied because they were not white Democrats. The question here was whether racial distinctions can exist in the primary election process, considering the Fourteenth, Fifteenth, and Seventeenth Amendments. In *Newberry v. United States*, Justice Pitney declared that the primary election should not be treated as a separate thing from the general election but should be considered so closely related that proper regulation is required. The present court held this view and stated that racial distinctions could not exist in the machinery that elects the officers and lawmakers of the United States. All citizens are equally entitled to vote, so the court granted judgment in favor of the plaintiff and enjoined the Democratic Party from excluding qualified voters based on race. Robert Lee Carter and Thurgood Marshall represented the plaintiff in the case.[153]

In *Wrighten v. Board of Trustees of the University of South Carolina*, the plaintiff was a black student who applied to the University of South Carolina Law School. He was fully qualified in academic achievement and character and was denied solely on the grounds of race. South Carolina state laws forbid any school to admit both white and black students. However, the University of South Carolina was the only institution in the state that operated a law school. There was no law school operated by an institution that admitted solely black students. Under the Fourteenth Amendment of the United States, the plaintiff claimed he had a right to equal opportunities in education. The plaintiff asked the court to declare injunctive relief, whereby he would be entitled to receive a legal education at the University of South Carolina Law School. Additionally, the plaintiff asked that money damages be paid for him by reason of deprivation of his rights. The court decided that the question of damages would be heard at another time. The question of this case was whether the plaintiff was entitled to admission at the University of South Carolina Law School and whether the state should be given ample time to provide equal law school facilities at a separate institution in the state. The state claimed that the State College for black students had received no applications for legal education and only recently had inquiries been made. The court responded that this was an excuse for delay but not denial of a legal education for black students. They ordered that the state of South Carolina provide law school facilities for black students equal to those at the University of South Carolina, either at the university itself or at another institution of the state, or provide none to anyone. The state was granted until the next law school semester, September 1947, to comply with these orders.[154]

In Alabama, Marshall lost his case—*Mitchell v. Wright*—before the Alabama federal trial court. The plaintiff, a black citizen of Macon County, Alabama, sought injunctive relief, declaratory judgment, and nominal damages because of the alleged failure of the Board of Registrars of Macon County to register him as a qualified elector solely because of his race and color. This, he claimed, was contrary to the antidiscrimination provisions of the Fifteenth Amendment of the U.S. Constitution. The plaintiff possessed all the qualifications necessary to become a qualified voter of the state. He properly filled out his application and listed the names of two references to vouch for him as a bona fide resident of the address stated on his application. The Board of Registrars required that two names be listed and at least one of them appear before the board to vouch for the applicant. However, neither of the two names listed on the plaintiff's application ever appeared before the board. One claimed that the plaintiff never informed him that he was listed as a reference. He had before given seven other black citizens reference before the board. The other reference appeared at the courthouse one day, saw a crowd, and left without ever returning. The court found no instance of a person who was registered by the board as a qualified voter without first having a reference appear on his or her behalf. No white or black voter was ever given this privilege. The board did not require that black voters give white references. The court held that the rules and regulations of the board were nondiscriminatory. The plaintiff failed to present evidence of discrimination by the Board of Registrars.[155]

In *Westminster School District of Orange County v. Mendez*, Carter and Marshall won their case before the Ninth Circuit Court of Appeals. Westminster School District appealed the judgment of the district court, which had ruled that the segregation of Mexican schoolchildren was unconstitutional. They appealed because there was no federal question put at issue, as the school officers were not acting under a state law or statute and thus could not be violating the Fourteenth Amendment. The questions here were whether the acts of segregation were done under color of state law and if they violated constitutional rights. The appellees had originally contested that their children, as well as five thousand other children, were victims of unconstitutional discrimination by being forced to attend a separate school for Mexicans. The court decided that the school officials, though they acted beyond the scope of their power, were performing under the color or pretense of California state law. The appellants argued that other court cases had upheld school segregation, but the court decided that those cases were not controlling in this one. No California state law existed permitting the act of school segregation. It followed that the actions of the school officers were without merit to California state law. Therefore, the court affirmed the lower court's decision and declared the segregation unconstitutional.[156]

In the case of *Brotherhood Locomotive Firemen and Enginemen v. Tunstall*, Charles Hamilton and Joseph Cornelius Waddy, along with Oliver W. Hill (Omega Psi Phi), won their case before Fourth Circuit. Tunstall filed suit against the Brotherhood of Locomotive Firemen and Enginemen for a declaratory judgment, injunction, and other relief after he was determined ineligible for membership to the Brotherhood solely because of his race. Brotherhood engaged in collective bargaining with Tunstall's railroad employer as a representative of the entire craft. Negotiations were made without notifying Tunstall or other members of his class. Because of the negotiations, Tunstall was removed from his job post and assigned a more difficult, lower wage job. The federal trial court dismissed the case, and the Fourth Circuit affirmed because the federal courts lacked the jurisdiction over the case. The plaintiff, therefore, appealed to the U.S. Supreme Court, which in turn reversed the dismissal of the Circuit Court. On remand, the federal trial court declared that the Brotherhood was the exclusive representative of the firemen employed by the railway company for the purposes of collective bargaining under the Railway Labor Act, that it was the duty of the Brotherhood to represent impartially and without hostile discrimination the plaintiff and the other black firemen, that the Brotherhood had violated this duty by negotiating with the railway company, that the agreements were null and void since they deprived the plaintiff and other black firemen of seniority and employment rights, and that the plaintiff had been illegally removed from his run and was entitled to be restored thereto. The defendants were enjoined from giving force or effect to the agreements insofar as they interfered with the occupation of plaintiff or of the class represented by him and the railway company was ordered to restore his position. The Fourth Circuit affirmed the decision on appeal, finding discrimination in the actions of Brotherhood.[157]

In 1947, the U.S. Supreme Court heard *Patton v. Mississippi*, for which Thurgood Marshall represented the petitioner, a black man named Henry Clay Patton. Patton was indicted by an all-white jury for the murder of a white man and sentenced to death by electrocution. Citing the Fourteenth Amendment, Marshall noted that no black person had served on a jury in Mississippi in thirty years. Though at least twenty-five black male electors were qualified for jury service, not even one was selected. The question was whether there was systematic racial discrimination in the juror selection process. To quell the presumption that black voters were deliberately excluded from the jury pool, the state would be required to justify such exclusion for reasons other than racial discrimination. If jury selection proceeded in such a way to systematically exclude representation of any group of eligible voters, the verdicts of such juries could stand. The state claimed that the reason no black voters were included was due to the extremely low number of eligible black voters compared to white voters. However, the court reasoned that this low number was due to the discrimination against black voters in the making of registration lists. If the few eligible black voters had been disqualified for proper reasons, such as commission of crime or habitual drunkenness, there was no doubt that the state could have proved it. Because they did not provide evidence against purposeful discrimination, the court concluded that it was indeed discrimination that kept black voters out of jury service for more than thirty years. The decision of the lower courts was reversed, giving Marshall the victory.[158]

Individually, Alpha Phi Alpha members were on the front line of social change. Illustrating racial tensions in 1948, past general president of the fraternity Raymond W. Cannon turned down a position on the Twin City Draft Board because of the continued racial discrimination in the U.S. Army.[159] In Maryland, Charles Houston and his team of lawyers litigated several cases. In *Goetz v. Smith*, he and Donald Gaines Murray (Kappa Alpha Psi) won their case before the Court of Appeals of Maryland. The action involved two cases that were argued together in the court, involving the attempted enforcement of a restrictive covenant against the sale, lease, transfer, or permitted occupation of certain properties to or by "any negro, Chinaman, Japanese, or person of negro, Chinese or Japanese descent."[160] In the Circuit Court the plaintiffs in the first case were unsuccessful in their attempt to enforce the restrictive covenant, but the plaintiffs in the second case were successful. The losers of each case appealed. The losers of the second case appealed under the allegation of a violation of the Fourteenth Amendment. The decree in the first case was affirmed, the decree in the second case was reversed, and the bill of complaint dismissed, under protection of the Fourteenth Amendment.[161]

However, before the Maryland federal trial court, Houston lost two cases. In *Law v. Mayor and City Council of Baltimore*, members Houston and Joseph Cornelius Waddy, along with W. A. C. Hughes Jr., represented a plaintiff who sued for the enforcement of civil rights arising under the Fourteenth Amendment. The plaintiff alleged that he and other black golfers were not provided golf facilities equal to those given to white golfers. The defendants argued that they provided a golf facility specifically for black golfers that, considering there were far fewer black golfers than white golfers, was an equal facility. The court found the black golf facility to be far inferior to the white facility. Accordingly, the court suggested that the Board of Recreation and Parks devise a solution that would remedy the lack of equality exhibited in black and white facilities.[162]

In *Norris v. Mayor and City Council of Baltimore*, Houston, Fred E. Wiesgal, Harry O. Levin, and W. A. C. Hughes Jr. represented Leon A.

Norris. Norris applied to the Maryland Institute for the Promotion of the Mechanic Arts and was denied admission due to his race. Norris filed suit on the grounds of the Fourteenth Amendment. His complaint asked (1) for a declaratory judgment that the plaintiff is entitled to be received as a student in the Maryland Institute on the same terms as other citizens and residents of Baltimore City without regard to race or color; (2) that the institute be enjoined from excluding him from such instruction solely because of race or color; (3) in the alternative, if the plaintiff is not entitled to the above relief, then the other defendant, the mayor and City Council of Baltimore, a municipal corporation, be enjoined from appropriating any public money or allocating any public property or resources to the Art Institute if it is a private corporation not under the restraints of the federal Constitution; (4) for damages of twenty thousand dollars. The complaint was dismissed, with the court stating that the act of discrimination did not constitute state action because the institute was a private corporation because its officers were not appointed by and it was not subject to the control of a public authority. It was also dismissed because the alternative relief in the complaint lacked jurisdiction because an injunction against appropriations of public money to an educational institution was essentially a taxpayer's suit.[163]

In Louisiana Marshall won his case—*Whitmyer v. Lincoln Parish School Board*—before the federal trial court. The plaintiff, a black schoolteacher, brought a class action suit against the Lincoln Parish school board and its superintendent. Because he received a lower salary than white teachers of equal experience and qualification, he sought a declaration by the court that the rights of black teachers be equal to those of white teachers and an injunction against further discrimination. The defendants moved to dismiss the case because the plaintiff brought a class action suit when he was not a representative of all black schoolteachers and the suit was truly on his own behalf as an individual. The court ruled that the motions be denied and proper decree in favor of the plaintiff should be issued.[164]

In Oklahoma Carter and Marshall lost their case—*McLaurin v. Oklahoma Regents for Higher Education*—before the federal district court. The plaintiff sought to earn a postgraduate degree in education from the University of Oklahoma. He was fully qualified but rejected because the school did not admit black students. Oklahoma laws made it a criminal offense for any school or educational institution to allow both white and black students to attend. The court found that no other institution in the state of Oklahoma would afford the plaintiff the same opportunity for education in the same amount of time. This, they said, denied him his constitutional rights under the Fourteenth Amendment. Further, they claimed that the Oklahoma laws requiring segregation in this case were unconstitutional and unenforceable. However, this did not mean that these laws were incapable of constitutional enforcement. In this case, they were inoperative. As the governor of Oklahoma committed to a course of action that would provide equal facilities and opportunities for black students in this matter, the court decided to hold off judgment. They held it was not the place of the court to determine the way the state complied with its constitutional responsibilities to its citizens and therefore suspended judgment.[165]

In a subsequent case also litigated by Carter and Marshall, McLaurin was finally accepted into and attended the University of Oklahoma. However, the segregated conditions under which he attended violated his Fourteenth Amendment rights. Though he attended the same classes as white students, he was required to sit at a designated desk or area separate from most of the class. He could use the library books and facilities; however, he was required to bring his books to a designated desk on the mezzanine floor, while other students were permitted to use any floor or area of the library. Finally, though he was served in the same cafeteria and ate the same food, he was required to eat at different times and at a designated table. He claimed that this isolation from all the other students created a mental discomfiture that made concentration and study difficult, if not impossible. Additionally, he claimed that the badge of inferiority affixed to him by the university affected his relationships with other students and his professors. However, the court found no legal basis for his mental discomfiture and found that all educational facilities were equal for white and black students. They denied the relief McLaurin sought against the university.[166]

In Georgia, Carter and Marshall prevailed in *Davis v. Cook* before the federal trial court. Samuel L. Davis, a black schoolteacher in Atlanta, brought this class action suit on behalf of himself and other black teachers similarly situated. He claimed that the Board of Education of the City of Atlanta was practicing unfair and discriminatory salary schedules. Before this case, the school board had switched from a separate pay schedule for black and white schoolteachers to a single pay schedule that was intended to ensure fair pay among teachers of all races. The court determined the evidence showed that though the original intention of the single schedule was to provide equal pay, it was implemented in such a way to discriminate pay based on race. Statistical evidence was provided by statistics experts on the side of the plaintiffs and the defense, and the numbers showed that the mean salaries of black teachers were lower than the mean salaries of white teachers, even after controlling for experience and qualification. Only 1.5 percent of black teachers were earning over $189 per month, while 78.1 percent of white teachers were. Because there was no administrative remedy for removing the salary inequalities, it could not have been existed prior to the filing of the suit. While the power to assign salaries would remain in the hands of the defendants, the court decreed that such assignments could not be discriminatory because of race or color. Injunctive relief was granted, and the defendants were given a reasonable time to comply.[167]

In South Carolina, Carter and Marshall prevailed in *Brown v. Baskin* before the federal trial court. The plaintiff, David Brown, was a fully qualified voter in the state of South Carolina. He registered with the Democratic Party to vote in the primary election. His name, as well as those of other black voters, was stricken from the enrollment books. He was told he must present a general election certificate and take an oath that, among other things, included the assertion that he would vote in favor of segregation. This case was an issue under the Fourteen and Seventeenth Amendments of the U.S. Constitution. The court believed the actions of the defendant to be a clear and flagrant evasion of the law. A temporary injunction was issued to allow all qualified people in the state to register for enrollment in the Democratic Party.[168] On appeal, handled by Carter and Marshall, the federal appeals court for the Fourth Circuit found no reason to overturn or modify their decision or to defend the voting limitations imposed by the Democratic Party of South Carolina. They held that the right to vote is an essential feature of our form of government and could not be denied to any citizen as ensured by the Fourteenth and Fifteenth Amendments. These amendments had been added to the Constitution to ensure to all black citizens the equal protection of the laws and the right to full participation in government.[169]

In the court of appeals for the Fifth Circuit, Houston, along with Francis S. K. Whittaker and Oliver W. Johnson, appealed the matter of *Hampton v. Thompson*. The appellants were brakemen on the Kingsville Division of the St. Louis, Brownsville & Mexico Railroad Company and members of the Colored Trainmen of America. They sued for themselves and all other brakemen members of their union to enjoin the enforcement of an award of the First Division of the National Railroad Adjustment Board against San Antonio, Uvalde, Gulf Railroad Company, and subordinate lodges of the Brotherhood of Railroad Trainmen. The District Court believed it did not have jurisdiction but stayed the proceedings so plaintiffs would have the opportunity to present their grievances to the National Railroad Adjustment Board for its decision. The plaintiffs declined. The Fifth Circuit was to determine whether the fact that the appellants were black members of an all-black railway labor union entitled them to bypass the National Railroad Adjustment Board and sue directly in the federal courts. The Court of Appeals agreed with the trial court that they were not entitled, stating that "constitutional amendments and federal statutes, dealing with race or color, were written, they have been interpreted and applied, not to discriminate in favor of Negroes, but to prevent discrimination against them, not to make, but to prevent, a different rule for Negroes than for whites. . . . The dispute here involves no racial element whatever. The fact that the brakemen in one group are Negroes, in the other whites, has no bearing on the demands on the B.R.T. lodges."[170]

In *Hurd v. Hodge*, a case Houston and Phineas Indritz brought before the U.S. Supreme Court, the plaintiffs sought injunctive relief to enforce the terms on restrictive covenants. The federal trial court declared the deeds held by the black petitioners to be null and void, thereby enforcing the terms of the restrictive covenants. White property owners who sold the houses to the black petitioners were enjoined from selling, leasing, or conveying the properties to any black or colored person. Black petitioners were ordered to remove themselves and their belongings from the property. The Court of Appeals affirmed this decision, as it felt that the decision was consistent with earlier decisions of the Court of Appeals. The U.S. Supreme Court reversed the decision, finding it in violation of the Civil Rights Act.[171]

Shelley v. Kraemer, a case Marshall brought before the U.S. Supreme Court, dealt with the ability of state courts to uphold a private agreement that denied black citizens their equal rights under the Fourteenth Amendment. Thirty out of thirty-nine total owners of property in a certain neighborhood of St. Louis signed an agreement that stated that the property in the area would be restricted to use by only white citizens. Several parcels of land affected by this restrictive covenant were already owned by black individuals. The owners of the affected properties petitioned to have the agreement declared unconstitutional under the Fourteenth Amendment. However, the lower court ruled in favor of the respondents. The Supreme Court decided that although private agreements of this sort are not subject to the Equal Protection Clause, the fact that the lower court enforced such discrimination was, in fact, unconstitutional. They ruled in favor of the petitioners.[172]

Also in the late 1940s Omega Psi Phi member Harold R. Boulware Sr., litigated a number of race cases.[173] In 1947, he litigated *Rice v. Elmore*,[174] which arose when the Democratic Party in South Carolina refused to allow George Elmore, an African American, to vote in the primary elections.[175] The District Court for the Eastern District of South Carolina held that African Americans were entitled to vote in primary elections and enjoined defendants from excluding African Americans from the voting process.[176] On appeal, the two pertinent issues were whether the decree giving African Americans the right to vote in the South Carolina Democratic primary elections was valid and whether the corresponding injunction was binding.[177] The Fourth Circuit Court of Appeals held that citizens had a fundamental right to participate in the political process and affirmed the right of African Americans to vote in the South Carolina primaries.[178] Two years later, the *Baskin v. Brown* case emerged similarly.[179] Resulting from the Fourth Circuit's ruling in *Rice II*, the South Carolina Democratic Party formed political clubs to control the primaries.[180] These clubs refused to admit African American applicants.[181] The District Court for the Eastern District of South Carolina subsequently granted an injunction against the South Carolina Democratic Party.[182] The Fourth Circuit Court of Appeals upheld the injunction by reasoning that political primaries were part of the election process and therefore subject to constitutional mandates prohibiting racial discrimination.[183]

As witnessed, BGLO members (mainly of Alpha Phi Alpha and Kappa Alpha Psi) litigated several cases related to civil and human rights for African Americans. However, many other organizations and their members engaged in racial uplift strategies through civic education, as the next section outlines.

Civic Education

At the 1940 Tuskegee (Alabama) Conclave the members of Phi Beta Sigma were still promoting civil rights through educational programs on African Americans civil duties, responsibilities, and rights, especially pertaining to enfranchisement and public office. During the 1940 fraternity Conclave, the Resolutions Committee drafted a proposition regarding African Americans and World War II. The proposition included condemnations of defense firms contracted by the United States for refusing to employ African American workers; condemnations of the Marine Corps for not allowing African Americans to serve in its ranks and of the Navy for limiting the roles of African American sailors; condemnations against the current policy of not allowing African American nurses to serve in the war effort; and a condemnation for the lack of African American pilots in the Aviation Corps.[184] J. L. S. Holloman's 1942 editorial in the *Crescent* condemned segregation as the "arch enemy of the American Republic," and many of Sigma's civil rights programs thereafter were committed to ending segregation in the United States.[185] Employment, de facto social segregation, police brutality, the segregation of the armed forces, and "anti-Negro propaganda" in the media were all identified as aspects of African American life that needed to be rectified.[186]

In the next year, 1941, Sigma Gamma Rho sorority continued in their administrative work from the previous two decades, proved worthwhile during wartime, as the national Boulés, which had become the birthplace of Sigma Gamma Rho service projects, were put on hold.[187] Sigma Gamma Rho canceled their national Boulés in 1942 and 1943 and instead urged members to dedicate themselves entirely to aiding in the war effort. Notably, members provided volunteer services for the Red Cross and the United Service Organizations (USO), and donated money to groups such as the Federated Women's Club of Newport News, Virginia. An example of the type of service that the members provided during the war effort was the Southwest Region Victory Drive. Mary S. Carter, of the Southwest Region, led the drive, which encouraged Sigma Gamma

Rho members to buy stamps and bonds, provided volunteer workers to the Red Cross and USO, and emphasized the rationing and sharing of automobiles and food supplies.[188] Community service projects such as the Victory Drive reflected the emphasis that Sigma Gamma Rho members placed on providing leadership and service to local communities. Sigma Gamma Rho adjusted to the conditions of the times and continued its mission through the sorority's individual chapters. These chapters carried on the sorority's service programs and dedicated resources toward the war effort but were able to do so only because of Sigma Gamma Rho's sound national structure.

Also in 1941, Elsie Austin presented a Delta Sigma Theta report titled "Jobs Analysis and Opportunities Project."[189] The aim of the project was to determine where African American women lacked job opportunities, then use Delta Sigma Theta resources to raise awareness and educate women on how to help.[190] Delta Sigma Theta launched its job opportunity program in 1941. Through this program Delta Sigma Theta set up clinics in high schools and colleges around the country educating youth about available job fields.[191] The job program eventually expanded to include teachers, guidance counselors, and parents. Its goal was to encourage parents and raise the aspirations of their children. Delta Sigma Theta also contacted prospective employers who were perpetuating discrimination to inform them that sorority members were working to end employment discrimination. In 1947 the sorority redoubled its efforts for fair employment and adopted a new resolution highlighting its efforts, which included promoting better training for African American workers, increasing awareness of the labor market challenges for African American workers, and instituting a stronger effort to enact policy changes that would improve the status quo for African American workers. The Beta Alpha Chapter of Delta Sigma Theta began lobbying the tobacco industry to promote equal rights for their mostly African American workforce.[192] In 1967 Delta Sigma Theta supported Job Opportunity Clinics in the southern region cosponsored by the Natural Urban League. In 1969 the sorority launched national programs—Delta Womanpower in the World of Work and the Career Motivation Program—conducted on forty college campuses.

In the *Sphinx* Alpha Phi Alpha members were calling for race consciousness and racial uplift. In a piece titled "Alpha Phi Alpha and National Defense," the author urged Alpha Phi Alpha's participation in the quest to see "colored citizens receive proportionate representation in all phases of the national defense program" to support the "abolishment of discriminatory practices and to the furtherance of democratic procedures."[193] In another piece, an author discussed the economic/industrial relegation of African Americans to the labor side of the equation. He went on to underscore that it was up to African Americans to support each other's businesses by harnessing their power as consumers and spending their money in those businesses. He closed by noting that Alpha Phi Alpha had gone on record "as favoring, wherever possible, industry and business owned and controlled by patrons of color."[194] In yet a third piece, an author noted that Alpha Phi Alpha had switched its outreach emphasis from academic to civic education. The author wished that the emphasis would again be changed to worker education—vocational instruction in terms of successful living—because the race was subject to confinement in unskilled laboring jobs that bring with them "low wages, long hours, recurrent unemployment, and lack of organizational and legislative protection."[195]

The *Sphinx* continued to play a crucial role in casting the fraternity's overarching vision across the entire brotherhood. Toward the close of 1941 two articles appeared in the journal that underscored this. In one piece, "The Negro in the New World Order," the author indicated that during the upcoming General Convention the fraternity would take considerable action "upon practical plans of procedure for participation in this new order of things, and out of these discussions should evolve a program for concerted action."[196] Another author described the areas where democracy was lacking for African Americans—for example, men could serve in the Navy only as servants; companies contracted by the government had discriminatory hiring procedures; soldiers were being brutalized in the South. He also highlighted the areas in which the U.S. government sought to combat discrimination and open more opportunities—such as the actions by President Roosevelt. The author believed that African Americans stood to benefit from the discussions of freedom and liberty that have been started because of the war.[197]

Race consciousness was palpable in the actions of fraternity members, as it was in the calls coming from articles in the *Sphinx*. For instance, Alpha Phi Alpha brother Reid E. Jackson emphasized the importance of the upcoming presidential election to the African American community, particularly in the face of rising reactionary measures in southern states that sought to limit the rights of people of color. He urged a deliberate consideration of the best candidates for their minority voice/issue as well as soliciting liberal white voters, particularly where they were deprived of the vote.[198] In another piece he discussed the trend to dehumanize African Americans by referring to them as Negroes using a lowercase "n." He contended that they must actively "resist positively and intelligently" this whenever they encountered it because it had deleterious effects that undermined the social status of African Americans.[199]

During World War II issues of race, inclusion, and democracy continued to be part of the fraternity's ongoing dialogue. In one article in the *Sphinx*, "For 'What' Are We Fighting?," the author reported some of the grievous wrongs that African American soldiers had to endure from southern white citizens and soldiers. There was a common practice not to hire African Americans in war-effort factories and other such jobs.[200] The author ultimately called for the race to continue to become more economically independent and stable, to use the ballot wherever possible, and to seek to develop educational opportunities to further the fight for "true democracy" in America while also fighting abroad.[201] He believed that all of these efforts should be led by the intellectually elite of both races as to avoid any violent conflict.[202] In another article, titled "The Negro in Post War Reconstruction," the author addressed the likely outcomes of society after World War II. The author made mention of the fight for equal rights moving toward resorting to more federal, especially executive, action and legal methods as suggested by recent U.S. Supreme Court cases. Not resting on the actions of government, the author also called for responsible mass action to bring about racial equality.[203] Looking to the work and obligations of Alpha Phi Alpha members, a third article—"Nobility Imposes Obligation"—underscored that Alpha Phi Alpha men must fight for victory abroad and domestically by fighting for democracy for the African American race. This fight had to be done through legitimate avenues of social pressure, and fraternity men should give the economic guidance and leadership that the race needs as well as help maintain morale during the war period.[204]

Adding to this work, Alpha Phi Alpha filed a complaint ("conceived, planned, and is prosecuting this case in its own right") against the Interstate Commerce Commission on behalf of Elmer W. Henderson (Kappa Alpha Psi).[205] Henderson was traveling first class on the Southern Railway during his employment for the government when he was denied service in the train's dining car. The protocol in the dining car was to seat African Americans in one of two reserved corner tables and draw curtains to separate them from white diners. If all the other tables were full, the curtains were opened and white passengers were seated at those two corner tables. When Henderson sought to eat in the dining car, there was an available seat at one of these designated tables, but a white passenger was seated in that section. Therefore, if the waitress sat Henderson at that table, she could not draw the curtains to isolate him. Instead, she told him that she would notify him when a table was opened. Henderson was never notified, even after returning to the dining car twice. The dining car was removed on one of the next train stops, without Henderson being served a meal.[206] The complaint alleged that there were two violations of the Interstate Commerce Act. First, Henderson was denied the same dining service offered to white passengers. Second, isolating African Americans with a drawn curtain in the corner of the dining car caused humiliation and embarrassment, depriving these passengers of their rights, privileges, and immunities as citizens of the United States. Furthermore, the complainant argued that customary practices within the dining car are not sufficient to justify segregation, and neither is the low volume of colored traffic on the train, as this is a personal constitutional rights issue.[207]

In its national organ, the *Sphinx*, Alpha Phi Alpha continued to shape the dialogue around race and justice vis-à-vis its members. In "Alpha's Program of Action," J. Rupert Picott, chairman of the National Committee on Publicity,[208] noted that one of the new planks of the organization's program of action was to "pool resources with other fraternities and sororities for establishment of a powerful research and lobby program in Washington."[209] Further, the fraternity's goal was to make a "constant attack upon the breastwork of the citadel of privilege and Jim Crowism which are the worst enemies of the common man."[210] Members challenged chapters to alter strategies for fighting against inequality. For example, in his announcement of the next General Convention, general president Belford V. Lawson urged Alpha men "to translate mere debate and protest, vague skepticism, tired cynicism, and national self-praise into angry dissatisfaction, courageous determination and a liberal, fighting program of action which are necessary to preserve the battlement of human integrity, equality, and dignity."[211] He went on to say that "we cannot wait in philosophical serenity or deadly inaction for a generation of unprejudiced men to be born . . . liberty and equality are not boons granted to dilettantes. They are the hard-earned possessions of fighting men."[212] Other BGLOs worked together in the fight for civil rights in 1946.

In December 1948 Kappa Alpha Psi would see an initial push toward becoming civically engaged nationwide. At a banquet in Windsor, Ontario, Kappa Alpha Psi member Dr. Martin D. Jenkins called upon his listeners to dedicate themselves to "programs of human welfare larger than the social interests of the average fraternity."[213] One of the ways that this manifested itself was in the authorization for the fraternity's affiliation with the ACHR.[214] On March 19, 1949, Kappa Alpha Psi's affiliation with the ACHR was authorized at the Thirty-Eighth Grand Chapter Meeting in Detroit.[215] The ACHR was known as one of the organizations that worked to defeat the recent filibuster rule against civil rights in the U.S. Senate. Other affiliated Greek organizations included Alpha Kappa Alpha, Alpha Phi Alpha, Delta Sigma Theta, Phi Beta Sigma, Sigma Gamma Rho, and Zeta Phi Beta. The ACHR was established to garner the extension of fundamental human and civil rights to all citizens and works through the U.S. Congress and federal government. The ACHR vigorously worked toward the passage of civil rights legislation and amendments to general legislation that would lead to the eradication of racial distinctions, benefitting all people. The legislative program agenda pushed for the passing of a fair employment practices bill that would enable equal job opportunities without discrimination, the anti–poll tax bill, the anti-lynching bill, and other civil rights measures presented in Congress. They also advocated for nondiscrimination provisions to be included in legislation such as housing bills, the repeal of the Taft-Hartley Act, and the Federal Aid to Education Bill.[216] Among the Kappa Alpha Psi members who would go on to serve in leadership positions were James E. Scott, selected in 1951 as board chairman, and Elmer W. Henderson, who served as the executive director.[217]

Public Policy

Many of the BGLOs engaged in racial uplift strategies by prodding federal and state lawmakers to write civil and human rights legislation, while also pushing prosecutors to practice the equitable laws that were slowly coming on the books. Moreover, under the principle of self-determination, BGLOs pushed for the expansion of policies that would allow for the development of their own businesses and institutions. For instance, at the 1941 Philadelphia Conclave of Phi Beta Sigma, member Lynwood Brown proudly announced that the fraternity had become a permanent member of the National Negro Business League. Immediately following Brown's announcement and on the advice of the Resolutions Committee, the fraternity prepared and circulated a pamphlet among the National Negro Business League's delegates titled "Sigma Exalts Bigger and Better Business."[218] The fraternity also linked its Bigger and Better Business Program with the U.S. Department of Commerce in its promotion of small business.[219] By 1942 the Bigger and Better Business Week program had grown to such an extent that it was observed twice a year, once in April and once in October. An editorial in the Phi Beta Sigma journal, the *Crescent* urged every active chapter to "sponsor at least two Bigger and Better Business Programs in 1942."[220]

A separate article appeared later in the *Crescent*, specifying exactly what a Bigger and Better Business Program should consist of. According to the article, Monday should begin the week with a speaker in all the local public schools, acquainting the students with the program. Tuesday included a roundtable discussion on problems facing businessmen in the community, and Wednesday was Woman's Day, in which Sigma's sister sorority, Zeta Phi Beta, and the Housewives' League would conduct a program. Thursday and Friday involved exhibits of business models and tours of all the businesses within a certain locality. Saturday was devoted to urging that "all the citizens of your community make as many purchases from Negro businesses as possible and check to see if the results of your efforts did not increase sales." On Sunday, a Mammoth Public Program took place, in which "a Sigma man or an outstanding business or professional man or educator" would speak on the subject of Bigger and Better Business.[221] This well-defined model evidently produced results, as in 1949 at the thirty-fifth Conclave, under the leadership of national president Ras O. Johnson, Phi Beta Sigma voted to continue all three phases of the national program, including Bigger and Better Business, Education, and Social Action.[222] Phi Beta Sigma also voted to give increased support to all phases of the program.[223]

By 1942 Alpha Phi Alpha's Committee on Public Opinion, under the leadership of chairman Howard H. Long, was urging members to support "the movement afoot in Congress to enact a bill for the prevention of the use of the poll tax as a qualification for voting for Federal officers" by contacting their senators and representatives.[224] Oliver Hart Jr. called for individual chapters to organize days to make cleanup efforts in African American neighborhoods that needed repair as a program for the general welfare of the race.[225] Alpha Upsilon Chapter started Sunday forums at Alabama State Teachers' College to invite speakers from the community to discuss relevant social issues.[226] Beta Eta Chapter (Southern Illinois Normal University) held a round table with multiple other Greek-letter organizations to discuss the topic "Post War Effects upon the Negro."[227] Beta Gamma Lambda Chapter (Richmond, Va.) planned to concentrate their citizenship program on one area of the city to reach all citizens there through a coordinated effort between social groups, churches, and schools. They aimed to disseminate information pamphlets as well as drive people to registration centers and help them pay their poll taxes.[228]

As 1942 ended the fraternity held its General Convention in Washington, D.C. Members outlined the educational campaign for the upcoming year—specifically, the fraternity's scholarship program, which awarded eleven out of the nineteen applicants financial assistance.[229] The Public Opinion Committee pledged to keep chapters informed on national interest topics such as "new bills proposed in Congress [and] racial discrimination in employment" as well as urge chapters to act quickly wherever racial welfare was at stake.[230] For example, chapters were urged to contact government representatives and officials to make known their displeasure over the postponing of a hearing "on discrimination in employment in the railroads."[231] Additionally, the Public Opinion committee continued to keep close contact with "proponents of the Anti–Poll Tax Bill."[232] General President Rayford Logan reported his activities for the past year—including the submission of a memorandum to the State Department concerning the establishment of a mandate system, attending speaking engagements on "The Negro and Post-War Problems," and speaking with the national director of educational activities about expanding Alpha Phi Alpha's program.[233]

In 1944 fraternity president Rayford Logan urged every chapter to appoint a committee to become thoroughly versed in the G.I. Bill so that they could aid returning members and other eligible people in receiving and taking advantage of the benefits thereby offered to them.[234] At the Thirtieth General Convention in 1944, the Committee on Public Opinion discussed efforts to secure the passing of the Fair Employment Practices Act. In achieving this, letters and telegrams were continuously sent to Senate members and prominent leaders in Congress.[235] Similarly, discussions were dedicated to Alpha Phi Alpha's role in improving racial conditions more broadly.[236]

On the chapter front, the Kappa Chapter had been distributing materials to local organizations and churches urging people to write to their Washington representatives concerning the Fair Employment Practice Committee and Poll Tax issues.[237] Alpha Beta Chapter (Talladega College) conducted an Anti–Poll Tax program in which 137 letters were written to senators of forty-eight states and money was raised for the National Committee for the Abolishment of the Poll Tax.[238] Alpha Lambda Chapter (Louisville) appointed a committee "to work on Juvenile Delinquency problems."[239] Alpha Psi Lambda Chapter (Columbia, S.C.) "contributed a substantial sum" to a charity drive aimed at building a new hospital for African Americans in the area.[240]

Alpha Phi Alpha member Herbert T. Miller became the first African American foreman of a county grand jury when he was appointed to the Kings County Grand Jury in New York.[241] Judge Leibowitz, in his final address to the grand jury, stated, "For the first time in the history of America, in any County, in any State, a member of the Negro race was signally honored by being appointed foreman of such an important and dignified and honorable body."[242] Charles W. Anderson, a Kentucky state legislator, introduced a bill to "break down segregated school laws to the extent of permitting Negroes to attend the Graduate and Professional Schools of the U. of Kentucky and the U. of Louisville." The bill was passed by the house but stopped in Senate committees.[243] Hugh M. Gloster was appointed USO associate regional executive. He was charged with investigating USO services to African Americans, initiating action for the improvement of USO work among colored troops and industrial plant employees, coordinating the activities of USO agencies serving African Americans, representing the regional executive in certain negotiations, and working in close cooperation with Henry W. Pope, national director of USO services to African Americans.[244]

In 1944 Phi Beta Sigma member R. A. Billings, in a letter to the fraternity, announced that the fraternity had paid for and circulated thousands of copies of "A Declaration for Negro Voters," which, among other things, demanded that "every vestige of segregation and discrimination in the armed forces be forthwith abolished."[245] The declaration was sent to both the Republican and Democratic National Conventions in 1944. Representatives of more than twenty-five national African American organizations, one of which was Phi Beta Sigma, attended. In 1945 a special committee revamped the Social Action Program of Phi Beta Sigma. The new aspects of the program were that the national office would direct the general strategy while each chapter attacked local problems, a sustained drive would be made for equality on all levels, and cooperation with other civil rights groups would be urged.[246] Subsequently, at the 1946 Phi Beta Sigma convention in New Orleans new objectives for the Social Action Program were listed. The new goals were to increase the Bigger and Better Business and Education programs, fight for the unqualified right to vote in any election, and continue fighting for an adequate education for every African American child. Later in 1946 the Resolutions Committee demanded (1) that the Eightieth Congress immediately enact fair employment legislation, (2) that Congress enact more laws to adequately protect all Americans in the actual enjoyment of their civil rights, (3) that federal aid be given to state education programs, (4) that church leadership around the world adopt policies of nondiscrimination in the practice of religion, and (5) that the United Nations assume jurisdiction over the matter of racial discrimination in the United States.[247] Moreover, only two years earlier, at the 1944 Chicago Conclave, the fraternity pledged support for the United Negro College Fund.

The next year, 1945, at the Thirty-Fourth Grand Chapter Meeting, Kappa Alpha Psi took firmer steps toward internalizing and formalizing its efforts toward racial justice and reconciliation.[248] The Committee on Interracial Cooperation was established by grand polemarch Augustus G. Parker and chaired by Dr. G. Cecil Lewis, who was also a member of the Illinois Interracial Commission.[249] The committee was considered a step in the right direction toward developing goodwill and interracial amity in the United States.[250] The slogan of the program was "Mutual Acquaintanceship."[251] Chairman Lewis of the Committee on Interracial Cooperation stated, "The field of race relations is, as of today, the most potent and vital element in the real democracy for which we have fought for the past four years, and has cost us the blood of some of our finest, regardless of race or creed. To make peace worthwhile, and the spirit of democracy something real we must all strive to foster a feeling of tolerance to all groups and a realization of that equality of all men so guaranteed by our form of government."[252] The committee attempted to cooperate and assist with the functioning of the fraternity and create organizations and programs involving both college men and campus activities where none previously existed.

The Committee on Interracial Cooperation explored how to use high school curricula in a way that would build healthy attitudes in human and intercultural relations. The experiment was carried out by the Commission on Community Interrelations, the American Jewish Congress, and representatives of the Board of Education of the City of New York at the Bronx High School of Science in New York during the school year. The experiment was to be carried out via a modification of the social science and biological science curricula at the school along intercultural lines. It was a more in-depth, broad-scale version of previous small-scale experimental work by Zachariah Subarsky, Morris Cohen, and Dr. Morris Meister in 1944 at the Bronx High School of Science. The modification of curriculum was expected to lead to deeper understanding of essential concepts of biology and social studies, and this knowledge was expected to "be translated into actual behavior changes which can be measured and evaluated."[253]

In 1946, at the Thirty-Sixth Grand Chapter Meeting in New York, Kappa Alpha Psi pushed for new resolutions: "(1) to support proposed legislation for a permanent Fair Employment Commission; (2) to support passage of an effective anti-lynching legislation by the 80th Congress; . . . (4) to support passage of a bill to provide increased aid to education by the federal government; . . . (7) to support the President's plan to appoint a Civil Rights Commission, and appeal to the commission to introduce a bill favoring enactment of a civil rights law by the Congress; . . ."[254] The fraternity also actively supported legislation to abolish the poll tax. Senator LaFollette proposed to institute a liberal government, which would reduce the southern representation in Congress, as it was focused on disenfranchising colored voters, and promoted the Dyer Anti-Lynching Bill.[255] Kappa Alpha Psi member G. Victor Cools pushed for support of LaFollette's initiative in part because LaFollette was against discrimination of all kinds and was the first senator to recognize African American men in the government of Wisconsin.[256]

In March 1948, Kappa Alpha Psi member James Egert Allen attended a conference called by the NAACP to create a draft document that postulated the wishes of African American voters and citizens.[257] Legislation on both state and national levels was called for. "Freedom to work, vote and live in the entire nation was considered of paramount importance. Abolition of segregation in the military forces and in education were made emphatic. . . . The fullest use of the ballot was urged."[258] That same year the fraternity called for a need to individually and collectively undertake the following actions:

(1) study the [President's Committee on Civil Rights' report, "To Secure These Rights"][;] (2) see that copies are in . . . libraries and in the hands of appropriate college officers and teachers, school superintendents, mayors, and preachers[;] (3) hold conferences and mass meetings to inquire into the state of local civil rights[;] (4) write letters to the editor and petition Government pointing out conditions that need corrections[;] (5) insist that vote-seekers take a stand on whether they will support legislation for fair employment, an anti-lynching bill, an anti–poll tax bill, etc.[259]

Philanthropy

While philanthropic endeavors reached their crescendo during the Great Depression, BGLO members continued their activities throughout World War II. For instance, Zeta Phi Beta members helped the federal government through the Housing Project, created by the efforts of Zeta Phi Beta member Georgia Johnson.[260] Zeta Phi Beta members conducted surveys to locate housing vacancies for war workers and registered the facilities with the National Housing Association of the United States.[261]

During the administration of Blanche Jackson Thompson (international grand basileus from 1939 to 1943), much of Zeta Phi Beta's philanthropy came in the form of financial assistance to local projects. In the 1940s Zeta Phi Beta members paid for a telephone, mirrors, and coats for an orphanage.[262] In 1942 the national organization sponsored Vacation School for girls aged four to fourteen and raised over seventeen hundred dollars for a community center.[263] Other chapters engaged in more common charity, such as distributing Christmas baskets to needy families.[264] In 1942 the Iota Zeta Chapter raised ninety dollars for a scholarship, and the Iota Alpha donated a hundred dollars to the Amanda Garrett Artificial Leg Fund.[265] Two years later the Psi Chapter raised over seven hundred dollars for Blue Revue, a program that gave needy kids glasses, and the Eta Zeta chapter established a scholarship fund for the Louisville community.[266]

Under the Lullelia W. Harrison administration (international grand basileus from 1943 to 1948), a project was developed called "The Prevention and Control of Juvenile Delinquency." Lillian Fitzhugh, of the Beta Zeta Chapter in Washington, D.C., and Phyllis O'Kelly were appointed to direct the project. Based on the recommendations of attorney Tom Clark's National Conference on Youth in November 1946, the project included foster home care, youth conferences, vocational guidance clinics, Tinker Shops (workshops offering crafts to keep children occupied in wholesome activities), and youth groups.[267] After World War II, as concerns about juvenile delinquency rose, the Dallas Zeta Phi Beta Chapter helped fund a study on this behavior.[268] Meanwhile, the Winston-Salem chapter helped with Zeta Phi Beta's national project, the Prevention and Control of Juvenile Delinquency, by sponsoring a shoe bank that gave pairs of shoes to needy elementary schoolchildren.[269]

Before the war, in 1937, Delta Sigma Theta began one of its largest, most ambitious projects—the National Library Project (NLP)—after seeing the lack of library facilities afforded to minorities in the South.[270] NLP was created at the Delta Sigma Theta National Conference, and the sorority appointed Anne Duncan as the first leader to guide the project until 1950, when it became incorporated into the Five-Points Program.[271] By 1940 there were only ninety-nine libraries that served African Americans throughout the South and only about 5 percent of rural African Americans had access to libraries.[272] Realizing a significant need, and with the NLP in place, Delta Sigma Theta mobilized its membership, and each chapter began purchasing books and organizing them into locked baskets for efficient transportation.[273] This work continued for decades, with the sorority implementing a bookmobile that traveled across the country, educating and encouraging reading among schoolchildren.[274] The bookmobile project soon earned the title Ride the Winged Horse and eventually won awards including a special Certificate of Merit, a Community School Improvement Award, and the coveted American Library Award.[275] Delta Sigma Theta also created a similar project on Saint Helena Island in South Carolina, where the local Delta Sigma Theta chapter created nine small libraries across the island to provide residents with access to library materials. Delta Sigma Theta incorporated the library service into the Five-Points Program. Many chapters across the nation continue to provide reading materials to those without access and now include communication skill seminars to provide services to communities lacking resources or that are geographically isolated.[276]

With the books purchased, the first question was where to begin. With the guidance of Mollie Houston Lee and Dr. Virginia Lacy Jones, the sorority chose numerous cities throughout the South, beginning in Franklin County, North Carolina, home to over forty schools, most having only one or two teachers. For this reason Delta Sigma Theta provided hundreds of books for the county. By the end of the project thank-you letters flowed in from across Franklin County for all that Delta Sigma Theta had provided. Franklin County even built a local library and named it after Delta Sigma Theta; in response the sorority provided five hundred dollars for the purchase of new books for the library. Carrolton, Georgia, created another library with the local Delta Sigma Theta Chapter providing five hundred dollars of start-up money, in addition to helping the local library raise two thousand dollars from other sources. After it was built, the library fell short on funds and could not provide film readers, furniture, or broad services to local residents. Delta Sigma Theta stepped in and covered the costs, which allowed the library to remain open and flourish.[277]

When the United States became involved in World War II, Delta Sigma Theta rose to the challenge and began a wide variety of war-related projects. At the group's 1942 National Convention, the sorority adopted the slogan "Delta Dynamic for Defense" and began investing in government bonds to support the war effort as well as bolstering support for USO, especially African American servicemen. Later Delta Sigma Theta began the Victory Book Drive, led by Victoria McCall, which collected books for servicemen overseas to provide them with entertainment while they spent time in their camps. Delta Sigma Theta further provided countless Red Cross kits and even purchased an ambulance to help the servicemen fighting the war. As the war ended and the new United Nations was readied, Delta Sigma Theta authorized Bertrell Wright to send a letter to each member of the Dumbarton Oaks delegation from the United States and advocated for a more robust proposal to further promote equal rights for people in the United States and across the world.[278] In 1947 Sadie T. M. Alexander was appointed to the Presidential Commission on Human Rights.[279]

In 1943 Alpha Phi Alpha took a moment to pause and reflect on its work in the community and society more generally. The work included the Go-to-High-School, Go-to-College movement, Education for Citizenship, A Voteless People Is a Hopeless People, assistance with the Southern Tennant Farmers Union, the entrance of Negroes into borderline and southern colleges and universities, support to the NAACP, and the Negro in the Post-War Society program.[280]

At Alpha Phi Alpha fraternity's Thirty-First General Convention, the Commission on Scholarships and Educational Activities presented a proposal to award scholarships to plaintiffs of Equal Educational Opportunity lawsuits, and the activities of the Education for Citizenship campaign were put under a magnifying glass.[281] During discussions members were presented three choices for the designated slogan for that year's convention: (1) "Education for Participation in World Citizenship, (2) Education for Participation in America Citizenship, or (3) Go-to-High-School, Go-to-College." As suggested, the slogan for the 1946 year was "Education and Citizenship" because that correlated well with multiple themes of Alpha from the prior year.[282] Further, scholarships and fellowships were awarded to numerous members and individuals.[283] Between 1927 and 1945 Alpha Phi Alpha awarded $10,100 in scholarships, while also awarding $6,225 in fellowships and grants-in-aid to scholarly applicants between 1934 and 1945.[284]

Delta Sigma Theta members frequently engaged in presentations and held beauty pageants to raise money for various philanthropic causes. In 1946 the Beta Beta Chapter in Texas raised over $7,000 through various activities and events to help build a child welfare center in Houston, and the Beta Kappa Chapter in Virginia raised $1,070 to help build a nursery school. Two chapters in Michigan, Alpha Pi Sigma and Tau, worked together to raise money to build a boarding house for delinquent young women and girls. The Delta Home for Girls, as it would be called, soon became operational and housed numerous troubled women, two of which were accepted into a Catholic institution.[285]

The philanthropy of Sigma Gamma Rho women extended to civil rights, to no great surprise, as the twentieth century dwelled on the problem of the color line. In 1946, under the direction of Grand Basileus Ethel Ross Smith, Sigma Gamma Rho made a $150 donation to the "Permanent Fair Employment" movement.[286] The donation followed President Franklin Roosevelt's creation of Executive Order 8802 in 1941, which sought to eliminate employment discrimination based on race. Also in 1946 the sorority pledged a commitment to the preservation of a permanent "Fair Employment Practice Commission."[287] The donation and pledge reflected Sigma Gamma Rho's efforts to advance civil rights by encouraging Congress to act on President Roosevelt's initiative. Almita S. Robinson, a Sigma Gamma Rho member, wrote in 1948, "I can remember how something akin to asphyxiation gripped me from within when I read of the brutal lynching's and uncalled-for mistreatment of Negroes . . . that I was a member of this kicked-around and downtrodden group made me apprehensive of the future."[288] As educated women, the sorority members believed that they held a particular responsibility. Robinson wrote about the upcoming national elections, "Our children and thousands of unlearned Negroes are expecting us to point the way to freedom and opportunity. This message is trying to warn against lethargy in the use of the ballot. . . . We should serve in our communities as blockades to any encroachments on civil liberties of any and all groups by giving our financial and moral support toward efforts that seek to weed out the germ of hatred and misunderstanding."[289] Both sororities held membership in the National Council of Negro Women and the NAACP.[290]

Community Service

In 1944, Sigma Gamma Rho sorority donated five hundred dollars to both the NAACP and the Negro College Fund.[291] Further, in 1945 the Gamma Sigma chapter donated twenty-five dollars to the local Fair Employment Practices drive in Houston, twenty dollars to the United College Fund Drive, and twenty-five dollars to the scholarship given to Jewel Anderson at Wiley College.[292] Other Sigma scholarships included the Gregg Scholarship, which was awarded to teachers who displayed "growth and professional interest" throughout the year, and a fifteen-dollar scholarship created by the Omicron Chapter for the Nursery School at Dillard University. Sigma Gamma Rho also donated five hundred dollars to the United College Fund at the Boulé (convention) in this year.

At the Thirty-Third Boulé over twenty-five thousand dollars' worth of scholarship awards were awarded to deserving young people from across the country.[293] Significant is the fact that by 1957 Sigma Gamma Rho scholarships presented to high school students and nonmembers totaled about twenty-five thousand dollars each year, while scholarships presented to members totaled about three thousand dollars each year.

Sigma Gamma Rho's National Boulé resumed in 1946, and with it so did their national projects, like their literary contest. Naomi G. Coulter became the chairman of the annual literary contest. The contest was originally a mechanism through which Sigma Gamma Rho encouraged its members to engage in educational writing on subjects pertinent to the times. For example, the theme in 1946 was "Juvenile Delinquency," and contestants wrote on subjects such as "Delinquency: Its Treatment and Prevention," "Delinquency Threatens Victory," and "Here's How Youth Can Curb Delinquency."[294] The literary contest also proved versatile; the following year contestants could submit an original play based on African American life instead of a formal essay. The contest expanded in 1947 by dividing the contest into two categories: a high school division and a college division. Lydia Robinson and Vivian Hedgewood became the chairpersons of each division, respectively.[295] This new format allowed members of the community who were not part of Sigma Gamma Rho to partake in the benefits of the contest.

At Sigma Gamma Rho's Golden Anniversary the literary contest transformed again into the "Golden Anniversary Literary Competition."[296] The *Aurora's* editor-in-chief, Lillie Wilkes, and associate editor, Marjorie Brown Wright, created this special literary competition. The competition was open to college and high school students and provided educational awards totaling five hundred dollars. The theme of the contest was "The Issues—Service and Progress," and entries were to focus on "Black Community Development."[297] The benefits of a versatile literary competition were multifaceted: Sigma Gamma Rho could spark the creation of educational literature that informed the public on hot-button issues, while also advancing scholarship among participants.

Some of Sigma Gamma Rho's programs in its first few decades of existence contained echoes of racial uplift. Racial uplift began as a philosophy among aspirational middle-class African Americans, dating back to the late nineteenth century, that had been popularized by Booker T. Washington. It asserted that whites judged blacks according to the lowest elements of the race. For blacks to acquire rights, the race needed to be uplifted. Therefore, elite blacks such as the sorority members offered instruction to working-class blacks to uplift the race. However, these working-class blacks did not always cheerfully accept the notion that they needed instruction or uplift. For example, in 1947 the Jackson, Mississippi, chapter of Sigma held a Charm School for teenagers. The children were taught eating for charm, good grooming, use of cosmetics, hair styling, care of hands and nails, skincare, dining at home, and dining away from home.[298] The offspring of the sorority women presumably already knew how to groom, keep clean, and dine at home, so there was a clear element of elitism in this program.

Sigma Gamma Rho members also performed individual instances of community service while the National Boulés were on hold. Sigma Gamma Rho member Robbie Scott, of Delta Sigma Chapter in Chicago, worked for the Army as the director of the Scott Field Center in East St. Louis, Illinois. Sallie Parham of the Zeta Sigma Chapter in St. Louis volunteered for the YWCA to develop activities for both African American and Caucasian female youths. C. M. Pitts of the Eta Sigma chapter in Atlanta ran a home for the youths of the city. Pitts won an award from the NAACP for outstanding woman of the year for her services.[299] Individual efforts such as these were typical of Sigma Gamma Rho service during World War I because the direction previously provided by the National Boulés transferred to regional syntaktes (regional heads) and the local chapters.

Sigma Gamma Rho pushed its members to provide volunteer services for the Red Cross and the USO and to buy war bonds during World War II.[300] The Kansas City chapter, Psi Sigma, focused on winning the war by investing 10 percent of member earnings in bonds. Psi Sigma also operated war bond sales booths in drug stores, collected fat for use in explosives manufacturing, collected paper, and attempted to clarify rationing points to those in need of assistance.[301] Both national sororities sent money to the Negro College Fund.[302]

Sigma Gamma Rho decided in 1944 that its national project would establish centers for the prevention of juvenile delinquency. Nationwide, the project included foster home care, craft workshops for children, youth groups and conferences, and vocational guidance clinics.[303] Under the direction of Ethel Ross Smith (international grand basileus from 1944 to 1948), the national project known as Teen Towns served as a mechanism through which Sigma Gamma Rho could effectively combat juvenile delinquency following World War II. Grand basileus Ethel Ross Smith of Delta Sigma chapter in Chicago created the program in 1944. Sigma Gamma Rho's National Project Committee managed the program. The national program had a flexible structure, allowing individual chapters to form their own version of the program to best suit their local community. Teen Towns aimed to provide a safe and constructive place for African American youth to congregate and lead them away from a path of juvenile delinquency. Examples of individual chapters' Teen Towns can be seen in Birmingham and Memphis. In Birmingham, the Chi Sigma Chapter opened a Teen Town that included a lounge, game room, art room, and snack bar for the youths of the community. In Memphis, the Omicron Sigma Chapter adjusted the national project to serve crippled youths by purchasing beds, crutches, and transportation for children receiving treatment at the local Collins Chapel Hospital. Over twenty communities had a Teen Town of their own by 1947.[304] In 1945 the Sigmas in Chicago raised four thousand dollars for the South Side Community Committee on Juvenile Delinquency.[305]

In 1947, Delta Sigma Theta teamed up with the National Urban League and created experimental programs in Atlanta and Detroit that worked to compare the vocational counseling needs of young people in segregated and nonsegregated communities. When Founder Jessie Dent sued the Galveston Independent School District, Delta Sigma Theta members in the area mobilized to help with Dent's landmark victory to gain equal pay for African American teachers in the district. In 1954 the Supreme Court handed down the historic *Brown v. Board of Education* decision, which led many African American teachers to question their position in this new system. Delta Sigma Theta answered those questions by issuing reports on what this decision would bring and providing support to African American teachers around the nation as they faced an uncertain future.[306] Delta Sigma Theta also sent numerous members from all over the country to the South to participate in the Freedom Summer—a move designed to help enforce the newly minted Voting Rights Act and ensure all eligible voters were registered properly.

Community Organizing

At the dawn of a new decade Delta Sigma Theta women were making great strides in the area of anticolonial activism. The Council on African Affairs (CAA), until 1941 called the International Committee on African Affairs (ICAA), was a volunteer organization founded in 1937. It was the leading voice of anticolonialism and pan-Africanism in the United States and internationally before the Cold War. Among its founders and early key members were Alpha Phi Alpha members Paul Robeson and W. E. B. Du Bois as well as Max Yergan, Alphaeus Hunton Jr., Raymond Leslie Buell, and Ralph J. Bunche. Robeson's wife and Delta Sigma Theta member Eslanda Goode Robeson was an active member of the CAA, which articulated and promoted the connection between the struggle of African Americans in the United States and the destiny of colonized, indigenous peoples around the world.[307]

In 1941 Alpha Phi Alpha members were on the move. Lester Blackwell Granger assumed the helm of the National Urban League from Jewel Eugene Kinckle Jones.[308] Randall Tyus was appointed as assistant field secretary of the NAACP.[309] Charles H. Wesley addressed the Oklahoma Association of Negro Teachers, urging that they give African American youth the dynamic leadership that they need—teaching them how to think, encouraging them to believe in themselves, and preparing them for the future.[310]

Individual chapters, too, were still on the front lines, doing the work of Alpha. Psi Chapter urged its fellow members to participate wholeheartedly in national defense preparation because the current situations had created many novel opportunities that would allow the race to make strides forward.[311] Beta Omicron Lambda Chapter aligned itself with the local NAACP branch to fight for free use of the ballot by African Americans in the South and against police brutality and inequality in teaching salaries.[312] Beta Xi Lambda Chapter raised funds to send a student to university and also held a youth meeting, giving instruction to attendees concerning how to properly apply for work. They also formed a committee to investigate the possibility of placing a member of the race in the personnel department of the Federal Housing Office.[313] Theta Lambda Chapter, through the Committee on Negro Employment, investigated "industries doing national defense work in Dayton."[314]

The fraternity continued its direct action on the racial justice front and helped provide structure for chapters and members to do similar work. A new general subcommittee was established to address questions raised about the race and labor relations during this unique period. Indeed, Alpha Phi Alpha wished to play a leading role in "preparations for the consideration of the Negro BEFORE this war shall have ended."[315] In partnership with other African American fraternities and sororities, the fraternity promoted African American participation in the war to save democracy even if our country did not always practice democratic principles domestically. They also called upon the institutions and elected officials involved in national defense to end practices of discrimination and segregation.[316] Alpha Phi Alpha's Southern Region also established a committee focused on the integration of African Americans in the national defense program. They worked to "bring pressure to bear necessary groups in Washington to alleviate" the unequal conditions.[317] It was clear that Alpha Phi Alpha was shifting its priorities when it changed the focus of its national education program from the "Go-to-High-School, Go-to-College" program to emphasizing citizenship and the use of the ballot.[318]

Beta Mu Lambda chapter of Alpha Phi Alpha (Salisbury-Statesville, N.C.) reported focusing its efforts on an extensive program to improve local conditions for Negroes.[319] Kappa Lambda chapter of Alpha Phi Alpha (Greensboro, N.C.) reported a successful citizenship program that "was made through active and aggressive participation in the

Greensboro councilman election, which saw an African American getting further in the election than ever before in the history of the council (through primaries). Although he was ultimately unsuccessful in winning the election, it was a success for African Americans in the city and the chapter voted to continue their program year-round instead of limiting it to one week."[320]

The long history of Alpha Phi Alpha members battling to attain civil rights, coupled with liberal changes within schools and universities, gave rise to a new spirit within and outside the fraternity's walls. Members at the 1946 General Convention voiced this new spirit,[321] which was a reverberation of what was seen fraternity-wide throughout the year. For example, at the General Convention, Alpha men were challenged to put into action their ideals locally, nationally, and internationally. The extension of the right to suffrage was one area of this newfound liberalism within the fraternity.[322] Alpha members worked together in voting campaigns and citizenship programs, using the slogan "A Voteless People Is a Hopeless People" throughout the country. Members pledged support to the fraternity's National Committee to Abolish the Poll Tax program, which gained active interest throughout the fraternity.[323] Over the years, including 1946, the fraternity remained loyal to the NAACP, providing contributions to their activities in national and local areas.[324]

Demonstrating its commitment to collective action, in 1947 Alpha Phi Alpha assisted the Congress on Racial Equality in an effort to integrate the YMCA cafeteria in Washington, D.C., by organizing a sit-in.[325] The general president of the fraternity was quoted as saying, "I think the direct, non-violent approach is historically significant in racial relation in this country. I think the fraternity ought to be in all worthwhile inter-racial movements."[326] The fraternity was thought to have a duty "to stay in the vanguard of those organizations which are fighting to lead public opinion toward a sound and just appraisal of the importance of our struggle for economic and political liberty."[327] Not surprisingly, that year at its Thirty-Third General Convention, the director of educational activities, H. Council Trenholm, reported considerable activity in the Education for Citizenship Program. Moreover, Howard Long, chair of the Committee on the Program, reported the following recommendations for the fraternity:

1. Creating a social climate in which the membership could enrich themselves for effective living and leadership in a democratic society stemming from the nobler religious impulses;
2. Stimulating an understanding of and an appreciation for our place in domestic affairs, as a fraternity, and as people;
3. Contributing in whatever way that subjects the members individually and collectively to a more effective democracy;
4. Promoting brotherhood among members, one, which is posed and balanced in the great interplay of social, economic, and cultural interests of our members.[328]

Conclusion

In the 1940s BGLOs continued their community service and organizing work. However, a major triumph of this era was the way in which BGLOs turned toward legal reform. The fraternities—especially members of Alpha Phi Alpha, Omega Psi Phi, and Kappa Alpha Psi—took to the courts. Their efforts sought to dismantle Jim Crow and continue to vindicate African Americans' right to vote. Their work also reflects something seminal about this era—sex discrimination in the legal profession—as civil rights lawyers within the sororities' ranks remained almost nonexistent. However, sororities led the way on another major triumph—policy work. Alpha Kappa Alpha's lobbying efforts set the stage for a joint effort—the ACHR—that would last into the 1960s, fighting for African Americans' rights in a range of areas and employing various approaches.

6

At the Forefront

Civil Rights and Social Change (1949–1963)

In this chapter we explore a time of rapid civil rights changes. While covering racial uplift praxis in general, this chapter focuses specifically on partnerships between and individual initiatives of the eight major BGLOs to make recommendations to the U.S. government concerning civil rights legislation.[1] The collective effort of these BGLOs resulted in the American Council on Human Rights (ACHR), founded in 1948.[2] We first examine the ACHR's work from 1949 to 1953 in the areas of employment, housing, and broader civil rights issues like integration, international relations, and voting. In so doing we investigate the ways in which the ACHR attempted to broaden its reach into African American communities via its public relations efforts and how the organization did its work, focusing on the local councils in various cities. Second, we cover how BGLOs were also working independently during this same time. Third, we cover how the ACHR's work changed in the post–*Brown v. Board* era, from 1954 to 1963, when the organization ultimately ended, showing how BGLOs were slowly pulling away from the ACHR during that same period.

The American Council on Human Rights and Direct Social Action: 1949–1953

The ACHR's direct social action program focused on a range of issues.[3] It initially adopted five targets: (1) nondiscrimination in employment; (2) nondiscrimination in housing; (3) legislation that would lead to (1) and (2), as well as revision of the U.S. Senate's cloture rule in order to facilitate such legislation; (4) connection of international issues to the goals of the ACHR; and (5) promotion of racial integration.[4] In 1951 the ACHR further detailed these five targets areas as focusing on (1) passage of a Fair Employment Practice Act; (2) integration and equality in the armed services; (3) passage of an anti–poll tax bill and the safeguarding of voting rights; (4) passage of an anti-lynching bill and measures to end mob violence; (5) ending of discrimination and segregation in Washington, D.C.; (6) integration of public transportation; (7) passage of an antidiscrimination in housing act; (8) passage of a federal aid to education bill with safeguards against discrimination; (9) revision of the U.S. Senate's cloture rule in order to end the filibuster; (10) representation of African Americans in federal appointments; and (11) the end of discrimination in immigration and naturalization.[5]

ACHR's plan was to "dedicate itself to a constant urging of the Congress and the Government to correct [the evils of racial discrimination] and through positive action bring into being a fuller realization of the basic principles of American democracy."[6] Recognizing that "reasoned argument is not sufficient to get action in Washington," the director of ACHR, Elmer W. Henderson, asked that the individual members of the sororities and fraternities making up ACHR place "constant pressure on individual Congressmen, Senators and Government officials."[7]

In September 1949 ACHR began publishing its bulletin, *Congress and Equality*, which covered the ACHR's progress in the current session of Congress.[8] In the year since its creation the ACHR had thrown its support behind several major civil rights bills, as well as housing and education social legislation.[9] Not satisfied with its member participation, the bulletin called on the members to place more pressure on Congress regarding civil rights.[10] Additionally, the bulletin called out members of the Senate, indicating who was up for reelection in 1950 and who had voted against one of the most recent civil rights bills to enter the Senate floor, stating that they had "betrayed democracy, betrayed the cause of civil rights, betrayed the spirits of the platforms of both political parties and betrayed [African Americans] and other minorities who looked to them for redress from discriminations under which they have suffered so long."[11]

By early 1950 the ACHR had secured Secretary of the Interior Julias A. Krug's public promise that "public facilities under the jurisdiction of the Department of Interior are going to be open to all on an equal basis and I don't mean 'separate but equal.'"[12] The ACHR was heavily involved in the case *Henderson v. S. Railway Co.*, which was to be argued in front of the Supreme Court in the coming year.[13] It additionally became involved in the Fair Employment Practices bill, which was defeated in the House of Representatives by a coalition of Southern Democrats and Northern Republicans.[14] Although the ACHR considered the bill to be "merely a pious resolution,"[15] it nevertheless devoted its resources to breaking what it predicted as "the inevitable filibuster,"[16] as well as "passing an FEPC bill with enforcement powers."[17] The ACHR's efforts proved to be fruitless, however: in 1950 the Eighty-First Congress "expired without enacting the Fair Employment Practices Act, the anti-lynch and anti-poll tax bills."[18]

The ACHR was successful, however, in its support of the policy to end segregation of D.C. swimming pools, as Secretary of the Interior Oscar L. Chapman ordered that all swimming pools be operated on a non-segregated basis.[19] In addition to its work with senators and congressmen, the ACHR also asked President Truman to "end Army Jim-Crow, to act against colonialism, to step up the activity of his civil service Fair Employment Board and create machinery to enforce the non-discrimination provisions in all defense contracts."[20] In October 1950 the ACHR's board of directors met with President Truman and called on him "to act against racial and religious job discrimination in industries producing war materials and to set up an agency similar to the Fair Employment Practices Committee which operated during World War Two."[21]

In addition to its work in Congress, the ACHR continued to emphasize the need for the creation of local human rights councils in communities across the country, which were to be made up of local chapters of the member fraternities and sororities.[22] In 1950 one such council, the Howard University Council of the ACHR, held a series of informal teas for students from Catholic University, George Washington University, and Miner Teachers College as part of its project on "What Students Can Do to Further Human Rights in the District of Columbia."[23] Another local council, the New York Local ACHR, created a voter education plan for the 1950 primary and general elections and organized registration drives whereby the NY ACHR provided babysitting and transportation services to allow for increased registration.[24] In May 1950 the NY ACHR discussed starting a program meant to "convince realty interests that colored persons are good risks as property owners and to report evidences of discrimination by mortgage banks to the Justice Department as violations of the anti-trust laws."[25] By June 1951 there were twenty-three operating local councils and twenty-five councils still undergoing the formation process.[26] Accordingly, in what follows we detail many of the ACHR activities.

Employment Issues

The ACHR focused its efforts in the employment arena on (1) promoting fair employment practices generally, (2) ending discriminatory federal employment practices, and (3) ensuring that employers who had federal government contracts engaged in nondiscriminatory employment practices.

Employment Practices

The ACHR's employment program sought to achieve fair employment practices and eradicate discrimination in respect to obtaining a job and advancing within a career. More specific objectives included creating nondiscrimination clauses in contracts between government and industry, creating a fair employment program in the national government, increasing employment of African Americans within the national government, and pursuing the appointment of African Americans in policy-making roles in government. To realize these goals, the ACHR recommended a multipronged approach that addressed both private contracts and governmental regulations.[27]

In the legislature, initial steps toward positive federal regulation began under the Wartime-Roosevelt Fair Employment Practice Committee (FEPC), culminating in HR 4453 (1949).[28] The ACHR testified before the House in support of legislation that, while employment discrimination was a reality and African Americans were backsliding from the progress that had been made, whites and African Americans could successfully work together.[29] The ACHR used its own network to contact and persuade congressmen to vote for HR 4453. They reached out to the Los Angeles ACHR chapter to persuade Richard Nixon, and they contacted Louisville Greek-letter chapters to persuade Kentucky congressmen. The group contacted ACHR congressmen and encouraged

ACHR members to write their own congressmen to ask that they attend the House vote for the FEPC without weakening amendments. This effort was eviscerated by a McConnell amendment, so that its eventual House passage did little to satisfy the bill's original proponents. Subsequently, the Senate discussion of the federal Fair Employment Practice Act encountered substantial procedural resistance, eventually falling to a cloture vote in the summer of 1950. In the end the Senate did not take up the matter. In 1949 the Senate amended the cloture Rule 22 by requiring a constitutional two-thirds vote instead of the previous simple two-thirds. The effect of this amendment was to immobilize any action seeking to end racial discrimination. The ACHR condemned the rule and instead advocated for a majority cloture vote as the rule instead.[30]

Federal Employment

The ACHR also pressed for changes to discriminatory federal employment practices. These efforts targeted the Department of Labor, the Housing and Home-Financing Agency, the Office of Defense Mobilization, and the Office of Price Stabilization.[31] The ACHR, acting with other civil rights organizations—e.g., NAACP, Brotherhood of Sleeping Car Porters, and National Council of Negro Women—pressed for nondiscriminatory employment opportunities, vocational education, and apprentice training.

At the State Department, representatives met with both Secretary Acheson and director of personnel for the department, Raymond T. Martin. Conventionally, the State Department had not employed African Americans. After repeated urgings, the department adopted a policy of "expanded Recruitment of Negroes" and appointed Dr. John A. Davis of Lincoln University, a historically black college, as part-time consultant. The ACHR also took up matters with the Department of the Interior, urging it to strengthen the fair employment and fair promotion programs within the department, simplify and publicize fair employment procedures, and ensure employment officers and officials are fair and sympathetic to the cause. Similarly, the ACHR urged the Department of Labor to strengthen the fair employment procedures governing the department's hiring and promotion policies to ensure that effective action would be taken if a discrimination case arose. Before the Senate Labor and Public Welfare Committee, the ACHR argued for (1) the withholding of certification by the National Labor Relations board to unions that refused membership because of race or religion and (2) a ban on the closed shop in cases where unions refused membership based on race or segregated African Americans.[32]

Advocacy work also resulted in the opposition of unfavorable legislation, which was blocked with the assistance of Senator Lehman. When President Truman included Annabel Matthews in his Federal Fair Employment Board, the ACHR strongly opposed Matthews's inclusion because she had voted against the admission of Mary Church Terrell into the American Association of University Women. The ACHR also questioned the board's operating procedure and called on President Eisenhower to strengthen the power of the board and make its services more accessible to those seeking employment. Senator Lehman blocked the passage of unfavorable legislation that would have impeded promotions of African Americans within the Federal Fair Employment Board. Other actions by the ACHR included (1) recommending to the Senate Labor and Public Welfare committee that racial safe-guards be provided, (2) recommending to the Senate Committee on Finance that it approve additional unemployment compensation benefits in limited cases to workers employed during a national emergency, (3) intervening in the employment protest of a psychologist in the Veterans Administration, and (4) creating a proposal that President Eisenhower raise the issue of fair employment with governors so that states could begin to work for fair employment.[33]

In addition, the ACHR made strong recommendations to President Truman to appoint an African American to the Board of Commissioners of D.C., to the Interstate Commerce Commission, to the United Nations as a delegate from the United States, and to the Point Four advisory committee. The ACHR was rewarded with the appointment of George Weaver to the Congress of Industrial Organizations. The ACHR continued advocating for the appointment of many persons of color to various government positions. The ACHR urged for the appointment of an African American to the Supreme Court and to policy positions in the defense program. Successes included two African Americans selected to the President's Committee on Government Contract Compliance.[34]

As part of its efforts in employment, the ACHR's director, Elmer W. Henderson, met with two cabinet officers in the Eisenhower administration during the spring of 1953. During that meeting, Secretary of Labor Martin P. Durkin stated that he would ensure fair employment policies in his department and would continue to support the Contract Compliance Committee's work to develop enforcement procedures for the nondiscrimination in employment clauses of federal contracts with private companies. Secretary of the Interior Douglas McKay likewise promised to continue his department's fair employment policies.[35]

Government Contracts

More specifically, the ACHR also advocated to reform government contracts. This effort was particularly focused on ensuring that war-controlled employers engaged in fair contracting arrangements. The ACHR advocated for government contracts to contain a nondiscrimination provision and to have a mechanism to enforce contract compliance. Through the efforts of the ACHR's memorandum, meetings, and conferences with President Truman, the president established the President's Committee on Government Contract Compliance to improve enforcement of nondiscrimination clauses in government contracts.[36]

ACHR director Henderson submitted the following recommendations to the Government Contracts Committee to assist them in carrying out President Eisenhower's Order to ensure compliance with nondiscrimination clauses in federal contracts with private companies: the committee should utilize the experience of officials from earlier government commissions and establish an independent locus for receiving complaints; procurement agencies should undertake a study of current practices; informative posters should be developed for display in contract plants; periodic inspection should be used to ensure compliance; public hearings should be conducted where serious violations are found; the question of cancellation or renegotiation of the contract should be raised immediately where violations are found and liquidated damages considered; and the committee should employ staff that are sympathetic to the objectives of the order.[37] Through such memoranda and testimony to President Eisenhower, the ACHR later successfully lobbied for a stronger Committee on Government Contracts to improve contract compliance.[38] This committee included a member of the ACHR board of directors as a vice-chairman.[39]

Housing Issues

On May 20, 1950, the ACHR joined four other organizations in sponsoring a Housing Conference.[40] Forty national African American organizations were invited.[41] During that conference, the national organizations set out to (1) formulate a blueprint for community action to be conducted by local counterparts in their communities and (2) formulate recommendations to policy makers of federal agencies regarding minority considerations in the execution of their programs. The organizations reached the conclusion that all actions taken must be taken with the goal to increase the land area open to African Americans and that land developed be unsegregated.[42] The ACHR's efforts in the area of housing were aimed at eliminating racial discrimination in America's housing practices.[43] Its specific agenda focused on (1) providing sufficient new housing for African Americans; (2) opening housing, particularly public housing, without regard to race or religion; (3) financing the construction and purchasing of homes free from racial or religious discrimination; (4) providing housing for the homeless; and (5) redeveloping slums with a policy of "open occupancy."[44]

Constructing New Housing

The ACHR faced two great struggles in the fight to better "Negro housing": achieving an adequate housing program and preventing loss in the construction program. The ACHR set out in the late 1940s to present an estimate of the housing needs of the nonwhite population to Congress. They estimated 2.4 million housing units would be needed over the next twelve years. As a result, Congress authorized 810,000 public housing units, but according to the report the "Negro community" still faced the problem of getting into the units. Thus, ACHR asked that a racial policy be established to "enable Negros to obtain a fair proportion of the new housing developed."[45]

In constructing new housing, the ACHR had several notable achievements. Henderson wrote to the Housing and Home Finance Agency shortly after the formation of ACHR to propose improvements. In 1949 Henderson testified at the U.S. Senate Committee on Banking and Currency to support housing programs and to express concerns of racial discrimination. Two months later the ACHR presented the same statement to the House Committee. African Americans, however, were still having trouble getting in housing units. In May 1951 supporters of public housing faced a sharp slash in the 1949 housing program.

In 1951 the ACHR took another step for public housing, after the Korean conflict caused emergency housing problems in defense areas. The ACHR emphasized that housing should not be limited to immigrants in defense areas, that there should be permanent construction for housing, and that there should be no discrimination against large families. Unfortunately, however, public housing later faced serious cuts and the ACHR pleaded with public officials "to use [their] influence to restore cuts made in housing appropriation by House of Representatives so that the original goal of 75,000 public housing units may be realized."[46]

Not getting the response they needed, the ACHR turned directly to President Truman in 1952 to urge that a formal commission be appointed by the president to appraise housing needs and to make recommendations to the president as necessary.[47] That same year the ACHR contacted President Truman as part of the National Housing Conference to plea for a commission on housing needs. The following year a congressional fight developed over the authorized housing units.

Housing People without Race Discrimination

According to the report, "better housing for Negroes" would be accomplished when more public housing was constructed and the cost of financing was fixed within reach of more people. In the past, the ACHR had supported new public housing without specifically focusing on nondiscrimination. However, this was unsuccessful because issues like redevelopment, slum clearance, and financing were directly tied to racial barriers.[48] Thus, the ACHR later made direct pleas to Congress and President Truman for assurance of nondiscrimination in public housing bills.[49] These requests were completely ignored. Part of the thought behind these requests being ignored was that a nondiscrimination clause would kill the passage of the 1949 Housing Bill.[50]

This denial was nothing new for the council. The ACHR had previously, on multiple occasions, urged the administration and the Senate Banking and Currency Committee to include a nondiscrimination clause in housing legislation.[51] The ACHR continued its struggle throughout much of 1949 without success. The group continued this struggle from 1950 to 1953, making small gains along the way.[52]

Financing Housing for All People

While working to achieve nondiscrimination in public housing, ACHR also argued for financing that would produce "better housing for Negroes."[53] They tried to achieve this through (1) clear policy statements prohibiting discrimination in housing financing, (2) denial of financing to any "racially restricted properties," (3) direct government loans to builders as well as to veterans' cooperatives, and (4) liberalization of the general rules of financing.[54] Over the years the ACHR made several recommendations documenting the needs of racial minorities in housing and financing. This gained considerable attention of the "colloquy between Senator Capehar and the ACHR Director."[55] Over time ACHR's efforts began to pay off. For example, the Federal Housing Administration amended its rules to abandon all racial considerations in mortgage insurance and financial assistance.[56]

In financing housing the ACHR had several noted achievements. The Bricker Amendment was drawn to establish nondiscrimination of both housing and financing. Congress rejected the amendment in 1949 when it approved the General Housing Policy. In 1953 the Senate Committee on Banking and Currency heard testimony from Elmer Henderson on the issue. These discussions drew considerable attention from the papers. Congress also took a favorable position on the extension of "advance commitment authority" and authorized the Federal National Mortgage Association to make commitments for up to 17.5 million dollars' worth of mortgage insurance arrangements for constructing low-rent housing for minority groups.

Slum Clearance and Redevelopment

Finally, the ACHR had concerns about what would happen to those "cleared" from slum areas and with who would be housed in the redeveloped section.[57] ACHR proposed that (1) preference be given in new projects to families displaced from the area because of slum clearance and (2) redevelopers be required to write in their contracts a covenant running with the land so that no person could be barred because of race or color.[58] Like before, ACHR made many attempts to implement its proposed ideas but faced resistance from the legislative and executive branches. Henderson testified that even though the ACHR desired passage of the slum clearance bill, amendments were necessary to protect families displaced from the clearance. Although ACHR was able to get the Powell Amendment added, at the Senate Committee Hearing the amendment was stricken as a result of the Senate-House Conference. Thus, ACHR again turned its attention to executive agencies to try to make change. Eventually, in 1953, the Housing and Home Finance Agency recognized that the clearance of slums would have a detrimental effect and would further compromise the housing conditions of racial-minority families. The resulting policy, however, neither improved nor denied housing for racial minorities.[59]

Broader Civil Rights Issues

More broadly, the ACHR focused its efforts on (1) civil rights issues such as voting rights and access to public accommodations, (2) desegregating the armed forces, and (3) situating African Americans' fight for civil rights within a broader international context.

Civil Rights

The efforts toward reformation of civil rights primarily comprised two movements: (1) legislative goals, including the 1952 and 1953 efforts to amend the Senate cloture rule and progress toward security of person and abolition of poll tax, to include nondiscrimination clauses in the federal aid to education bills and require nonsegregation in public accommodations; and (2) advocacy in areas of general welfare, including social security, housing, rent control, economic and social development, and immigration.[60]

The ACHR saw federal legislation as the traditional approach to preventing mob violence and lynching and testified as such before the House Judiciary Committee in 1949.[61] Two years later the ACHR and other groups met with Attorney General J. Howard McGrath to get federal relief of the 1951 Cicero, Illinois, riots; McGrath promised to convene a grand jury in response.[62]

Not all efforts were successful. The ACHR was disappointed with the amount of civil rights and progressive legislation included in record leading up to the end of the first session of the Eighty-First Congress. Of the numerous civil rights efforts made by the ACHR, its housing bill was the only measure passed to date.[63]

Moreover, civil rights in Congress took a major step back in March 1949 when the southern Democrats and most Republicans teamed up to defeat a proposed filibustering amendment. Filibustering has long been used to block progressive legislation (e.g., civil rights proposals) by talking them to death. In an effort to line up as many senators as possible for a favorable vote, the ACHR wrote all ninety-six. Although the failed effort was a major setback, the organization did not view it as fatal one. The ACHR urged stronger efforts be taken to put an end to the device utilized by "rabid anti-Negro southern Senators."[64] The ACHR cited the lack of pressure on senators from their home states as a major factor in the filibuster defeat. Thus, the organization expressed the need for energizing the members of local chapters affiliated with them; at the March meeting the ACHR board recommended that special attention be given to the formation of Local Councils on Human Rights.[65]

In July 1950, the U.S. Senate succumbed to intimidations of filibustering and gave up on the FEPC. The *New York Times* stated on July 14, "This does not, of course, mean that the fight should be abandoned . . . eventual victory in this effort is inevitable."[66]

In other areas the ACHR testimony before the House Committee on Administration focused on poll taxes, but that legislation (like the anti-lynching legislation) died in committee.[67] More efforts were directed toward generating access to nondiscriminatory education, which was guaranteed by the U.S. Supreme Court's interpretation of the Fourteenth Amendment. The ACHR sought to end discrimination in education through legislative and judicial means and supported federal aid to education with equitable provisions to safeguard minority children, yet these efforts could not push a bill to passage by Congress.[68]

The ACHR also sought to end discrimination in public accommodations (e.g., hotels, trains, etc.) and found more success. Alpha Phi Alpha's general president, Belford V. Lawson, acting as counsel for ACHR, argued before the U.S. Supreme Court against Southern Railway.[69] The Supreme Court found unreasonable prejudice and held in favor of the plaintiff. In response, Southern Railway passed internal policies of seating "Negroes with Negroes." When the railway was challenged in court again by the same plaintiff, the ACHR's suit pressured the railway to revoke its own policy before a judicial resolution of the matter. The ACHR scored another civil rights victory against Hotel Phillips, forcing the Kansas City establishment to stop discriminating against Negroes. The ACHR also supported several social programs, including rent control, improved housing, immigration, and social development. The ACHR testified to the marginalization of African Americans from social security, and Congress voted to extend social security coverage to most domestic and farm workers, which greatly benefited the large African American populations in those occupations who had previously been excluded from social security coverage. The ACHR also supported better housing and rent control for Americans regardless of race or religion. In the field of immigration, the ACHR criticized a proposed bill that would limit immigration from British colonies including Negro-populated countries such as Jamaica and Trinidad. The final legislation reflected the ACHR's position of extending citizenship to Japanese aliens and not restricting British colony immigration.[70]

The ACHR also made efforts to abolish segregation and discrimination in Washington D.C., including a home-rule provision for the citizens of the city.[71] Resultantly, in 1950 the federal swimming pools in the district announced that they would operate without regard to race.[72] Before the desegregation could take place, a bill had to be passed transferring the pools from the Interior Department to the District Recreation Board and a plan for administering the pools had to be created. The ACHR suggested steps for safe use and operation of the pools, helping the desegregation to be successful.[73] Additionally, the ACHR helped stop a bill to transfer the swimming pool operation from going to the House floor. In 1950 the District Commissioners proclaimed that old antidiscrimination municipal ordinances still on the books were in full effect. A southern congressman introduced a bill to repeal these ordinances, and the ACHR staunchly opposed his measure. The ordinances became the basis for litigation, in relation to which the ACHR was a party to two amici curiae briefs. In a unanimous decision, the eight-judge Supreme Court ruled that the measures were valid. The ACHR also worked to improve employment opportunities for African Americans in D.C. with a focus on the Fire Department, the Transit Company, the U.S. Park Police, and the appointment of an African American commissioner. The ACHR proposed integration in the Fire Department, but despite support from the District Commissioners, the integration was not achieved. The ACHR brought awareness of employment discrimination by the Capital Transit Company and helped resolve the problem of promotion discrimination within the U.S. Park Police. The ACHR also supported bills to end segregation and petitioned President Eisenhower to announce nonsegregation as the public policy in D.C. and to help enforce the policy throughout the District.[74]

Armed Forces

A major ACHR objective had been to abolish segregation and to ensure equal opportunity in the armed services. The ACHR proposed removing all traces of discrimination from the armed services, preventing discrimination in industries producing defense materials, and creating a bipartisan joint committee of the House and Senate to help abolish discrimination.[75] One prong in this attack was direct testimony before the President's Committee on Equality of Treatment and Opportunity in the Armed Services. This was unfortunately met with reactionary moves by southerners.[76] Repeated attachments of pro-segregation amendments to the Draft Bill were defeated, eventually resulting in the assignment of an African American medical officer into the previously all-white Thirty-First Infantry Division.[77]

By 1951 President Truman's administration had not issued a Fair Employment Practice Order (FEPO)—"banning discriminatory employment practices by Federal agencies and all unions and companies engaged in war-related work."[78] The White House had not given any rea-son as to why there had been a delay in issuing the FEPO.[79] Moreover, at the time of the Korean War, it arguably needed to be issued before the U.S. defense program could become crystallized, with plants staffed and hiring completed.[80]

On February 28, 1951, conferees met with President Truman to dis-cuss major racial problems. During this meeting, the group requested the president take specific action on the following six points:

1. To abolish, immediately, racial segregation in the nation's capital
2. To appoint qualified African Americans on the administrative and policy-making levels of the U.S. government
3. To integrate African Americans in all new agencies that were being established and would be established as a result of this emergency
4. To appoint African Americans more widely in the foreign and diplomatic service of the county
5. To issue an executive order guaranteeing the maximum use of all manpower in all production efforts irrespective of color, race, or national origin in the defense emergency and provide adequate machinery for its enforcement (FEPC)
6. To abolish the racial segregation of African American soldiers in the U.S. Army once and for all

Although the president expressed sympathy and stated no discrimi-nation was in his office, he did not commit himself to any specific proposal. However, ACHR's director, Elmer W. Henderson, felt that the meeting with President Truman was valuable because it put major issues that concern African Americans on the table in front of the president in a constructive manner. Henderson also noted a major task to counter any pressure exerted by the southerners who sit on powerful positions in Congress because the conference alone was not, in his opinion, suf-ficient to cause any action to be taken on the points raised.[81]

On April 13, 1951, the Winstead Amendment to the Draft-Universal Military Training Bill, which would have allowed inductees to state a preference for service in racially segregated units, was defeated, but by a very narrow margin of 138 to 123. In combatting this proposal, ACHR local councils rallied and sent wires and letters to congressmen.[82]

International Affairs

In April and May 1952 Elmer Henderson expanded the ACHR's interest in international affairs when he visited France, England, Germany, Italy, and Switzerland. While on his trip Henderson investigated the effect of racial discrimination in the United States on the perception and standing of our country abroad, the effectiveness of the State Department's informational program in counteracting anti-American propaganda, the use of Point Four funds in non-self-governing areas, and conditions among African American troops stationed in Europe. Upon his return, after meeting with various European government officials and American officials stationed there, Henderson declared that race discrimination had become a critical issue in international relations and that the longer American people refused to act on major problems at home, the more likely the failure of U.S. foreign policy would become.[83]

Additionally, the ACHR constantly sought a close working relationship with the United Nations Commission on Human Rights and the UNESCO.[84] The ACHR was granted "observer status" with the United Nations General Assembly.[85] The group joined efforts to decry South African apartheid.[86] In its work with the UN, ACHR developed several strategies for effective international advocacy.[87] First, it appeared that America's racial discrimination received much more press in England and France than it did in Italy and Germany.[88] Awareness in Europe of American racial discrimination was met with disapproval and anti-American opinions.[89] In response, people believed that employment of American racial minorities by the U.S. government would lead to much more effective international awareness.[90] This seemed to be validated by the acceptance of recently integrated American soldiers by German civilians.[91] Work with the UN led to the conclusion that the ACHR must continue working toward a declaration of human rights, using its influence to abolish the colonial system and informing minorities in the United States of these changes abroad.[92] Finally, the ACHR repeatedly lobbied the executive department to include more minorities in the public affairs staff of certain target countries, England and Italy in particular.[93] So far, these requests had not been successful.[94]

The ACHR Public Relations Apparatus

When the ACHR began to take shape, one purpose that seemed to have a high degree of importance was the "education and public relations" function of the organization.[95] These seemingly distinct functions, however, were not easily separated, and the ACHR proceeded with the notion that carrying out the education and public relation functions would often work hand in hand.[96] Through a number of mediums— public meetings, staff-developed informational articles, articles in newspapers and periodicals, and other miscellaneous aspects of education and public relations[97]—the ACHR worked to effectively collect and disseminate information during its history.

Public Meetings

"Selling social action for civil rights goals and selling ACHR have been key matters in many public meetings."[98] Meetings came in a variety of forms, including public forums, panels, and workshops, as well as formal dinners and receptions.[99] Board members were effective in giving talks in both formal and informal settings, in many places urging the constituent members of the ACHR to "carry out the work of the ACHR."[100] Other board members used large gatherings, such as sorority- or fraternity-sponsored events, to disseminate the "goals and aims of the ACHR's program to the broad community."[101] Where the ACHR issues intersected with issues of civil rights, members and leaders often talked extensively about the ACHR program.[102] For example, Henderson gave talks to countless groups around the country, from Greek organizations in Baltimore to the Annual Teacher's Association Convention in Ohio to the NAACP Banquet in Chicago.[103]

In addition to speaking engagements, the ACHR utilized forums and workshops to disseminate information and instill attitudes.[104] These events, generally conducted by ACHR local councils, dealt with both the role of the ACHR as well as various human rights problems.[105] Like the speaking engagements, the forums and workshops were conducted all over the country.[106]

A final, vital method of carrying out the education and public relations program was ACHR dinners. "Each year the American Council on

Human Rights presents annual awards for distinguished service to the cause of human rights to those most deserving."[107] The first dinner, held in October 1948,[108] and those that followed presented opportunities to highlight significant civil rights achievements and provided opportunities for far-reaching observations.[109] At the inaugural dinner, President Harry S. Truman remarked, "It has been particularly gratifying to see the growth of public interest during the year for, in the last analysis, the extension of freedom depends on a change in the minds and hearts of men."[110]

A particularly memorable moment was in 1949 when Secretary of the Interior Julius Krug declared that all public facilities under the jurisdiction of the Department of Interior would be "open to all on an equal basis," not just "separate but equal."[111] The civil rights dinners served four notable functions in advancing the ACHR's goals: (1) honored deserving people and their actions, (2) put a spotlight on civil rights advancements and issues, (3) gained widespread press coverage, and (4) broadened opportunity for African Americans in the hotels of Washington, D.C.[112]

The annual conventions of the six ACHR member organizations in December 1952, held in Cleveland, were "unprecedented,"[113] and the ACHR provided coordination for these conventions as well as two open meetings to be held in conjunction.[114] With the objectives of stimulating interest in membership, demonstrating the willingness and ability of Greek-letter organizations to fight for equality and justice, furthering cooperation for specific goals between the member organizations, and providing the first opportunity for mutual cooperation among the members of these organizations, the ACHR sought to further its educational programs.[115] The two public meetings included a presentation of an award to Secretary of the Interior Oscar Chapman, accepting on behalf of President Truman,[116] as well as a talk by Sir Zafrulla Khan, minister of foreign affairs of Pakistan.[117] The outcomes of the meetings in Cleveland were "expectedly satisfying."[118] Not only had the members learned more about the goals of the ACHR, but numerous daily and weekly publications had publicized the event, allowing hundreds of thousands of people to learn about the organization.[119] In the end, the convention was "an essential step in the ACHR's program of motivational and informational public relations,"[120] spotlighting the fight of African Americans for human rights.[121] Real values were gained toward fraternal good will, and the convention even turned a profit.[122]

The convention adopted four resolutions. The first was to support Senators Ives and Humphrey to amend the Senate Rule 22 to limit debate to a reasonable time and allow cloture to be imposed by a majority vote. This action would reduce the effectiveness of the filibuster, a measure historically used by southern Democrats to prevent civil rights legislation from coming to a vote. The second resolution was to call for long-overdue action from Congress on the issue of fair employment and other civil rights legislation.[123] The third resolution was to call on President Eisenhower to work with Congress to enact federal fair employment and civil rights legislation, to include African Americans in policy-making positions in his administration, to see that all departments in the federal government adopt fair employment policies, to eliminate segregation in the District of Columbia, and to eliminate segregation in all branches of the armed forces. The fourth resolution was for ACHR to fully support President Eisenhower and his administration in effectuating these resolutions.[124]

Staff-Developed Informational Materials

The ACHR also distributed printed and mimeographed materials, including its principal publication, *Congress and Equality*,[125] and released publications describing various human rights issues and goals and highlighting the ACHR's program to achieve the "extension of civil rights."[126] In addition, the ACHR sought to inform membership about various civil rights issues through brochures and leaflets. Among these publications was *What the Negro Wants*,[127] published in 1952 as a "statement of political objectives," including a federal FEPC, anti-lynching legislation, protection of the right to vote, an end to discrimination in the military, and the abolishment of segregation in interstate travel.[128] Through brochures, the public was informed about the roots, goals, and logistics of the ACHR.[129] And through staff memoranda the executive director regularly informed officers about anything from information requests to contests and matters of particular interest to councils.[130]

Articles in Newspapers and Periodicals

Aside from printing its own materials, the ACHR was the subject of hundreds of articles in daily and weekly newspapers, Greek-letter journals, and picture magazines.[131] These articles "reflect both good will and recognition of the program."[132] Many news stories were motivated by ACHR's own press releases. These releases were sent on a "full" or "limited" scale, where some were distributed very widely across the country, while others were sent only to local presses depending on content.[133] Newspapers from Atlanta to Tucson and from Charleston, South Carolina, to Charleston, West Virginia, all received ACHR press releases and proceeded to published stories.[134]

While most publicity was favorable, some writings were unfavorable.[135] For example, in August 1950 Stanley Robert criticized the ACHR and Henderson in a column in the *Pittsburgh Courier*.[136] Louis Lautier also published a criticism of the ACHR in 1952 in the *Norfolk Journal and Guide* and proposed sending money to the NAACP to improve lobbying efforts.[137] In Greek-letter journals, member organizations carried eighty-five articles regarding ACHR, thoroughly covering the action and education programs.[138] Finally, the ACHR was given attention in other publications such as *Ebony, Scoop,* and *Color* magazines and *Report of the American Council on Race Relations*.[139]

Miscellaneous Aspects of Education and Public Relations

The ACHR used various other means to undertake public relations and education goals. In 1949 the ACHR sponsored a contest on college campuses to choose a slogan that "best epitomized its ACHR's ideals and objectives."[140] When the display of Confederate flags became prevalent in late 1951, the ACHR undertook a movement to issue thousands of window and car stickers with the message "Our flag is the American flag."[141] This movement resulted in several papers carrying a picture of Howard University's Gridiron Queen attaching the sticker to a car. Among other public relations approaches were a portable exhibit displaying the purpose and membership of the ACHR; a montage about council activities, providing information about human rights goals to the Department of State; and republication of an article for the yearbook of the *Journal of Negro Education*.[142]

The ACHR's education and public relations function was a vital aspect of the organization's operation. Being able to effectively communicate the ACHR's message, instill attitudes in members in the public, and educate members as to the goals and objectives of the ACHR were all achieved through effective education and public relations programs. Through meetings, forums, dinners, printed brochures and informational packets, news releases and publications, and miscellaneous projects, contests, and programs, the ACHR found methods to carry out the education and public relations function effectively, to advance the objectives of the group.

Community Organizing and Local Councils

The original format for local councils was that "each chapter of each member organization [would] establish four local non-partisan committees to serve as a channel for social action and as a connecting link between the central office and local communities."[143] Finding this system to be too cumbersome, the execution director recommended the creation of local councils consisting of formal voluntary combinations of the representatives of each chapter.[144]

The local councils were formed to facilitate cooperation.[145] The organizations had three main goals. The first goal was to contact nationally elected officials on legislative initiatives and increase awareness of congressionally significant issues in the local community.[146] The second goal was to support movements on the state level.[147] And the final goal was to execute social action programs to improve human rights in the local communities.[148] The local council operation was unique in its diversity and breadth.[149] It had councils in a number of cities where member organizations had chapters; there were a number of chapters belonging to the ACHR member groups and a number of participating members of Greek-letter organizations.[150] Local councils spread to 105 cities with chapters of ACHR member organizations.[151]

Local councils were composed of delegates from each member chapter that had representation on ACHR's national Board of Directors.[152] Each council elected its own officers, but the ACHR encouraged that officers be elected from various member organizations whenever possible.[153]

The local councils conducted letter writing and telegraphing campaigns, mass meetings and forums, held large workshops and small conferences, and participated in testimony at open hearings and court trials.[154] Councils were encouraged to engage in these types of activities at the national, state, and local levels.[155] The success of these is demonstrated by the wide press attention they garnered.[156] The ACHR's work at the local level was more notable and diverse.[157] The local councils led voter registration drives, raised money for legal fees, and conducted campaigns to integrate schools and other public accommodations, as well as campaigns to get blacks elected to office.[158] Councils in Baltimore, Charleston (W.Va.), Chicago, Cleveland, Indianapolis, Kansas City, Los Angeles, Miami, Nashville, New York, Washington, D.C., and Winston-Salem all conducted successful local initiatives.[159] The ACHR also worked to achieve national objectives, including those in employment, housing, armed services, civil rights, and international affairs.[160]

The local council model also had several areas in which it could have been more effective. Chiefly, despite their breadth of potential, no more than thirty-five local councils were ever active at one time.[161] Additionally, several chapters of member organizations expressed interest in creating a local council by writing letters to the ACHR, but many of these councils never came to fruition.[162]

The ACHR also had several problems at the local level. There was a fear that the attorney general classified the ACHR as "Red."[163] Some individuals, particularly those who were employed by government entities, worried about the ACHR's disfavor with governmental authorities because of its methods and were thus hesitant to be outspoken participants.[164] There was also a problem of "scope-creep" or duplication with other established organizations, including local pan-Hellenic groups, the NAACP, and the Urban League.[165] However, despite these concerns about duplication of efforts, a council was established in each locality where members raised the concern.[166] The local councils also struggled with challenges in conducting their social action program, including defining the problem and which program objective to choose, defining and executing a strategy to achieve goals, maintaining interest between major national and state initiatives, and publicizing their programs.[167] The ACHR councils also faced structural issues such as fostering cooperation among previously autonomous organizations and local organizers who ignored the national structure of the ACHR.[168] Another structural challenge arose when members of local chapters who were not part of the ACHR's member organizations wanted to create local councils.[169] Last, some councils were concerned about their "inability to get support for local council programs from individual members of local chapters."[170] The local councils enjoyed a number of successes and identified several areas for improvement.

The ACHR's operations were a vital aspect to study, specifically considering *how* the ACHR achieved its objectives and goals.[171] The commission focused on three important factors in determining the "how":

1. How well has the ACHR concentrated its activities in the government or in nongovernmental enterprises and institutions? Have its activities been directed to national or international problems?
2. What are the methods of the ACHR? Is it a "lone wolf" organization, or does it work in concert with others? What are the procedures—letter, conference, and testimony or picket line? Are its actions always of a "positive" nature, or does it use the *protest* to a great extent?
3. How does the ACHR operate? Financial support? The office operation, particularly relating to staff, facilities, and equipment?[172]

Areas of Social Action

The ACHR primarily used the federal government as a venue to carry out its goals and objectives.[173] Traditionally, the goal was to use the federal government to act or place prohibitions on certain activity that was believed to be wrong.[174] The ACHR used each branch of the federal government for assistance.

The Legislative Branch is responsible for drafting and creating all laws, a power granted by the U.S. Constitution.[175] Because of this fundamental power, the ACHR used Congress to discuss various programs of concern, including "housing, employment, anti-lynching, anti–poll tax, public accommodations, [and] certain areas of general welfare."[176] Despite great efforts, it should be noted that during the ACHR's lifetime at the time of the study, Congress had not yet "been induced to pass any civil rights legislation."[177]

The Executive Branch consists of the president and his cabinet members, who are responsible for carrying out the laws—another power granted by the Constitution. The ACHR brought hundreds of matters to the president, his cabinet members, and the administration. Most notably were the discussions with President Truman regarding employment and housing. Henderson was also able to communicate with the subsequent president, Dwight D. Eisenhower, although not through personal meetings but rather through the drafting of memoranda on matters of concern. Aside from meeting and communicating with presidents, the ACHR made great efforts to work with all other members of the Executive Branch, including testifying before presidential administration committees and attending conferences with Department of Justice officials. The ACHR used these opportunities to discuss topics including employment, housing, segregation, discrimination, and others.[178]

Some of the most significant accomplishments of the ACHR have taken place within the Justice Branch, through the ACHR's participation in litigation. One of the ACHR's proudest moments thus far was when "the Supreme Court agreed with the contention of ACHR (and Alpha Phi Alpha) Counsel Belford Lawson that the Southern Railway unlawfully discriminated against Elmer W. Henderson in depriving him of the right to eat in a railroad dining car." As previously mentioned, the ACHR was also a sponsor in another case against a hotel accused of discrimination; this case ended with an out-of-court settlement by the hotel. Apart from direct involvement in litigation, the ACHR, on numerous occasions, has submitted joint amici curiae briefs with other organizations. Some of these briefs reached the Supreme Court, and others were submitted in landmark cases like *Bolling v. Sharpe*.[179]

The ACHR also used the political parties to help advance their objectives. In the 1948 and 1952 election years, the ACHR "took its civil rights program to the major political parties in convention." In addition, during the years between conventions, the ACHR "called on the party leadership to live up to the platform pledges and the candidates' promises." During the Republican National Convention, Henderson made a statement to the Resolutions Committee of the party that included five major recommendations primarily relating to the "elimination of discrimination and segregation."[180] Unfortunately, the ACHR did not have much luck with gaining the Republican Party's support, and the party did not include "a strong plank on civil rights or those supporting civil rights to make a strong fight." The ACHR was certainly more successful with the Democratic National Convention, particularly building a strong relationship with Democratic nominee Adlai Stevenson. Henderson met with Stevenson privately and concluded he was "perfectly sincere in his pronouncement . . . and has given careful study to the subject of civil rights and the role of the Federal Government and the Congress."[181]

Although its efforts were not as extensive, the ACHR also worked to eliminate discrimination in international relations and used the State Department, the president, and the United Nations to assist in its efforts.[182]

Methods of Operation

The ACHR used two primary approaches for attaining its goals and objectives: individual action and group action. The ACHR was "an independent organization working specifically toward its own objectives and 'target aims.'" For example, the ACHR made presentations to a senator regarding improvement of housing financing for African Americans. The ACHR also worked with various other groups to help accomplish its goals. It worked with both federally and privately sponsored organizations from all different sectors of its field of work.[183]

The ACHR took several approaches to the procedures it used within its social action. It used basic procedures such as "writing letters and telegraphing, meeting with other group representatives and conferring with one or two people and offering oral testimony." As mentioned above, it also involved itself in lawsuits. However, it avoided action such as "picketing, boycotting overtly, encouraging strikes, 'waiting lines,' or 'sitdown' movement[s]."[184]

One of the ACHR's most strong-handed moves was its practice to "protest strongly and immediately (1) unsatisfactory appointments and actions of officers of the government, [and] (2) actions prejudicial to human rights." This powerful stance enabled the ACHR to actively and effectively advocate for its objectives.[185]

Means of Operation

The ACHR operated "financially on the basis of contributions from the member organizations and implements its program by means of a rather small office staff." The contributions consisted of seven-member organizations, each making an annual payment of twenty-five hundred dollars, paid quarterly. The ACHR maintained one office in Washington, D.C. and was able to afford all basic necessities for its maintenance with the member payments. There were also three staff members, including a director, assistant director, and office secretary.[186]

A War on Different Fronts: BGLO Activism from 1949 to 1953

While working with the ACHR, each organization developed different and independent foci during this period. In what follows we provide a brief overview of some of the organization's individual activities.

Alpha Phi Alpha Fraternity

As the first half of the twentieth century ended, the racial climate facing African Americans continued to be deeply problematic. In 1949 general president Lawson declared that Alpha Phi Alpha was translating its program and spirit to Negro progress all over America as part of a racial crusade.[187] Furthermore, the fraternity's general secretary urged every chapter to encourage their fellow students to exercise the franchise (voting).[188] By October 1949 members attended the board meeting of the ACHR in Washington, D.C.[189] Alpha men and the rest of the ACHR made efforts to push several civil rights bills, but to no avail.[190] That year's ACHR Report demonstrated Alpha Phi Alpha's commitment to racial equality and included the following:

1. Alpha Phi Alpha, as part of the ACHR, encouraged a new housing bill that supported FHA financing for middle-income groups—specifically, African Americans, who were discriminated against by the FHA.
2. Alpha Phi Alpha joined the NAACP to encourage improvement in the Fair Employment Board's approach to discrimination.
3. Alpha Phi Alpha worked with the President's Committee on Equality of Training and Opportunity in the Armed Services to address discrimination in the military. After the fraternity testified before the committee, several changes were made to the Navy and Air

Force, but not the Army, although the group pledged to continue its efforts as far as the Army was concerned.

4. The ACHR investigated the lack of African American participation in the federal Vocational Education and Apprenticeship Training program, which they believed to be a product of discriminatory hiring practices of the participating bureaus.[191]

5. Alpha Phi Alpha asked to help a group of African American members of the U.S. Park Police combat discrimination in employment and promotions within the police unit. After the fraternity took the matter up with the Secretary of the Interior, the issue was addressed and rectified.[192]

On other fronts, fraternity leadership urged members to cooperate and aid NAACP efforts and social campaigns. One example of such aid involved brother Billy Jones, who successfully fought alongside the NAACP for integration in the East St. Louis school system; he also took an active role in the local school discrimination cases.[193]

In New York, brother Thurgood Marshall lost his case in *Dorsey v. Stuyvesant Town Corporation*. Appellants were black tenants who had been denied the right to rent certain apartments by a certain developer in New York City. The appellees claimed that as a private corporation they reserved the right to decide who could and could may not rent apartments in their developments. The court considered whether a corporation organized under the Redevelopment Companies Law had the privilege to exclude black citizens from consideration as tenants. The appellants argued that Stuyvesant Town Corporation was subject to the restraints of the Equal Protection Clauses of the State and Federal Constitution and could not lawfully discriminate against by race or color. The court determined that the appellees, though receiving some state funding, could not be held to answer for their policy under the Constitution of the United States or of the state of New York. The aid was determined to not be sufficiently substantial enough to require action by the court. Thus, the judgment was affirmed.[194]

In Kentucky, brothers Marshall and Robert Carter, along with James Crumlin Sr. (Omega Psi Phi) and John Rose, litigated the case of brother Lyman T. Johnson in *Johnson v. Board of Trustees*. The case, brought before the federal trial court, involved a student who applied to the University of Kentucky's graduate program and was denied admission based on his race. The court found that "the refusal to admit plaintiff to the graduate school . . . solely because of his race and color constitutes a denial of rights secured under the Fourteenth Amendment."[195] Therefore, Kentucky's Day Law, banning whites and African Americans from attending the same school, was held unconstitutional because the basement set up by the university was not "substantially" equal.[196]

In a Kentucky federal court, brothers Charles Hamilton and Joseph Cornelius Waddy, along with Charles W. Anderson, prevailed in their case—*Salvant v. Louisville & Nashville Rail Road Company*. Salvant sought an injunction against the Louisville & Nashville Railroad Company and Brotherhood of Locomotive Firemen and Enginemen to enjoin them from further bargaining as his statutory representative. Salvant was a black resident of Mobile, Alabama, who was employed by Louisville & Nashville Railroad Company as a locomotive fireman. He brought this action as a class action on behalf of other black employees on the claim of jurisdiction under the Fifth Amendment, the Railway Labor Act, the Civil Rights Act, and the Judiciary Act. He worked under contract with his employer that was negotiated by the Brotherhood of Locomotive Firemen and Enginemen, as a representative of all members of the craft. Salvant filed a complaint with the Brotherhood that it was committed to eliminating black locomotive firemen from the railroad service. Salvant also sought an injunction pendente lite (awaiting the litigation), prohibiting negotiations proposed by a certain notice. The defendants filed a motion to dismiss on grounds of lack of jurisdiction. The motion for injunction pendente lite was sustained, and the defendants' motion to dismiss was overruled. The requested injunctive relief as to the railroad was denied, as the railroad was a public service corporation under obligation to run trains and serve the public. The railroad had no option other than to recognize the right of the union to bargain collectively or else it would have had to shut down, which was not an option. However, injunctive relief against the Brotherhood was granted to determine if the evidence sustained the allegations.[197]

Brother Marshall, in *Monk v. City of Birmingham*, prevailed before the federal trial court in Alabama. Mary Means Monk, the plaintiff in this class action suit, argued on her behalf and on behalf of any other black citizens of Birmingham similarly situated that certain zoning ordinances of the city were unconstitutional under the Fourteenth Amendment. The defendants were the City of Birmingham, James W. Morgan, a city commissioner, and H. E. Hagood, its building inspector. The sections of the zoning ordinance in question racially segregated certain residence districts. The ordinance made it a misdemeanor offense for a member of the prohibited race to move into the districts from which they were banned. The plaintiffs claimed that the zoning ordinances violated their right to use and occupy property solely based on race or color, as they already owned and paid for property in the prohibited district. Further, they claimed that the zoning and classification of the property was tantamount to its confiscation, and this threatened them with irreparable injury. Each of the plaintiffs owned a piece of real estate, purchased their property prior to the filing of the zoning ordinances, and was subject to the provisions of the zoning ordinance, and no black citizen including the plaintiffs would be permitted to occupy their property as a home or dwelling due to their race. The court found that the mere existence of the zoning ordinances deprived the plaintiffs of the free use of their property. As property consists of more than the thing the person owns and also includes the free use, enjoyment, and disposal of a person's acquisitions without control or diminution, save by the law of the land, the ordinance could not stand. Judge Mullins declared the ordinances unconstitutional.[198]

In Kansas, Marshall represented plaintiffs in *Webb v. School Dist. No. 90, Johnson County* who were the parents of black schoolchildren who had be reassigned to attend a new school in their district. This school was found to be unlawfully established, inadequate, insufficient, out of date, dilapidated, and not fit for learning. The district refused to allow the black students in question to attend the other school in the district, South Park Grade School, by claiming that they did not live in the district. However, it was found that the attendance areas were not divided by any reasonable means but meandered in such a way to force all black students to attend the dilapidated Walker School and all white students to attend the South Park Grade School. The differences in each facility were as follows: South Park Grade School had undergone a ninety-thousand-dollar reconstruction in 1947, while Walker School had no plans for renovation; Walker School had sanitation and fire hazards, while South Park Grade School was of the latest design and construction; neither school contained a gym, but South Park Grade School contained a large auditorium while Walker School had none; Walker School's playground equipment would be adequate if several missing parts were installed; no kindergarten existed at Walker School; South Park Grade School had both a lunch service and a kindergarten; Walker School had only two teachers while South Park had nine; the eight grades at Walker School were taught in two rooms, while South Park had a different room for each grade as well as a part-time music teacher, which Walker School lacked. Textbooks, teaching materials, and scholastic attainment were all judged to be the same. The bathrooms at Walker School were outside, while those at South Park were inside. The court ruled that the establishment of Walker School and its attendance areas were unreasonable and unlawful. The writ of mandamus to compel district officials to admit black students was allowed.[199]

In the Midwest, the federal court of appeals for the Sixth Circuit handed down its decision in *Whiteside v. Southern Bus Lines, Inc.*, a case litigated by brothers Carter and Marshall. The appellant, a black bus passenger, challenged the district court decision, which ruled the appellee bus company not liable. The appellant had been forcibly ejected from the bus she was riding from St. Louis to Paducah, Kentucky. She refused to move from her front seat to the rear of the bus and was then removed from the bus by the bus operator and a nearby police officer, whom the operator had enlisted for help. The appellant claimed that she was severely injured during this ordeal and lost several articles of personal property. The question for this court was whether the seating of passengers upon buses due to race and color imposed an undue burden on interstate commerce. The appellee bus company claimed that they reserved for themselves full control and discretion of the seating of passengers and reserved the right to change such seating at any time during the trip. The appellant challenged that rule as neither reasonable nor necessary for the safety, comfort, and convenience of its passengers and that the appellee had no legal or constitutional right to adopt or enforce it. Two previous decisions, controlling in this case, were *Hall v. DeCuir* and *Morgan v. Virginia*. The *Morgan* case reasoned that uniformity was

necessary for the functioning of commerce and that regulations desig-
nating seat assignments may be disturbing, particularly when they are
through territory where local regulations differ.[200] Thus, this court reversed the decision of the lower court and remanded to the district court
for trial.[201]

As 1949 came to a close, brother Belford Lawson reached out to Alpha
Phi Alpha brothers, requesting that they provide statements about their
experiences of segregation on the U.S. railways as part of the ongoing
Henderson v. U.S. case.[202] Lawson thought such statements would be
effective in conveying the "brutalizing and humiliating effects of this
type of public humiliation" to the court.[203] Specifically, Lawson solicited the aid of brothers Howard Hale Long, Rayford Wittingham Logan,
and Antonio Maceo Smith—Alpha's seventh, fifteenth, and seventeenth
general presidents, respectively. In a letter to Lawson, dated May 25,
1949, Logan—who was at that point a history professor at Howard
University—stated,

> Dear Brother Lawson:
> I am delighted to know that definite progress is being made with respect
> to the validity and reasonableness of the dining car regulations of the
> Southern railway. In response to your request I am submitting the fol-
> lowing statement which you may use in any way you deem best:
> Dr. Rayford W. Logan, officer of the United States Army in France in
> World War I, head of the Department of History at Howard Univer-
> sity, world traveler, author of several books and member of the United
> States, National Commission for UNESCO, states that the regulation
> which compels me to eat behind a curtain or partition in a dining car is
> the most humiliating and degrading experience in his entire life in the
> United States. He further states that by training and temperament it is
> impossible for him to be a communist but if there were any one thing in
> American society that would lead him to communism, it is the impact
> of the insult to his dignity as an individual arising from the dining car
> regulations.[204]

In a letter dated June 1, 1949, to Lawson, Smith—then a racial relations
advisor for the Federal Housing Administration—stated,

Dear Sir:

I understand that Alpha Phi Alpha Fraternity is prosecuting the case of Elmer Henderson v. United States, et al, in an effort to eliminate the vicious practices of Southern Railroads which require Negro passengers, who seek dining car accommodations, to be served at a table set off by curtain or partition. As one who travels extensively in the interest of the Government I wish to make some comments.

I have been exposed to these conditions many, many times and have never enjoyed equality in service at any time, while seated behind this curtain. Usually these four seats behind the curtain are occupied by whites because of overflow and congestion while there may be a single seat available elsewhere in the dining car. In the next place, the humiliating inconvenience and discomfort of such separate seats are not in use by whites during the early period of the meal, the dining car employees occupy them and leave them, usually, in complete disorder. Because of the discomfiture of such separate eating facilities on most Southern Railroads, many times I deny myself the privilege of a meal, rather than to engage in controversy with the Railroad employees in search of an available seat elsewhere in the dining car.[205]

And in a letter to Lawson dated June 11, 1949, Long—then an administrator at Central State University—wrote,

My dear Brother Lawson:
. . . I wish to advise that I have never eaten behind the curtain provided in dining cars which separate the tables where Negroes may eat from tables where all other human beings may eat. Several times I have had meals served in the Pullman car to avoid humiliation. At other times I have been fortunate enough not to eat at all rather than sit behind the curtain. I have talked to a goodly number of my friends and acquaintances who travel a good deal and I am advised in varying details that to them the separation by the curtain does something somewhat different from the other Jim-crow experiences they have had. In the first place, it seems so senseless that white persons should be satisfied to be served, by Negro waiters, food that has been cooked and prepared by Negro cooks but refuse to eat in the same car with other Negroes unless there

is some symbol of the inferior status imposed by circumstances over which Negroes themselves do not have control.[206]

These letters and others would ultimately be included in the petitioner's brief to the U.S. Supreme Court in *Henderson*.[207]

Alpha Kappa Alpha Sorority

In 1951 Alpha Kappa Alpha voted to continue supporting the ACHR for five years, and Alpha Kappa Alpha's supreme basileus, Laura Lovelace, called on all local chapters to adhere to and follow the "program targets set up for the year by A.C.H.R."[208] In her letter to the chapters, Lovelace stated that "efforts should be made at every opportunity to develop a readiness for integration."[209] Alpha Kappa Alpha's focus was to be on the creation and maintenance of a free and open housing market, and all legislative activity was to be aimed at ending the Senate rule that had led to the failure of the FEPC bill in 1950,[210] as the sorority worked to become "effective tools of human betterment on the local scene," and united "on the common cause of the rights of man."[211]

In 1951 local California ACHR councils began a letter writing campaign promoting a state FEPC bill,[212] and by September the National ACHR had gathered the support of many national leaders to appoint a "qualified Negro American to fill the post made vacant by the resignation of David Niles, administrative assistant to President Truman."[213] The director of ACHR urged Congress to "overhaul its legislative machinery" by creating standing Senate and House committees on civil rights; by revising Senate rules to eliminate the filibuster; by prioritizing elements of the majority party platform in Congress; and by developing a new system for the appointment of committee chairman.[214] By the end of 1951 ACHR had a list of eleven legislative and governmental objectives:

1. Passage of a Fair Employment Practice Act
2. Abolition of segregation and the assurance of equality of training and opportunity in the armed services
3. Passage of an anti-poll-tax bill and the adoption of any and all legislative and administrative measures to insure voting rights

4. Passage of an anti-lynching bill and the adoption of any and all administrative measures to end mob violence and protect the security of the person

5. Abolition of segregation in public transportation

6. Abolition of segregation and discrimination of all forms in the nation's capital

7. Passage of a Defense Housing Act with safeguards against discrimination

8. Passage of a federal aid to education bill with safeguards against discrimination

9. Revision of the cloture rule to eliminate the undemocratic filibuster in the U.S. Senate

10. Fair representation of Negroes and other minorities in federal appointments

11. Abolition of racial discrimination in immigration and naturalization[215]

By December 1951 the organization was almost three years old and had accomplished many notable things, including (1) helping to defeat the pro-segregation amendments to the Selective Service Act; (2) preventing the passage of a bill that would have interfered with the non-segregated swimming pool policy in D.C.; (3) successfully urging the president to appoint an African American to the advisory committee on the Point Four program; (4) continuously carrying out a campaign against segregation in the Army and making several recommendations that led to positive change in the Armed Forces; (5) supporting the successful suit *Henderson v. United States et al*, which outlawed discrimination in dining cars; (6) fighting for the passage of the National Housing Act, which contained features to help end discrimination; (7) joining other organizations to expand the Social Security Act to cover a greater range of workers; (8) striving (but failing) to pass the FEPC bill and other civil rights bills in Congress; (9) testifying before Congress on legislation involving minority interests; (10) helping to draft the executive order to prevent employment discrimination in defense industries and working to hold the president accountable to it; (11) participating in a conference with President Truman discussing the needs of African American citizens; (12) leading the movement for the appointment of a qualified African American as White House aide to the president; (13) striving to ensure full participation of African Americans and other minorities in defense programs; (14) joining other organizational leaders in working to further the employment of African American professionals; and (15) joining an amicus curiae brief in the *Thompson Restaurant* case, which led to a revived antidiscrimination ordinance in D.C.[216]

In 1952 ACHR threatened to pursue the *Smith v. Hotel Phillips* case, which was an important step in the "fight for equal accommodations for all persons in public places."[217] The ACHR also filed an amicus curiae brief in the *Thompson Restaurant* case, "which aims to validate the antidiscrimination ordinance in the District of Columbia."[218] In an attempt to combat the "confederate flag craze" that was "sweeping the country," the ACHR began a movement "to encourage the public to fly the American flag as a symbol of faith in ultimate victory of the principles of equality of citizenship for all without regard to race or color in the United States."[219] The ACHR submitted presentations to the platform committees for both the Republican and the Democratic national conventions and was successful in keeping the issue of civil rights "in the ascendancy in both parties."[220] Although ACHR considered the Republican platform to be a "step backward" from its plan in 1948 and the Democratic Platform to be an "advance over 1948," the group strove to remain bipartisan and urged its members to implore all African Americans to vote during this election, regardless of their presidential choice.[221]

Through the 1950s the ACHR continued to work both with government officials as well as through local actions within communities.[222] In early 1953 ACHR sent nine proposals to President Eisenhower, including (1) to appoint African Americans to positions of responsibility within agencies; (2) to strengthen the Fair Employment Board of the Civil Service Commission, which was created in 1949 with the purpose of eliminating "discrimination throughout the federal establishment"; and (3) to reconstitute and strengthen the committee on contract compliance within the Department of Labor, whose job it was to prevent discrimination by government contractors.[223] The ACHR also cooperated with other organizations as amici curiae in support of the plaintiffs in the *Bolling v. Sharpe* school segregation case from D.C., one of the cases that joined *Brown v. Board of Education*, the landmark case in which the Supreme Court outlawed segregation in public schools in 1954.[224] In response to *Brown v. Board of Education*, in June 1954 the ACHR created a pamphlet to help local councils as well as cooperating organizations implement the decision and integrate public schools.[225] Recognizing that this case was the result of legal efforts put forth by the NAACP, the council nevertheless urged its local counsel to "take all possible steps and even to adopt as a major project the implementation and proper execution of this great decision."[226]

Kappa Alpha Psi Fraternity

In December 1948 Kappa Alpha Psi would see an initial push toward becoming civically engaged nationwide. At a banquet in Windsor, Ontario, Kappa Alpha Psi member Dr. Martin D. Jenkins called upon his listeners to dedicate themselves to "programs of human welfare larger than the social interests of the average fraternity."[227] One of the ways that this manifested itself was in the authorization for the fraternity's affiliation with the ACHR.[228] On March 19, 1949, Kappa Alpha Psi's affiliation with the ACHR was authorized at the Thirty-Eighth Grand Chapter Meeting in Detroit.[229]

The ACHR was known as one of the organizations that worked to defeat the recent filibuster rule against civil rights in the U.S. Senate. Other affiliated Greek organizations included Alpha Kappa Alpha, Alpha Phi Alpha, Delta Sigma Theta, Phi Beta Sigma, Sigma Gamma Rho, and Zeta Phi Beta. The ACHR was established to garner the extension of fundamental human and civil rights to all citizens and worked through the U.S. Congress and federal government. The ACHR vigorously worked toward the passage of civil rights legislation and amendments to general legislation that would lead to benefits for all people sans racial distinctions. The legislative program agenda pushed for the passing of a fair employment practices bill that would enable equal job opportunities without discrimination, the anti–poll tax bill, the anti-lynching bill, and other civil rights measures presented in Congress. Other legislation for which ACHR advocated for nondiscrimination provisions included housing bills, repeal of the Taft-Hartley Act, and the Federal Aid to Education Bill.[230] Among the Kappa Alpha Psi members who would go on to serve in leadership positions were James E. Scott, selected in 1951 as board chairman, and Elmer W. Henderson, who served as executive director.[231]

Kappa Alpha Psi members were seen pushing for social justice on all fronts, even from their bully pulpits in higher education. On December 17, 1949, Martin David Jenkins was inaugurated as the seventh president of Morgan State College.[232] In his speech he addressed goals for students, which included "to know the history and status of the Negro people and the goals toward which they are striving; . . . to be free of racial and national prejudices and petty social intolerances."[233] Furthermore, he made his stance clear regarding segregation: "I oppose segregation because I reject, as any self-respecting Negro must, the basic assumption underlying all phases of racial segregation, namely, that Negroes are inherently and inescapably inferior to other racial groups in our population. . . . I oppose it because its practice deprives Negroes of occupational, educational and other civic benefits and has thus served both to depress the general level of accomplishment of the group and to deprive our society of the value of the accomplishment which might have been."[234] Additionally, he remarked, "As a psychologist, I know that a free people cannot be forced to change ingrained attitudes and behavior patterns overnight; but I also know that attitudes and practices can be modified, and that they sometimes change with startling rapidity."[235] He claimed that the path for African American youth was becoming lined with more opportunities, particularly in terms of education and acceptance into the University of Maryland's Law School and other private institutions within the state.[236]

Back on the legal front, Earl B. Dickerson litigated *United States v. Sacher* in 1950. The U.S. Court of Appeals for the Second Circuit considered whether the district court was justified in holding Sacher and other attorneys who had represented several alleged Communist Party members—among those members, an African American—in contempt for their conduct throughout the proceedings of their clients' trials. The court of appeals held that the district court was justified in most of its findings of contempt and sentences for Sacher and others.[237]

William Ming was among a group of lawyers also fighting for social justice in the courts; however, higher education desegregation was his focus. One of his cases was *Sweatt v. Painter*, which involved Alpha Phi Alpha member Heman Sweatt applying to the University of Texas Law School and being denied admission because he was African American.[238] The law school created a facility for African American students that did not contain the same amount of staffing, textbooks, facilities, or prestige as the white educational facility. The Supreme Court held that the educational facility provided to the African American students was not equal to that provided to the white students; therefore, the policy of the University of Texas Law School violated the Fourteenth Amendment's Equal Protection Clause.[239]

Kappa Alpha Psi member Leon Ransom continued his diligent civil rights efforts in 1949 through the case *Carter v. School Board*.[240] The class action suit was brought on behalf of all African American students of high school age residing in the county. The complaint alleged discrimination against African American students by the school board failing to provide them, solely on account of their race or color, with facilities and opportunities for high school education equal to those furnished to the white students. Plaintiff Carter was a student who attempted to register for certain courses at an all-white high school not offered at her all-black high school but was denied registration on account of her race. African American students were denied equal facilities for instruction and extracurricular activities by the school board as well as course offerings in comparison to those offered to white students in the same school district. The court went on to perform a point-by-point analysis of the two schools and stated that there was no discrimination in this case because students were afforded an equal educational opportunity at either school but did not decide the broader question of whether segregation alone constituted discrimination. The Fourth Circuit found that the plaintiffs had made a sufficient showing of the differences between the two schools to defeat dismissal but remanded the case for further proceedings at the district court.[241]

In *Carr v. Corning*, Ransom represented Marguerite Daisy Carr, who sought injunctive relief to permit the attendance of African American students at an all-white junior high school to guarantee them the educational opportunities, facilities, and equipment equal to those allegedly afforded white students. The dispute arose out of overcrowding in the all-black school that separated the students' class sessions into two sessions of four and a half hours per day, rather than the six hours required by statute. The court of appeals found that statutes providing for separation of races in schools of the District of Columbia did not violate the U.S. Constitution. The court of appeals found that the same treatment would have occurred had plaintiffs been white; therefore, no unconstitutional discrimination on the basis of race occurred.[242]

Also in 1950 the U.S. Supreme Court handed down a critical opinion in the fight to end racial segregation. The groundwork, however, began eight years prior. On May 17, 1942, Elmer Henderson traveled to Atlanta from Washington, D.C., aboard a Southern Railway train. Southern's policy was for whites to be served ahead of blacks at the tables reserved for blacks if the dining car had already been opened and there were no seats available at white tables. At the opening of the dining car on the evening of May 17, no black passengers immediately arrived for service. As such, the curtain was pulled back and white passengers were allowed to sit at the end tables (those generally reserved for blacks). When Henderson arrived neither of the end tables was vacant (though seats were available among the whites sitting at the colored table), yet the steward refused to seat him among the whites. The diner was filled continuously with passengers from the line, taking seats as soon as others vacated them, so Henderson was forced to wait. The steward offered to serve Henderson in his seat back in the Pullman car, but Henderson declined the service and waited to be seated in the dining car. By the time the dining car was removed at nine o'clock that night, Henderson had not been served.

The following October Henderson filed a complaint with the Interstate Commerce Commission alleging that Southern had "unjustly discriminated against him in violation of the provisions of Section 3(1) of the Interstate Commerce Act, 49 U.S.C.A. § 3(1), and Section 2, Par. I of Article IV of the Constitution of the United States, by failing to furnish him with dining car service equal to that furnished White passengers."[243] The Commission ultimately dismissed the complaint, finding that, among other things, although Southern violated the Interstate Commerce Act (ICA) by subjecting Henderson to "undue and unreasonable prejudice," Henderson did not sustain any compensable damages.

Following the commission's decision, Belford V. Lawson Jr. and Josiah F. Henry—members of Alpha Phi Alpha and Kappa Alpha Psi, respectively—brought suit in the U.S. District Court for the District of Maryland on Henderson's behalf.[244] Citing *Plessy*, the court recognized that "it has been repeatedly declared by the Supreme Court that race segregation by State law is not *per se* an abridgment of any constitutional right secured to the citizen."[245] The court further noted that by virtue of the Commerce Clause Congress has the power to prohibit segregation in interstate travel, but has not done so, choosing rather to limit section 3 of the ICA prohibition to more general "undue or unreasonable prejudice or disadvantage."[246] The court concluded that the service was not equal.[247] Accordingly, it dismissed the commission's order and remanded.[248]

Following the remand, Southern adopted new regulations for its dining cars that provided that one of the behind-the-curtain tables was reserved *exclusively* for black passengers. The Interstate Commerce Commission, in reviewing Southern's new policy, affirmed its prior findings. Accordingly, the commission dismissed the complaint, and Henderson again sued in federal district court to set aside the order.

This time, the court agreed with the Interstate Commerce Commission and dismissed Henderson's complaint. First, the court reestablished that racial segregation of interstate passengers is not forbidden by the U.S. Constitution, the ICA, or any other act of Congress. Additionally, the court agreed with the commission's determination that the regulation allotting only one reserved table was adequate. Finally, the court observed that the principle of segregation was approved by the Supreme Court and that the curtains were merely a method of carrying it into execution, something that was proper for the commission to determine. Accordingly, it concluded curtains were a reasonable means of segregation.[249]

Following the district court's dismissal, Henderson appealed directly to the Supreme Court.[250] On brief for Henderson were six attorneys, among them three Alpha Phi Alpha members (Belford V. Lawson Jr., Jawn Sandifer, and Sidney A. Jones Jr.), two Kappa Alpha Psi members (Earl B. Dickerson and Josiah F. Henry Jr.), and one member of Alpha Kappa Alpha Sorority (Marjorie McKenzie).[251] There were also six of counsels; among them, five were Alpha Phi Alpha members (Aubrey E. Robinson Jr., Edward W. Brooke, William M. McClain, Theodore M. Berry, and George H. Windsor).[252] Charlotte R. Pinkett was not affiliated with a sorority.[253] Their collective work, like that of the ACHR, highlights the significant ways in which BGLO members worked together to vindicate African Americans' struggles for social equality and civil rights. Alpha Phi Alpha lawyers' significant role in working with a

Kappa Alpha Psi member to bring an end to racial segregation was not by accident. This case was the only major civil rights case of the era not funded by the NAACP Legal Defense and Educational Fund.[254] Rather, it was funded and litigated by Alpha Phi Alpha.[255]

The court determined that its decision was largely controlled by its recent decision in *Mitchell v. United States*.[256] In *Mitchell*, a black passenger was denied a seat in a Pullman car, although he held a first-class ticket, the seat was unoccupied, and the seat would have been available had Mitchell been white.[257] Railroad regulations allotted a limited amount of "Pullman space" to black passengers; because the allotment was met, Mitchell was required to ride in a second-class coach.[258] The court held that the passenger had been subjected to an unreasonable disadvantage, as the railroad violated section 3 of the ICA.[259] Likewise, the court observed that Henderson was denied a seat in the dining car that would have been available if he were white.[260] As in *Mitchell*, the court concluded that Southern's regulation subjected passengers to "undue or unreasonable prejudices" in violation of the ICA.[261]

The court emphasized that the right to be free from unreasonable discrimination under the ICA belongs to each particular person.[262] The court observed that denial of dining service to *any* passenger based on Southern's segregation by race regulation imposed deprivation upon white and black passengers alike.[263] Its terse holding granted life support to *Plessy* in that the Constitution still permitted segregation, but *Plessy*'s foundation was severely weakened. *Henderson* demonstrated "separate but equal" was an "undue or unreasonable prejudice"[264] and could provide for dicta in the movement to overrule *Plessy*.

This decision, along with the *Sweatt v. Painter* and *McLaurin v. Oklahoma State Regents for Higher Education* cases,[265] decided on the same day as *Henderson*, initially cracked the legal foundation of racial segregation established in *Plessy*.[266]

In 1953 Kappa Alpha Psi awarded its own Dr. A. M. Tinsley the Laurel Wreath for his work with civil rights.[267] Tinsley worked for many issues on behalf of blacks, "including the equalization of black teachers' salaries with those of white teachers, litigation to increase the state voting strength of the black, and opening all state-supported colleges and universities to blacks."[268] That same year, during the Forty-Third Grand Chapter Meeting in Chicago, resolutions were made to enact the following laws: "[A] Fair Employment Practices Bill with enforcement powers; an Anti–Poll Tax Bill designed to remove the tax as a prerequisite for voting; a bill to outlaw segregation in interstate travel; an Omnibus Civil Rights Bill to strengthen the authority of the Department of Justice in the protection of basic rights of citizens."[269]

Omega Psi Phi Fraternity

In 1949, grand basileus Dr. H. T. Penn announced in a pre-Conclave address that Omega Psi Phi had pledged their support to the ACHR, an organization composed of seven fraternities with the goal to secure human and civil rights to all American citizens.[270]

Also in the late 1940s and early 1950s, Harold R. Boulware Sr. litigated a number of race cases.[271] For example, *Rice v. Elmore* arose when the Democratic Party in South Carolina refused to allow George Elmore, an African American, to vote in the primary elections.[272] The District Court for the Eastern District of South Carolina held that African Americans were entitled to vote in primary elections and enjoined defendants from excluding African Americans from the voting process.[273] On appeal, the two pertinent issues were whether the decree giving African Americans the right to vote in the South Carolina Democratic primary elections was valid and whether the corresponding injunction was binding.[274] The Fourth Circuit Court of Appeals held that citizens had a fundamental right to participate in the political process and affirmed the right of African Americans to vote in the South Carolina primaries.[275] Two years later the *Baskin v. Brown* case emerged similarly.[276] Resulting from the Fourth Circuit's ruling in *Rice II*, the South Carolina Democratic Party formed political clubs to control the primaries.[277] These clubs refused to admit African American applicants.[278] The District Court for the Eastern District of South Carolina subsequently granted an injunction against the South Carolina Democratic Party.[279] The Fourth Circuit Court of Appeals upheld the injunction by reasoning that political primaries were part of the election process, and therefore subject to constitutional mandates prohibiting racial discrimination.[280]

Around this time, Hayzel B. Daniels was also fighting for school integration.[281] In 1952 he litigated *Phillips v. Phoenix Union High School District*.[282] At the time, Carver High School was the only legally segregated high school in Arizona.[283] With the support of the NAACP, Daniels served as pro bono counsel.[284] In an initial ruling the Superior Court of Arizona provided that there was no legal authority for segregation at Carver High School and that "a half century of intolerance is enough."[285] Daniels and Finn went on to obtain a broader ruling in 1953 with *Heard v. Davis*, a case against the Wilson Elementary School District, which established that school segregation was an unconstitutional deprivation of equal protection under the Fourteenth Amendment.[286] Many believe that this ruling was pivotal to the development of *Brown v. Board of Education* because the Supreme Court requested a copy of Judge Bernstein's opinion before issuing its landmark ruling in 1954.[287]

In the 1950s Omega men were involved in eliminating official racial discrimination, and the Conclaves were dominated by support for social activism.[288] George L. Vaughn and Francis Morse Dent litigated *Shelley v. Kraemer* and *McGhee v. Sipes*, respectively, which eliminated the enforcement of racial restrictive covenants on real property in courts.[289] The notion to challenge the constitutionality of racial segregation itself—instead of inequality in facilities—was crafted by James Nabrit, Spottswood Robinson, and Oliver Hill.[290]

The issue in *Shelley v. Kraemer* was whether a private restrictive covenant that discriminates on the basis of race is constitutionally prohibited by the Fourteenth Amendment's Equal Protection Clause.[291] More specifically, the court considered whether a judicial enforcement of such a covenant is a violation of the Fourteenth Amendment's Equal Protection Clause. The facts of the joint cases involved private restrictive covenants that prohibited African Americans from owning title to or occupying the premises of the restricted land. In both cases, one from Missouri and another from Michigan, African Americans purchased properties on the restricted land. In the Missouri case the trial court denied the request of the other restricted property landowners on the grounds that the covenant had not become final. However, the Supreme Court of Missouri reversed the judgment of the trial court. In the Michigan case the African Americans who acquired title to the property were ordered to vacate their properties within ninety days by the Circuit Court of Wayne County; the Supreme Court of Michigan affirmed.

On appeal, the Supreme Court held that a private restrictive covenant cannot be a violation of the Fourteenth Amendment, but that judicial enforcement of such a covenant constitutes a state action and is, therefore, a violation of the Equal Protection Clause. Thus, restrictive covenants were rendered effectively meaningless. The court reversed both the Missouri and Michigan decisions. The court first reasoned that the acquisition, enjoyment, ownership, and disposition of property are among the basic civil rights intended for protection by the Fourteenth Amendment as a precondition to the realization of other basic civil rights and liberties. The court noted that the issue in these cases—unlike previous cases in which statutory discrimination on racial grounds was invalidated—dealt with private agreements and not statutory regimes. Thus, the court could not invalidate the agreement. Citing *Twining v. New Jersey*, however, the court stated that "the judicial act of the highest court of the State, in authoritatively construing and enforcing its laws, is the act of the state." Therefore, judicial enforcement of a racially discriminatory covenant is state endorsement of a discriminatory covenant and a violation of the Equal Protection Clause.[292]

In Arkansas, Wiley Branton fought to ensure the Supreme Court's desegregation principles were upheld in schools.[293] In a voting rights case, Charles Gomillion, president of the Tuskegee Civic Association, successfully challenged Alabama's gerrymandering process by which African Americans' voting rights were violated.[294] In Ohio, notable Omega men—including Charles P. Lucas, NAACP secretary; Charles V. Carr, councilman; Charles White, Common Pleas Court judge; and Harry Bonaparte, attorney—along with Chester J. Gray of the Ohio State Employment Service paved the way for a Fair Employment Practices Commission.[295] Contributing to the desegregation of public facilities in Ohio by winning cases before the Ohio Supreme Court were Steve Simmons, president of the NAACP Dayton Branch, and William Howard.[296] Bringing about the *Morgan v. Virginia* decision, which found bus segregation to be a burden on interstate commerce, Bayard Rustin was a leader in the "Journey to Reconciliation."[297]

The issue in *Morgan v. Virginia* was whether a Virginia statute requiring all common motor vehicle carriers (interstate and intrastate) to separate "without discrimination" the passengers on a racial basis was unconstitutional.[298] Failure to comply with or enforce the statute constituted a misdemeanor. The facts involved an African American woman who traveled by common carrier from Virginia, through Washington

D.C., and into Baltimore. Upon refusing to move to a seat designated for nonwhites, the appellant was arrested and convicted under the Virginia statute. The Supreme Court of Appeals of Virginia affirmed the decision. Virginia claimed the policy was necessary to "avoid friction between the races." On appeal, the Supreme Court reversed the conviction under the Virginia statute and held the statute invalid.[299] The court found that if the state statute "unduly burdens" commerce where uniformity between and within states is necessary, then the statute is invalid.[300] The court held that the state's rationale was invalid because it prevented uniformity between the regulations for interstate travel, under the authority of Congress, and that the Virginia statute unduly burdened interstate commerce because of the lack of uniformity to which the statute contributed.[301] Justice Burton dissented.[302]

Between the late 1940s and late 1960s, member James Nabrit litigated numerous cases in state and federal courts in an effort to vindicate African American rights.[303] In the U.S. Supreme Court case *Sweatt v. Painter*, Alpha Phi Alpha member Heman Marion Sweatt "filed an application for admission to the University of Texas Law School for the February 1946 term."[304] "His application was rejected solely because he is a Negro. . . . Petitioner thereupon brought this suit for mandamus against the appropriate school officials, respondents here, to compel his admission. . . . At that time, there was no law school in Texas which admitted Negroes." The state had been permitted to supply substantially equal facilities.[305] "At the expiration of the six months, in December 1946, the court denied the writ on the showing that the authorized university officials had adopted an order calling for the opening of a law school for Negroes the following February. . . . While petitioner's appeal was pending, such a school was made available, but petitioner refused to register therein. . . . The Texas Court of Civil Appeals set aside the trial court's judgment and ordered the cause 'remanded generally to the trial court for further proceedings without prejudice to the rights of any party to this suit.'"[306] The court held that "the Equal Protection Clause of the Fourteenth Amendment requires that petitioner be admitted to the University of Texas Law School."[307] "The judgment is reversed and the cause is remanded for proceedings not inconsistent with this opinion."[308]

The 1953 *Terry v. Adams* case, argued by Nabrit, was the last in a string of cases that ruled white-only primaries violated the Fifteenth

Amendment.[309] Qualified black voters in Fort Bend County sued the Jaybird Democratic Association, a group that had organized white-only pre-elections for county offices since 1889.[310] The winners of these pre-elections invariably won the subsequent official elections.[311] The Jaybirds claimed that they were not a political party governed by state regulation, but a voluntary club.[312] The court ruled, however, that the group still fell within the Fifteenth Amendment because it covers any election in which public issues or public officials are elected.[313] Thus, barring blacks from voting in the primaries is a violation of the Fifteenth Amendment.[314]

Many fraternity members volunteered on NAACP state legal redress committees that investigated allegations of discrimination, including Reuben Lawson and Willmer Dillard, Roanoke; Ernest Perkins, Baltimore; Harold Flowers, Arkansas; Charles Carr, Cleveland; Willard Brown, West Virginia; Amos Hall, Tulsa; Floyd Skinner, Grand Rapids; Z. Alexander Looby, Nashville; Herbert Tucker, Boston; Tucker Dearing, Baltimore; James Rowland, Harrisburg; George R. Vaughns; Thomas Neuson; Charles L. Wilson; Charles H. Matthews; Clarence G. Smith, president, Ohio Conference of NAACP Branches; J. McKinley Neal, Missouri House of Representatives; and Frederick Yates, Michigan House.[315] A leader in the Missouri fight for equality, Neal sponsored legislation to eliminate school segregation, establish a Fair Employment Practices Commission, and allow African Americans to serve in the Missouri National Guard.[316] In Illinois, Corneal Davis, a twelve-year veteran of the Illinois legislature, sponsored legislation to block state funding for segregated schools in 1949.[317] Similarly, former national executive secretary H. Carl Moultrie testified before the board of education and the board of recreation on the integration of the Washington, D.C., School and Recreation System.[318] In 1952 Moultrie also represented the NAACP in investigations of police brutality. Charles E. Williams, an attorney living in Washington, D.C., made several unsuccessful attempts to end racial segregation in Virginia restaurants during the 1950s.[319] However, he played an integral role in the desegregation of the American Bar Association of the District of Columbia by filing suit against the association in 1958.[320] Generally, in the arena of civil rights activism, Omega Psi Phi attempted to strike a balance between the social obligations of the national fraternity and those of its individual members.[321] While Omega Psi Phi, as a national organization, was less directly involved in the civil rights movement, many chapters and individual members fought fierce battles against racial discrimination and segregation through litigation and legal support.[322]

In *Davis v. County School Board*,[323] Omega Psi Phi member Oliver Hill represented multiple plaintiffs in a suit that would eventually join to become *Brown v. Board of Education*.[324] Dorothy E. Davis brought an action against the County School Board of Prince Edward County to prevent the separation of white and colored children in schools.[325] The District Court of the Eastern District of Virginia held that policies requiring separate teaching for colored and white children were not unconstitutional, but noted inequities in facilities, curricula, and buses furnished to Negro children and white children.[326] Therefore, the court ordered the school district to eliminate racial inequality in buildings, facilities, curricula, and buses.[327] The district court's ruling on the first portion of Davis's argument was later overturned by the Supreme Court as a part of *Brown v. Board of Education*.[328]

In 1953, Jesse N. Stone Jr. represented appellees in *Bryce v. Byrd*, where the central issue was that qualified African American voters in Louisiana's Bossier Parrish were denied the right to register to vote on account of their race or color.[329] According to the 1950 census, the parish's population was 40,139, with whites accounting for 26,227.[330] In total, more than 9,000 individuals were registered voters in Bossier, but none were individuals of color.[331] In placing an immediate injunction on the parish's voting practice, the court held that the registrar of voters, Mary K. Brice, had "discriminated against the colored voters," and violated the Louisiana Revised Statutes of 1950's Section 37 of Title 18 by failing to give any weight and consideration when qualified Negroes applied to register.[332] The court reasoned that Brice "made registration favorable beyond the average insofar as the white applicants be concerned; but, as to Negro applicants, she never has been of the thought or conviction that they should receive from the office of the registrar the same opportunity to become voters."[333]

Wiley Branton litigated the 1954 *Brown v. Board of Education* case,[334] which held that the segregation of children in public schools solely on the basis of race deprived minority children equal protection of the laws under the Fourteenth Amendment,[335] thus overturning the "separate but equal" doctrine announced in 1896 in *Plessy v. Ferguson*. The case was a consolidation of several cases throughout the country where minority children were denied admission to public schools on a nonsegregated basis. In reaching its decision, the Warren Court focused on the importance of education in society and the negative psychological effects of segregation on minority children. The court wrote that segregation generates "a feeling of inferiority as to [minority children's] status in the community that may affect their hearts and minds in a way unlikely ever to be undone." Thus, the Warren Court unanimously concluded that "separate but equal" in the context of public education is inherently unequal and violates the Equal Protection Clause of the Fourteenth Amendment.[336]

In *Bolling v. Sharpe*, another case litigated by Nabrit and decided on the same day as *Brown v. Board*, a group of black students challenged D.C. school segregation.[337] The black students were not admitted to a school that was attended by white students because of their race. They challenged the law under a violation of Due Process Clause of the Fifth Amendment. This case was distinguished from *Brown* because the Fourteenth Amendment, which binds states to equal protection, does not apply in the District of Columbia. The Fifth Amendment was used to defend the students' due process rights, but unlike the Fourteenth Amendment, the Fifth Amendment does not have an Equal Protection Clause. The court rectified this by stating, "The concepts of equal protection and due process, both stemming from our American ideal of fairness, are not mutually exclusive. The 'equal protection of the laws' is a more explicit safeguard of prohibited unfairness than 'due process of law,' and, therefore, we do not imply that the two are always interchangeable phrases. But, as this Court has recognized, discrimination may be so unjustifiable as to be violative of due process." Therefore, the court ruled that segregation is a violation of the Due Process and Equal Protection Clause.[338]

While these men were litigating cases, individuals like Jesse Champion Sr. fought for African American civil rights on a different front.[339] During the 1950s and 1960s Champion became a familiar voice on Birmingham radio as one of the first African American news announcers in the city.[340] Champion proved controversial at the time on radio in the Deep South.[341] He broadcast against racial segregation and developed a genius strategy that encouraged civic participation and activism over the radio.[342] He became a key source of information concerning civil rights events and helped pave the way for greater equality over time.[343] Champion was ultimately forced to leave the city by Birmingham's infamous Sheriff Bull Connor as a result of his actions.[344]

Aaron Henry was another Omega Psi Phi member who fought for civil rights.[345] After graduating from the Pharmacy School at Xavier University, Henry returned to his hometown of Coahoma, Mississippi, and, with his wife Noelle Henry, opened the only black-owned drug store in the area, Fourth Street Drug Store.[346] Many civil right activists gathered there.[347] During that time Henry organized a boycott of stores in the Clarksdale area that refused to promote integration.[348] He and seven others were arrested for conspiring to withhold trade, but the charges were reversed.[349] Later Henry was charged with sexual harassment, but that charge was also reversed.[350] Henry's boycott remained active—even after his pharmacy's windows were broken and his house was firebombed—until the Civil Rights Act of 1964 was passed.[351] Henry organized the local branch of the NAACP in Mississippi and then was elected president in 1959.[352] He also helped pass the Voting Rights Act in 1965 by establishing the statewide Council of Federated Organizations and hosting a "freedom vote," a mock election that taught African American voters how to participate in the actual U.S. elections.[353]

Delta Sigma Theta Sorority

In 1948 Delta Sigma Theta formed an affiliation with the ACHR, which organized black opinion on numerous legislative and policy implications and provided a unified opinion in favor or in opposition to these policies.[354] Delta Sigma Theta's work with the ACHR lasted for a decade and a half. In 1952 Delta Sigma Theta members attended the ACHR meeting in Cleveland, Ohio, where three thousand delegates from various fraternities and sororities represented their organizations. Many Delta Sigma Theta members held positions in the ACHR. Patricia Roberts Harris, a graduate from Howard University and an Alpha Chapter initiate, was in charge of ACHR's social action programs. Other prominent members of the sorority held positions as well, including Mae Downs, first vice president; Dorothy Height, vice president in 1952; and Bertell Wright, president in 1953 and 1954. In the early 1960s Delta Sigma Theta participated in the Student Emergency Fund created by the ACHR. The fund was designed to pay fines and bonds for those arrested during the civil rights movement. The fund supported a variety of activities, including helping to pay the tuition of the first North Carolina Agricultural and Technical students to participate in a sit-in.[355] Other student activists, such as Charlayne Gault, a Delta Sigma Theta member from Georgia who worked to integrate the University of Georgia, were supported by the fund.[356]

The ACHR had both short- and long-term impacts on Delta Sigma Theta's internal organization. Several sorority activities—formerly delegated to sorority committees—were now channeled through the intrafraternal council. While national programs were running smoothly and some of the internal structures were coordinated through the ACHR, the sorority focused on its next stage of development. The group took this time to reevaluate itself; the result was a more streamlined sorority structure. Delta Sigma Theta was a dedicated member of ACHR, but by the 1960s the sorority believed its resources would better support other organizations. The ACHR leadership agreed to disband the council in 1963 due to financial reluctance among its allies and pressure from the NAACP.[357]

Under the presidency of Jeanne Noble, Delta Sigma Theta produced a project manual for its Delta Five-Points Project. This manual "present[ed] suggested blueprints for project organization" for any of the points in the Delta Five-Point Project. The Five Points in the project were library services, job opportunities, community volunteerism, mental health, and international affairs.[358] It was intended that this project be a "flexible and expressive vehicle to confront and help eradicate the problems of the day."[359] Moreover, chapters showed creative approaches to motivate youth through job opportunity and library outreach programs; chapters also shared skills and goods through the Volunteers for Community Service.[360]

As Delta Sigma Theta chapters worked to combine civil rights, job readiness, and education efforts in their communities, their work was recognized and supported by the federal government. For example, Berkeley's chapter secured a four-thousand-dollar federal grant used to help motivate junior high school students toward college and future careers. A chapter in St. Louis received federal funding to assist with the costs of college entrance exams and college application fees for low-income students. Delta Sigma Theta members did not limit scholarship offers to only their membership. The sorority consistently provided money to young women looking to pursue studies overseas, such as Dorothy Maynor, a young woman seeking to conduct music and study in Europe.[361]

Kumari Paul was another young woman who received money from Delta Sigma Theta, in her case to study in India. Also, Delta Sigma Theta gave money to graduates of Lincoln and Virginia Union Universities to enable women to further their studies after graduation.[362] The sorority also supported efforts to increase literacy in underserved areas and schools. In 1950 the Delta Sigma Theta Bookmobile extended service in northwest Georgia as part of the West George Regional Library.[363] In 1956 Delta Sigma Theta gifted a sewing machine to a young woman from Ghana while she visited the United States. Once the young lady returned to Ghana, she reported that she had become a leader in African fashion and was wildly successful due to Delta Sigma Theta's donation. In 1959, under national president Jeanne Noble, Delta Sigma Theta sponsored Lucy Lameck, a young political leader of the Tanganyika African National Union who was working to promote women's rights in many of the new African nations.[364]

In 1951 the Urban League conducted a study to determine the prevalence of discrimination among downtown hotels and restaurants in Portland, Oregon. As a member of Delta Sigma Theta, Ellen T. Law volunteered to be a human "guinea pig" for the discrimination study. As a member of the study, Law visited restaurants and took notes about her dining experience. From that survey Oregon enacted a state law against discrimination in public accommodations in 1953; it was later broadened in 1957. These events led to the founding of the Civil Rights Division at the U.S. Department of Justice, which was established to replace the Fair Employment Practices Division in 1957.[365]

Ignited by student protests, the civil rights movement caught fire nationwide. Less than two years later, over 35 percent of Delta Sigma Theta's membership had participated in sit-ins. When conditions turned violent in Little Rock, Delta Sigma Theta president Jeanne Noble paid a visit to the city to survey the scene. She found numerous members active in the cause and attempting to maintain order among the more violent factions. Delta Sigma Theta chapters across the nation also continued to run advertisements in the *Arkansas State Press*—a pro–equal rights paper run by the husband of Daisy Bates that lost all of its funding during this time.[366]

Through the chapters' generous donations, the paper was able to stay afloat and continue business for a few more months.[367] Delta Sigma Theta women worked with "black families in Albany, Georgia, whose means of income had been cut off due to their efforts to obtain the right to vote."[368] Moreover, Delta Sigma Theta members in Albany were often in the middle of protest activities, which placed them at risk. The chapter president, Marion King, was attacked by police officers who knocked her to the ground as she delivered food to peaceful teenage protesters. King was six months pregnant and lost her baby as a result of the police attack.[369]

In 1953 Delta Sigma Theta sponsored a town meeting with Stanley High, editor of *Reader's Digest*, and Dr. Charles S. Johnson, the founder of the National Urban League's *Opportunity* magazine and president of Fisk University. The goal of the town meeting was to discuss the moral fabric of the community and determine whether it was eroding. The sorority held another town meeting in Detroit and discussed the role of race in America on an international scale. Both meetings served the purpose of providing knowledge and awareness to the community of problems Delta Sigma Theta believed needed attention.[370] The sorority also sponsored the Portland Conference on Counseling Minority Youth. The Delta Workshop directed attention to the less tangible—and some of the most fundamental—needs of Negro youth.[371]

Phi Beta Sigma Fraternity

At the 1948 Los Angeles Conclave Phi Beta Sigma decided to raise a special tax in support of the ACHR and "other civil rights expenses."[372] At the 1949 Conclave the fraternity passed a number of civil rights resolutions, among which were that "Brother [Ndame] Azikiwe's [president of Nigeria] program in particular and the African peoples' liberation movement in general be supported," "Social Action in general and the American Council on Human Rights in particular be supported," "Federal Aid to Education be urged on Congress," "the Civil Rights fight be pushed," "curbs on civil liberty by federal authorities (such as loyalty oaths and F.B.I. persecutions) be stopped," and finally "Washington, D.C. have home rule and its people citizenship rights."[373] At the 1950 New York City Conclave, and for the third year in a row, the fraternity donated twenty-five hundred dollars to the ACHR.[374] During this time the fraternity also closely followed independence movements in several African countries, including the Gold Coast (Ghana) and Nigeria. The famous sociologist and Phi Beta Sigma member John Gibbs St. Clair Drake stated, "Our interest in African independence is not a mere sentimental one. A number of free Negro African states will mean more black faces on United Nations Commissions; more black ambassadors in Washington to embarrass the Jim Crow system there; friends in international circles who can speak out, without fear, about the plight of the American Negroes. . . . We shall all profit by this."[375] Phi Beta Sigma's approach to civil rights was clearly international in addition to its focus on the United States.

In 1951 the annual Conclave was held in Birmingham, Alabama, led by national president Dr. Felix J. Brown.[376] At the 1951 Conclave the Resolutions Committee called for the governors of Texas and Florida to take immediate steps to put an end to the bombing of African American homes. Additionally, the fraternity asked Attorney General J. Howard McGrath to punish those responsible for the cruel bombings.[377] The fraternity made strong pushes for fair employment by lobbying Democrats and Republicans to do more than talk about the fair employment practice legislation and enact more laws that would make it effective by creating a Fair Employment Practices Commission.[378] The fraternity also called on Congress to pass legislation preventing segregation in the public school system and called upon the president to place qualified African Americans in "positions of counsel and responsibility."[379] The Resolutions Committee commended college presidents who would not let their teams play in racist contests and condemned the Sugar Bowl Committee for its Jim Crow attitude toward the game.[380] At the 1952 Conclave the fraternity again adopted anti-lynching resolutions, with the theme of "Full Democracy—Nothing Less."[381] It adopted several other resolutions, among them unqualified support for the NAACP, a call for the strengthening of the civil rights section of the Department of Justice and the enactment of fair employment practices, revision of Congress's investigative procedure and the McCarran Internal Security

Act, and establishment of a plan that would lead to the "granting of the just demands of the people of Africa for self-government."[382]

Additionally, in 1952 Phi Beta Sigma would become the only college fraternity listed by the Department of Commerce as having a well-defined program promoting better business.[383] That same year at the Richmond Conclave, the Bigger and Better Business Program gave a report encouraging African Americans to conduct their businesses so well that anyone would buy their products or services or have work done at their shops.[384] In 1955 Phi Beta Sigma witnessed how much their Bigger and Better Business Program had grown and how important it had become. The fraternity held a Bigger and Better Business Banquet at the Stratford Hotel, and it was so successful it reached an estimated half million people.[385] In addition to business, Phi Beta Sigma continued to emphasize the importance of education; the theme for the 1954 Conclave, held under the leadership of national president Dr. George L. Hightower, was "Education—The Key to Freedom."[386] The event was held in Norfolk, Virginia, in 1954 and featured more than six hundred delegates and collaboration with Alpha Phi Alpha in the presentation of a distinguished service award to Hulan E Jack.[387]

Zeta Phi Beta Sorority

After the end of World War II, Zeta Phi Beta members helped the federal government through the Housing Project, created by the efforts of Zeta Phi Beta member Georgia Johnson.[388] Zeta Phi Beta members conducted surveys to locate housing vacancies for war workers and registered the facilities with the National Housing Association of the United States.[389]

During the administration of Blanche Jackson Thompson (international grand basileus from 1939 to 1943), much of Zeta Phi Beta's philanthropy came in the form of financial assistance to local projects. In the 1940s Zeta Phi Beta members paid for a telephone, mirrors, and coats for an orphanage.[390] In 1942 the national organization sponsored Vacation School for girls aged four to fourteen years and raised over seventeen hundred dollars for a community center.[391] The Jacksonville, Florida, chapter purchased an artificial limb for a tenth grade girl with a peg leg.[392] Other chapters engaged in more common charity, such as distributing Christmas baskets to needy families.[393] In 1942 the Iota Zeta Chapter raised ninety dollars for a scholarship, and the Iota Alpha Chapter donated a hundred dollars to the Amanda Garrett Artificial Leg Fund.[394] Two years later the Psi Chapter raised over seven hundred dollars for Blue Revue, a program that gave needy kids glasses, and the Eta Zeta Chapter established a scholarship fund for the Louisville community.[395]

Under the administration of Lullelia W. Harrison (international grand basileus from 1943 to 1948), the Prevention and Control of Juvenile Delinquency project was developed. Lillian Fitzhugh, of the Beta Zeta Chapter in Washington, D.C., and Phyllis O'Kelly were appointed to direct the project. Based on the recommendations of attorney Tom Clark's National Conference on Youth in November 1946, the project included foster home care, youth conferences, vocational guidance clinics, Tinker Shops (workshops offering crafts to keep children occupied in wholesome activities), and youth groups.[396] After World War II, as concerns about juvenile delinquency rose, the Dallas Zeta Phi Beta chapter helped fund a study on this behavior.[397] Meanwhile, the Winston-Salem chapter helped with the Zeta Phi Beta's national project, the Prevention and Control of Juvenile Delinquency, by sponsoring a shoe bank that gave pairs of shoes to needy elementary schoolchildren.[398]

Over the years individual sorority members sacrificed their jobs and put themselves at great personal risk by pushing for equal pay with whites, equal job opportunities, and other equivalent treatment. Zeta Phi Beta members advocated equal recreational opportunities for black soldiers during World War II, among other acts.[399] Both sororities held membership in the National Council of Negro Women and the NAACP.[400]

In 1947 Zeta Phi Beta and Sigma Gamma Rho accepted Alpha Kappa Alpha's offer to join their lobbying project, the ACHR.[401] In 1952 both sororities joined their partner organizations at the ACHR's Joint Convention in Cleveland.[402] The conference produced a wide range of results including stimulating interest among membership of each Greek-letter society, demonstrating the willingness of Greek-letter organizations to join forces to fight for equality and justice and fostering cooperation between the six organizations.[403] Both sororities were involved with ACHR and participated fully in all of its programs.[404] For example, Zeta Phi Beta was heavily involved with the ACHR and adopted it as one of their national projects.[405] In addition, Deborah Cannon Wolfe of Zeta Phi Beta was elected vice-president of the ACHR at a 1960 Board of Directors meeting.[406]

The 1950s were marked by the challenges of desegregation and the Cold War. As governors blocked the doorways of schools to black students in the wake of the *Brown* decision, the Soviets took note and publicized American hypocrisy about freedom. Meanwhile, the Soviet Union launched Sputnik into orbit in 1957 and succeeded in both being the first country to enter space and scaring the daylights out of complacent Americans. The United States continued to move slowly on integration, yet sped to enter the Space Race.

During the same period Zeta Phi Beta was led primarily by teachers or social workers. Dr. Deborah Cannon (Partridge Wolf)—the first African American full-time professor at the City University of New York, visiting professor at Teachers College, Columbia University, and professor of education at Tuskegee Institute—took the helm.[407] In 1962 she would go on to be appointed education chief for the House of Representatives Education Committee.[408] Through that position Wolf was able to introduce Zeta Phi Beta to government participation on a higher level. She created an awareness of the influence of government and how to benefit from the political system.[409]

In a 1955 directive from Wolf, Zeta Phi Beta's international grand basileus at the time, she urged chapters to racially integrate membership to demonstrate the sorority's belief in integration in all areas of life.[410] In 1956 Wolf said, "This goal of integration should permeate not only our school life and activities but our sorority life as well. We must accept responsibilities that accompany this achievement, realizing always that integration, like democracy, is a great social achievement, not a legacy; therefore, it may not simply be inherited."[411] Article after article in the *Archon* highlighted Zeta Phi Beta members for being the first to present before specific integrated groups or for serving in completely integrated offices. For example, Zeta Phi Beta member Tommie Morton-Allen became the first black to graduate from George Peabody College in Nashville by earning her master's degree in 1955.[412]

In the late 1950s Zeta Phi Beta continued to push its community service and philanthropy efforts. In 1957 the Rho Zeta chapter sponsored a shoe bank for delinquent and underprivileged children.[413] The same year the Tau Zeta chapter awarded fifty-dollar scholarships to three high school graduates.[414] Alpha Phi Zeta awarded several hundred dollars in scholarships, while Shreveport's Zetas awarded three hundred-dollar scholarships to local high school graduates.[415] In addition, Alpha Eta Zeta awarded seventeen hundred dollars' worth of scholarships, and Alpha Chi Zeta awarded a two-hundred-dollar scholarship to Sybil Buckley.[416] The Midwestern Regional organization also gave Lesceilla Marie Webb and Phoebe Eloise Hall hundred-dollar scholarships.[417]

Sigma Gamma Rho Sorority

In the Jim Crow era black professional women engaged in socially responsible individualism that balanced private and public sphere responsibilities. Historian Stephanie Shaw examined these women "who stood for something" in her book, *What a Woman Ought to Be and to Do*.[418] Although some, if not many, of Shaw's subjects probably belonged to sororities, she did not examine these organizations. Zeta Phi Beta and Sigma Gamma Rho members, however, clearly saw themselves as part of this cohort of women. As educated women, they bore a special obligation to change the world for the better. Privilege brought responsibility. While Shaw's study stops with the 1950s, Sigma Gamma Rho and Zeta Phi Beta members saw the responsibility as being timeless.[419]

In 1950 Sigma Gamma Rho member Kate J. Hicks founded a Vocational Guidance Program in New York City. This program specialized in the area of vocational guidance and aimed at meeting the needs of the community.[420] The most significant engagement for both sororities, however, came in the late 1940s with their membership in the ACHR.[421] Its objective was to secure the basic human rights for all citizens, national and international, regardless of race, color, or creed; to urge passage of legislation for the good of mankind; and to oppose legislation detrimental to mankind.[422] This collaboration was undertaken by the grand basileus Lullelia W. Harrison and Ethel Ross Smith from Zeta Phi Beta and Sigma Gamma Rho, respectively. However, it was the administrations of Zeta Phi Beta's Nancy B. Woolridge McGhee and Deborah Cannon P. Wolfe (international grand basileus from 1948–53 and 1953–65, respectively) as well as Sigma Gamma Rho's Sallie Edwards Johnson, Edna Douglas, Lorraine A. Williams, and Cleo Surry Higgins (grand basileus from 1948–54, 1954–59, 1959–62, and 1962–63, respectively) that carried the initiative forward.

In 1947 Sigma Gamma Rho, like Zeta Phi Beta, accepted Alpha Kappa Alpha's offer to join their lobbying project, the ACHR, and by 1952 Sigma Gamma Rho joined as a partner organization.[423] Sigma Gamma Rho required its chapters to include ACHR's agenda into their activities.[424] In addition, members of Sigma Gamma Rho participated in ACHR's Workshop on Planning for Integration.[425]

Drifting Apart: The ACHR and BGLOs from 1954 to 1963

With *Brown v. Board of Education* decided in 1954, Jim Crow was toppled, at least under the formal law. What remained was to bring into effect and relief the impacts of segregating resources, power, status, and rights from African Americans.

By March 1954 the Committee on Evaluation released "The American Council on Human Rights: An Evaluation."[426] The committee's report consisted of "an objective appraisal of the organization's work" and was "measured . . . in light of our purpose—the elimination of racial discrimination and segregation in employment, armed services, international affairs, accommodations and transportation, and other areas of Civil Rights."[427] In keeping with this directive, the report was divided into three parts: the first focusing on the history of the ACHR, the second detailing the program and activities of the ACHR, and the third consisted of a summary and evaluation of the findings of the committee as well as recommendations to the ACHR. The discussion of the ACHR's program was further divided into five areas that the ACHR had focused on, namely lobbying efforts in Congress promoting the passage of civil rights legislation, an end to racial discrimination and segregation in housing, educational and public resources programs, the activities of the local councils of the ACHR, and the "how of the ACHR operation."[428] The results of the evaluation were presented at the annual board meeting in March 1954, which also saw the election of new national officers.[429]

Individually, Delta Sigma Theta members also worked to integrate public educational institutions. As a teenager, Daisy Bates met her husband Christopher, who was an experienced journalist. They married and moved to Little Rock, where they operated the *Arkansas State Press*, a weekly African American newspaper that championed civil rights. Bates also became president of her NAACP chapter in 1952. After the landmark *Brown v. Board of Education* decision, when school segregation continued in Arkansas, Bates and her husband used their media presence to report on these events. In 1957 Daisy Bates used her authority as NAACP chapter head and as a reputable newspaper publisher to help the famous Little Rock Nine become the first African American students to attend Central High School in Little Rock. On September 4, 1957, Arkansas governor Orval Faubus sent members of the Arkansas National Guard to prevent the Little Rock Nine from entering the school. Undeterred, the students had their first integrated day of school on September 25, 1957, guarded by U.S. soldiers sent by President Dwight D. Eisenhower.

Throughout the 1950s Omega Psi Phi helped World War II veterans find permanent employment through the Veterans' Welfare Committee. James M. Nabrit supervised the committee of district representatives who were responsible for providing veterans with employment information and working to place African Americans in employment with the Veterans Administration.[430] Additionally, the fraternity went on record in support of the Urban League's efforts to increase quality jobs for African Americans in the United States.[431]

When *Brown v. Board of Education* was issued, Sigma Gamma Rho members published a statement by black southern educators in support.[432] However, Sigma Gamma Rho members did not take this opportunity to publish a statement specifically from the sorority. Grand basileus Edna Douglas (serving from 1954 to 1959) later noted that she discussed the ramifications of the Supreme Court decision with integrated workshops of churchwomen, possibly referring to Church Women United, but she did not clearly state her view.[433] Because many Sigma Gamma Rho members taught in public schools, the sorority may have been in a bind. To express support for integration might imply that black schoolteachers were not as good as white ones and could also place members in difficult positions with respect to white-controlled, segregationist school boards in the South that firmly opposed *Brown*. Additionally, if all-black schools closed, black teachers were not likely to be hired by formerly all-white schools, thus eliminating the jobs of some Sigma Gamma Rho members. In 1955, in reaction to these educational challenges, the Zeta Sigma Chapter sent a financial contribution to the Committee for a Representative School Board, worked with the United Negro Organization and the Committee on Racial Equality, volunteered in the YMCA's Second Century Fund Campaign, and donated to the NAACP at its annual mammoth tea.[434]

In 1954 Sigma Gamma Rho expanded its 1940s successful Teen Towns project by adopting a new national project at the Twenty-Third Boulé. Honorary member Alma Illery was named supervisor of Camp Achievement, a forty-eight-acre campground outside of Pittsburgh, left to the National Achievement Clubs by a friend of Illery.[435] While Sigma Gamma Rho did not create the camp, the sorority pledged to provide financial support for Camp Achievement and to take an active role in volunteering at the camp.[436] Sigma Gamma Rho adopted the practice of providing a thousand dollars annually to the camp by 1956.[437] The sorority's efforts at Camp Achievement advanced Sigma Gamma Rho's involvement in social development of youths. Sigma Gamma Rho also showed dedication to youth development in other ways. For example, in 1958 the Kappa Sigma chapter sponsored a hundred and fifty children at their Christmas party and donated twenty-five dollars to the Red Shield club of the Salvation Army.[438]

In addition to conducting an internal review, the ACHR also conducted an external evaluation of sorts in the form of Elmer Henderson's tour of a plethora of states in various regions of the country. In early 1954 Henderson spent six weeks visiting South Carolina, Georgia, Kentucky, Mississippi, Texas, Missouri, California, Colorado, Nebraska, Illinois, New York, and New Jersey. He spoke with hundreds of individuals from all walks of life regarding issues such as housing, employment, and civil rights. Significantly, Henderson noted "all over the south there is a belief among both Negroes and whites that an end to segregation is inevitable regardless of the outcome of the present school cases before the Supreme Court." He also observed "a growing political consciousness among Negroes and a determination to act independently."[439] Henderson made a full report of his findings to the ACHR board at the annual board meeting in March 1954.

In addition to the 1954 *Brown* decision, the U.S. Supreme Court ruled in *Bolling v. Sharpe*.[440] In *Bolling*, a case litigated in part by Kappa Alpha Psi member George Edward Chalmer Hayes, the court ruled that although the Fourteenth Amendment's Equal Protection Clause applied exclusively to the states to prevent segregation in state public schools, the District of Columbia was subject to the Fifth Amendment of the U.S. Constitution. The Fifth Amendment's Due Process Clause was not interchangeable with the Fourteenth Amendment's Equal Protection Clause, but the court found that the discrimination prohibited by the Fourteenth Amendment also violated the Fifth Amendment's Due Process Clause. The court reasoned that segregation of schools in the District of Columbia did not serve a reasonable government interest and posed an undue burden on citizens. Therefore, the court held that the Fifth Amendment required desegregation of schools in the District of Columbia based on the Due Process Clause.[441]

Despite the effort put forth by both the fraternity and its members, ultimately this avid engagement would be threatened. During the Forty-Sixth Grand Chapter Meeting banquet, the fraternity's leading and significant role in the ACHR was questioned when it seemed that the members at the Grand Chapter Meeting would not vote to continue membership. However, because of the advocacy of Kappa Alpha Psi member James E. Scott and other proponents of the program, the fraternity voted to continue membership in the council. The fraternity was not uninterested in the fight for civil rights; however, it was gradually realizing the need for critical self-examination and improvement within the fraternity. Reform for Kappa Alpha Psi was inevitable, and the new image for the organization was being created.

Interest in the ACHR continued to wane, and in its Forty-Seventh Grand Chapter Meeting banquet, the fraternity voted to discontinue membership in the council. This was the tipping point for the unrest and great discontent that had been growing for several years within the ACHR. Following this meeting, interest in the ACHR waned and membership dropped. The fraternity emphasized that it was not uninterested in the rights of all peoples; instead, its decision was motivated by the fact that the fraternity spent large sums of money in its affiliation with the ACHR, which it believed might be better "used in support of other national civil rights organizations."[442] Kappa Alpha Psi had been a proud participant in the ACHR for eight years and had provided significant support. Though the national organization discontinued its official membership in the ACHR, the fraternity did not prohibit its individual chapters from participating with the ACHR on a local basis or from giving financial support to the council. Indeed, individual members pressed on in the fight for civil rights. By way of example, in 1955 Ralph David Abernathy and his close friend and Alpha Phi Alpha member Dr. Martin Luther King Jr. cofounded the Montgomery Improvement Association, an organization that would go on to lead the Montgomery Bus Boycott.[443]

By 1955 the ACHR had revamped its campaign to energize voters around civil rights issues for the 1956 general election. Many resources were made available to voters wanting to become more proactive in local, state, and federal politics: such as the "Political Action Handbook" published by the Friends Committee on National Legislation in 1955. This handbook detailed many ways to effectively participate in the political process, mainly through working with organizations on local and national levels, joining a political party, voting, and maintaining communication with elected officials on subjects of interest. The handbook also provided practical guidance on contacting elected officials and information on legislative processes, as well as aspects of Congress such as the respective roles and areas of influence of various House and Senate committees.[444]

That same year the resolutions for Phi Beta Sigma's 1955 Conclave focused on not only education, in terms of the need for federal aid and desegregation, but also housing and equal opportunity in employment as well as ongoing resolutions relating to de jure segregation and civil rights, most importantly suffrage. The National Social Action program was the focus of Phi Beta Sigma's efforts to achieve improvement in the areas listed and had as its theme for 1956 "Full-Fledged Freedom for Every American Citizen."[445]

Also in 1955 Delta Sigma Theta implemented the Delta Volunteers for Community Service program, in conjunction with the Five-Point Project. The Five-Point Project was designed to motivate Delta Sigma Theta chapters to become more involved in their community and increase volunteerism with Delta Sigma Theta partners like the YWCA, American Red Cross, National Urban League, Girl Scouts of America, and National Community Chest and Councils. As part of the mental health initiative for the Five-Point Project, Delta Sigma Theta chapters throughout the Midwest raised money to provide radios, television sets, toiletries, games, and magazines to local mental health patients. Many chapters also held informative sessions on mental health to provide the public with knowledge of what remains a shrouded problem.[446]

Under the goals of the Five-Point Program, Delta Sigma Theta also established the Southern Regional Project, an endeavor led by Cecil Edwards designed to improve services to children with impaired hearing. Delta Sigma Theta members located in Atlanta—the site of the Southern Regional Project—contributed to the programs by helping the specialists involved and running the center's day-to-day needs. Continuing its programs in the South, Delta Sigma Theta began the Ride the Winged Horse program in Tuskegee, Alabama. The program was designed to foster good reading habits in area children; the local Delta Sigma Theta chapter ran the entire program. This program eventually spread to chapters in St. Petersburg and Bradenton, Florida, where the local chapters would continue to run the program.[447] Delta Sigma Theta continued to make notable strides in literacy and education with support and services related to education as one of the primary community service activities.

Delta Sigma Theta possessed a large national influence as well. The newly created International Project, a part of the Five-Point Program, grew significantly. In 1955 Hurricane Hazel hit Haiti and caused millions of dollars' worth of damage. Delta Sigma Theta had recently established a chapter there and felt the need to contribute. The sorority sent a thousand dollars to the heavily damaged village of Jeremie to provide tools, sewing machines, food, and other necessities. The economic level of the village was raised so much by this donation that Delta Sigma Theta was not allowed to give any more money to the region for fear of unbalancing the region.[448]

Under the administration of Edna Douglas, Sigma Gamma Rho also continued their scholarship awards for high-achieving women. In 1955 the Kappa Sigma Chapter of Sigma Gamma Rho awarded Jacqueline Scott a scholarship so she could attend Howard University. This same year the Alpha Nu Sigma chapter awarded Mahalie Poteat a seventy-five-dollar scholarship.[449] Additionally, the Beta Sigma chapter awarded Stella Marie Baker a scholarship to attend Alabama State, the Rho Sigma chapter gave Constance Halliburton and Charlesetta Andrews scholarships, the Eta Chapter awarded Sigma Gamma Rho member Gloria Wells a scholarship, and the Alpha Nu Sigma chapter awarded Minnie Dixon a scholarship.[450]

By 1955 Omega Psi Phi's philanthropic work, limited by financial resources, consisted mainly of donations to national lobbies and scholarship efforts. Omega Psi Phi supported many national organizations in their work for equality. Much of this support was financial. For example, under the sixteenth grand basileus, Albert Dent, the fraternity contributed its first five-hundred-dollar lifetime membership in the NAACP.[451] Between the years 1955 to 1959 Omega men provided thirty-six thousand dollars to the NAACP in lifetime memberships. By supporting organizations such as the NAACP, Omega Psi Phi intended to avoid wasteful spending and to cut down on duplicating uplift efforts.[452]

These individual efforts were having an effect on the ACHR. By early 1955 the ACHR experienced "depletions in membership and finance," and Alpha Phi Alpha left the organization.[453] Focusing on three areas of concern, "(1) strengthening and improving human resources in staff personnel; (2) increasing financial support; and (3) reactivating and expanding the program of the Council in necessary areas, particularly with reference to grass roots participation,"[454] the Council's Board of Directors strove to increase its membership numbers.[455] The results were positive: Alpha Phi Alpha voted to reconsider its withdrawal, Zeta Phi Beta voted to continue its support through 1956, and, in 1956, Kappa Alpha Psi voted to continue its support as well.[456] Success was also found in expanding the council's grassroots participation,[457] but by 1956 the organization was still not seeing the financial gains it wanted.[458] In response, the council began to discuss new ways to increase financial support without relying on memberships.[459]

The year 1956 saw an increased push by the ACHR behind campaigns such as the Registration and Vote Campaign, an initiative backed by the ACHR's board of directors' slogan, "Your Vote Is Your Voice."[460] At its annual meeting in March 1956, the Board of Directors reaffirmed its campaign to get sorority and fraternity members registered to vote. To aid this effort the board released a booklet, "Getting Out the Vote in 1956," and distributed it to over two hundred fifty sorority and fraternity chapters in sixty cities. The board also called upon Congress to enact legislation protecting the right to vote and voter registration.[461] The ACHR joined several other organizations in successfully encouraging Congress to reject the Daniel-Mundt-Thurmond proposal to change the electoral college system. Although ACHR recognized that a change in electoral system was needed, this proposed legislation would have been "a vote against civil rights" and a "step away from democracy."[462] In an attempt to get the Citizens Councils and other Klans under congressional scrutiny, the Washington Alumni Chapter of Kappa Alpha Psi sent a letter to Representative Scherer of Cincinnati urging investigation of the councils. ACHR's campaign to get the House Un-American Activities Committee (HUAC) to investigate the councils had not met with success.[463]

A new ACHR director, John T. Blue Jr., was appointed in 1956, assuming duties on June 1.[464] The Spring 1956 *ACHR Bulletin*, now renamed *ACHR and Equality*, featured stories on the ACHR's efforts to increase voter registration and awareness of civil rights issues. In particular, the Board of Directors released a booklet titled "Getting Out the Vote" in early 1956 in preparation for the November 1956 elections.[465] The bulletin also reported on developments within the organization such as meetings held with local councils, contact with various government officials, the unanimous reelection of Dr. Nancy McGhee as president of the Board of Directors of the ACHR, and member sorority Alpha Phi Alpha's establishment of a commission to study the efficacy of the ACHR. Furthermore, the bulletin also featured a piece intended to increase its readers' awareness of measures they could take in order to fight racial discrimination: the Voluntary Home Mortgage Credit Program to fight loan and housing discrimination, the President's Committee on Government Employment Policy to report employment discrimination for government employees, and the Committee on Government Contracts for government contractors who are discriminated against.[466] The ACHR served as a liaison and sponsor for those who wished to file complaints.[467] The Board of Directors also made a concerted effort to centralize the goals and leadership of the ACHR, holding dozens of meetings with local council leaders and other Greek organizations.[468] Finally, the Spring 1956 bulletin lauded the "substantial" gains made in moving civil rights bills toward passage, many of which were successfully cleared by the House Judiciary Committee and were held in the House Rules Committee; this legislation would represent "substantial gains" in the civil rights movement if passed.[469]

Following its October 1956 board meeting, the ACHR submitted a list of problems, including the fact that school desegregation was "being denied citizens by threats, violence, and deceits,"[470] as well as the fact that there was a "continued policy and practice of racial discrimination in housing finances and urban re-development."[471] In response, the council urged the president to "put the full force of the Executive Offices behind school de-segregation," and to establish "a President's Committee on Fair Housing" for the "express purpose of eliminating segregated housing."[472] Additionally, in 1957 the council hosted a National Workshop on Leadership Responsibilities and Techniques, focusing on "(1) newer problems in racial discrimination; (2) techniques in the solution of these problems; and (3) the transition from desegregation to integration."[473]

In the midst of these activities, Omega Psi Phi member Oliver Hill represented plaintiffs in *Thompson v. County School Board*[474]—a suit to enjoin a county school board and superintendent from denying African American children access to Arlington County schools despite *Brown v. Board of Education*.[475] The district court granted the injunction, but defendants appealed to the Fourth Circuit, which upheld the district court's ruling.[476] Despite initial injunction, the school board continued to deny the seven children from the initial lawsuit access to the Arlington schools pursuant to Virginia's Pupil Placement Act.[477] Plaintiffs then asked for a supplemental decree to direct admission of qualified students into white schools despite the school board's rejection.[478] The district court granted the plaintiffs' supplemental decree because "although the school representatives believed they were following the law under the Pupil Placement Act, the injunction is paramount in the present circumstances and the schools can no longer refuse admittance to the plaintiffs."[479] On a second appeal to the Fourth Circuit, the district court's ruling was affirmed.[480]

Oliver Hill then argued for the plaintiff in *NAACP v. Patty*.[481] The NAACP originally brought this action against the attorney general of Virginia alleging irreparable injury through enactment of Chapters 31, 32, 33, 35, and 36 of the Virginia Assembly Acts. The enactments infringed on rights under the Fifth and Fourteenth Amendments, and petitioners sought an injunction against the statutes enforcement. Chapter 32 involved activities relating to the passage of racial legislation, advocacy of "racial integration or segregation," and the expenditure of funds in connection with racial litigation.[482] "Declaring that the continued harmonious relations between the races are essential to the welfare, health and safety of the people of Virginia," the chapter finds it "vital to the public interest" that registration be made with the State Corporation Commission by "persons, firms, partnerships, corporations and associations whose activities are causing or may cause interracial tension and unrest."[483] Chapter 35 is a "barratry" statute defined as "the offense of stirring up litigation."[484] The district court held Chapters 31, 32, and 35 unconstitutional and permanently enjoined their enforcement against the NAACP.[485] Chapters 33 and 36, on the other hand, the court unanimously found vague and ambiguous.[486] "It accordingly retained jurisdiction as to those Chapters, without reaching their constitutionality, and allowed the complaining parties a reasonable time within which to obtain a state interpretation."[487] The Supreme Court, in a subsequent decision, held that the district court should have abstained from passing on the validity or constitutionality of the Virginia statute until Virginia courts had an opportunity to construe the statute as they saw fit to protect the independence of the state courts.[488]

With these legal endeavors afoot, the ACHR published a specific list of target aims for achievement in the January 1957 issue of *ACHR and Equality*.[489] These aims included amending Senate Rule 22 (which would make it more difficult to filibuster civil rights bills), "seeking legislation that makes Federal aid to schools . . . available only to school districts that do not segregate by race," and urging President Eisenhower to establish a President's Committee on Fair Housing.[490] The ACHR's member Greek organizations were largely successful in getting citizens registered to vote for the 1956 elections.[491] Local council activities, such as the voter registration efforts of the local Atlanta council, were highlighted, and in order to motivate members, this issue of *ACHR and Equality* contained a detailed list of things to *not* do in order to keep the local councils running (for example, not attending meetings, not offering input, not paying dues, etc.).[492]

Members and staff of the ACHR continued to press the reelected president Eisenhower and his administration on matters of employment discrimination, continuing demands declared years earlier to take desegregation steps further and permanently end all employment discrimination.[493] In this vein the issue also reported on interactions between the ACHR and government officials such as Dr. Ross Clinchy, director of the President's Committee on Government Employment Policy. At

the semiannual board dinner in October 1956, Dr. Clinchy addressed
the ACHR Board of Directors in reference to the progress made by the
Eisenhower administration and the challenges that remained regarding
equal opportunity in employment.[494] Furthermore, members of Kappa
Alpha Psi met with President Eisenhower's cabinet secretary, Maxwell
Rabb, in a meeting arranged by the ACHR to express their support for
civil rights aims such as integration in schools, voting rights, and an end
to racial discrimination in housing.

The Civil Rights Act of 1957 was signed by President Eisenhower on
September 9, 1957. ACHR lobbied extensively, with the director visiting
members of Congress almost daily. In addition to the director's lobbying efforts on Capitol Hill, ACHR orchestrated a letter writing campaign
and numerous press releases. ACHR urged that civil rights not be limited to protecting voting rights, and that the right to trial by jury was un-
necessary in the civil rights legislation. The Civil Rights Act of 1957 also
authorized the creation of a Civil Rights Commission and appointment
of an additional attorney general to aid in prosecution of civil rights
violations.[495]

The Winter 1957 issue of *ACHR and Equality* also featured an expanded legislative program for the ACHR for 1958. "The Committee
voted to support a wide range of legislative proposals and to have persons representing ACHR to testify at every hearing on civil rights legislation or on legislation in any way affecting the Negro."[496] The legislative
agenda for the ACHR included the following ten items:

1. Amendment of the Civil Rights Act of 1957
2. Federal aid for scholarships for minorities, particularly for scientific study
3. Federal aid for school construction (particularly the Powell
   Amendment, which denies aid to school districts refusing to
   integrate)
4. Udall bill on school integration (aids school districts seeking to
   integrate)
5. ACHR Bill on School Aid (ACHR's own bill to extend federal aid
   to school districts that lose their state aid when and because they
   integrate)

6. Housing (particularly public housing, redevelopment, slum clearance, urban renewal)
7. Hospital construction, appropriation, and other federal aid
8. Amendment of the Senate Cloture Rule (Rule 22)
9. Rural libraries (funding for libraries that do not discriminate against patrons based on race)
10. Investigations of Citizens Councils, the Ku Klux Klan, etc.[497]

Despite these endeavors, by 1957 Alpha Phi Alpha had still not rejoined the council.[498] Still, the ACHR pressed on.

In the midst of these activities, future Omega Psi Phi member Ernest G. Green became one of the African American students known as the Little Rock Nine in 1957.[499] He and eight other students integrated Little Rock's Central High School in the shadow of the *Brown v. Board of Education* case. Green then became the first black student to graduate from the racially desegregated Little Rock High School.[500] He would go on to work toward improving civil rights.[501] While advocating for racial equality, he became director of the A. Philip Randolph Education Fund and assistant secretary of labor during the Carter administration.[502] He also served on the Council on Foreign Relations.[503] Green was a recipient of a Congressional Gold Medal, along with the rest of the Little Rock Nine, given by President Bill Clinton for their contributions to security, prosperity, and racial equality in society.[504]

In 1958 the ACHR voted to support legislation that would allow the Justice Department to act on "behalf of parents seeking to enter their children in a school," and to act on "behalf of any person denied his civil rights."[505] That same year the Washington, D.C., ACHR council compiled and released a guide detailing the nonsegregated public accommodations available in the city.[506] This list of accommodations ranged from hotels to transportation and recreation, from barber shops to restaurants and schools; this bulletin was meant to highlight the nonsegregated amenities available in the city and to support the businesses that had embraced civil rights gains. The bulletin made a point of noting "the law is on our side," and that one could expect cooperation from the metropolitan police department in enforcing the laws regarding integration in public facilities.[507]

Such employment and housing changes in the post–World War II era brought new demands for women. In the new bedroom communities outside of the city, black men often spent most of their waking hours away from their homes and communities. As Sigma Gamma Rho member Gwen Cherry would go on to state in 1959, "If the community is to have good schools, responsible local government, the cultural advantages of public recreation areas and local libraries, and information on aspects of the world beyond the local community, women through their organized activities will have to work for these ends and bear the brunt of the load."[508] That same year Zeta Phi Beta joined the new Committee to Salvage Talent in response to an invitation by a biracial group of prominent Americans, including singer and Alpha Kappa Alpha member Marian Anderson, baseball executive Branch Rickey, and Senator John F. Kennedy. In the midst of the Cold War, loss of talent had national security implications. The committee, focused on New York City, Washington, D.C., and Philadelphia, aimed to encourage black youth to enter higher education by providing guidance and financial aid. Citing an educated population as "our most valuable resource for assuring national growth and survival," the committee observed that the "largest known loss occurs among racial minorities whose economic and cultural handicaps—compounded by poor schools—lessens ambition."[509] While forming 10 percent of the U.S. population, blacks represented only 1 percent of the students in interracial colleges. Zeta Phi Beta members, already experienced in locating young women of promise, now also searched for bright young men to push toward college.

On top of pursuing basic necessities, civil rights activism was not lost. Sigma Gamma Rho participated in a 1958 ACHR board meeting where member Emma Manning Carter was elected president.[510] The respective national presidents went on record to support the student sit-ins.[511] They asked local chapters to immediately cancel plans for formal dances and hold a fund-raiser instead to send proceeds to the ACHR's Student Emergency Fund. The money would go toward paying fines, bails, and aid to students arrested for peaceful protest demonstrations.[512] Members were also asked to send the money that they would have spent on a spring hat to the fund. (Earlier generations of black women placed great importance on hats, so this was not a frivolous request by any means.)[513] However, unlike civil rights activism, philanthropy came with fewer risks for sororities.

Fraternity members, like Omega Psi Phi member Wiley Branton, litigated *Cooper v. Aaron* in 1958, which held that the states were bound to obey the court's order in *Brown v. Board of Education* to end racial segregation in public schools.[514] While the Little Rock District School Board was working toward desegregation, the Arkansas General Assembly adopted a state constitutional amendment opposing desegregation and relieving schoolchildren from compulsory attendance at racially mixed schools. Additionally, on the day before minority students were to integrate into Central High School, the governor dispatched the Arkansas National Guard and "placed the school 'off limits' to colored students." Due to this opposition from the Arkansas government and public hostility, the school board and superintendent of schools filed a petition to postpone their program for desegregation. Despite the board's good-faith intentions, the court rejected its request for postponement. Citing *Marbury v. Madison*, the court noted that its interpretation of the Fourteenth Amendment in *Brown v. Board of Education* is the supreme law of the land and binding upon the states.[515] Therefore, the board had to effectuate its plan for desegregation.[516]

Also in 1959 Branton litigated *Aaron v. McKinley*.[517] The case arose out of a subsequent attempt by the governor and General Assembly of Arkansas to preserve racial segregation in public schools and evade the Supreme Court's rulings in *Brown v. Board of Education* and *Cooper v. Aaron*.[518] At issue were Acts 4 and 5, which were passed in 1958.[519] Act 4 closed all of the senior high schools in Little Rock,[520] which were to remain closed unless a majority of qualified electors of the school district voted in favor of integration in an election called by the governor.[521] Act 5 complemented Act 4 in that it withheld government funds from the closed school and diverted them to other public and nonprivate schools attended by students from the closed schools. While the Arkansas Supreme Court concluded that both of these acts were constitutional, the district court concluded that, particularly in light of the Supreme Court's recent decisions, Act 4 was clearly unconstitutional under the Due Process and Equal Protection Clauses of the Fourteenth Amendment.[522] Because Act 5 depended upon Act 4, the court effectively invalidated Act 5.[523]

In order to elaborate further upon the nature of the ACHR and its activities, the Publications Committee of the ACHR released "The American Council on Human Rights: What It Is and How It Operates."

The brochure, published in December 1959, described the ACHR as "a cooperative Social Action program of five major sororities." It discussed the founding of the organization as well as its goals and objectives, and provided answers to a series of "Frequently Asked Questions." Finally, it explained the structure and activities of the ACHR, outlined the organization's plans for 1960, and listed the officers and members of the board of directors at the time. The year 1959 also saw the formal addition of national sorority Phi Delta Kappa to the national council of the ACHR,[524] but both Kappa Alpha Psi and Phi Beta Sigma had left, leaving only the Alpha Kappa Alpha, Delta Sigma Theta, Phi Delta Kappa, Sigma Gamma Rho, and Zeta Phi Beta sororities.[525]

ACHR's Fourth Annual Workshop was held in October 1960 and approximately five hundred participants from diverse regions of the country attended. The theme was "A Political Primer for 1960—Education-Understanding-Action," and senator and soon to be president-elect Kennedy was one of the consultants. The participants voted to "unanimously reaffirm [their] dedication to the democratic ideals which undergird [their] nation," and passed a series of resolutions relating to registration and voting, social action techniques, and an international focus on human relations.[526]

In 1960 Sigma Gamma Rho grand basileus Lorraine A. Williams (serving from 1959 to 1962 and then from 1967 to 1971) and member Annie Lee Whitehead Neville (grand basileus from 1963 to 1967) attended the White House Conference on Children and Youth. The goal of the program was to "promote opportunities for children and youth to reach their full potential for a creative life in freedom and dignity."[527] Williams and Neville reflected Sigma Gamma Rho's emphasis on youth service and education by representing the sorority at the conference. In the 1960s pan-Africanism also gained strength, and both Zeta Phi Beta and Sigma Gamma Rho increased their ties to Africa. Zeta Phi Beta was the first BGLO to establish chapters in Africa, with its initial chapter in Liberia.[528] In 1960 an officer modestly stated, "You will find that most women of importance in Africa are Zetas."[529] That same year Zeta Phi Beta chapters were asked to obtain toys, books, and games to send to Africa to better the understanding between Africans and Americans. Zeta Phi Beta members wanted to further their African program to strengthen the bonds of friendship and to encourage black Africans as they fought for freedom and self-government. Sigma Gamma Rho chapters shipped educational and medical journals to African students in dire need of research materials.[530] The Eta Sigma Chapter donated four hundred pounds of fabric to "Linen for Africa."[531] However, as usual the older sorority stayed less expressly political than Zeta Phi Beta. Philanthropy without clear political ties proved simpler.

Also in 1960 Omega Psi Phi member Charles Gomillion and Fred D. Gray participated in the *Gomillion v. Lightfoot* Supreme Court case.[532] In 1957, the Alabama State Legislature passed Special Act 140, which redefined the boundaries of the City of Tuskegee, from a square to a twenty-eight-sided, irregular figure.[533] This gerrymandering resulted in a drop from a population of four hundred African American eligible voters in Tuskegee down to four or five.[534] Many African American Tuskegee citizens claimed that Special Act 140 was unconstitutional because it discriminated against African Americans in violation of the Due Process Clause, the Equal Protection Clause, and the right to vote as guaranteed by the Fifteenth Amendment. The district court dismissed the case, claiming it had "no control over, no supervision over, and no power to change any boundaries of municipal corporations fixed by a duly convened and elected legislative body, acting for the people in the State of Alabama."[535] Subsequently, the Fifth Circuit upheld the district court's ruling on the grounds that Special Act 140 did not have racial or class discrimination appearing on its face and therefore did not violate the Fourteenth or Fifteenth Amendment.[536] The Supreme Court granted certiorari to review the case because "serious questions were raised concerning the power of a State over its municipalities in relation to the Fourteenth and Fifteenth Amendments."[537] Upon review, the court stated that "when a legislature singles out a readily isolated segment of a racial minority for special discriminatory treatment, it violates the Fifteenth Amendment." Thus, the court held that a local act that altered the shape of a city from a square to a twenty-eight-sided figure and drastically decreased the numbers of Negro voters while not removing a single white voter or resident constituted a violation of the Due Process Clause, the Equal Protection Clause, and the right to vote as guaranteed by the Fifteenth Amendment.[538]

In 1960 the ACHR objectives were social action that would continue to work to eliminate discrimination and segregation based on race, color, religion, or national origin, as well as continuing to educate both the council's members and the public through workshops as well as registration and voting campaigns.[539] The ACHR and the Non-Partisan Council significantly influenced the grassroots support for the civil rights movement.[540] The ACHR sponsored campaigns for both voter registration and education,[541] and a drive collecting funds for students whose education finances were withheld as punishment for their participation in desegregation activities.[542] Included in these students were the "young men who staged the first sit-ins in North Carolina."[543]

Funds raised by ACHR's Sacrifice for Rights campaign were put into their newly created Student Emergency Fund to provide scholarships to students who faced hardship due to their participation in sit-ins or other peaceful demonstrations.[544] To follow up on issues addressed by President Kennedy at the October 1960 Political Workshop and Leadership Conference, more than forty ACHR leaders met in the Capital on January 7, 1961. A goal of the meeting was to prepare a position paper concerning voting rights, employment, housing, and education. Attendees sought to congratulate the president on his use of distinguished African American women in his campaign and to appoint a committee to him in further employing African American women in the federal government.[545]

The ACHR published a bulletin of highlights in February 1961 that featured the achievements and general happenings of ACHR members during 1960. It was clear that the 1961 bulletin aimed to emphasize campaigns of sit-ins and grassroots efforts such as the Write for Rights letter-writing campaigns and workshops to educate and energize voters. The Write for Rights campaign involved citizens writing letters to Congress in support of legislation to implement the Supreme Court's desegregation rulings as well as seeking additional powers for the attorney general to pursue civil injunctions "against all violations of civil rights," and federal action to ensure voting rights for all citizens.[546] A number of Greek and civil rights organizations supported this initiative. The ACHR's bulletin noted, "Indications are that the ACHR campaign provoked the greatest avalanche of Congressional mail in history."[547] Efforts to support student sit-ins financially through the Student Emergency Fund of ACHR, established to pay fines, bails, and scholarships to students "suffering reprisals as a result of their participation in the 'Student Sit-Down

Movement,'" as well as programs to educate voters were at the forefront of the ACHR's 1960 efforts. During 1960 the director of the ACHR, Mrs. Aretha B. McKinley, asked the approximately fifty thousand members of the ACHR to "Sacrifice for Rights," that is, to forgo holding formal functions and instead hold fund-raising events in order to contribute to the Student Emergency Fund.[548]

The ACHR also made efforts to communicate with the Kennedy administration regarding the group's goals and concerns about civil rights progress.[549] In the spring of 1961 the ACHR submitted to President Kennedy a list of forty distinguished black women whom the ACHR considered to be qualified to serve in policy-making decisions within the government. The list was commissioned by the ACHR and compiled by New York University's Center of Human Relations under the guidance of Dr. Jeanne L. Noble, president of Delta Sigma Theta. The only name specifically recommended for a certain position was Mrs. Marjorie McKenzie Lawson, described as "President Kennedy's campaign adviser on Negro affairs"; the ACHR suggested she be appointed to the U.S. Federal District Court in D.C. The ACHR said in a statement that "ACHR is . . . disappointed in the fact that very few Negro women have been placed in policy-making positions . . . there is an excellent womanpower potential among the 157,000 Negro women college graduates in this country."[550]

In 1961, the ACHR continued to assist student sit-in protests in the form of financial support. Miss Marie Barksdale, a member of the executive committee of ACHR and executive director of Delta Sigma Theta, donated a thousand dollars to the Atlanta Women's Steering Committee. The committee had been formed in response to the sit-in demonstrations in order to "provide guidance and financial aid."[551] While the ACHR continued to focus on domestic issues, many of the BGLOs began to also focus on international issues and ideologies of pan-Africanism. For instance, in that same year of 1961, under the presidency of Jeanne L. Noble, Delta Sigma Theta again used its philanthropic arm to fund another project—this time in Kenya. Using money from various sources, Delta Sigma Theta contributed five thousand dollars and helped build the maternity ward in the Njore Mungai Hospital in rural Kenya.[552] In 1962 forty-five members went on the African Study Tour and took Friendship Trees with them.[553] Following the study tour, Delta

Sigma Theta projects involving international affairs emerged. The sorority presented over fifteen hundred dollars to the National Council of Women in Liberia and the Women's Association for Aid to Rwanda Women for village developments that taught girls vocational and educational skills. They also pledged five thousand dollars to the Thika Hospital that opened in 1964. Not only does that hospital provide medical services, it also trains nurses and midwives. New York's Queen Alumnae Delta Sigma Theta chapter underwrote the education of six children in Kenya.[554]

Still, Delta Sigma Theta chapters did not abandon domestic programs. The sorority held annual Christmas parties across the United States where the chapter provided underprivileged children with Christmas presents, food, and holiday cheer.[555] Across the nation Delta Sigma Theta has held these annual parties to support those in need. As tensions rose in Little Rock, Delta Sigma Theta provided gifts and money to students who endured the tedious situation. When an entire class of African American students were refused graduation at Prince Edward County High School in Virginia because the school shut down to avoid integration, Delta Sigma Theta provided all fifty-seven seniors with a Christmas party that raised scholarship money for them to attend school elsewhere. In 1961 Delta Sigma Theta gave Christmas gifts to seventy high school students in McComb, Mississippi, who were expelled after refusing to sign a pledge to stop their nonviolent demonstrations against the arrest of a fifteen-year-old student named Brenda Travis, who violated travel segregation laws.[556]

During the early 1960s individual Delta Sigma Theta members flew the sorority banner in their social justice work. Among them was Joan Trumpauer Mulholland, who participated in the Mississippi Freedom Ride during the summer of 1961. She had arrived in Jackson by train from New Orleans. She was shortly arrested by Jackson police and taken to a waiting paddy wagon; she was refused bail and transferred to Parchman State Prison Farm. There she was put on trial and found innocent. After the Freedom Rides Trumpauer Mulholland studied at Tougaloo College and was a Freedom Summer organizer in 1964. As one of the first white women to become a Delta Sigma Theta member, Mulholland set an example of white-black solidarity with respect to social justice activism.

Similarly, Delta Sigma Theta member Joyce Barrett joined the civil rights movement in the early 1960s. She was one of the few white northerners involved. When she was in college she joined the Student Non-violent Coordinating Committee and worked to promote voting rights. In the spring of 1963 she was jailed in Albany, Georgia, for handing out voter registration forms. For her activism and service to the civil rights movement, she was inducted as an honorary member of Delta Sigma Theta, one of the only white women to receive such an honor.

In 1962 the ACHR published a fact sheet detailing the important civil rights actions that were taken in the District of Columbia between 1948 and 1962. The fact sheet, which was broken down into the categories of government, education, recreation, employment, housing, and public accommodations, outlined measures that reduced or stopped segregation and/or discrimination in each category. Some of the more noteworthy advances included President Truman's executive order desegregating the military in 1948; the U.S. Department of the Interior's prohibition on segregation of public parks and swimming pools in D.C. in 1949–50; the integration of D.C.'s public school system in 1954, following the Supreme Court's ruling in *Brown v. Board of Education*; and the end of racial discrimination in restaurants and hotels throughout 1953–54. Furthermore, in 1957 the U.S. Civil Service Commission ended the racial designation of employees on personnel forms, and in 1961 "Qualified Negroes were integrated in the Federal and District of Columbia governments." The fact sheet made a point of noting that this integration extended to all levels of government, and particularly to those in "policy-making positions."[557]

In November 1962 the ACHR held its sixth annual Leadership Conference at Howard University Law School. Subjects such as the mobilization of voters in D.C. and Atlanta, where the involvement of black voters culminated in the defeat of the "arch-segregationist" James C. Wilson in the Democratic primary, were the focus of the conference, in addition to issues like state reapportionment.[558]

As the ACHR disbanded in 1963, that same year Zeta Phi Beta adopted Project Challenging Times.[559] This six-point African project was conducted jointly by chapters in America and Africa; under the program, the Domestic Science Center opened in Monrovia, Liberia, in October 1965. Working with CARE, a humanitarian organization that serves the poorest communities in the world, Zeta Phi Beta members ran the community development program out of a house provided by William Tubman, who was president of Liberia and a Phi Beta Sigma brother.[560]

Conclusion

The ACHR played an ongoing and important role in the fight for civil rights until its dissolution in 1963. By the time it disbanded it consisted of four member organizations: Alpha Kappa Alpha, Phi Delta Kappa, Sigma Gamma Rho, and Zeta Phi Beta. Alpha Kappa Alpha summed up the decision to dissolve as follows: "In the course of time, the increasing acceptance of responsibility by more widely based groups was reflected in some modifications in the viewpoint of ACHR constituents. . . . These groups, realizing that as the focus and characteristics of ACHR had been modified, its supporters had changed in their approach to problems and in the resources available to them, promulgating the recommendation to terminate."[561] With the ACHR finally recognizing that "the focus and characteristics of ACHR had been modified, [and] its supporters had changed in their approach to problems and in the resources available to them," members of the four remaining sororities decided to recommend termination to the council.[562] The Board of Directors accepted this recommendation.

To mark the organization's dissolution and to distribute remaining funds, the ACHR planned a public reception gala on November 22, 1963. This date is, of course, better known as the day of Kennedy's assassination, and the speakers at the ACHR gala paid tribute to the fallen president and his support for civil rights objectives, in addition to remarking upon the ACHR's achievements. Former Alpha Kappa Alpha supreme basileus and ACHR president Marjorie Parker stated,

> It is by surrendering one's personal portion of life that the individual becomes part of the vast wonder of unlimited life eternal. And this we would believe not only for our President but for this organization which has been the embodiment of our best dream and the focus of our finest efforts for all these years. As other speakers have noted the dedication of the President to this cause and called upon it to finish the fight in which he has fallen, our commitment to the unfinished struggle for freedom

and dignity is no less. . . . So we hold that it is not mere rationalization . . . to say tonight that ACHR is not dead but, because we all continue to be . . . active, functioning, effective supporters and participants in the climactic efforts for freedom in peace and dignity, this organization, like the individual, moves into the larger vastness of eternal life.[563]

At the conclusion, the council's funds were distributed amongst the Prince Edward County Free School Association, the Student Nonviolent Coordinating Committee, and the Leadership Conference on Civil Rights.[564]

Throughout its fifteen-year history the ACHR helped to achieve significant progress in the struggle for civil rights. The activities of the ACHR included campaigns for voter registration and education, mobilization of public opinion in favor of or against pending legislation, and dedicated lobbying of legislators and government officials to promote the passage of laws and implementation of policies that would end racially based discrimination. The ACHR also played a role in supporting court cases that would advance civil rights—in particular the *Henderson* case in which the Supreme Court forbid segregated seating in railway dining cars. Finally, the ACHR also sponsored drives for funds to aid students whose finances had been negatively affected by their participation in sit-in demonstrations. Grants by the ACHR included funds toward the tuition of the young men who took part in the first sit-in in Greensboro, North Carolina. Essentially, the ACHR "played no small part in the swell of the grassroots support for the civil-rights revolt, particularly as it spread among students and other popularly based groups."[565] Legislators, college presidents, and other public figures recognized the contributions of ACHR. Paul H. Douglas, a U.S. senator from Illinois, told the ACHR, "Your objectives aim at the very heart of those denials of democratic rights which not only bar the way to personal advancement, but also weaken the respect for American democracy in other free nations." Furthermore, the president of the City College of New York, Buell Gallagher, described the work of the ACHR as "an important contribution to the effort to bring about the day when all people will be accepted on the basis of their own merits as persons."[566]

The ACHR arose within the context of broader initiatives around civil rights on the part of other BGLOs.[567] What distinguished the ACHR's work, however, was its breadth of strategies (e.g., lobbying, litigation, and philanthropy), duration (e.g., fifteen years), and ability to unify several large, national organizations around a common objective. Its work, strategy, and organization had not been seen before it emerged on the American scene and have not been seen since. It died out, unsurprisingly, around the same time that the social justice and civil rights initiatives of the other BGLOs also petered out. After the passage of the Civil Rights Act of 1964, the Voting Rights Act of 1965, and the Fair Housing Act of 1968, the civil rights movement itself, it can be argued, died out.

Conclusion

Where to Now? The Future of Black Greek Racial Uplift

As noted at the outset of this book, a confluence of factors gave rise to black Greek-letter organizations (BGLOs) and shaped their collective identity. From their inception BGLOs were fashioned as organizations through which college-educated African American men and women could work to address the needs of African Americans. Time would clarify exactly the nature of that work as well as how broad and deep it would be. It spanned social action, public policy, litigation, community service, and philanthropy. In fact, the chapters in this book bear witness to that. However, after the passage of the Civil Rights Act of 1964, the Voting Rights Act of 1965, and the Fair Housing Act of 1968, BGLOs—like many other African American organizations concerned with racial uplift—shifted their work largely to community service and philanthropy. Litigation gave way to mentoring; public policy work surrendered to scholarships.

This shift should be no surprise. In fact, it seems to be quite consistent with how organizations and movements evolve. For example, Herbert Blumer, one of the earliest scholars to study group action—that is, social movement processes—identified four stages of social movements' lifecycles: (1) social ferment, (2) popular excitement, (3) formalization, and (4) institutionalization.[1] Today, scholars recast those stages as (1) emergence, (2) coalescence, (3) bureaucratization, and (4) decline.[2] With regard to the last component, "decline," such may take place because the movement succeeded in what it intended to accomplish.[3] As such, in the context of BGLOs, assuming that their membership and leadership believed that the goals of the civil rights movement were achieved in the 1960s, organizational success was largely achieved.

Even still, many important questions remain: Did BGLOs ever truly test their limits? Did they do all they could to uplift the race? Did they draw exhaustively on their human and intellectual capital to help bring about social change for African Americans, or did they simply do what they could? The same questions can and should linger today. Unlike in generations past, we now live in an age in which information abounds—information that could aid BGLOs in discerning whether they are simply doing a few good things to address African Americans' needs or are testing their every capacity as organizations. If we might, we suggest that BGLOs do some good work, but that work is far from what they could do. In fact, this work is hampered by several challenges that BGLOs face.

Academic Achievement

Though BGLOs have worked to inculcate their members with the importance of scholastic achievement, evidence does not support the notion that members gain any advantage over their nonaffiliated counterparts in the classroom. In a review of university grade reports, Shaun Harper and colleagues found that a large percentage of GPAs of African American fraternities are well below the overall average GPAs of other college fraternities.[4] In their study, Chambers and colleagues found that the mean GPAs of BGLOs members were between 2.59 and 2.97.[5] With the exception of Alpha Phi Alpha, sororities statistically outperformed every other fraternity observed in the study.[6] These achievement gaps were not indicative of students' propensity to perform, as they were enrolled in flagship, research-intensive institutions and their GPAs were relatively strong prior to college enrollment.[7]

Harper and colleagues provide a cautionary, though not alarmist, perspective.[8] For example, research illustrates a link between BGLO membership and positive gains in the ability to acquire and apply knowledge in complex ways.[9] In a more obvious and direct way, poor academic achievement, along with poor critical thinking and weak problem-solving capabilities, may negatively affect BGLOs' ability to positively influence the social and cultural capital—network, access to resources, and ability to acquire knowledge—of their members.[10] Poor academic performance can lessen students' opportunity to expand their social and cultural capital.[11] In turn, when African American students' social and cultural capital is limited, there is a decrease in their ability to secure top internships, admission to graduate and professional school, and employment opportunities.[12] In this way, poor academic performance can negatively impact BGLOs' ability to advocate for African Americans from a position of power and influence, where a portion of their membership may be professionally and financially constrained. This constraint may limit the amount of time and financial resources members can allocate to their organization in the service of the greater community good.

Even more, contemporary racial uplift activism may require creative and nontraditional solutions to recurring problems. Thus, BGLO members should, but may not, possess the requisite level of critical-thinking and innovative skills needed to be effective community problem solvers. Without a motivated force of critical and innovative thinkers, BGLOs may lack the ability to effectively design and develop socially based projects that successfully address the diverse set of needs that are prevalent in the African American community.

Brotherhood and Sisterhood

"A house divided against itself cannot stand,"[13] and a BGLO with deep fissures among its membership is likely to be ineffective in its work. In their research, Michael Stern and Andrew Fullerton indicate that social networking and civic activity are interconnected.[14] Social networks are formed when individuals feel a sense of belonging within a group. Social identity—the process people use to classify themselves and others in the social world—helps to shape these networks.[15] The "oneness" felt within the social network creates a sense of belonging for the members of the group and creates an exclusive environment.[16]

Fissures may arise within social networks based upon individual characteristics, including age, race, religion, and sexual orientation. For example, within any given BGLO, age and generational differences may play a role in undermining the organization's racial uplift work.[17] Age gaps have been particularly relevant for younger members identifying with hip-hop culture and for older members with more "traditional and mainstream views" on how their organization should promote itself.[18] Diverging expectations on issues such as organizational reputation, the representation of organizational symbols, presentation of self, and academic attainment can augment and undermine interactions between younger and older members.

While interracial pledge classes have existed within BGLOs since the 1950s, some members still debate the propriety of admitting nonblack members.[19] The potential fissures created by racial issues within BGLOs are quite varied. Some fear the loss of tradition with the initiation of nonblacks, while others are concerned about the commitment to civic engagement with nonblacks as members.[20]

Religious affiliation also may create fissures in civic involvement within BGLOs. The vast majority of BGLO members are Christians, of various denominations.[21] However, there is a small subset of members who believe that there is a tension between their BGLO affiliation and Christian identity.[22] Frequently, these individuals renounce their membership.[23] In their exploration of the experiences of non-Christian, non-heterosexual, and nonblack BGLO members, Rashawn Ray and Kevin Spragling found that religion is an important dimension that influences members' social interactions with and treatment from other members.[24] Ray and Spragling found that over half of non-Christian Alpha Phi Alpha members, for example, report experiencing forms of mistreatment and isolation from Christian members based on their religious beliefs.[25]

Sexual orientation is the third-rail issue within BGLOs, especially fraternities.[26] While religious interpretations of homosexuality vary, in keeping with traditional Christian beliefs, many BGLO members struggle with the notion of homosexuality. BGLO membership, especially in fraternities, carries with it a strong sense of collective and personal masculinity, which many members perceive as contrary to homosexuality.[27] One study found that homophobia within black Greek-letter fraternities (BGLFs) is not an unexamined prejudice, but rather an ideology in keeping with a belief system that is "discussed, debated, and refined."[28] While homosexuality may appear contrary to ideals of black masculinity cultivated by BGLFs, homophobia will only exclude potential leaders in the ongoing crusade for social justice and equality.

In a study of social capital formation within a voluntary youth association, researchers found that white participants exhibited a tendency toward racial homophily, while black participants were equally likely to form interracial ties with socially dissimilar peers as with socially similar peers.[29] Thus, whites were shown to be less likely to create relationships that transcended race, gender, and educational boundaries, thereby limiting their ability to create network ties and accumulate social capital.[30] BGLOs place a similar limitation on their ability to foster network ties across all social boundaries where age, race, and religious chasms exist.[31] This may be no more evident than in the context of BGLOs vis-à-vis how they reconcile themselves with lesbian, gay, and bisexual members.

Activist Mindedness

Brian Christens and colleagues find that the correlation between individuals' self-report of community and organizational participation with their actual participation in community activities, though positive, is not very strong.[32] The study of social action is key in that community participation is a requisite for both capital formation and a functioning civil society. However, what has been found is that the measurement of such participation remains underdeveloped.[33] Conceptualizations of community and public participation range from narrow definitions of behaviors (e.g., voting) to an "aggregation of related but questionably integral activities such as reading newspapers, informal conversations with neighbors, and memberships in voluntary associations."[34] The point is that participation in social and collective action is measurable and required in order to determine how organizations, like BGLOs, are making their mark.

Katie Corcoran and colleagues found that participation in high-cost collective action is more likely for those who both are efficacious and perceive structural disadvantage as unjust.[35] The concern for collective action stems from political participation and recent activism for the long-standing concerns about social inequality and injustice.[36] Stemming from relative deprivation theory, perceptions of structural disadvantage and injustice are predicted to lead to collective action when people view disadvantage as rooted in societal structures that are unjust. Further, value-expectancy theory (i.e., an individual's belief that she can create change and achieve a valued outcome) proposes that one's motivation to engage in collective action is the product of efficacy and the perceived value of the collective good.[37] One possible reason for the mobilization around inequality/injustice in recent years is that there has been a convergence of an ever-growing perception of injustice with a stronger sense that these injustices can be rectified through the use of high-cost tactics.[38] Within BGLOs, this begs the question, "What percentage of financially, active members hold views that make them likely to be engaged in social and collective action?" What may be troubling is that those numbers may be quite small.

In fact, what we may see within BGLOs is a fairly large portion of financially, active members—at best—engaged in low-grade social activism on social media. For example, Jessica Vitak and colleagues studied the impact of political activities on Facebook on the 2008 U.S. presidential election.[39] More specifically, they sought to determine if such social network site (SNS) politics had a substantial impact on the political behavior of young people, or if instead it allowed such activists only to feel good about themselves without truly creating a real-world impact. The researchers identified three determining factors for political participation: psychological engagement, campaign recruitment, and access to resources. For the purposes of this study, they focused primarily on access to and utilization of resources.[40] What they found was that the relationship between young people's political involvement and their use of social media is complex. The most common form of political participation tended to be informational and low in resource necessity. This finding supports the argument that young voters are becoming "slacktivists," by participating in ways that allow them to feel good but have little or no substantial impact. However, an alternative explanation views SNS politics as a form of "practice" for developing civic skills with minimal time and effort commitment. In this way, SNS politics increases political participation, rather than diminishes it, by providing young people with a highly accessible outlet for activism. Moreover, views of appropriate activity on Facebook are nuanced; participants tend to view self-expression as appropriate but persuasion as inappropriate. This further supports the idea that Facebook provides an appropriate context for developing civic skills.[41] The proverbial jury is still out on what such findings mean for BGLOs.

Race Consciousness

For decades, psychologists and political scientists have researched the extent to which individuals identify with their own racial group and the influence that such identity has on political engagement. Donald

Matthews and James Prothro examined the attitudes and behaviors of African Americans as well as the reactions and attitudes of whites in the southern United States. In their assessment of the prerequisites of African American leadership, they identified "an interest in and identification with other members of the race."[42] Such racial "interest and identification" can more broadly be conceptualized in the context of group identity, racial identity, and race consciousness.[43]

Group identification is "an individual's awareness of belonging to a certain group and having a psychological attachment to that group based on a perception of shared beliefs, feelings, interests, and ideas with other group members."[44] Group identity has further been framed within the context of social identity theory such that an individual's identity is largely defined by group membership.[45] In turn, racial identity is the "awareness of and identification with a racial group based on feelings of in-group closeness."[46] Black racial identity is the extent to which blacks identify with blacks. Psychologist William Cross articulated a five-stage theory of black racial identification, called Nigrescence, which translates as "the process of becoming Black."[47]

The model progresses through the pre-encounter, encounter, immersion, emersion, and internalization stages.[48] In the pre-encounter stage, the individual is unaware of his or her race and the social implications that come with racial categorization.[49] In the encounter stage, the individual experiences a situation that suddenly and sharply raises race as an issue; it is generally an awakening to race consciousness. This encounter makes the individual open to a new, racialized worldview.[50] In the immersion stage, the individual becomes consciously black, though this consciousness is often provincial where blackness is oversimplified.[51] The emersion stage is characterized by a growth from the oversimplified ideologies.[52] During the internalization stage, an individual has internalized his or her blackness and no longer feels the need to "wear it on their sleeve."[53] In turn, he or she is comfortable rejoining society with a strong sense of his or her racial self to be able to forge relationships with members from other racial/ethnic groups.[54] Not surprisingly, researchers have found that black racial identity predicts community outreach such that the pre-encounter stage negatively (i.e., weaker racial identity) and the immersion-emersion and internalization stages positively (i.e., stronger racial identity) predict community outreach among black college students.[55]

Moving beyond simply group and racial identity, race consciousness is the "willingness of an individual not only to identify with her racial group but also to work with the collective group."[56] Other scholars have defined it as "in-group identification politicized by a set of ideological beliefs about one's group's social standing, as well as a view that collective action is the best means by which the group can improve in status and realize its interests."[57] Internal and external influences shape the ways in which an individual develops his or her racial identity, including social norms and social institutions. Group consciousness plays a pivotal role in racial uplift activism, as it is utilized to mobilize blacks to confront racism and protect the interests of the community.[58] Research has demonstrated that blacks' race consciousness explains black political involvement in the 1960s and 1970s.[59]

The question for BGLOs is the extent to which their members' racial identity and race consciousness advance their organizations' racial uplift agenda. For example, participation in BGLOs has shaped the ways in which members progress through the racial identity development process. Shaun Harper and colleagues have explored how Cross's Nigrescence theory and Parham and Helm's theory of blacks' self-actualization highlight the importance of providing black students with the space to conceptualize and experience blackness.[60] Those who viewed their racial identity in favorable terms developed higher levels of self-esteem and effectively achieved their academic goals.[61] According to Harper and colleagues, BGLOs serve as an important vehicle for the exploration of racial identity and provide African American students with the opportunity to negotiate their understandings of race within a safe environment.[62]

Implicit, subconscious racial bias offers a counternarrative to research that suggests that BGLO members have stronger racial identities than African Americans who are nonmembers. Expressions of implicit racial bias among BGLO members may go unrecognized by those possessing bias.[63] According to measures like the Implicit Association Test (IAT), approximately 70 percent of whites in the United States maintain automatic, implicit anti-black/pro-white biases.[64] Similar studies have established that 50 to 60 percent of blacks harbor similar biases, though less consistently than whites.[65] When BGLO members took the race IAT during one study, nearly 23 percent reported implicit racial

bias for whites.[66] When college-age members were more closely scruti-
nized, 40 percent demonstrated an implicit anti-black/pro-white bias.[67]
In contrast, no participant expressed an explicit preference for whites
over blacks.[68] This research suggests that implicit racial biases may undermine a significant portion of BGLO members' race consciousness
and, in turn, commitment to racial uplift activism.

Organizational Commitment

There is no guarantee that BGLO members will remain financially
and physically engaged in their organizations for life. For example, we
know that BGLOs hemorrhage a majority of financially active members
within just a few years of initiation. Accordingly, at best—if all financially active members were engaged in community uplift activity—that
would be a paltry number. In fact, as organizational theorists suggest,
"organizational effectiveness is multidimensional."[69] Although a solid
infrastructure contributes to an organization's success, effectiveness
is not ensured by "organizational design alone. . . . Members of the
organization [must] behave in a manner supportive of organizational
goals."[70] Organizational effectiveness depends upon the willingness
of its members to remain active and display "dependable role behavior, as prescribed by the organization, and spontaneous and innovative
behavior which go beyond explicit behavioral prescriptions."[71] In sum,
a committed member's participation and production promote organizational effectiveness.

Within BGLOs, three problems seem to undermine their racial uplift
work. First, many, if not most, financially active members are disen-
gaged from the external work of their organization. Second, the masses
of duly initiated members are not even active with their organization
such that said organization could nudge them toward this kind of work
and community engagement. Third, BGLO membership retention rates
are abysmal, and there has not been a meaningful, data-driven approach
to reclamation in years, if ever.

Ultimately, soaring rhetoric and even formalized mentoring, philanthropy, social action, and civic engagement activities likely will do
little to allow BGLOs to make the kind of community impact that they
could make. Indeed, fundamental changes within BGLOs likely need

to be made for them to be what they once were, if not better and more effective. As noted above, there are a range of significant issues that BGLOs need to address to be the social change powerhouses they present themselves to the world to be. These issues are not only multiple but likely interacting and complex. While not noted previously, take for example hazing. It is a problem that bogs down national executive council meetings, undermining more strategic thinking. It saps BGLOs of financial resources. It imperils BGLOs fiscally over the long term. It likely drives some duly initiated members away from BGLOs. As such, it also seems to be part of the reason why BGLOs have a drain on their human, intellectual, and social capital needed to advance BGLOs racial uplift mission.

Turning the corner on these issues will not be easy. It would require BGLOs taking a drastically different approach to how they do almost everything. Members, in large numbers, could fight to bring about changes. However, they may not have an incentive or broader resources to bring about such a massive overhaul of BGLOs. What seems to be true is that the elected leaders would have to decide to bring about such a sweeping cultural shift. However, they may have neither the will nor the skill to do so.

Ultimately, the linchpin issue revolves around how BGLOs and their members conceptualize leadership, particularly the uppermost leaders. In many respects BGLOs operate like benevolent dictatorships—a theoretical form of government in which an authoritarian leader exercises absolute political power over the state but does so for the benefit of the population as a whole. Within a benevolent dictatorship, the dictator may allow for some democratic decision making, such as through elected representatives with limited power, and often prepares for a transition to genuine democracy during or after his or her term. Within such a regime, it might be seen as a republican form of enlightened despotism.

Within BGLOs, each organization's national head holds a significant amount of quasi-power. For example, the power is not sufficient to effectuate real change within BGLOs around critical issues or to mobilize members. Rather, there is (1) the power to preside—such as, members standing when the leader walks in the room, the ability to silence members during business sessions when merely tired of hearing what they are saying; (2) the power to exercise control over organizational resources—for example, dictate to some extent how money will be spent; and (3) the power to not be questioned by most members. Undoubtedly, the national heads of these organizations and surrogates see this power as being for the greater good of the organization and its membership. While there are other members of these national boards, and the members can exercise authority through their delegates at national conventions, to a large extent both seem to acquiesce to the office of the national head. The former may do so to preserve that office's power for the day when they run for and obtain that seat. The latter may acquiesce simply out of habit; they do not want to shift substantially from the status quo.

The point is not whether it is good or bad for the office of the national head to have such tremendous authority. Rather, the point is that given that it is imbued with such, a bottom-up change within BGLOs is unlikely. Instead, if BGLOs are to move beyond rhetoric and fairly hollow initiatives and partnerships, they will need to elect transformational leaders—particularly national heads. Within the context of campaigns for BGLOs' national board positions, the term "transformational leader" is bandied about without much thought as to what it truly means. In the context of what BGLOs need with respect to fundamentally changing their course and trajectory regarding racial uplift, for example, what seems to be required is something quite specific.

A transformational leader is one who projects idealized influence, inspirational motivation, intellectual stimulation, and individualized consideration.[72] Even more, such a leader must understand and capitalize on the randomness and seeming unpredictability of interactions within the system to create positive change.[73] Such a leader must see the relationships between individual, interpersonal, and organizational dynamics within BGLOs and how they impact BGLOs' racial uplift work. Moreover, the leader must possess the ability to substantively address those multilevel and often complex dynamics. For example, a national head who lacks a vision and strategy for addressing reclamation and retention will not be able to draw upon a large enough body of members to do the intellectual and physical work of racial uplift. In addition, a transformational leader must be able to innovate—to identify, recruit, and unleash the potential of highly innovative organizational members.[74]

The risk in national heads' failure to be and do these things is that they may lose the credibility needed within their organization to make their vision reality.[75] In fact, national heads who are billed as transformational but who lack the ability to augment the broader internal dynamics within their organization that undermine its racial uplift work may get the applause when they enter a room. However, they may find that they cannot command the proverbial troops to bring about the types of societal changes they desire. Additionally, members may come to see their ability to do effective racial uplift work through the organization as limited not because the work is not valuable. Rather, they may not perceive the broader dynamics that impact their own organization's racial uplift work. Accordingly, such repeated failures may leave many members experiencing a sense of organizational learned helplessness.[76] This in turn may lead to increased disengagement from racial uplift work on the part of an increasing number of members.

Ultimately, and in closing, two concepts may animate why BGLOs find themselves in a bind with regard to elevating truly transformational leaders who can help their organizations realize their racial uplift potential in this day and age. The first is that within the BGLOs leaders tend to be promoted to positions based on their performance in their current role, rather than on abilities relevant to the intended role.[77] For example, BGLOs do not ask what a national head should be or offer to dramatically and positively shift the trajectory of their organization. Rather, they simply ask—at best—whether the candidates did a "good" job in their prior leadership posts. Even there, accomplishment is vague and measured at a low threshold—such as chapters in compliance, revenue raised from convention/conference, money given to March of Dimes. Ultimately, many national heads likely maintain the status quo simply because they do not know how to bring about change, and this impacts the organization's ability to do its racial uplift work.

Second, national board members—especially the national head—are individuals who rise through the ranks of leadership within their organization. In his research, Gautam Mukunda studied the extent to which leaders are and are not indispensable—to what extent they are one of a kind and ultimately transformational. What he found was that across a host of institutions, organizations, and countries, there are essentially two types of leaders. One type, which he calls highly filtered, rise through the ranks, holding numerous offices and titles. Some subset of these leaders then compete for the top position. According to Mukunda, members of that institution or organization could almost select from this group of competitors randomly because the competitors likely have the same vision and outlook for the institution. After all, they emerged from the same pool.[78] Within Alpha Phi Alpha, for example, it should be no surprise that candidates for general president largely have the same platform—if they present one—and talking points. They emerge from the ranks of chapter presidents, state heads, and regional heads. According to Mukunda, the second thing that is observed with such leaders is that they are adept at maintaining the status quo. This is because they have spent many years operating within the system and have thought little about and have not developed the skills needed to bring about dramatic and fundamental change within the institution.[79]

The other type of leader Mukunda identified in his research was the one who emerges from nowhere—the leader who did not rise through the ranks. He called this leader the unfiltered leader. If the filtered leader was in the middle of the leadership bell curve, he or she was two standard deviations away. The unfiltered leader had not adopted the traditional ways of the institution. He or she could more easily innovate and think outside the proverbial "box." He or she was more risky and not bound by orthodoxy. Two examples would likely be Barack Obama and Donald Trump. According to Mukunda, there is no such thing as a perfect leader. Rather, an organization must ask itself what its needs are—status quo or change. Depending on its needs, a certain type of leader is best.[80] However, within BGLOs, we seem deeply committed to the same models of leadership that we have used for decades, if not generations.

Within BGLOs, the ways in which we must commit to and execute on community service, philanthropy, social action, shaping public policy, and even community organizing and mobilization turn on our ability to fundamentally address a broad set of complex dynamics. "Sound and fury, signifying nothing,"[81] will not suffice. Even new initiatives and partnerships will prove themselves to be anemic. Most crucial to our ability to turn a sharp corner on these issues is whom we elect to lead us. The choices predict the outcome. Only time will tell if these organizations are willing to make different choices.

ACKNOWLEDGMENTS

This is our second book together on black fraternalism, following *Black Greek-Letter Organizations 2.0: New Directions in the Study of African American Fraternities and Sororities,* in 2011. Compiling the material, reading, writing, and editing are no small matter and could not have been accomplished without a large amount of assistance from capable hands. Accordingly, we thank the editorial board of New York University Press who saw the big picture in our proposal and preliminary sketches. To Clara Platter, our acquisitions editor, we are extremely grateful for your support of our endeavor and strong shepherding of this process. Thank you also to editorial assistants Constance Grady, Amy Klopfenstein, and Veronica Knutson for all your labors. We also are indebted to the peer reviewers who helped sharpen our focus and make a better text in the end. We appreciate the library assistance of Mary Susan Lucas. Thank you to our research assistants: Alena Baker, Samantha Berner, LaRita Dingle, Jordan Dongell, Ashley Eng, Ashley Escoe, Steven Franklin, Ashlee Johnson, Brian Kuppelweiser, Katherine Law, Eli Marger, Ryan McIntrye, Morgan McPherson, Valerie Mock, Tenika Neely, Adam Nyenhuis, Chineze Osakwe, Justin Philbeck, Kevin Rothenburg, Hannah Rudder, Angela Sheets, Kimberly Sokolich, and Sarah Walton.

Lastly and probably most importantly, we thank the readers—most of whom are likely members of black fraternities and sororities—for your support. It is our intent not that our work simply sit on shelves nor that it rest in the minds of readers. Rather, we hope that the information gained from this book will translate into the betterment of not only our organizations, but the larger black diaspora and all the globe's citizens.

NOTES

CHAPTER 1. THE PRECONDITIONS FOR UPLIFT (1865–1905)

1 Kenneth M. Stampp, *The Peculiar Institution: Slavery in the Ante-Bellum South* (New York: Vintage, 1956).

2 Booker T. Washington, *Up from Slavery: An Autobiography* (1901; New York: Doubleday, Page, 1907), 19–21.

3 Felix L. Armfield et al., "Defining the 'Alpha' Identity," in *Alpha Phi Alpha: A Legacy of Greatness, the Demands of Transcendence*, ed. Gregory S. Parks and Stefan M. Bradley (Lexington: University Press of Kentucky, 2012), 23, 28.

4 Armfield et al., "Defining the 'Alpha' Identity."

5 C. Vann Woodward, *Reunion and Reaction: The Compromise of 1877 and the End of Reconstruction* (Boston: Little, Brown, 1951), 3–15.

6 Armfield et al., "Defining the 'Alpha' Identity," 28–29.

7 Armfield et al., "Defining the 'Alpha' Identity," 29.

8 Armfield et al., "Defining the 'Alpha' Identity," 32.

9 Henry Lyman Morehouse, "The Talented Tenth," *Independent*, April 23, 1896, www.webdubois.org; Evelyn Brooks Higginbotham, *Righteous Discontent: The Women's Movement in the Black Baptist Church, 1880–1920* (Cambridge, Mass.: Harvard Univ. Press 1993).

10 W. E. B. Du Bois, "Talented Tenth," in *The Negro Problem: A Series of Articles by Representative Negroes of To-day* (New York: James Pott, 1903); Rashawn Ray, "W. E. B. Du Bois: Pioneering Social Theorist, Methodologist, and Public Sociologist," in *Oxford Bibliographies Online: Sociology*, ed. Jeff Manza (New York: Oxford University Press, 2011).

11 Angel L. Harris, *Kids Don't Want to Fail: Oppositional Culture and the Black-White Achievement Gap* (Cambridge, Mass.: Harvard University Press, 2011).

12 Armfield et al., "Defining the 'Alpha' Identity," 40.

13 Armfield et al., "Defining the 'Alpha' Identity," 40.

14 Jessica Harris and Said Sewell, "Faith and Fraternalism: A History," in *African American Fraternities and Sororities: The Legacy and the Vision*, 2nd ed., ed. Tamara L. Brown, Gregory S. Parks, and Clarenda M. Phillips (Lexington: University Press of Kentucky, 2012), 63.

15 Harris and Sewell, "Faith and Fraternalism," 65.

16 Harris and Sewell, "Faith and Fraternalism," 63.

17 Harris and Sewell, "Faith and Fraternalism," 66–67.

18 Armfield et al., "Defining the 'Alpha' Identity," 37.

19 Anne S. Butler, "Black Fraternal and Benevolent Societies in Nineteenth-Century America," in Brown, Parks, and Phillips, *African American Fraternities and Sororities*, 76–77; Harris and Sewell, "Faith and Fraternalism," 66.

20 Butler, "Black Fraternal and Benevolent Societies," 75, 77 (noting black secret societies "grew steadily" in part because they provided spiritual nourishment, a sense of hope, and material support).

21 Butler, "Black Fraternal and Benevolent Societies," 86.

22 Butler, "Black Fraternal and Benevolent Societies," 76.

23 Butler, "Black Fraternal and Benevolent Societies," 82.

24 Butler, "Black Fraternal and Benevolent Societies," 78–79.

25 Harris and Sewell, "Faith and Fraternalism," 66–67.

26 Harris and Sewell, "Faith and Fraternalism."

27 Harris and Sewell, "Faith and Fraternalism," 76.

28 Butler, "Black Fraternal and Benevolent Societies," 88–91, 94–95.

29 Harris and Sewell, "Faith and Fraternalism," 66–67.

30 Butler, "Black Fraternal and Benevolent Societies," 74.

31 Butler, "Black Fraternal and Benevolent Societies," 76.

32 Butler, "Black Fraternal and Benevolent Societies," 68.

33 Butler, "Black Fraternal and Benevolent Societies," 89.

34 Butler, "Black Fraternal and Benevolent Societies," 89.

35 Butler, "Black Fraternal and Benevolent Societies," 89.

36 Butler, "Black Fraternal and Benevolent Societies," 89.

37 Butler, "Black Fraternal and Benevolent Societies," 75–76.

38 See Butler, "Black Fraternal and Benevolent Societies," 75 (noting that fraternal groups had a "structure for uniting local, district, or national bodies").

39 Butler, "Black Fraternal and Benevolent Societies."

40 Sigma Pi Phi Fraternity, "History of Sigma Pi Phi Fraternity" (2015), http://zetaboule.com/sigma-pi-phi.html.

41 Craig L. Torbenson, "The Origin and Evolution of College Fraternities and Sororities," in Brown, Parks, and Phillips, *African American Fraternities and Sororities*, 38.

42 Armfield et al., "Defining the 'Alpha' Identity," 34; Torbenson, "Origin and Evolution," 37.

43 Torbenson, "Origin and Evolution," 38–39, 55.

44 Clarence Bacote, *The Story of Atlanta University: A Century of Service, 1865–1965* (Atlanta: Atlanta University, 1969), 240; H. M. Bond, *Education for Freedom: A History of Lincoln University Pennsylvania* (Princeton, N.J.: Princeton University Press, 1976), 414–15; Rodney T. Cohen, *Fisk University* (Charleston, S.C.: Arcadia, 2001), 29.

45 Armfield et al., "Defining the 'Alpha' Identity," 34.

46 Torbenson, "Origin and Evolution," 38–39.

47 Torbenson, "Origin and Evolution," 38–39.

48 Torbenson, "Origin and Evolution," 39.

49 Armfield et al., "Defining the 'Alpha' Identity," 36.

50 Torbenson, "Origin and Evolution," 38.

51 Torbenson, "Origin and Evolution," 56.

52 Torbenson, "Origin and Evolution," 56–57.

53 Torbenson, "Origin and Evolution," 56–57.

54 Rayford W. Logan, *Howard University: The First Hundred Years, 1867–1967* (New York: New York University Press, 1969), 4.

55 Logan, *Howard University*, 4.

56 Logan, *Howard University*, 6–8.

57 Logan, *Howard University*, 25.

58 Logan, *Howard University*, 12.

59 Jacqueline M. Moore, *Leading the Race: The Transformation of the Black Elite in the Nation's Capital, 1880–1920* (Charlottesville: University of Virginia Press, 1999), 131.

60 Carl L. Becker, *Cornell University: Founders and the Founding* (Ithaca, N.Y.: Cornell University Press, 1943), 133.

61 Armfield et al., "Defining the 'Alpha' Identity," 40.

62 Armfield et al., "Defining the 'Alpha' Identity," 41.

63 Carol Kammen, *Part & Apart: The Black Experience at Cornell, 1865–1845* (Ithaca, N.Y.: Cornell University Press, 2009), 123.

64 Kammen, *Part & Apart*, 123.

65 W. Drew Perkins, producer, *Alpha Phi Alpha: A Century of Leadership* (DVD; Baltimore: Rubicon Productions, 2006).

66 Charles H. Wesley, *Henry Arthur Callis: Life and Legacy* (Baltimore: Foundation Publishers, 1997), 4, 7.

67 Wesley, *Henry Arthur Callis*, 7.

68 Wesley, *Henry Arthur Callis*, 7.

69 Wesley, *Henry Arthur Callis*, 16.

70 Wesley, *Henry Arthur Callis*, 16.

71 Wesley, *Henry Arthur Callis*, 17.

72 Wesley, *Henry Arthur Callis*, 17.

73 Perkins, *Alpha Phi Alpha*.

74 Perkins, *Alpha Phi Alpha*.

75 Perkins, *Alpha Phi Alpha*.

76 Wesley, *Henry Arthur Callis*, 18.

77 Wesley, *Henry Arthur Callis*, 18.

78 Wesley, *Henry Arthur Callis*, 18.

79 Wesley, *Henry Arthur Callis*, 17.

80 Perkins, *Alpha Phi Alpha*.

81 Perkins, *Alpha Phi Alpha*; see also Wesley, *Henry Arthur Callis*, 1.

82 Wesley, *Henry Arthur Callis*, 1.

83 Wesley, *Henry Arthur Callis*, 1.

84 Wesley, *Henry Arthur Callis*, 1.

85 Wesley, *Henry Arthur Callis*, 190.

86 See Wesley, *Henry Arthur Callis*, 190, 205 (discussing the purposes of establishing the fraternity).

87 Wesley, *Henry Arthur Callis*, 190, 205.

88 Wesley, *Henry Arthur Callis*, 191. "Alpha Phi Alpha became an exclusive social set that was accused of snobbishness toward the darker students and those not from prominent families." E. Franklin Frazier, *The Negro in the United States* (New York: Macmillan, 1949), 383.

CHAPTER 2. THE GENESIS OF BLACK GREEK-LETTER ORGANIZATIONS (1906–1922)

1 Charles H. Wesley, *The History of Alpha Phi Alpha: A Development in College Life, 1906–1979* (Chicago: Foundation Publishers, 1991), 1.

2 Wesley, *History of Alpha Phi Alpha*, 1.

3 Wesley, *History of Alpha Phi Alpha*, 1–2.

4 Wesley, *History of Alpha Phi Alpha*, 2.

5 Wesley, *History of Alpha Phi Alpha*, 2.

6 Wesley, *History of Alpha Phi Alpha*, 2.

7 Wesley, *History of Alpha Phi Alpha*, xvii.

8 Ralph E. Johnson et al., "The Quest for Excellence: Reviewing Alpha's Legacy of Academic Achievement," in *Alpha Phi Alpha: A Legacy of Greatness, the Demands of Transcendence*, ed. Gregory S. Parks and Stefan M. Bradley (Lexington: University Press of Kentucky, 2012), 189.

9 W. Drew Perkins, producer, *Alpha Phi Alpha: A Century of Leadership* (DVD; Baltimore: Rubicon Productions, 2006).

10 Perkins, *Alpha Phi Alpha*.

11 Wesley, *History of Alpha Phi Alpha*, 59.

12 Wesley, *History of Alpha Phi Alpha*, 61.

13 Haynes was an honorary member of the fraternity. *Sphinx*, April 1918, 10.

14 *Sphinx*, April 1918, 10.

15 *Sphinx*, April 1918, 10.

16 Wesley, *History of Alpha Phi Alpha*, 83.
17 Wesley, *History of Alpha Phi Alpha*, 85.
18 Wesley, *History of Alpha Phi Alpha*, 85.
19 Wesley, *History of Alpha Phi Alpha*, 85.
20 *Sphinx*, March 1914, 21.
21 *Sphinx*, March 1914, 6.
22 *Sphinx*, March 1914, 7.
23 *Sphinx*, March 1914, 7.
24 *Sphinx*, March 1914, 8.
25 Perkins, *Alpha Phi Alpha*.
26 Perkins, *Alpha Phi Alpha*.
27 Roscoe C. Giles, *Sphinx*, June 1914, 5–6.
28 *Sphinx*, June 1914, 5–6.
29 *Sphinx*, June 1914, 11.
30 F. H. Miller, "To Alumni," *Sphinx*, April 1916, 9.
31 Miller, "To Alumni," 9.
32 *Sphinx*, October 1916, 3–4.
33 *Sphinx*, October 1916, 11.
34 *Sphinx*, October 1916, 10.
35 *Sphinx*, December 1916, 21.
36 Numa P. G. Adams, "The Aim of Alpha Phi Alpha Fraternity," *Sphinx*, December 1916, 12.
37 Adams, "Aim of Alpha Phi Alpha Fraternity," 12.
38 *Sphinx*, February 1917, 10.
39 *Sphinx*, February 1917, 10.
40 *Sphinx*, April 1917, 19.
41 *Sphinx*, April 1917, 22–23.
42 *Sphinx*, April 1917, 22–23.
43 *Sphinx*, April 1917, 29.
44 *Sphinx*, April 1917, 29.
45 *Sphinx*, February 1917, 15.
46 *Sphinx*, April 1917, 19.
47 J. M. Sampson, "Ideals for Which Alpha Phi Alpha Stands," *Sphinx*, April 1917, 11.
48 Numa P. G. Adams, "The Place of Fraternity Life in Negro College Life," *Sphinx*, April 1917, 5.
49 Adams, "Place of Fraternity Life in Negro College Life," 6.
50 Geo B. Kelley, "The History and Purpose of Alpha Phi Alpha," *Sphinx*, April 1917, 9.
51 Wesley, *History of Alpha Phi Alpha*, 104.
52 Wesley, *History of Alpha Phi Alpha*, 105.
53 Wesley, *History of Alpha Phi Alpha*, 105.
54 Wesley, *History of Alpha Phi Alpha*, 105.
55 Wesley, *History of Alpha Phi Alpha*, 105.
56 Wesley, *History of Alpha Phi Alpha*, 105–6.
57 Wesley, *History of Alpha Phi Alpha*, 107.
58 Wesley, *History of Alpha Phi Alpha*, 108.
59 Daniel D. Fowler, "Letter in the Case of Negro College Men vs. White Officer Commanding S.A.T.C.," *Sphinx*, April 1918, 5–6. For further details of this incident, see Wesley, *History of Alpha Phi Alpha*, 112.
60 Fowler, "Letter in the Case," 5–6.
61 Fowler, "Letter in the Case," 5–6.
62 Fowler, "Letter in the Case," 5–6.
63 Fowler, "Letter in the Case," 7.
64 *Sphinx*, April 1918, 15.

65 Judson MacLaury, "The Federal Government and Negro Workers under President Woodrow Wilson" (paper, Society for History in the Federal Government, Washington, D.C., March 16, 2000), www.dol.gov.

66 Perkins, *Alpha Phi Alpha*; Felix L. Armfield, *Eugene Kinckle Jones: The National Urban League and Black Social Work, 1910–1940* (Urbana: University of Illinois Press, 2012), 75.

67 Perkins, *Alpha Phi Alpha*; Armfield, *Eugene Kinckle Jones*, 75.

68 *Sphinx*, October 1919, 13.

69 *Sphinx*, October 1919, 13.

70 *Sphinx*, October 1919, 17.

71 "For Action on Race Riot Peril," *New York Times*, October 5, 1919, https://timesmachine.nytimes.com.

72 *Sphinx*, March 1919, 4.

73 *Sphinx*, February 1920, 5. Scott was secretary-treasurer of Howard University.

74 *Sphinx*, February 1920, 5.

75 *Sphinx*, February 1920, 5.

76 Roscoe C. Giles, "Suggestions and Questions for the 12th Convention to Consider," *Sphinx*, December 1919, 13–14.

77 Giles, "Suggestions and Questions," 13–14.

78 Giles, "Suggestions and Questions," 13–14.

79 Wesley, *History of Alpha Phi Alpha*, 123.

80 Wesley, *History of Alpha Phi Alpha*, 123.

81 Wesley, *History of Alpha Phi Alpha*, 123.

82 "The Go-To High School, Go-To College Movement," *Sphinx*, April 1923, 5, 42–43.

83 *Sphinx*, February 1920, 9.

84 Wesley, *History of Alpha Phi Alpha*, 127.

85 Wesley, *History of Alpha Phi Alpha*, 127.

86 Wesley, *History of Alpha Phi Alpha*, 127, 129–30 (16th ed., 1996).

87 Wesley, *History of Alpha Phi Alpha*, 130.

88 Wesley, *History of Alpha Phi Alpha*, 135.

89 Wesley, *History of Alpha Phi Alpha*, 135.

90 Wesley, *History of Alpha Phi Alpha*, 135–36.

91 Wesley, *History of Alpha Phi Alpha*, 136.

92 *Sphinx*, May 1920, 27.

93 *Sphinx*, May 1920, 27.

94 *Sphinx*, February 1921, 3.

95 *Sphinx*, February 1921, 3.

96 *Sphinx*, February 1921, 3.

97 *Sphinx*, February 1922, 5.

98 "Douglas We're Here," *Sphinx*, February 1922, 9.

99 "At Anacostia," *Sphinx*, April 1922, 4.

100 "One Conclave of Collegians," *Sphinx*, February 1922, 6.

101 *Sphinx*, May 1922, 9.

102 "General President Issues Advance Notice of Legislative Program for the 15th Convention," *Sphinx*, November 1922, 1.

103 "Negro Business Today," *Sphinx*, December 1922, 6–7.

104 Benjamin T. Johnson, "Negro Business the Bedrock of Progress," *Sphinx*, October 1922, 3–4.

105 Johnson, "Negro Business the Bedrock of Progress," 3–4.

106 Johnson, "Negro Business the Bedrock of Progress," 3–4.

107 Johnson, "Negro Business the Bedrock of Progress," 3–4.

108 Marjorie H. Parker, *Past Is Prologue: The History of Alpha Kappa Alpha 1908–1999* (Washington, D.C.: Marjorie H. Parker, 1999), 3.

109 Parker, *Past Is Prologue*, 3, 40.
110 Parker, *Past Is Prologue*, 3, 40.
111 Tamara L. Brown, Gregory S. Parks, and Clarenda M. Phillips, eds., *African American Fraternities and Sororities: The Legacy and the Vision*, 2nd ed. (Lexington: University Press of Kentucky, 2012).
112 Parker, *Past Is Prologue*, 4.
113 Brown, Parks, and Phillips, *African American Fraternities and Sororities*, 53.
114 Parker, *Past Is Prologue*, 4.
115 Columbia University, "Lucy Diggs Slowe, Columbia Celebrates Black History and Culture," https://blackhistory.news.columbia.edu.
116 Parker, *Past Is Prologue*.
117 Parker, *Past Is Prologue*, 5.
118 Parker, *Past Is Prologue*.
119 Earnestine G. McNealey, *Pearls of Service: The Legacy of America's First Black Sorority, Alpha Kappa Alpha* (Chicago: Alpha Kappa Alpha Sorority, 2006).
120 "Angelina Weld Grimke (1880–1958)," *BlackPast*, www.blackpast.org.
121 Alpha Kappa Alpha Sorority, "AKA Centennial Timeline," http://hustorage.wrlc.org.
122 Alpha Kappa Alpha Sorority, "AKA Centennial Timeline."
123 Alpha Kappa Alpha Sorority, "Alpha Kappa Alpha Sorority, Inc.—Service to All Mankind since 1908," http://aka1908.com.
124 Alpha Kappa Alpha Sorority, "AKA Centennial Timeline."
125 *Ivy Leaf*, 1922, 24.
126 *Ivy Leaf*, 1922, 19.
127 *Ivy Leaf*, 1922, 19.
128 *Crescent of Gamma Phi Beta*, 1904, 134.
129 Michael E. Jennings, "The Pride of All Our Hearts: The Founders of Kappa Alpha Psi Fraternity," in *Black Greek-Letter Organizations in the Twenty-First Century: Our Fight Has Just Begun*, ed. Gregory S. Parks (Lexington: University Press of Kentucky, 2008), 115.
130 John Bartlow Martin, *Indiana: An Interpretation* (New York: Knopf, 1992), 189.
131 Jennings, "Pride of All Our Hearts," 115–21, 188–90.
132 André McKenzie, "In the Beginning: The Early History of the Divine Nine," in Brown, Parks, and Phillips, *African American Fraternities and Sororities*, 188–89.
133 William L. Crump, *The Story of Kappa Alpha Psi: A History of the Beginning and Development of a College Greek Letter Organization, 1911–1999* (Philadelphia: Kappa Alpha Psi, 2003); McKenzie, "In the Beginning"; Jennings, "Pride of All Our Hearts."
134 Jennings, "Pride of All Our Hearts," 118.
135 McKenzie, "In the Beginning," 189–90.
136 Jennings, "Pride of All Our Hearts," 121–22.
137 Kappa Alpha Psi Fraternity, Mu Epsilon Chapter, "Kappa Alpha Nu Becomes Kappa Alpha Psi."
138 Kappa Alpha Psi Fraternity, "Kappa Alpha Psi (KAΨ) Founding History."
139 Herman Dreer, *The History of the Omega Psi Phi Fraternity: A Brotherhood of Negro College Men, 1911–1939* (Washington, D.C.: Omega Psi Phi Fraternity, 1940), 12 (establishing the fraternity in 1911).
140 McKenzie, "In the Beginning," 189.
141 McKenzie, "In the Beginning," 191 ("Omega Psi Phi was formed from the initials of the Greek phrase meaning 'Friendship is essential to the soul'").
142 Robert L. Gill, *A History of the Omega Psi Phi Fraternity* (Washington, D.C.: Omega Psi Phi Fraternity, 1963), 1 ("Alpha Phi Alpha Fraternity's Beta Chapter had been established at Howard University in 1907").
143 Dreer, *History of the Omega Psi Phi Fraternity*, 19.

144 Dreer, *History of the Omega Psi Phi Fraternity*, 12–13, 19–24.

145 U. of Minn. Omega Psi Phi Fraternity, "History: This Is Ξ Chapter," www.xiques1921.com.

146 Paula J. Giddings, *In Search of Sisterhood: Delta Sigma Theta and the Challenge of the Black Sorority Movement* (New York: William Morrow, 1988), 48; Michael Livingston II, "Delta Sigma Theta Sorority Celebrates 100 Years of Black Sisterhood in D.C.," *Washington Post*, January 11, 2013, www.washingtonpost.com.

147 Giddings, *In Search of Sisterhood*.

148 Giddings, *In Search of Sisterhood*.

149 Giddings, *In Search of Sisterhood*.

150 Giddings, *In Search of Sisterhood*, 50–51.

151 Giddings, *In Search of Sisterhood*, 48.

152 Giddings, *In Search of Sisterhood*, 53.

153 See Marybeth Gasman, "Passive Activism: Empirical Studies of Black Greek-Letter Organizations," in *Black Greek-Letter Organizations 2.0: New Directions in the Study of African American Fraternities and Sororities*, ed. Matthew W. Hughey and Gregory S. Parks (Jackson: University Press of Mississippi, 2011), 27–41.

154 Mary E. Vroman, *Shaped to Its Purpose: Delta Sigma Theta—The First Fifty Years* (New York: Random House, 1965), 9.

155 Giddings, *In Search of Sisterhood*, 57, 112.

156 Giddings, *In Search of Sisterhood*, 64, 70, 96.

157 Giddings, *In Search of Sisterhood*, 296.

158 Giddings, *In Search of Sisterhood*, 63, 131.

159 W. Sherman Savage and L. D. Reddick, eds., *Our Cause Speeds On: An Informal History of the Phi Beta Sigma Fraternity* (Atlanta: Fuller Press, 1957), 13.

160 I. L. Scruggs, "I Knew A. Langston Taylor in His Early Years," *Crescent* 38, no. 1 (Spring 1954): 15.

161 L. F. Morse, "As I Remember Them," *Crescent* 33, no. 1 (Spring 1949): 8.

162 *The Mirror* (Howard University Yearbook, 1915).

163 A. L. Taylor, "The First Four Years," *Crescent* 33, no. 1 (Spring 1949): 10.

164 Savage and Reddick, *Our Cause Speeds On*, 14; Taylor, "First Four Years," 10.

165 This date is incorrectly listed as October 8, 1913, in the *Sigma Light*, 4th ed. (1981), 25. The actual date is October 18, 1913. This is evidenced by A. L. Taylor's words: "It was in the afternoon of the next to the last Saturday of October 1913 . . . Saturday, October 18, 1913, therefore, is important in that at this time the idea of the new fraternity was proposed and agree to by two persons" (cited in Savage and Reddick, *Our Cause Speeds On*, 14). Accordingly, the next to last Saturday in October 1913 was the 18th; the 8th was a Wednesday.

166 Savage and Reddick, *Our Cause Speeds On*, 14; Taylor, "First Four Years," 10.

167 *The Mirror* (Howard University Yearbook, 1915).

168 *Crescent* 37, no. 1 (Spring 1953): 7.

169 *Crescent* 37, no. 1 (Spring 1953): 7.

170 Savage and Reddick, *Our Cause Speeds On*, 14.

171 Morse, "As I Remember Them," 8.

172 Phi Beta Sigma Fraternity, "Who We Are," www.pbs1914.org.

173 Savage and Reddick, *Our Cause Speeds On*, 14.

174 Brother T. L. Alston's name is sometimes misspelled as "Austin." For instance, in the *Sigma Light*, 4th ed. (1981), 10, his name is spelled "Austin," but in the *Crescent* 33, no. 1 (Spring 1949), 9–10, his name is spelled "Alston" by both founders, Taylor and Morse.

175 Savage and Reddick, *Our Cause Speeds On*, 14.

176 Savage and Reddick, *Our Cause Speeds On*, 15.

177 Savage and Reddick, *Our Cause Speeds On*, 15; Lawrence C. Ross Jr., *The Divine Nine: The History of African American Fraternities and Sororities* (New York: Dafina Books, 2000), 103.

178 Savage and Reddick, *Our Cause Speeds On*, 15–16.
179 Savage and Reddick, *Our Cause Speeds On*, 18.
180 The phrase "talented tenth" was written by W. E. B. Du Bois in September 1903 and was published in *The Negro Problem: A Series of Articles by Representative Negroes of To-day* (New York: James Pott, 1903). Du Bois argued that social change could be accomplished by developing the small group of college-educated, elite blacks he called "the Talented Tenth." He wrote, "Three tasks lay before me; first to show from the past that the Talented Tenth as they have risen among American Negroes have been worthy of leadership; secondly to show how these men may be educated and developed; and thirdly to show their relation to the Negro problem." Du Bois later recounted his words and took up another position advocating against the elitism of his prior argument.
181 "The Philosophy of Phi Beta Sigma," *Sigma Light*, 4th ed. (1981): 17.
182 Savage and Reddick, *Our Cause Speeds On*, 19. It is interesting to note that when I. L. Scruggs graduated from medical school in 1919, he married Ruth Trappe, a member of the Alpha Chapter of Zeta Phi Beta Sorority. Seven years later, in 1926, Ruth Trappe Scruggs was elected grande basileus of Zeta Phi Beta Sorority and served with distinction until 1930.
183 Savage and Reddick, *Our Cause Speeds On*, 22.
184 Savage and Reddick, *Our Cause Speeds On*, 22.
185 Savage and Reddick, *Our Cause Speeds On*, 22.
186 Savage and Reddick, *Our Cause Speeds On*, 7–8.
187 Savage and Reddick, *Our Cause Speeds On*, 21.
188 Savage and Reddick, *Our Cause Speeds On*, 23.
189 Savage and Reddick, *Our Cause Speeds On*, 23.
190 Savage and Reddick, *Our Cause Speeds On*, 25.
191 Savage and Reddick, *Our Cause Speeds On*, 25.
192 Jessica Harris and Vernon C. Mitchell Jr., "A Narrative Critique of Black Greek-Letter Organizations and Social Action," in Parks, *Black Greek-Letter Organizations in the Twenty-First Century*, 143, 7. Phi Beta Sigma helped create the Central Committee of Negro College Men as a response to segregation. Harris and Mitchell, "Narrative Critique." Black soldiers were being led by white officers without any integration of black and white soldiers. Harris and Mitchell, "Narrative Critique." This was unfair to the black soldiers; if they could not receive integration, then they had every right to be led by black officers. Harris and Mitchell, "Narrative Critique." With the suggestion of T. Montgomery Gregory, the Central Committee of Negro College Men became a committee with Mr. C. Benjamin Curley as the secretary to send out letters and telegrams over the country fighting the War Department for the appeal for an "Officers' Reserve Training Camp for Colored Men." Emmett Scott, "Colored Officers and How They Were Treated," in *Scott's Official History of the American Negro in the World War* (1919), http://net.lib.byu.edu. Finally, their cries were heard and the Central Committee of Negro College Men established an officers' training camp for African Americans on May 19, 1917. Central Committee of Negro College Men, "Training Camp for Negro Offices" (Sagamore Hill National Historic Site), www.theodorerooseveltcenter.org.
193 Harris and Mitchell, "Narrative Critique," 143, 7.
194 Robert V. Morris, "Black Officers at Fort Des Moines in WWI," *Iowa Pathways*, www.iptv. org. On May 19, 1917, the U.S. War Department created a military training program for college-age Negro men; this became known as the Seventeenth Provisional Reserved Officer Training Corps (ROTC). In June 1917, the Seventeenth Provisional Training Regiment was organized at Fort Des Moines, Iowa. Over sixteen hundred Negro men from all over the United States were accepted, making the Seventeenth the first training regiment for Negro officers to lead Negro troops in American history. Morris, "Black Officers." Captain G. E. Goodrich, Thirtieth Infantry, was assigned as the senior instructor of the Seventeenth Provisional Training Regiment with his adjutant Major Wm. *Plattsburg* 19 (1917), https://books.

google.com. Together with other educated black cadets in different units, the Seventeenth enlisted hoping to fight Germany in World War I. Morris, "Black Officers."

195 Savage and Reddick, *Our Cause Speeds On*, 26.
196 Savage and Reddick, *Our Cause Speeds On*, 32.
197 *Sigma Light*, 4th ed. (1981): 8.
198 *Sigma Light*, 4th ed. (1981): 13.
199 *Sigma Light*, 4th ed. (1981): 9.
200 Donald J. Jemison, international executive director, Phi Beta Sigma Fraternity, originally written by Gerald D. Smith, executive director (1978–90), Phi Beta Sigma Fraternity, "Founders' Day Speech" (Tuskegee Institute, 2006).
201 McKenzie, "In the Beginning," 184–86. Some scholars have focused on the work of these groups in the area of civil rights activism and efforts to shape public policy. See Gregory S. Parks et al., "Complex Civil Rights Organizations: Alpha Kappa Alpha Sorority, An Exemplar," *Alabama Civil Rights and Civil Liberties Law Review* 6 (2014): 125–66. Others have also explored the role of these groups in the areas of community service and philanthropy in addition to civil rights activism and efforts to shape public policy. See Marcia Hernandez and Gregory S. Parks, "Fortitude in the Face of Adversity: Delta Sigma Theta's History of Racial Uplift," *Hastings Race and Poverty Law Journal* 13, no. 2 (2016): 273; McKenzie, "In the Beginning."
202 "History of the Zeta Phi Beta Sorority," *Crescent*, April 1929, 57.
203 "History of the Zeta Phi Beta Sorority."
204 Jemison, "Founders' Day Speech."
205 Rubye G. Watts, "Highways of Sigma," *Aurora* 17, no. 1 (1947): 3.
206 See Marcia D. Hernandez, "Sisterhood Beyond the Ivory Tower: An Exploration of Black Sorority Alumnae Membership," in Parks, *Black Greek-Letter Organizations in the Twenty-First Century*, 253, 286.
207 Clarenda M. Phillips, "Sisterly Bonds: African American Sororities Rising to Overcome Obstacles," in Brown et al., *African American Fraternities and Sororities*, 139.
208 McKenzie, "In the Beginning," 184–86.
209 McKenzie, "In the Beginning," 184–86.
210 McKenzie, "In the Beginning," 184–86; Bernadette Pruitt et al., "Seven Schoolteachers Challenge the Klan: The Founders of Sigma Gamma Rho Sorority," in Parks, *Black Greek-Letter Organizations in the Twenty-First Century*, 127.

CHAPTER 3. FINDING THEIR WAY
1 See Henley L. Cox, "Current Thought among Modern College Students Part II," *Kappa Alpha Psi Journal*, March 1924, 9.
2 Cox, "Current Thought," 9.
3 Cox, "Current Thought," 9–10.
4 Cox, "Current Thought," 25.
5 Paula J. Giddings, *In Search of Sisterhood: Delta Sigma Theta and the Challenge of the Black Sorority Movement* (New York: William Morrow, 1988), 87, 106.
6 Mary E. Vroman, *Shaped to Its Purpose: Delta Sigma Theta—The First Fifty Years* (New York: Random House, 1965), 26–27.
7 Vroman, *Shaped to Its Purpose*, 82–83.
8 "Go to High School, Go to College Movement," *Sphinx* 10, no. 2 (April 1924): 5–9.
9 "Go to High School," 5–9.
10 "Go to High School," 5–9.
11 "Go to High School," 5–9.
12 "Go to High School," 9.
13 "Go to High School," 32.

14 "Go to High School," 32.
15 Nelson E. Woodley, "Activities of Chapters: Upsilon Chapter," *Sphinx* 10, no. 3 (June 1924): 10.
16 W. Sherman Savage and L. D. Reddick, eds., *Our Cause Speeds On: An Informal History of the Phi Beta Sigma Fraternity* (Atlanta: Fuller Press, 1957), 38.
17 Savage and Reddick, *Our Cause Speeds On.*
18 Savage and Reddick, *Our Cause Speeds On,* 39.
19 J. S. Hughson, "Our Fraternity's Place in Society," *Crescent,* 1924, 14.
20 "The Eleventh Annual Conclave," *Crescent,* April 1925, 1–2.
21 "Eleventh Annual Conclave," 1–2.
22 "Fannie Jackson Coppin, Heroine," *Crescent,* April 1925, 10–13.
23 "Fannie Jackson Coppin," 10–13.
24 *Ivy Leaf* 2, no. 1 (1922–23): 28.
25 *Ivy Leaf* 2, no. 1 (1922–23): 39.
26 *Ivy Leaf* 2, no. 1 (1922–23): 46.
27 William L. Crump, *The Story of Kappa Alpha Psi: A History of the Beginning and Development of a College Greek Letter Organization, 1911–1999* (Philadelphia: Kappa Alpha Psi, 2003), 198; J. J. Peters, "The Guide Right Movement," *Kappa Alpha Psi Journal,* 1925, 12.
28 Crump, *Story of Kappa Alpha Psi,* 198.
29 Crump, *Story of Kappa Alpha Psi.*
30 J. Jerome Peters, "Guide Right—How the Idea Began: Yellowed Notes Reveal Original Drafts of Program Made for St. Louis Alumni," *Kappa Alpha Psi Journal,* April 1938, 319.
31 Crump, *Story of Kappa Alpha Psi,* 198.
32 "Guide Right Week," *Kappa Alpha Psi Journal* 10, no. 7 (April 1924): 1.
33 Lionel F. Artis, *Kappa Alpha Psi Journal,* 1926.
34 "Upsilon Chapter News, 'Guide Right' Movement Launched Here," *Kappa Alpha Psi Journal,* 1924, 7.
35 Peters, "Guide Right Movement," 12.
36 F. B. Ransom, "The Negro Sanhedrin," *Kappa Alpha Psi Journal,* March 1924, 3; see also C. Alvin Hughes, "The Negro Sanhedrin Movement," *Journal of Negro History* 69, no. 1 (Winter 1984).
37 Ransom, "Negro Sanhedrin," 3.
38 Ransom, "Negro Sanhedrin," 3–4.
39 *Thurman-Watts v. Bd. of Edu.,* 222 P. 123 (Kan. 1924); "Significant Victory Won by Topeka Brothers in Coffeyville Case," *Kappa Alpha Psi Journal,* December 1924, 9.
40 See "Prelude to Brown—1924: Thurman-Watts v. Coffeyville" (Brown Foundation), http://brownvboard.org.
41 *Thurman-Watts,* 124; "Significant Victory," 9.
42 *Thurman-Watts,* 124; "Significant Victory," 9.
43 *Thurman-Watts,* 124 (citing *Woolridge v. Bd. of Educ.,* 157 P. 1184 [Kan. 1916]).
44 *Thurman-Watts,* 125; "Significant Victory," 9–10.
45 "Significant Victory," 9–10.
46 "Negro Education in the South," *Kappa Alpha Psi Journal,* January 1927, 1.
47 *Ivy Leaf* 3, no. 1 (1924): 44.
48 Savage and Reddick, *Our Cause Speeds On,* 59.
49 "Report of the 13th Annual Conclave of Phi Beta Sigma Fraternity Held At A. & T. College, Greensboro, N.C., Dec. 26–29, 1926," *Crescent* 5, no. 1 (1927):10.
50 "Report of the 13th Annual Conclave."
51 *Sphinx,* February 1924, 10; Charles H. Wesley, *The History of Alpha Phi Alpha: A Development in College Life, 1906–1979,* 16th ed. (Baltimore: Foundation Publishers, 1996), 153.

52 "The Negro Sanhedrin," *Sphinx*, February 1924, 18; see also "The Sanhedrin," *Sphinx* 10, no. 2 (April 1924): 8–10.

53 "Negro Sanhedrin," 18.

54 "Negro Sanhedrin."

55 V. E. Daniels, "Opinion-Forming among Negro Americans," *Sphinx*, April 1925, 6–7.

56 Daniels, "Opinion-Forming," 6–7.

57 Daniels, "Opinion-Forming," 6–7.

58 Daniels, "Opinion-Forming," 6–7.

59 Charles West, "The Colored World in Athletics," *Sphinx* 11, no. 4 (October 1925): 4–6.

60 "Lest They Forget," *Sphinx* 11, no. 4 (October 1925): 8–9.

61 *Sphinx*, December 1924, 30.

62 *Sphinx*, April 1925, 27.

63 *Sphinx*, April 1925, 28–29.

64 "A Successful Educational Campaign," *Sphinx* 11, no. 3 (June 1925): 4.

65 Julian H. Lewis, "The Public Session," *Sphinx* 12, no. 1 (February 1926): 6–9.

66 Lewis, "Public Session," 6–9.

67 Lewis, "Public Session," 6–9.

68 Victor R. Daly, "The Educational Movement and Endowment Plan," *Sphinx* 13, no. 2 (April 1927): 17.

69 *Sphinx*, June 1927, 20.

70 Savage and Reddick, *Our Cause Speeds On*, 47. It is important to note that "Education" and "Social Action" were adopted as the additional two national programs in 1934 and 1945, respectively.

71 The program was created by the Phi Beta Sigma Fraternity at the 1924 Fraternal Conclave in Philadelphia. While it started out as an exhibit, it was very successful and was made the official public program of the fraternity at the 1925 conclave in Richmond, Virginia. Today the program is dedicated to supporting and promoting minority businesses and services. Dr. I. L. Scruggs, "Excerpts from Our Cause Speeds On" (Phi Beta Sigma Fraternity, Eastern Region), www.pbseast.org/bbb/.

72 Savage and Reddick, *Our Cause Speeds On*, 42. Woodhouse was president from 1923 to 1925. He was also a member of the Zeta Sigma service chapter.

73 Savage and Reddick, *Our Cause Speeds On*, 45.

74 Savage and Reddick, *Our Cause Speeds On*, 46.

75 Savage and Reddick, *Our Cause Speeds On*, 53.

76 "Bigger and Better Business Week, Its Value in the Economic Outlook of the Negro," *Crescent*, March 1927, 5–7.

77 "Bigger and Better Business Week," 5–7.

78 "Bigger and Better Business Week," 5–7.

79 "Bigger and Better Business Week," 5–7.

80 W. Clemmons Burnett, "Alpha Phi Alpha and Opportunity for Service," *Sphinx* 12, no. 1 (February 1926): 29–30.

81 Burnett, "Alpha Phi Alpha," 29–30.

82 Raymond W. Cannon, "Origin, Purpose and Operation of the Go-to-High-School-and-College Movement," *Sphinx* 12, no. 2 (April 1926): 3–4.

83 "Editorial: Inter-Fraternal 'Super Service,'" *Sphinx* 12, no. 5 (December 1926): 5.

84 John E. Oakes, "Study Business College Men," *Sphinx* 12, no. 5 (December 1926): 25.

85 Oakes, "Study Business College Men," 25.

86 Oakes, "Study Business College Men," 25.

87 Oakes, "Study Business College Men," 25.

88 Oakes, "Study Business College Men," 25.

89 Oakes, "Study Business College Men," 25.

90 Oakes, "Study Business College Men," 17.

91 *Ivy Leaf*, 1924, 44.

92 *Ivy Leaf*, 1925, 23.

93 *Ivy Leaf*, 1926, 64.

94 *Ivy Leaf*, 1926, 31.

95 *Ivy Leaf*, 1926, 31.

96 *Ivy Leaf*, 1926, 67.

97 Savage and Reddick, *Our Cause Speeds On*, 22.

98 Savage and Reddick, *Our Cause Speeds On*, 22.

99 "Clean Speech Movement," *Crescent*, 1925, 4.

100 "Clean Speech Movement," 4.

101 "Clean Speech Movement," 4.

102 Savage and Reddick, *Our Cause Speeds On*, 46–47.

103 "Report of the 13th Annual Conclave of Phi Beta Sigma Fraternity Held at A&T College, Greensboro, N.C., Dec. 26–29, 1926," *Crescent*, 1927, 5, 10.

104 Savage and Reddick, *Our Cause Speeds On*, 59.

105 Savage and Reddick, *Our Cause Speeds On*, 61.

106 "Heritage" (Zeta Phi Beta Sorority), www.zphib1920.org.

107 "Incorporators" (Zeta Phi Beta Sorority), www.zphib1920.org.

108 Robert L. Gill, *A History of the Omega Psi Phi Fraternity* (Washington, D.C.: Omega Psi Phi Fraternity, 1963), 65.

109 "The Achievement Project," *Oracle*, 1927, 78.

110 Gill, *History of the Omega Psi Phi Fraternity*, 65.

111 Gill, *History of the Omega Psi Phi Fraternity*, 65; "Our Negro Achievement Project," *Oracle*, 1926, 107.

112 Gill, *History of the Omega Psi Phi Fraternity*, 65.

113 Gill, *History of the Omega Psi Phi Fraternity*, 67.

114 Albertus B. Conn, "Epsilon Chapter," *Sphinx* 10, no. 3 (June 1924): 3.

115 H. G. Tolliver, "Zeta Chapter," *Sphinx* 10, no. 3 (June 1924): 5.

116 "'Go-to-High-School, Go-to-College' Movement Brings on More Talk," *Sphinx* 10, no. 4 (October 1924): 22–25, 29.

117 Raymond W. Cannon, "To All Our Sororities and Fraternities, Greetings," *Sphinx* 8, no. 1 (February 1927): 27.

118 Raymond W. Logan, "Negro History Week," *Sphinx* 8, no. 1 (February 1927): 33.

119 Raymond W. Logan, "The Fourth Pan-African Congress," *Sphinx*, June 1927, 8–10.

120 Robert S. Abbot, "We Must Cease Segregating Ourselves," *Sphinx* 8, no. 1 (February 1927): 30–31.

121 Abbot, "We Must Cease Segregating Ourselves," 30–31.

122 W. Drew Perkins, producer, *Alpha Phi Alpha: A Century of Leadership* (DVD; Baltimore: Rubicon Productions, 2006).

123 Giddings, *In Search of Sisterhood*, 113.

124 Giddings, *In Search of Sisterhood*, 123, 126.

125 Giddings, *In Search of Sisterhood*, 144.

126 Vroman, *Shaped to Its Purpose*, 34.

127 Giddings, *In Search of Sisterhood*, 144.

CHAPTER 4. BLACK GREEK-LETTER ORGANIZATIONS AS SOCIAL WELFARE NETS (1930–1939)

1 For example, in the section titled "Along the Color Line: Social Uplift," an announcement in the March 1912 edition of the *Crisis* (vol. 3, no. 5) states, "The fourth annual convention of the Alpha Phi Alpha Fraternity was held at Ann Arbor, Mich. This is a colored Greek-letter

fraternity, which has twelve active chapters in the best universities of the country. Charles H. Garvin of Howard was elected president" (185).

2 Patricia Sullivan, *Lift Every Voice: The NAACP and the Making of the Civil Rights Movement* (New York: New Press, 2009), 152.

3 Kenneth Robert Janken, *Walter White: Mr. NAACP* (Chapel Hill: University of North Carolina Press, 2006), 166.

4 Sullivan, *Lift Every Voice*, 155.

5 Richard Kluger, *Simple Justice: The History of* Brown v. Board of Education *and Black America's Struggle for Equality* (New York: Vintage, 2004), 170.

6 Library of Congress, "Race Relations in the 1930s and 1940s," www.loc.gov.

7 Library of Congress, "Race Relations in the 1930s and 1940s."

8 Library of Congress, "Race Relations in the 1930s and 1940s."

9 An important, albeit personal, detail for readers: the co-author of this book, Matthew W. Hughey, was named after Matthew W. Bullock (1881–1972), who was also among the first African American members, and leaders, of the Baha'i Faith.

10 National Pan-Hellenic Council, "Our History," www.nphchq.org.

11 Walter Kimbrough, *Black Greek 101: The Culture, Customs, and Challenges of Black Fraternities and Sororities* (Madison, N.J.: Fairleigh Dickinson, 2003), 36.

12 Kimbrough, *Black Greek 101*, 36.

13 "Sorority News: Chapter Installs Its New Officers," *New York Amsterdam News*, January 25, 1936, 6.

14 "Iota Phi Lambda Sorority Meets in Washington," *New York Amsterdam News*, September 10, 1938, 4.

15 "Pan-Hellenic Council Meets: Eight Greek-Letter Societies to Assemble Here for 11th Confab," *New York Amsterdam News*, August 26, 1939, 5.

16 Deborah E. Whaley, *Disciplining Women: Alpha Kappa Alpha, Black Counterpublics, and the Cultural Politics of Black Sororities* (Albany: State University of New York Press, 2010), 41.

17 Marcia Hernandez and Harriet Arnold, "'The Harvest Is Plentiful but the Laborers Are Few': An Interdisciplinary Examination of Career Choice and African American Sororities," *Journal of African American Studies* 16 (2012): 666.

18 Hernandez and Arnold, "'Harvest Is Plentiful,'" 660.

19 Hank Nuwer, *Wrongs of Passage: Fraternities, Sororities, Hazing, and Binge Drinking* (Bloomington: Indiana University Press, 1999), 178.

20 Hernandez and Arnold, "'Harvest Is Plentiful,'" 663.

21 Marybeth Gasman and Halima Leak, "Leadership of Philanthropy through African American Sororities and Fraternities," in *Leadership in Nonprofit Organizations: A Reference Handbook*, ed. Kathryn A. Agard (Thousand Oaks, Calif.: Sage, 2011), 286.

22 Gasman and Leak, "Leadership of Philanthropy," 289–90.

23 Pearl Schwartz White, *Behind These Doors—A Legacy: The History of Sigma Gamma Rho Sorority* (Chicago: Sigma Gamma Rho Sorority, 1974), 32.

24 White, *Behind These Doors*, 19.

25 White, *Behind These Doors*, 26.

26 Lullelia W. Harrison, *Torchbearers of a Legacy: A History of Zeta Phi Beta Sorority, Inc. 1920–1997* (Washington, D.C.: Zeta Phi Beta Sorority, 1998), 159.

27 Harrison, *Torchbearers of a Legacy*, 159–60.

28 Harrison, *Torchbearers of a Legacy*, 31–32, 159.

29 Harrison, *Torchbearers of a Legacy*, 47.

30 "Nu Alpha Chapter," *Archon* 8, no. 2 (1939): 20.

31 "Dickson Recreational and Religious Education Project," *Archon* 10, no. 3 (1942): 7.

32 "Chapter Chatters," *Archon* 8, no. 2 (1939): 21.

33 Myrtle C. Griffin, "Possible Goal of Achievement as Women," *Archon* 8, no. 2 (1939): 2.

34 Dorothy M. Hendricks, "Our Three Fields," *Archon* 8, no. 2 (1939): 19.

35 Hendricks, "Our Three Fields," 19.

36 Hendricks, "Our Three Fields," 19.

37 "Zeta Phi Beta Southern Regional Conference," *Archon* 8, no. 2 (1939): 7.

38 "Chapter Chatters," *Archon* 8, no. 2 (1939): 20.

39 "Chapter Chatters," 20.

40 "Chapter Chatters," 22.

41 Paula J. Giddings, *In Search of Sisterhood: Delta Sigma Theta and the Challenge of the Black Sorority Movement* (New York: William Morrow, 1988), 159, 161, 180.

42 Tom Ward, "Medical Missionaries of the Delta: Dr. Dorothy Ferebee and the Mississippi Health Project, 1935–1941," *Journal of Mississippi History* 63, no. 3 (2001): 189–203; Whaley, *Disciplining Women*, 47.

43 Giddings, *In Search of Sisterhood*, 180.

44 Mary E. Vroman, *Shaped to Its Purpose: Delta Sigma Theta—The First Fifty Years* (New York: Random House, 1965), 101.

45 *Delta*, 1979, 9.

46 *Ivy Leaf*, December 1931, 12.

47 *Ivy Leaf*, December 1931, 12.

48 *Ivy Leaf*, December 1931, 14.

49 *Ivy Leaf*, December 1932, 16.

50 *Ivy Leaf*, December 1932, 3.

51 *Ivy Leaf*, March 1933, 105.

52 *Ivy Leaf*, March 1933, 110.

53 *Ivy Leaf*, March 1933, 107.

54 *Ivy Leaf*, March 1933, 111.

55 *Ivy Leaf*, December 1933, 13.

56 Ida Louise Jackson, "Service Project: 'Summer School for Teachers'—Saints Industrial School, Lexington, Mississippi," *Ivy Leaf*, June 1934, 20.

57 *Ivy Leaf*, June 1935, 11.

58 *Ivy Leaf*, December 1935, 15.

59 *Ivy Leaf*, December 1935, 18.

60 Dorothy Boulding-Ferebee, "Alpha Kappa Alpha's Health Project," *Ivy Leaf*, September 1939, 20.

61 *Ivy Leaf*, June 1939, 10.

62 "Mississippi Health Project," *Ivy Leaf*, September 1936, 18.

63 Dorothy Boulding-Ferebee, "Our 1937 Mississippi Health Project," *Ivy Leaf*, September 1937, 4.

64 Marjorie Holloman, "Concerning the Health Project," *Ivy Leaf*, December 1938, 5–6.

65 *Ivy Leaf*, December 1935, 18.

66 *Ivy Leaf*, July 1936, 50.

67 *Ivy Leaf*, December 1937, 24.

68 *Ivy Leaf*, September 1937, 10.

69 *Ivy Leaf*, December 1937, 24.

70 *Ivy Leaf*, December 1937, 6.

71 Mary Church Terrell, "Conference on the Participation of Negro Women and Children in Federal Welfare Programs," *Ivy Leaf*, June 1938, 16.

72 Terrell, "Conference on the Participation," 16.

73 Terrell, "Conference on the Participation," 16.

74 Terrell, "Conference on the Participation," 16.

75 "In the Community," *Ivy Leaf*, June 1939, 6.

76 "Alpha Kappa Alpha at the Conference of the NAACP," *Ivy Leaf*, September 1939, 1–2.

77 "In the Community," *Ivy Leaf*, June 1939, 7.

78 "In the Community," *Ivy Leaf*, September 1939, 12–13.

79 Lionel F. Artis, *Kappa Alpha Psi Journal*, 1930.

80 R. J. Reynolds, "Marked Guide Right Interest Seen," *Kappa Alpha Psi Journal*, March 1940; "Guide Right Calls Us Again: Every Chapter and Every Kappaman Expected to Do His Part for Movement," *Kappa Alpha Psi Journal*, March 1940, 137–38.

81 Robert L. Gill, *A History of the Omega Psi Phi Fraternity* (Washington, D.C.: Omega Psi Phi Fraternity, 1963), 24.

82 Gill, *History of the Omega Psi Phi Fraternity*, 223–24.

83 Gill, *History of the Omega Psi Phi Fraternity*, 223–24.

84 Gill, *History of the Omega Psi Phi Fraternity*, 224.

85 Charles H. Wesley, *The History of Alpha Phi Alpha: A Development in College Life, 1906–1979*, 16th ed. (Baltimore: Foundation Publishers, 1996), 253–54.

86 Wesley, *History of Alpha Phi Alpha*, 253.

87 O. Wilson Winters, "Fraternity Fun," *Sphinx* 27, no. 3 (August 1939): 26.

88 Charles H. Wesley, "The Message and Convention Call," *Sphinx* 27, no. 3 (August 1939): 3, 38.

89 John F. Cuyjet, "Achievements Cited: Alpha Zeta Chapter," *Sphinx* 27, no. 3 (August 1939): 37.

90 George R. Arthur, "An Address Made by George R. Arthur to Chicago Brothers," *Sphinx* 27, no. 3 (August 1939): 24–25.

91 Arthur, "Address," 24–25.

92 Ewwart Gunier Papers, New York Public Library, Schomburg Center for Research in Black Culture.

93 Arthur, "Address," 225.

94 Arthur, "Address," 123–29. Cast against the backdrop of the Great Depression, white tenant farmers had exhibited hostility toward blacks in many parts of Texas. In May 1930, George Hughes, a black farmhand, was accused of raping an unidentified white woman. Hughes admittedly went to the farm just southeast of Sherman, Texas, in search of the woman's husband, who owed him wages. Hughes reportedly demanded his wages at gunpoint and raped the woman. He ultimately surrendered to authorities and was indicted for criminal assault by a grand jury. In the days just before the trial, rumors spread about the case, among them that Hughes's alleged victim was unlikely to survive her injuries. A medical examination of the woman and of Hughes proved the rumors to be false. In the midst of the jury trial, a white mob forced its way into the courtroom. Despite Rangers' efforts to secure Hughes, he was seized and dragged behind a car to the front of a drugstore in the black business section. There, he was hanged from a tree by the mob. Furnishings from local black businesses were used to fuel a fire under Hughes's hanging corpse. The mob also burned down various black businesses in the area and prevented firemen from saving the burning buildings. By daybreak, most of the town's black businesses and a residence were in ashes. See Texas State Historical Association, "Sherman Riot of 1930," https://tshaonline.org.

95 Giddings, *In Search of Sisterhood*, 136.

96 Roger Keeran, "National Groups and the Popular Front: The Case of the International Workers Order," *Journal of American Ethnic History* 14, no. 3 (1995): 23.

97 Keeran, "National Groups and the Popular Front."

98 Keeran, "National Groups and the Popular Front," 128.

99 Vroman, *Shaped to Its Purpose*, 35.

100 Vroman, *Shaped to Its Purpose*, 42.

101 Giddings, *In Search of Sisterhood*, 161.

102 *Ivy Leaf*, March 1934, 12.

103 *Ivy Leaf*, June 1934, 3.

104 *Ivy Leaf*, March 1936, 33.

105 "In the Community," *Ivy Leaf*, September 1939, 12.

106 "Our Lobby Project," *Ivy Leaf*, September 1939, 6.

107 *Ivy Leaf*, March 1939, 18.

108 W. Sherman Savage and L. D. Reddick, *Our Cause Speeds On: An Informal History of the Phi Beta Sigma Fraternity* (Atlanta: Fuller Press, 1957), 87.

109 Savage and Reddick, *Our Cause Speeds On*, 91.

110 Savage and Reddick, *Our Cause Speeds On*, 93.

111 Savage and Reddick, *Our Cause Speeds On*, 95.

112 "Retail Merchandising among Negroes," *Crescent*, December 1929, 5–7.

113 "Retail Merchandising among Negroes," 5–7.

114 Savage and Reddick, *Our Cause Speeds On*, 106.

115 Savage and Reddick, *Our Cause Speeds On*, 116.

116 Savage and Reddick, *Our Cause Speeds On*, 120.

117 Hugo Black, a senator from Alabama, sponsored the administration bill in the senate, and William P. Connery a representative from Massachusetts, sponsored the bill in the House. In general terms, the bill provided for a forty-cents-an-hour minimum wage, a forty-hour maximum workweek, and a minimum working age of sixteen except in certain industries outside of mining and manufacturing. The Black-Connery bill had wide public support. However, there were strong opponents who argued that it was poorly drawn legislation that would lead the country to turmoil. The Senate passed a weakened version of the bill in 1937, but a coalition of Republicans and conservative Democrats kept it in the House Rules Committee, and it was never voted on. U.S. Department of Labor, "Fair Labor Standards Act of 1938: Maximum Struggle for a Minimum Wage," www.dol.gov.

118 Robert F. Wagner, a senator from New York, and Frederick Van Nuys, a senator from Indiana, introduced this bill to the Senate. The main goal of this legislation was to provide punishment for any legal officer "whose negligence leads to the lynching of a person entrusted in his custody." Additionally, it would fine any political subdivision that failed to protect and provide a fair trial for an individual suspected or accused of a crime. United Press, "Anti-Lynching Bill Offered in Senate," *Pittsburgh Post-Gazette*, February 25, 1937, https://news.google.com.

119 Savage and Reddick, *Our Cause Speeds On*, 109.

120 Peter Irons, "Jim Crow's Schools" (American Federation of Teachers), www.aft.org.

121 "The Negro's Best Champion," *Crescent*, April 1929, 12.

122 George W. Lawrence was an attorney in Chicago. National Pan-Hellenic Council, "NPHC Presidents," www.nphchq.org. Lawrence was a charter member of the Upsilon Sigma Chapter located in Chicago in 1927. Upsilon Sigma Chapter, "About Upsilon Sigma Chapter," www.dwaynedixon.com. He served as the national president of Phi Beta Sigma Fraternity from 1938 to 1940. Additionally, he was president of the National Pan-Hellenic Council from 1941 to 1943. National Pan-Hellenic Council, "NPHC Presidents."

123 William L. Crump, *The Story of Kappa Alpha Psi: A History of the Beginning and Development of a College Greek Letter Organization, 1911–1999* (Philadelphia: Kappa Alpha Psi, 2003), 56–57.

124 Crump, *Story of Kappa Alpha Psi*, 56–57.

125 Crump, *Story of Kappa Alpha Psi*, 56–57. "Lynch Law," says the *Virginia Lancet*, "as known by that appellation, had its origin in 1780 in a combination of citizens of Pittsylvania County, Virginia, entered into for the purpose of suppressing a trained band of horse thieves and counterfeiters whose well concocted schemes had bidden defiance to the ordinary laws of the land, and whose success encouraged and emboldened them in their outrages upon the community. Col. Wm. Lynch drafted the constitution for this combination of citizens, and hence 'Lynch Law' has ever since been the name given to the summary infliction of punishment by private and unauthorized citizens."

126 J. William Harris, "Etiquette, Lynching, and Racial Boundaries in Southern History: A Mississippi Example," *American Historical Review* 100, no. 2 (April 1995): 391.

127 William Ziglar, "The Decline of Lynching in America," *International Social Science Review* 63, no. 1 (Winter 1988): 14–25.

128 Harris, "Etiquette, Lynching, and Racial Boundaries," 393.

129 Harris, "Etiquette, Lynching, and Racial Boundaries." This typology is drawn from the work of W. Fitzhugh Brundage, *Lynching in the New South: Georgia and Virginia, 1880–1930* (Urbana: University of Illinois Press, 1993), 36–45.

130 Arthur, "Address," 97–98.

131 Arthur, "Address," 156–58.

132 Crump, *Story of Kappa Alpha Psi*, 61.

133 "Problems of Race Attacked in Kappas Numerous Resolutions," *Kappa Alpha Psi Journal*, February 1938, 28.

134 Crump, *Story of Kappa Alpha Psi*, 64.

135 "Anti-Lynching Legislation," *Kappa Alpha Psi Journal*, October 1937, 197.

136 "Anti-Lynching Legislation," 197.

137 Jeffrey A. Raffel, "History of School Desegregation," in *School Desegregation in the 21st Century*, ed. Christine H. Rossell, David J. Armor, and Herbert J. Walberg (Westport, Conn.: Praeger, 2020), 20.

138 White, *Behind These Doors*, 18.

139 White, *Behind These Doors* , 18.

140 *Ivy Leaf*, September 1937, 10.

141 George A. Singleton, "The Idea of Progress," *Sphinx* 17, no. 3 (October 1930): 24.

142 Singleton, "Idea of Progress," 24.

143 Singleton, "Idea of Progress," 24.

144 Raymond W. Cannon, Director of Education, "Messages from Our General Officers: Information Wanted," *Sphinx* 16, no. 5 (December 1930): 14.

145 Cannon, "Messages from Our General Officers," 14.

146 Cannon, "Messages from Our General Officers," 14.

147 Charles W. Anderson Jr., "What Led to Freedom," *Sphinx* 17, no. 1 (February 1930): 10, 12.

148 Anderson, "What Led to Freedom," 21.

149 Charles H. Wesley, *Henry Arthur Callis: Life and Legacy* (Baltimore: Foundation Publishers, 1997), 1.

150 *Nixon v. Condon*, 286 U.S. 73 (1932).

151 *Nixon v. Condon*.

152 *Nixon v. Condon*.

153 *Nixon v. Condon*, 82.

154 *Nixon v. Condon*.

155 *Nixon v. Condon*.

156 *Nixon v. Condon*, 34 F.2d 464 (W.D. Tex. 1929).

157 *Nixon v. Condon*, 49 F.2d 1012 (5th Cir. 1931).

158 *Nixon v. Condon*, 286 U.S. 73 (1932).

159 *Nixon v. Condon*.

160 *Nixon v. Condon*.

161 *Nixon v. Condon*, 226.

162 *Nixon v. Condon*.

163 *Nixon v. Condon*.

164 *Nixon v. Condon*, 227.

165 Wesley, *History of Alpha Phi Alpha*, 227.

166 Rawn James Jr., *Root and Branch: Charles Hamilton Houston, Thurgood Marshall, and the Struggle to End Segregation* (New York: Bloomsbury, 2010), 66.

167 Leland B. Ware, "Setting the Stage for Brown: The Development and Implementation of the NAACP's School Desegregation Campaign, 1930–1950," *Mercer Law Review* 52 (Winter 2001): 644.

168 James, *Root and Branch*, 67.

169 James, *Root and Branch*, 67; Wesley, *History of Alpha Phi Alpha*, 217–18.

170 James, *Root and Branch*, 68.

171 James, *Root and Branch*, 68. It has been noted that there was a competition between Charles Houston and Belford Lawson to see who would file the *Murray* case. See Oliver W. Hill Sr., *The Big Bang:* Brown v. Board of Education *and Beyond—The Autobiography of Oliver W. Hill, Sr.*, ed. Jonathan K Stubbs (Winter Park, Fla.: Four-G, 2000), 158.

172 Wesley, *History of Alpha Phi Alpha*, 227.

173 Wesley, *History of Alpha Phi Alpha*, 226–27.

174 Wesley, *History of Alpha Phi Alpha*, 226–27.

175 *Pearson v. Murray*, 169 Md. 478, 182 A. 590 (1936).

176 Wesley, *History of Alpha Phi Alpha*, 223.

177 James, *Root and Branch*, 185.

178 "Rural Policeman Who Slew Unarmed Motorist 'Not Guilty,'" *Negro Star*, May 17, 1935.

179 "Rural Policeman."

180 Wesley, *History of Alpha Phi Alpha*, 227–28.

181 *Missouri ex rel. Gaines v. Canada*, 305 U.S. 337 (1938).

182 Wesley, *The History of Alpha Phi Alpha*, 220.

183 Wesley, *History of Alpha Phi Alpha*, 220.

184 Wesley, *History of Alpha Phi Alpha*, 236.

185 *Williams v. Zimmerman*, 192 A. 353 (Md. 1937).

186 J. M. Gandy, "The Annual Fraternity Address," *Sphinx* 13, no. 1 (February 1927): 6, 9.

187 *Missouri ex rel. Gaines*, 305 U.S. 337.

188 *Missouri ex rel. Gaines*.

189 *Gilbert v. Highfill*, 190 So. 813 (Fla. 1939).

190 *Gilbert v. Highfill*.

191 *Gilbert v. Highfill*.

192 *Mills v. Lowndes*, 26 F. Supp. 792 (D. Md. 1939).

193 *Mills v. Lowndes*.

194 *Mills v. Lowndes*.

195 "Black Voter Education Project," *Wichita Times*, May 13, 1976, 2. Roy Wilkins was a noted journalist and civil rights leader in the United States for five decades. NAACP, "NAACP History: Roy Wilkins," www.naacp.org.

196 NAACP, "NAACP History."

197 For example, in 1950 Wilkins co-founded the Leadership Conference on Civil Rights, a civil rights coalition that has organized and executed a national legislative campaign for every major civil rights law since 1957. Wilkins is perhaps best known for his leadership of the NAACP from 1955 to 1977. He became the executive secretary of the organization in 1955, before ultimately becoming the executive director in 1964. Wilkins had extensive roles in the passage of key civil rights legislation, such as *Brown v. Board of Education*, the Civil Rights Act of 1964, and the Voting Rights Act of 1965. He also met and advised presidents Kennedy, Johnson, Nixon, Ford, and Carter on civil rights legislation.

198 NAACP, "NAACP History."

199 Gill, *History of the Omega Psi Phi Fraternity*, 21.

200 Gill, *History of the Omega Psi Phi Fraternity*, 21.

201 *Grovey v. Townsend*, 295 U.S. 45 (1935).

202 *Grovey v. Townsend*, 46–47, 52, 54.

203 *United States v. Classic*, 313 U.S. 299 (1941) ("Interference with the right to vote in the Congressional primary . . . [is] in fact an interference with the effective choice of the voters at the only stage of the election procedure when their choice is of significance"). More specifically, the primary issue in *United States v. Classic* was whether there is a constitutional right of qualified voters to vote in the Louisiana primary, and by extension primaries in all states, to have their ballots counted. *United States v. Classic*, 308. The Democratic Party of Louisiana altered eighty-three primary election ballots cast for one candidate and fourteen cast for another by changing the votes to a third candidate. *United States v. Classic*. The allegation is that this deprived voters of their right to select a congressman. *United States v. Classic*, 308–9. The Eastern District of Louisiana sustained a demurrer to the allegations that was appealed directly to the Supreme Court under the Criminal Appeals Act, which provides that the invalidity or construction of the statute upon which the indictment is founded can be appealed directly. *United States v. Classic*, 309.

   The Supreme Court reversed the district court by holding that the right to participate through the primary in choice of congressional representation is secured by the Constitution to the same extent and manner as the general election. *United States v. Classic*, 323–24. When officials manipulated the votes of ninety-seven voters in the Democratic primary, the voters were deprived of their constitutional right to select their representatives. *United States v. Classic*, 324. The key rationale behind this holding is that the practical operation of the primary election is to secure the election of the Democrat candidate for Congress; thus, interference with voter selection for a desired candidate affects voters' ability to have any meaningful choice in representation in Congress. *United States v. Classic*, 313–14. In other words, "The primary is by law made an integral part of the election machinery, whether the voter exercises his right in a party primary which invariably, sometimes, or never determines the ultimate choice of the representative." *United States v. Classic*, 313.

204 *Smith v. Allwright*, 321 U.S. 649 (1944); Gill, *History of the Omega Psi Phi Fraternity*, 21. Hastie was born in Knoxville, Tennessee, on November 17, 1904. Donna Batten, ed., *The Gale Encyclopedia of American Law*, 3rd ed. (Detroit, Mich.: Gale Research, 2010), 212.

205 *Smith v. Allwright*, 650–51.

206 *Smith v. Allwright*, 652, 664, 666.

207 See, e.g., *Mills v. Bd. of Educ. of Anne Arundel Cty.*, 30 F.Supp. 245 (D. Md. 1939) (holding that black teachers in Maryland deserve the same pay as white teachers).

208 *Mills v. Bd. of Educ. of Anne Arundel Cty.*, 246–49, 251.

209 *University v. Murray*, 182 A. 590 (Md. 1936), Carol T. Bond, 593, www.courtlistener.com.

210 *University v. Murray*, 590–94.

211 Juan Williams, *Thurgood Marshall: American Revolutionary* (New York: Three Rivers Press, 1998), 75–78.

212 "Praises Radio Protest," *Kappa Alpha Psi Journal*, February 1938, 287. Wellington Holland was elected polemarch of the southwestern province at the Twentieth Grand Chapter Meeting in 1930. Crump, *Story of Kappa Alpha Psi*, 42.

213 "Hotel Refusing to Accommodate Conclave Delegate Is Sued," *Kappa Alpha Psi Journal*, February 1938, 287.

214 *Hale v. Kentucky*, 303 U.S. 613, 613, 616 (1938).

215 *Hale v. Kentucky*, 615.

216 James M. Coggs, "Wins Jury Case in Highest Court: Kentucky Reversed, Youth's Life Saved as Ransom Argues Exclusion of Race Jurors," *Kappa Alpha Psi Journal*, May 1938, 345.

217 *Hale v. Kentucky*, 614–16.

218 *Mills v. Bd. of Educ. of Anne Arundel Cty.*, 245–50.

219 *Bone v. State*, 129 S.W.2d 240, 240, 244 (Ark. 1939).

220 Hugh Henson, "If Bloomington Were in Germany! Only One Place Where Indiana University Students May Eat—If They Are Colored," *Kappa Alpha Psi Journal*, March 1939, 111.

221 Henson, "If Bloomington Were in Germany!," 111.

222 "Congress Memorialized to Lower Bars Which Keep Negroes Out of Regular Army," *Kappa Alpha Psi Journal*, March 1939, 120.

223 Michele F. Pacifico, "'Don't Buy Where You Can't Work': The Negro Alliance of Washington," *Washington History* 6, no. 1 (1994): 68.

224 Nina Mjagkij, *Organizing Black America: An Encyclopedia of African American Associations* (New York: Routledge, 2001), 447.

225 Pacifico, "Don't Buy Where You Can't Work," 69.

226 Mjagkij, *Organizing Black America*, 447.

227 Pacifico, "Don't Buy Where You Can't Work," 70.

228 Pacifico, "Don't Buy Where You Can't Work," 70.

229 Gilbert Ware, *William Hastie: Grace under Pressure* (Oxford: Oxford University Press, 1984), 66.

230 "Definition of Clerk Bars Negroes from Office under CWA," *Cleveland Plain Dealer*, December 22, 1933.

231 Pacifico, "Don't Buy Where You Can't Work," 67.

232 Jonathan Scott Holloway, *Confronting the Veil: Abram Harris, Jr., E. Franklin Frazier, and Ralph Bunche, 1919–1941* (Chapel Hill: University of North Carolina Press, 2002), 50–51; see also Ware, *William Hastie*, 66–67.

233 Pacifico, "Don't Buy Where You Can't Work," 73.

234 Pacifico, "Don't Buy Where You Can't Work," 73.

235 Holloway, *Confronting the Veil*, 52; Pacifico, "Don't Buy Where You Can't Work," 72–73.

236 Pacifico, "Don't Buy Where You Can't Work," 74.

237 Pacifico, "Don't Buy Where You Can't Work," 74.

238 Holloway, *Confronting the Veil*, 53.

239 Ware, *William Hastie*, 67.

240 Pacifico, "Don't Buy Where You Can't Work," 74.

241 Pacifico, "Don't Buy Where You Can't Work," 74.

242 Pacifico, "Don't Buy Where You Can't Work," 77.

243 Pacifico, "Don't Buy Where You Can't Work," 77.

244 Ware, *William Hastie*, 74.

245 "Arrest Negro Pickets in Chain Store Boycott," *Cleveland Plain Dealer*, October 6, 1933.

246 Pacifico, "Don't Buy Where You Can't Work," 77.

247 Pacifico, "Don't Buy Where You Can't Work," 77.

248 Pacifico, "Don't Buy Where You Can't Work," 77.

249 Pacifico, "Don't Buy Where You Can't Work," 77.

250 Pacifico, "Don't Buy Where You Can't Work," 77.

251 *New Negro Alliance v. Kaufman*, 78 F.2d 415 (1935).

252 *New Negro Alliance v. Kaufman*.

253 *New Negro Alliance v. Kaufman*, 415–16.

254 *New Negro Alliance v. Kaufman*.

255 *New Negro Alliance v. Kaufman*.

256 *New Negro Alliance v. Kaufman*.

257 *New Negro Alliance v. Kaufman*.

258 Sanitary Grocery Stores would go on to become Safeway Stores. Hill, *Big Bang*, 83.

259 *New Negro Alliance et al. v. Sanitary Grocery Co.*, 92 F.2d 510 (1937).

260 *New Negro Alliance et al. v. Sanitary Grocery Co.*

261 *New Negro Alliance et al. v. Sanitary Grocery Co.*

262 *New Negro Alliance et al. v. Sanitary Grocery Co.*

263 *New Negro Alliance et al. v. Sanitary Grocery Co.*

264 *New Negro All. v. Sanitary Grocery Co.*, 303 U.S. 552, 559–60, 58 S. Ct. 703, 706, 82 L. Ed. 1012 (1938).

265 *New Negro Alliance et al. v. Sanitary Grocery Co.*, 513.

266 Pacifico, "Don't Buy Where You Can't Work," 78.

267 Pacifico, "Don't Buy Where You Can't Work," 78.

268 Monroe Friedman, *Consumer Boycotts: Effecting Change through the Marketplace and the Media* (London: Routledge, 1999), 115; Pacifico, "Don't Buy Where You Can't Work," 79.

269 Pacifico, "Don't Buy Where You Can't Work," 82.

270 Ware, *William Hastie*, 78.

271 Brief for the petitioner at cover, *New Negro Alliance et al. v. Sanitary Grocery Co., Inc.*, 303 U.S. 552 (1938) (No. 511).

272 *Sanitary Grocery Co.*, 303 U.S. 552.

273 *Sanitary Grocery Co.*, 561.

274 *Sanitary Grocery Co.*

275 *Sanitary Grocery Co.*, 563.

276 Ware, *William Hastie*, 79–80.

277 "Obituary: Rites for Belford Lawson, 1st Black Atty. in U.S. to Win Supreme Court Case," *Jet Magazine*, March 11, 1985, 5.

278 Savage and Reddick, *Our Cause Speeds On*, 74.

279 "A Program for the Negro Race," *Crescent*, December 1930, 10.

280 "Program for the Negro Race," 10.

281 "Will the Depression Bring the Negro to His Senses?," *Crescent*, December 1931, 29.

282 J. C. Coleman, "A Reminiscence You'll Enjoy," *Sphinx* 17, no. 1 (February 1930): 8.

283 Forrester B. Washington, "Headway in Social Work," *Sphinx* 16, no. 2 (April 1930): 14, 15.

284 Tom Young, "Where Are We Going, Brothers?," *Sphinx* 16, no. 3 (June 1930): 5, 6.

285 Young, "Where Are We Going, Brothers?," 5, 6.

286 A. A. Taylor, "Why Go to College?," *Sphinx* 17, no. 3(October 1930): 6, 7.

287 Dr. John M. Gandy, "The Virginia Negro," *Sphinx* 17, no. 3 (October 1930): 8, 9.

288 Tom Young, "The Case of Tackle Bell," *Sphinx* 16, no. 5 (December 1930): 7.

289 Associate Editors to the *Sphinx*, "The Sphinx Speaks," *Sphinx* 16, no. 3 (June 1930): 26, 28, 29, 30, 32, 36.

290 Louis B. White, "The Sphinx Speaks: Alpha Theta's Radio Broadcast a Success," *Sphinx* 16, no. 2 (April 1930): 24.

291 White, "Sphinx Speaks," 24.

292 Pacifico, "Don't Buy Where You Can't Work," 28, 33, 36.

293 Kenneth Robert Janken, *Rayford Logan and the Dilemma of the African American Intellectual* (Amherst: University of Massachusetts Press, 1993), 101.

294 Janken, *Rayford Logan*, 101.

295 Janken, *Rayford Logan*, 101.

296 Janken, *Rayford Logan*, 101.

297 Janken, *Rayford Logan*, 101.

298 Janken, *Rayford Logan*, 101.

299 Janken, *Rayford Logan*, 102, 103.

300 Janken, *Rayford Logan*, 103.

301 Janken, *Rayford Logan*, 103.

302 Janken, *Rayford Logan*, 103, 104.

303 Janken, *Rayford Logan*, 104.

304 Janken, *Rayford Logan*, 104.

305 Janken, *Rayford Logan*, 104.

306 Janken, *Rayford Logan*, 104, 105.

307 Janken, *Rayford Logan*, 100.
308 Janken, *Rayford Logan*, 100.
309 Janken, *Rayford Logan*, 104.
310 Janken, *Rayford Logan*, 100, 101.
311 Janken, *Rayford Logan*, 100, 101.
312 Janken, *Rayford Logan*, 101.
313 Janken, *Rayford Logan*, 101.
314 Wesley, *History of Alpha Phi Alpha*, 223.
315 Wesley, *History of Alpha Phi Alpha*, 228.
316 Wesley, *History of Alpha Phi Alpha*, 228.
317 Janken, *Rayford Logan*, 105.
318 Wesley, *History of Alpha Phi Alpha*, 229.
319 Wesley, *History of Alpha Phi Alpha*, 229.
320 Wesley, *History of Alpha Phi Alpha*, 229.
321 Wesley, *History of Alpha Phi Alpha*, 242–43.
322 Wesley, *History of Alpha Phi Alpha*, 243.
323 W. Drew Perkins, producer, *Alpha Phi Alpha: A Century of Leadership* (DVD; Baltimore: Rubicon Productions, 2006).
324 Milton S. J. Wright, "Does the Negro Really Care?," *Sphinx* 24, no. 2 (May 1938): 9, 44–45.
325 Wright, "Does the Negro Really Care?," 9, 44–45.
326 Rayford W. Logan, "Alpha's Educational Program," *Sphinx* 24, no. 2 (May 1938): 4.
327 Logan, "Alpha's Educational Program," 6.
328 Barbee Wm. Durham, "Voice of the Sphinx: Alpha Rho Lambda," *Sphinx* 24, no. 2 (May 1938): 18.
329 Bill Crawford, "Voice of the Sphinx: Alpha Phi Lambda Chapter," *Sphinx* 24, no. 2 (May 1938): 21.
330 Sigma Gamma Rho's most significant resource when shaping public policy may have been its beloved publication, the *Aurora*, generally used as a mechanism to spark sorority action throughout its existence. For instance, in Sigma Gamma Rho's second era, member Ethel Smith authored an article, "Woman's Place in the Negro's Forward March," that urged members to take a part in the "revolutionary changes" of the times. White, *Behind These Doors*, 14. Beginning in 1942, the *Aurora* began printing articles that would prove influential to the public at large. Two articles led the charge: "The Negro in the Defense Program" and "The Negro Women in Civilian Defense Work." Both were aimed at informing African Americans of community resources and protesting areas in which racial discrimination was found. White, *Behind These Doors*, 35. By the 1970s the *Aurora* had published a variety of articles addressing human needs, such as "Don't Pigeon Hole People," "New Dimensions for Black Greek Organizations," and "The Key to Relevance." White, *Behind These Doors*, 126. The *Aurora* reflected "sisterhood, human concern, and youth dedication." White, *Behind These Doors*, 140.
331 See Michael H. Washington and Cheryl L. Nuñez, "Racial Uplift, and the Rise of the Greek-Letter Tradition: The African American Quest for Status in the Early Twentieth Century," in *African American Fraternities and Sororities: The Legacy and the Vision*, 2nd ed., ed. Tamara L. Brown, Gregory S. Parks, and Clarenda M. Phillips (Lexington: University Press of Kentucky, 2012), 141.
332 James L. Roark et al., *The American Promise: A History of the United States*, 5th ed. (Boston: Bedford/St. Martin's, 2012), 809.
333 William A. Sundstrom, "Last Hired, First Fired? Unemployment and Urban Black Workers during the Great Depression," *Journal of Economic History* 52, no. 2 (1992): 415.

334 "Reports on Negro Women: Labor Department Says Ratio of Workers in Twice That of White," *Aurora* 33, no. 4 (1964): 2.

335 White, *Behind These Doors*, 11.

336 White, *Behind These Doors*, 21.

337 White, *Behind These Doors*, 17.

338 White, *Behind These Doors*, 18.

339 White, *Behind These Doors*, 19.

340 White, *Behind These Doors*, 18.

341 See "Amelia Boynton Biography," Biography.com, www.biography.com; Margalit Fox, "Amelia Boynton Robinson, a Pivotal Figure at the Selma March, Dies at 104," *New York Times*, August 26, 2015, www.nytimes.com.

342 Savage and Reddick, *Our Cause Speeds On*, 71.

343 Savage and Reddick, *Our Cause Speeds On*, 79.

344 Savage and Reddick, *Our Cause Speeds On*, 102.

345 "Our National Social Action Program," *Crescent*, Spring 1956, 9.

346 "The Haitian-Virgin Isle Commission," *Crescent*, 1927, 3.

347 Savage and Reddick, *Our Cause Speeds On*, 74–75.

348 Savage and Reddick, *Our Cause Speeds On*, 83.

349 Zeta Omega Chapter Omega Psi Phi Fraternity, "History of Achievement Week," http://zetaomega.com.

350 Maudelle B. Bousfield, "Remarks for Radio Broadcasting Station WLW," *Ivy Leaf*, December 1932, 34.

351 *Ivy Leaf*, June 1934, 17.

352 *Ivy Leaf*, March 1934.

353 *Ivy Leaf*, September 1934, 22.

354 *Ivy Leaf*, September 1934, 28–29.

355 Marjorie H. Parker, *Past Is Prologue: The History of Alpha Kappa Alpha 1908–1999* (Washington, D.C.: Marjorie H. Parker, 1999), 194.

356 Parker, *Past Is Prologue*, 195; Howard H. Long, *The American Council on Human Rights: An Evolution* (Washington, D.C.: American Council on Human Rights, 1954), 3; ACHR: Mobilization for Human Rights (1952), 7; Edna Over Campbell, "The American Council on Human Rights: What It Is and How It Operates" (Washington, D.C.: American Council on Human Rights, 1959), 1.

357 Jeanetta Welch and Kathryn Johnson, "National Non-Partisan Council on Public Affairs," *Ivy Leaf*, March 1941, 10.

358 Welch and Johnson, "National Non-Partisan Council," 10.

359 Norma E. Boyd, "National Non-Partisan Council on Public Affairs—Planning for Tomorrow," *Ivy Leaf*, March 1944, 7.

360 Parker, *Past Is Prologue*, 195.

361 Norma E. Boyd and Thomasina Johnson, "The Non-Partisan Council on Public Affairs," *Ivy Leaf*, June 1943, 6.

362 Boyd and Johnson, "National Non-Partisan Council," 8. The budget for the organization was $17,000. Long, *American Council on Human Rights*, 118. The consistent goal, however, was $25,000. Long, *American Council on Human Rights*, 121.

363 Parker, *Past Is Prologue*, 4.

364 Parker, *Past Is Prologue*, 4.

365 Parker, *Past Is Prologue*, 4.

366 Parker, *Past Is Prologue*, 4.

367 Parker, *Past Is Prologue*, 4.

368 Parker, *Past Is Prologue*, 4.

CHAPTER 5. SPREADING THE WORD

1 Eve Tobey, "Executive Order 8802 and Executive Order 10730," *Prezi*, https://prezi.com.

2 Marjorie H. Parker, *Past Is Prologue: The History of Alpha Kappa Alpha 1908–1999* (Washington, D.C.: Marjorie H. Parker, 1999), 4.

3 Parker, *Past Is Prologue*.

4 Parker, *Past Is Prologue*, 196.

5 Norma E. Boyd and Thomasina Johnson, "National Non-Partisan Council on Public Affairs," *Ivy Leaf*, December 1943, 8.

6 Norma E. Boyd, "National Non-Partisan Council on Public Affairs," *Ivy Leaf*, December 1943, 5 (hereinafter Boyd, December 1943).

7 Boyd, December 1943.

8 Boyd, December 1943.

9 Norma E. Boyd, "The Non-Partisan Council on Public Affairs," *Ivy Leaf*, September 1943, 8 (hereinafter Boyd, September 1943).

10 Boyd, September 1943.

11 Boyd, September 1943, 7–8.

12 Norma E. Boyd and Thomasina Johnson, "National Non-Partisan Council on Public Affairs," *Ivy Leaf*, March 1945, 8.

13 Zatella R. Turner, ed., "National Non-Partisan Council on Public Affairs," *Ivy Leaf*, December 1943, 8.

14 Turner, "National Non-Partisan Council."

15 Parker, *Past Is Prologue*, 196.

16 Parker, *Past Is Prologue*.

17 Norma E. Boyd, "Dear Sorors . . . ," *Ivy Leaf*, June 1947, 18.

18 Parker, *Past Is Prologue*, 196.

19 Parker, *Past Is Prologue*, 197.

20 J. H. Calhoun Jr., "How Can Negro Greek-Letter Societies Cooperate?," *Sphinx*, December 1945, 8–9.

21 Calhoun, "How Can Negro Greek-Letter Societies Cooperate?," 28–29.

22 Calhoun, "How Can Negro Greek-Letter Societies Cooperate?"

23 Robert P. Watts, "Program of the National Pan-Hellenic Council," *Sphinx*, October 1946, 20.

24 Howard H. Long, *The American Council on Human Rights: An Evolution* (Washington, D.C.: American Council on Human Rights, 1954), 3; Edna Over Gray, "Report of President at Annual Meeting," *Congress & Equal*, Summer 1949, 1; Edna Over Campbell, "The American Council on Human Rights: What It Is and How It Operates" (Washington, D.C.: American Council on Human Rights, 1959), 1; see generally ACHR: Mobilization for Human Rights (1952), 7. During Alpha Phi Alpha's General Convention in 1946, fraternity members recommended that the fraternity take the lead in coordinating with other fraternities and sororities on a national social action program for human rights. Charles H. Wesley, *The History of Alpha Phi Alpha: A Development in College Life, 1906–1979*, 16th ed. (Baltimore: Foundation Publishers, 1996), 283. Belford V. Lawson expressed the view that the concerted action should work to lobby in Washington or revitalize and reorganize the National Pan-Hellenic Council. Wesley, *History of Alpha Phi Alpha*, 283.

25 Long, *American Council on Human Rights*, 3; Gray, "Report of President," 2.

26 Gray, "Report of President," 2.

27 Long, *American Council on Human Rights*, 3; Gray, "Report of President," 2. Kappa Alpha Psi initially was not a member but joined the ACHR shortly after it was formed, with Ernest Wilkins, James E. Scott, and Victor Ashe on the ACHR board. Long, 3. Omega Psi Phi decided not to participate in this joint effort at its 1949 Chicago Grand Conclave because the fraternity's leaders believed the ACHR was a "mediocre duplication," presumably of other civil rights organizations. Accordingly, it decided to put its financial support behind the

NAACP. Letter from J. H. Calhoun to Walter A. White, December 17, 1950 (on file with the *Journal of Gender, Social Policy & the Law*). Phi Beta Sigma ceased to be engaged with the ACHR in 1951. See *Congress and Equality* 1 (Summer 1951) (note the listing of organizations), contra *Congress and Equality* 1 (Fall 1952) (note listing of organizations) (Washington, D.C.: American Council on Human Rights, 1951); Long, *American Council on Human Rights*, 106.

28 Long, *American Council on Human Rights*, 3; Gray, "Report of President," 2 (contends that the meeting was in Washington, D.C.). Campbell, "American Council on Human Rights," 1. With regard to Kappa Alpha Psi, for example, in December 1948, at a banquet in Windsor, Ontario, Dr. Martin D. Jenkins called upon his listeners to dedicate themselves to "programs of human welfare larger than the social interests of the average fraternity." William L. Crump, *The Story of Kappa Alpha Psi: A History of the Beginning and Development of a College Greek Letter Organization, 1911–1999* (Philadelphia: Kappa Alpha Psi, 2003), 210. One of the ways that this manifested itself was in the authorization for the fraternity's affiliation with the American Council on Human Rights. Crump, *Story of Kappa Alpha Psi*, 210.

29 Long, *American Council on Human Rights*, 3.

30 Long, *American Council on Human Rights*.

31 Long, *American Council on Human Rights*. Among the members of the first Board of Directors were Bertell Collins Wright (president), Sally Nuby Edwards (vice president), Laura T. Lovelace (corresponding secretary), Evelyn B. Pope (recording secretary), W. Henry Greene (treasurer), Aubrey E. Robinson Jr. (general counsel), Emma Manning Carter, Beatrice W. Fox, Edna Over Gray, Dorothy I. Height, Howard H. Long, Patricia Roberts, James E. Scott, A. Maceo Smith, Arnetta G. Wallace, J. Ernest Wilkins, Julia B. Wilson, and Nancy B. Woodridge. Long, *American Council on Human Rights*, ii.

32 Long, *American Council on Human Rights*, 3.

33 "By 1940, the block-level 'index of dissimilarity' for nonwhite-white segregation stood at 88.0, indicating that at least 88 percent of all minorities would have had to change their place of residence in Kansas City to live in an integrated neighborhood." Kevin Fox Gotham, "Missed Opportunities, Enduring Legacies: School Segregation and Desegregation in Kansas City, Missouri," *American Studies* 43, no. 2 (2002): 5–42.

34 Wesley, *History of Alpha Phi Alpha*, 242.

35 Wesley, *History of Alpha Phi Alpha*, 236.

36 "Alpha's Aid in Building Southern Negro Youth Congress," *Sphinx*, October 1940, 19–20.

37 William A. Robinson, "The Role of Alpha in Aviation Is First of All in This Field," *Sphinx*, May 1940, 9.

38 *Alston v. School Bd. of City of Norfolk*, 112 F.2d 992 (4th Cir. 1940).

39 *Alston v. School Bd. of City of Norfolk*.

40 *Alston v. School Bd. of City of Norfolk*.

41 *Alston v. School Bd. of City of Norfolk*.

42 Crump, *Story of Kappa Alpha Psi*, 73. The Pepper-Geyer bill repealed the poll tax laws as they referred to primary and general elections of nominees and candidates to federal offices. Poll tax states included Alabama, Arkansas, Georgia, Mississippi, South Carolina, Tennessee, Texas, and Virginia. Susan Green, "Congress Filibuster Threatens to Kill Anti-Poll Tax Bill," *Labor Action* 6, no. 47 (1942): 1–2, https://perma.cc.

43 *Hansberry v. Lee*, 311 U.S. 32, 37–38, 44–46 (1940).

44 *Chambers v. Florida*, 309 U.S. 227, 229, 230–35 (1940).

45 *State ex rel. Bluford v. Can.*, 153 S.W.2d 12 (Mo. 1941).

46 *State ex rel. Bluford v. Can.*

47 *State ex rel. Bluford v. Can.*

48 *McDaniel v. Bd. of Pub. Instruction for Escambia Cty.*, 39 F. Supp. 638 (N.D. Fla. 1941).

49 *McDaniel v. Bd. of Pub. Instruction for Escambia Cty.*

50 *McDaniel v. Bd. of Pub. Instruction for Escambia Cty.*

51 "Kappa's Voice in War Time . . . : Letter from Grand Polemarch and Grand Chapter Meeting Resolutions Sent to President," *Kappa Alpha Psi Journal*, February 1942, 75.
52 "Kappa's Voice in War Time."
53 *Durkee v. Murphy*, 29 A.2d 253 (Md. 1942).
54 *Durkee v. Murphy*.
55 *Durkee v. Murphy*.
56 *Durkee v. Murphy*.
57 *Thomas v. Hibbitts*, 46 F. Supp. 368 (M.D. Tenn. 1942).
58 *Thomas v. Hibbitts*.
59 *Thomas v. Hibbitts*.
60 *Smith v. Allwright*, 131 F.2d. 593 (5th Cir. 1942).
61 *Smith v. Allwright*.
62 *Smith v. Allwright*.
63 *State ex Rel. Michael v. Witham*, 179 Tenn. 250, 257 (Tenn. 1942).
64 *State ex Rel. Michael v. Witham*, 253–54.
65 Crump, *Story of Kappa Alpha Psi*, 77.
66 Crump, *Story of Kappa Alpha Psi*, 77.
67 *Turner v. Keefe*, 50 F. Supp. 647 (S.D. Fla. 1943).
68 *Turner v. Keefe*.
69 *Turner v. Keefe*.
70 *Turner v. Keefe*.
71 *James v. Marinship Corp.*, 155 P.2d 329 (Cal. 1944).
72 *James v. Marinship Corp.*
73 *James v. Marinship Corp.*
74 *Morris v. Williams*, 59 F. Supp. 508 (E.D. Ark. 1944).
75 *Morris v. Williams*.
76 *Morris v. Williams*.
77 *Morris v. Williams*.
78 *Morris v. Williams*.
79 *Railway Mail Ass'n v. Corsi*, 267 A.D. 470 (N.Y. App. Div. 1944).
80 *Railway Mail Ass'n v. Corsi*.
81 *Railway Mail Ass'n v. Corsi*.
82 *Railway Mail Ass'n v. Corsi*.
83 *Davis v. Cook*, 55 F. Supp. 1004 (N.D. Ga. 1944).
84 *Davis v. Cook*.
85 *Davis v. Cook*.
86 *Davis v. Cook*.
87 *Steele v. Louisville & Nashville R.R. Co.*, 323 U.S. 192 (1944).
88 *Steele v. Louisville & Nashville R.R. Co.*
89 *Steele v. Louisville & Nashville R.R. Co.*
90 *Steele v. Louisville & Nashville R.R. Co.*
91 *Smith v. Allwright*, 321 U.S. 649 (1944).
92 *Smith v. Allwright*.
93 *Smith v. Allwright*.
94 *Smith v. Allwright*.
95 *Smith v. Allwright*, 652.
96 *Thompson v. Gibbs*, 60 F. Supp. 872 (E.D.S.C. 1945).
97 *Thompson v. Gibbs*.
98 *Thompson v. Gibbs*.
99 *Mitchell v. Wright*, 62 F. Supp. 580 (M.D. Ala. 1945).
100 *Mitchell v. Wright*.

101 *Mitchell v. Wright.*
102 *Mitchell v. Wright.*
103 *Mitchell v. Wright.*
104 *Kerr v. Enoch Free Libr. of Balt. City*, 149 F.2d 212 (4th Cir. 1945).
105 *Kerr v. Enoch Free Libr. of Balt. City.*
106 *Kerr v. Enoch Free Libr. of Balt. City.*
107 *Morris v. Williams*, 149 F.2d 703 (8th Cir. 1945).
108 *Morris v. Williams.*
109 *Morris v. Williams.*
110 *Morris v. Williams.*
111 *Morris v. Williams.*
112 *Chapman v. King*, 154 F.2d 460 (5th Cir. 1946).
113 *Chapman v. King.*
114 *Chapman v. King.*
115 *Chapman v. King.*
116 *Mitchell v. Wright*, 154 F.2d 924 (5th Cir. 1946).
117 *Mitchell v. Wright.*
118 *Mitchell v. Wright.*
119 *Mitchell v. Wright.*
120 *Mitchell v. Wright.*
121 *Mitchell v. Wright.*
122 *Morgan v. Commonwealth of Va.*, 328 U.S. 373 (1946).
123 *Morgan v. Commonwealth of Va.*
124 *Morgan v. Commonwealth of Va.*
125 *Morgan v. Commonwealth of Va.*
126 *Morgan v. Commonwealth of Va.*
127 Carroll Van West, "Columbia Race Riot, 1946," in *The Tennessee Encyclopedia of History and Culture*, December 25, 2009, https://tennesseeencyclopedia.net.
128 Van West, "Columbia Race Riot."
129 Charles K. Grant, "From the President: On Moving Forward," *Nashville Bar Journal*, November 2013, 2.
130 Van West, "Columbia Race Riot."
131 Catherine Roth, "Reynolds, Grant (1908–2004)," *BlackPast*, www.blackpast.org.
132 Roth, "Reynolds."
133 Harry S. Truman, "Special Message to the Congress on Civil Rights," February 2, 1948, www.presidency.ucsb.edu.
134 "Lincoln J. Ragsdale, 69, a Pilot Who Broke Many Color Barriers," *New York Times*, June 16, 1995, www.nytimes.com.
135 Matthew C. Whitaker, "Ragsdale, Lincoln J, Sr. (1926–1995)," *BlackPast*, www.blackpast.org.
136 "Lincoln J. Ragsdale."
137 Whitaker, "Ragsdale."
138 *Dorsey v. Stuyvesant Town Corp.*, 74 N.Y.S.2d 220 (N.Y. Sup. Ct. 1947).
139 *Dorsey v. Stuyvesant Town Corp.*
140 *Dorsey v. Stuyvesant Town Corp.*
141 *Dorsey v. Stuyvesant Town Corp.*
142 *Dorsey v. Stuyvesant Town Corp.*
143 *Dorsey v. Stuyvesant Town Corp.*
144 *Nw. Civic Ass'n v. Sheldon*, 27 N.W.2d 36 (Mich. 1947).
145 *Nw. Civic Ass'n v. Sheldon.*
146 *Nw. Civic Ass'n v. Sheldon.*
147 *Nw. Civic Ass'n v. Sheldon.*

148 *Nw. Civic Ass'n v. Sheldon.*
149 *Kennedy v. State*, 186 Tenn. 310 (1947).
150 *State v. Perkins*, 31 So.2d 188, 192 (La. 1947).
151 *Sipuel v. Bd. of Regents*, 199 Okla. 36 (1947).
152 *Sipuel v. Bd. of Regents of Univ. of Okla.*, 332 U.S. 631 (1948).
153 *Elmore v. Rice (Rice I)*, 72 F. Supp. 516 (E.D.S.C. 1947).
154 *Wrighten v. Bd. of Trustees of Univ. of S.C.*, 72 F. Supp. 948 (E.D.S.C. 1947).
155 *Mitchell v. Wright*, 69 F. Supp. 698 (M.D. Ala. 1947).
156 *Westminster Sch. Dist. of Orange Cty. v. Mendez*, 161 F.2d 774 (9th Cir. 1947).
157 *Bhd. of Locomotive Firemen and Enginemen v. Tunstall*, 163 F.2d 289 (4th Cir. 1947).
158 *Patton v. State of Miss.*, 332 U.S. 463 (1947).
159 *Sphinx*, December 1948, 15.
160 *Goetz v. Smith*, 62 A.2d 602, 602 (Md. 1948).
161 *Goetz v. Smith.*
162 *Law v. Mayor and City Council of Balt.*, 78 F. Supp. 346 (D. Md. 1948).
163 *Norris v. Mayor and City Council of Balt.*, 78 F. Supp. 451 (D. Md. 1948).
164 *Whitmyer v. Lincoln Parish Sch. Bd.*, 75 F. Supp. 686 (W.D. La. 1948).
165 *McLaurin v. Okla. Regents for Higher Educ.*, 87 F. Supp. 526 (W.D. Okla. 1948).
166 *McLaurin v. Okla. State Regents for Higher Educ.*, 87 F. Supp. 124 (W.D. Okla. 1949).
167 *Davis v. Cook*, 80 F. Supp 443 (N.D. Ga. 1948).
168 *Brown v. Baskin*, 78 F. Supp. 933 (E.D.S.C. 1948).
169 *Baskin v. Brown (Baskin II)*, 174 F.2d 391 (4th Cir. 1949).
170 *Hampton v. Thompson*, 171 F.2d 535, 538 (5th Cir. 1948).
171 *Hurd v. Hodge*, 334 U.S. 24 (1948).
172 *Shelley v. Kraemer*, 334 U.S. 1 (1948).
173 "Harold R. Boulware, Lawyer; Was a Pioneer in Civil Rights," *New York Times*, January 30, 1983.
174 *Rice v. Elmore (Rice II)*, 165 F.2d 387, 388 (4th Cir. 1947).
175 *Rice I*, 51.
176 *Rice I*, 528.
177 *Rice II*, 388.
178 *Rice II*, 389.
179 *Brown v. Baskin (Baskin I)*, 80 F. Supp. 1017, 1018 (E.D.S.C. 1948).
180 *Baskin I*, 1019.
181 *Baskin I.*
182 *Baskin I*, 1021.
183 *Baskin II*, 394.
184 W. Sherman Savage and L. D. Reddick, eds., *Our Cause Speeds On: An Informal History of the Phi Beta Sigma Fraternity* (Atlanta: Fuller Press, 1957), 131.
185 "The American Negro and the Challenges of Segregation," *Crescent*, December 1942, 24.
186 "The Negroes Tale of Four Cities," *Crescent*, April 1944, 14–15.
187 "Negroes Tale of Four Cities," 30.
188 Pearl Schwartz White, *Behind These Doors—A Legacy: The History of Sigma Gamma Rho Sorority* (Chicago: Sigma Gamma Rho Sorority, 1974), 35.
189 "Library," *Delta*, June 1960, 10.
190 Paula J. Giddings, *In Search of Sisterhood: Delta Sigma Theta and the Challenge of the Black Sorority Movement* (New York: William Morrow, 1988), 195.
191 "Library," 10.
192 Giddings, *In Search of Sisterhood*, 197, 205, 209.
193 "Alpha Phi Alpha and National Defense," *Sphinx*, October 1940, 5, 12.
194 Kenneth L. Bright, "Fraternity Buy Power 'A Social Mechanism,'" *Sphinx*, October 1940, 10.

195 Furman L. Templeton, "Worker Education a Needed Program," *Sphinx*, October 1940, 11.

196 *Sphinx*, October 1941, 5.

197 Sidney A. Jones, "Democracy and World War II," *Sphinx*, October 1941, 6.

198 Reid E. Jackson, "A Forge for Freedom," *Sphinx*, May 1944, 6, 9.

199 Reid E. Jackson, "Are We Lower Than Skunks?," *Sphinx*, October 1944, 6, 9.

200 Dr. Reid E. Jackson, "For 'What' Are We Fighting?," *Sphinx*, October 1942, 11–12, 24.

201 Jackson, "For 'What' Are We Fighting?," 11–12, 24.

202 Jackson, "For 'What' Are We Fighting?," 11–12, 24.

203 Thomas Posey, "The Negro in Post War Reconstruction," *Sphinx*, May 1942, 14, 42.

204 George W. Gore Jr., "Nobility Imposes Obligation," *Sphinx*, October 1942, 40, 42.

205 Gore, "Nobility Imposes Obligation," 40, 42.

206 Gore, "Nobility Imposes Obligation," 40, 42.

207 Gore, "Nobility Imposes Obligation," 40, 42.

208 J. Rupert Picott, "Alpha's Program of Action," *Sphinx*, May 1946, 5–6.

209 Picott, "Alpha's Program of Action," 5–6.

210 Picott, "Alpha's Program of Action," 5–6.

211 "The Convention Call," *Sphinx*, October 1946, 5.

212 "Convention Call."

213 Crump, *Story of Kappa Alpha Psi*, 85 (internal quotation marks omitted).

214 Crump, *Story of Kappa Alpha Psi*, 85.

215 "United for Human Rights . . . Kappa Adds Its Strength to Council Working for Fuller Civil Liberties," *Kappa Alpha Psi Journal*, May 1949, 43–44.

216 "United for Human Rights," 43–44. The Taft-Hartley Act was one of more than 250 union-related bills pending in both houses of Congress in 1947. It was seen as a means of demobilizing the labor movement by imposing limits on labor's ability to strike and by prohibiting radicals from attaining leadership positions. The law was promoted by large business lobbies including the National Association of Manufacturers. The Taft-Hartley Act was the first major revision to the Wagner Act, and after much resistance from labor leaders and a veto from President Harry S. Truman, it was passed on June 23, 1947. The Taft-Hartley Act provided the following: it allowed the president to appoint a board of inquiry to investigate union disputes if he believed a strike would endanger national health or safety and to obtain an eighty-day injunction to stop the continuation of a strike; it declared all closed shops illegal; it permitted union shops only after a majority of the employees voted for them; it forbade jurisdictional strikes and secondary boycotts; it ended the check-off system whereby employers collect union dues; and it forbade unions from contributing to political campaigns. Although many politicians sought to repeal the act, the Taft-Hartley Act stayed in effect until 1959, when the Landrum-Griffin Act amended some of its features.

"Federal aid to education" is a blanket term for the federal government's assistance to education, including the G.I. Bill of Rights, National Defense Education Act, and Elementary and Secondary Education Act.

217 Crump, *Story of Kappa Alpha Psi*, 97, 99. For information on Henderson's work with ACHR, see Gregory S. Parks, "'Lifting as We Climb': The American Council on Human Rights and the Quest for Civil Rights," *American University Journal of Gender, Social Policy & the Law* 25, no. 3 (2017).

218 Savage and Reddick, *Our Cause Speeds On*, 137.

219 Savage and Reddick, *Our Cause Speeds On*.

220 "Bigger and Better Business Program," *Crescent*, April 1942, 20.

221 "Bigger and Better Business Program."

222 "Bigger and Better Business Program." Johnson was president from 1948 to 1950 and a member of the Lambda Sigma service chapter.

223 "Conclave Highlights," *Crescent*, Spring 1950, 42.

224 "Alpha Men in the News," *Sphinx*, May 1942, 11–12.

225 "Alpha Men in the News," 12.

226 "Alpha Men in the News," 16.

227 "Alpha Men in the News," 12.

228 "Alpha Men in the News," 33.

229 Wesley, *History of Alpha Phi Alpha*, 268–69.

230 "Washington D.C. Conference," *Sphinx*, February 1943, 7–8.

231 "Washington D.C. Conference."

232 "Washington D.C. Conference."

233 "Washington D.C. Conference," 6, 30.

234 Dr. Rayford W. Logan, "Call for the Thirtieth General Convention," *Sphinx*, October 1944, 5.

235 Wesley, *History of Alpha Phi Alpha*, 280.

236 Wesley, *History of Alpha Phi Alpha*, 280.

237 "Kappa Chapter Columbus Ohio," *The Sphinx*, May 1944, 27.

238 "Kappa Chapter Columbus Ohio," 30.

239 "Kappa Chapter Columbus Ohio," 19.

240 "Kappa Chapter Columbus Ohio," 27.

241 "Democracy Functions in Selection of Negro as Grand Jury Foreman," *Sphinx*, May 1944, 11.

242 "Democracy Functions in Selection of Negro as Grand Jury Foreman," 12.

243 "Democracy Functions in Selection of Negro as Grand Jury Foreman," 16.

244 "Alpha Men in the News: Brother Dr. Hugh M. Gloster Appointed USO Associate Regional Executive," *Sphinx*, October 1944, 9.

245 Savage and Reddick, *Our Cause Speeds On*, 143. The declaration was sent to both Republican and Democratic National Conventions in 1944. It was made by representatives of more than twenty-five national African American organizations, one of which was the Phi Beta Sigma. Jessie P. Guzman et al., eds., *Negro Year Book: A Review of Events Affecting Negro Life, 1941–1946* (Department of Records and Research, Tuskegee Institute, 1947), 281.

246 Savage and Reddick, *Our Cause Speeds On*, 146.

247 Savage and Reddick, *Our Cause Speeds On*, 149.

248 G. Cecil Lewis, "For Better Race Relations . . . : Kappa Alpha Psi Adopts New Public Service Program for National Welfare," *Kappa Alpha Psi Journal*, October 1945, 47.

249 "Purpose: Interracial Amity," *Kappa Alpha Psi Journal*, October 1945, 41.

250 "Purpose: Interracial Amity," 41.

251 Lewis, "For Better Race Relations."

252 G. Cecil Lewis, "Good First Year Seen for Inter-racial Work," *Kappa Alpha Psi Journal*, February 1946, 11.

253 "Experiment in Democracy . . . : Study to Promote Better Intercultural Relations Gets School Board Backing," *Kappa Alpha Psi Journal*, October 1946, 61.

254 Crump, *Story of Kappa Alpha Psi*, 83–84.

255 G. Victor Cools, "Which Way Are We Going?," *Kappa Alpha Psi Journal*, October 1924, 15. In response to an epidemic of lynchings, especially in the South, Republican congressman Leonidas Dyer of Missouri introduced an anti-lynching bill in 1918. The main effect of the proposed bill was to classify lynching as a federal felony crime, which would have moved prosecution from the states to the federal government. The bill included provisions to imprison officials who refused to prosecute those involved in lynching and a mandatory minimum sentence of five years for anyone involved in the lynching itself. The bill passed through the House of Representatives in 1922 but was halted by a filibuster in the Senate. Though dozens of anti-lynching bills were subsequently introduced, none were passed, mainly because of the strong opposition of the southern Democratic voting bloc. See generally Barbara Holden-Smith, "Lynching, Federalism, and the Intersection of Race and Gender in the Progressive Era," *Yale Journal of Law & Feminism* 8, no. 1 (1996): 31.

256 Cools, "Which Way Are We Going?"

257 James Egert Allen, "Rebuttal: Not Just Politics! . . . : Political Charge Against Civil Rights Report Called 'Fallacy,'" *Kappa Alpha Psi Journal*, August–October 1948, 63.

258 Allen, "Rebuttal," 63.

259 "'To Secure These Rights'—Project for Study and Action," *Kappa Alpha Psi Journal*, February 1948, 1.

260 Lullelia W. Harrison, *Torchbearers of a Legacy: A History of Zeta Phi Beta Sorority, Inc. 1920–1997* (Washington, D.C.: Zeta Phi Beta Sorority, 1998), 46.

261 Harrison, *Torchbearers of a Legacy*, 46–47.

262 "Twenty-Second Annual Boule Held in Jacksonville, Florida," *Archon* 10, no. 3 (1942).

263 "Dickson Recreational and Religious Education Project," *Archon* 10, no. 3 (1942): 7, 8.

264 "Twenty-Second Annual Boule."

265 "Iota Alpha Chapter," *Archon* 10, no. 3 (1942): 19, 18.

266 "Eta Zeta Establishes Memorial Scholarship Fund," *Archon* 11, no. 1 (1944): 20; "Psi Chapter Presents Annual Zeta Blue Revue," *Archon* 11, no. 1 (1944): 16.

267 Harrison, *Torchbearers of a Legacy*, 161.

268 "Kappa Zeta Strong in Dallas," *Archon* 24, no. 2 (1959).

269 "Shoe Bank Is Sponsored by Rho Zeta Chapter," *Archon* 22, no. 1 (1957): 23.

270 "Library," 8.

271 Mary E. Vroman, *Shaped to Its Purpose: Delta Sigma Theta—The First Fifty Years* (New York: Random House, 1965), 110.

272 Giddings, *In Search of Sisterhood*, 183.

273 Vroman, *Shaped to Its Purpose*, 110.

274 "Appraising Values," *Delta*, 8.

275 "Appraising Values." See also "National Deltas Hire Associate Director Washington," *Los Angeles Tribune*, May 8, 1959.

276 Vroman, *Shaped to Its Purpose*, 52, 110.

277 Vroman, *Shaped to Its Purpose*, 47–49.

278 Vroman, *Shaped to Its Purpose*, 199–200, 207.

279 "Corporate Report," *Delta*, 1949, 40.

280 *Sphinx*, October 1943, 6.

281 Wesley, *History of Alpha Phi Alpha*, 285.

282 Wesley, *History of Alpha Phi Alpha*, 285.

283 Wesley, *History of Alpha Phi Alpha*, 287–88.

284 Wesley, *History of Alpha Phi Alpha*, 289.

285 Giddings, *In Search of Sisterhood*, 209–10.

286 White, *Behind These Doors*, 43.

287 White, *Behind These Doors*, 44.

288 Almita S. Robinson, "The Negro Press and Our Children," *Aurora* 17, no. 2 (1948): 7.

289 Almita S. Robinson, "Sigma Gamma Rho Members and National Affairs," *Aurora* 17, no. 3 (1948): 9.

290 Rubye G. Watts, "Highways of Sigma," *Aurora* 17, no. 1 (1947): 4.

291 *Boule Digest*, Boule issue of *Aurora*, 1944, 10.

292 "Gamma Sigma Chapter, Houston, Texas," *Aurora* 15, no. 1 (1945): 15.

293 White, *Behind These Doors*, 118.

294 White, *Behind These Doors*, 42.

295 White, *Behind These Doors*.

296 White, *Behind These Doors*, 138.

297 White, *Behind These Doors*, 42.

298 "Tau Sigma Chapter Sponsors Charm School for Teen-Age Group," *Aurora* 17, no. 2 (1948): 10.

299 "Tau Sigma Chapter," 39.

300 White, *Behind These Doors*, 35.

301 "Psi Sigma: Kansas City, Mo, Chapter Activities for Year 1944," *Aurora*, November 1944, 21.

302 White, *Behind These Doors*, 36.

303 "Kappa Zeta Strong in Dallas," *Archon*, no. 2 (1959): 24.

304 White, *Behind These Doors*, 49.

305 "Sigmas in Chicago Help Combat Juvenile Delinquency," *Aurora* 24, no. 3 (1945): 7.

306 "Sigmas in Chicago," 206, 208, 232–33.

307 "Sigmas in Chicago," 110.

308 Guichard Parris and Lester Brooks, *Blacks in the City: A History of the National Urban League* (Boston: Little, Brown, 1971).

309 *Sphinx*, October 1941, 18.

310 *Sphinx*, March 1941, 12, 14.

311 *Sphinx*, October 1941, 22.

312 *Sphinx*, March 1941, 14.

313 *Sphinx*, March 1941.

314 *Sphinx*, March 1941.

315 *Sphinx*, November 1941, 5.

316 "Pan-Hellenic Council Takes Stand for Negros in National Defense," *Sphinx*, March 1941, 13.

317 *Sphinx*, 16.

318 *Sphinx*, 6.

319 *Sphinx*, February 1943, 25.

320 *Sphinx*, October 1943, 29.

321 *Sphinx*, October 1943, 300.

322 *Sphinx*, October 1943, 301.

323 *Sphinx*, October 1943.

324 *Sphinx*, October 1943, 296.

325 *Sphinx*, October 1947, 6.

326 *Sphinx*, October 1947.

327 *Sphinx*, October 1947, 9.

328 Wesley, *History of Alpha Phi Alpha*, 309.

CHAPTER 6. AT THE FOREFRONT

1 The organizations consisted of Alpha Phi Alpha Fraternity, Alpha Kappa Alpha Sorority, Delta Sigma Theta Sorority, Kappa Alpha Psi Fraternity, Sigma Gamma Rho Sorority, and Zeta Phi Beta Sorority. Howard H. Long, *The American Council on Human Rights: An Evaluation* (Washington, D.C.: American Council on Human Rights,, 1954), i (hereafter *ACHR: An Evaluation*).

2 Robert L. Harris Jr., "Lobbying Congress for Civil Rights: The American Council on Human Rights, 1948–1963," in *African American Fraternities and Sororities: The Legacy and the Vision*, 2nd ed., ed. Tamara L. Brown, Gregory S. Parks, and Clarenda M. Phillips (Lexington: University Press of Kentucky, 2012), 211–32.

3 In a general sense, the ACHR's specific efforts emerged out of the organizations' collective disappointment with the amount of civil rights and progressive legislation included in the record leading up to the end of the first session of the Eighty-First Congress. "Civil Rights Can Be Won but Pressure Needed," *Congress and Equality* 1, no. 1 (Summer 1949): 1.

4 Long, *ACHR: An Evaluation*, 6; ACHR: Mobilization for Human Rights (1952), 8–9.

5 Long, *ACHR: An Evaluation*, 6; ACHR: Mobilization for Human Rights, 8–9; Edna Over Campbell, "The American Council on Human Rights: What It Is and How It Operates" (Washington, D.C.: American Council on Human Rights, 1959), 2. Much of this work apparently began at least a year earlier. See "ACHR and Leading Senators Analyze Civil Rights Failure in Congress," *Congress and Equality* (Winter 1950): 1.

6 Lucille McAllister Scott, ed., "Your ACHR News," *Ivy Leaf*, September 1948, 22.

7 Scott, "Your ACHR News," September 1948, 22. The constituency is estimated to have included over 100,000 college students and graduates. Marjorie H. Parker, *Past Is Prologue: The History of Alpha Kappa Alpha 1908–1999* (Washington, D.C.: Marjorie H. Parker, 1999), 199.

8 Scott, "Your ACHR News," *Ivy Leaf*, September 1949, 6. The bulletin was distributed to the local chapters and members of the Greek organizations making up ACHR. Scott, "Your ACHR News," September 1949, 6.

9 Scott, "Your ACHR News," September 1949.

10 Scott, "Your ACHR News," September 1949.

11 Scott, "Your ACHR News," September 1949.

12 Scott, "Your ACHR News," *Ivy Leaf*, December 1949, 6. The Bulletin was distributed to the local chapters and members of the Greek organizations making up ACHR. Scott, "Your ACHR News," December 1949, 6.

13 Scott, "Your ACHR News," December 1949.

14 Scott, "Your ACHR News," *Ivy Leaf*, March 1950, 6.

15 Scott, "Your ACHR News," March 1950.

16 Scott, "Your ACHR News," March 1950.

17 Scott, "Your ACHR News," March 1950.

18 Scott, "Your ACHR News," *Ivy Leaf*, March 1951, 8; *Congress and Equality* cited these actions as virtually amounting "to criminal negligence." Scott, "Your ACHR News," *Ivy Leaf*, September–December 1950, 10.

19 Scott, "Your ACHR News," September–December 1950, 10.

20 Scott, "Your ACHR News," September–December 1950.

21 Scott, "Your ACHR News," March 1951, 8.

22 Scott, "Your ACHR News," March 1950, 6.

23 Scott, "Your ACHR News," March 1950.

24 Scott, "Your ACHR News," March 1951, 11.

25 Scott, "Your ACHR News," March 1951.

26 Scott, "Your ACHR News," *Ivy Leaf*, June 1951, 4.

27 Long, *ACHR: An Evaluation*, 7.

28 Long, *ACHR: An Evaluation*, 8; "Local Councils on Human Rights," *Congress and Equality* (Summer 1949): 4; "ACHR to Press for Passage of the FEPC in January," *Congress and Equality* (Fall 1949): 1–2.

29 Long, *ACHR: An Evaluation*, 7.

30 Long, *ACHR: An Evaluation*, 7–10.

31 Long, *ACHR: An Evaluation*, 11.

32 Long, *ACHR: An Evaluation*, 11–12.

33 Long, *ACHR: An Evaluation*, 12–13.

34 Long, *ACHR: An Evaluation*, 13–14.

35 "Henderson Holds Satisfactory Talks with New Secretaries of Labor and Interior," *Congress and Equality* 4, no. 2 (Spring 1953): 2.

36 Long, *ACHR: An Evaluation*, 10–11.

37 "Recommendations Submitted on Procedure to Government Contracts Committee," *Congress and Equality* 5, no. 1 (Fall 1953): 4, 4–5.

38 Long, *ACHR: An Evaluation*, 11.

39 Long, *ACHR: An Evaluation*.

40 "ACHR Joins in Sponsoring Housing Conference," *Congress and Equality* 2 (1950): 1, 6–7. For a broader analysis of the ACHR's efforts in the area of housing, see "ACHR Joins in Sponsoring Housing Conference," 1, 6–7.

41 "ACHR Joins in Sponsoring Housing Conference," 6.

42 "ACHR Joins in Sponsoring Housing Conference," 6–7.

43 Long, *ACHR: An Evaluation*, 30.

44 Long, *ACHR: An Evaluation*, 31.

45 Long, *ACHR: An Evaluation*, 31–32.

46 Long, *ACHR: An Evaluation*, 32–33.

47 Long, *ACHR: An Evaluation*, 32–33.

48 Long, *ACHR: An Evaluation*, 33–35.

49 Long, *ACHR: An Evaluation*, 36; "Civil Rights Can Be Won but Pressure Needed," 1.

50 Long, *ACHR: An Evaluation*, 33–34.

51 Long, *ACHR: An Evaluation*, 37–38.

52 Long, *ACHR: An Evaluation*, 34.

53 Long, *ACHR: An Evaluation*, 40.

54 Long, *ACHR: An Evaluation*, 41.

55 Long, *ACHR: An Evaluation*, 44.

56 "ACHR Efforts and Recognition in Federal Housing Progress," *Congress and Equality* 5, no. 1 (Fall 1953): 2.

57 Long, *ACHR: An Evaluation*, 45–46.

58 Long, *ACHR: An Evaluation*, 50.

59 Long, *ACHR: An Evaluation*, 53.

60 Long, *ACHR: An Evaluation*, 15.

61 Long, *ACHR: An Evaluation*; "Local Councils on Human Rights," 4.

62 Long, *ACHR: An Evaluation*, 15–16.

63 "Civil Rights Can Be Won but Pressure Needed," 1.

64 "Civil Rights Can Be Won but Pressure Needed," 1.

65 "Local Councils on Human Rights," 6–8.

66 "Failure of Congress on Civil Rights Scored," *Congress and Equality* 2 (Summer 1950): 1, 7.

67 Long, *ACHR: An Evaluation*, 16. For a discussion of the poll tax issue in the Senate and Congress, see "Local Councils on Human Rights," 6.

68 Long, *ACHR: An Evaluation*, 16–17.

69 Long, *ACHR: An Evaluation*, 18. The ACHR had a particular interest in the Henderson case because the plaintiff, chief attorney, and associate counsel were largely prominent members of ACHR. "Supreme Court Strikes Hard Blows at Segregation," *Congress and Equality* 2 (1950): 1, 8. Moreover, the Henderson case was largely funded from the treasuries of the Alpha Phi Alpha Fraternity and the ACHR. "Supreme Court Strikes Hard Blows at Segregation," 1.

70 Long, *ACHR: An Evaluation*, 18–20.

71 For a discussion of the issues with regard to segregation and discrimination in Washington, D.C., see "Local Councils on Human Rights," 6.

72 Long, *ACHR: An Evaluation*, 20; "D.C. Swimming Pools Non-Segregated," *Congress and Equality* (Summer 1950), 2; "ACHR Takes Lead in Defeating Pro–Jim Crow Bills in Congress," *Congress and Equality* (Winter 1950).

73 Long, *ACHR: An Evaluation*, 20.

74 Long, *ACHR: An Evaluation*, 20–22.

75 Long, *ACHR: An Evaluation*, 24; see also "Truman Urged to End Army Jim-Crow, Act against Colonialism," *Congress and Equality* (Summer 1950).

76 Long, *ACHR: An Evaluation*, 24.

77 Long, *ACHR: An Evaluation*, 25; "ACHR Takes Lead in Defeating Pro–Jim Crow Bills in Congress."

78 "Issue the Fair Employment Practice Order," *Congress and Equality* (1951), 1; Executive Order No. 8802, 6 *Fed. Reg.* 3109 (June 27, 1941).

79 "Issue the Fair Employment Practice Order," 1.

80 "Issue the Fair Employment Practice Order," 1.

81 "Henderson Report on Conference with Truman on Major Racial Problems," *Congress and Equality* (1951): 1, 3.

82 "Pro-Segregation Beaten in Draft Bill," *Congress and Equality* (1951).

83 "Henderson Completes Fact-Finding Visit to Five European Countries," *Congress and Equality* (1952): 1, 7.

84 Long, *ACHR: An Evaluation*, 26.

85 Long, *ACHR: An Evaluation*, 25.

86 Long, *ACHR: An Evaluation*, 26.

87 Long, *ACHR: An Evaluation*, 27.

88 Long, *ACHR: An Evaluation*.

89 Long, *ACHR: An Evaluation*.

90 Long, *ACHR: An Evaluation*.

91 Long, *ACHR: An Evaluation*.

92 Long, *ACHR: An Evaluation*, 28.

93 Long, *ACHR: An Evaluation*.

94 Long, *ACHR: An Evaluation*, 29.

95 Long, *ACHR: An Evaluation*, 54.

96 Long, *ACHR: An Evaluation* ("ACHR activities in the 'clearing house' and 'Education' functions, for sound reasons, cannot be classified in rigid compartments").

97 Long, *ACHR: An Evaluation*, 54.

98 Long, *ACHR: An Evaluation*, 55.

99 Long, *ACHR: An Evaluation*.

100 Long, *ACHR: An Evaluation* (describing a time when the national president of one of ACHR's member organizations disseminated this message on tours of his chapters across five states).

101 Long, *ACHR: An Evaluation*, 55.

102 Long, *ACHR: An Evaluation*.

103 Long, *ACHR: An Evaluation*, 55–57 (listing Mr. Henderson's numerous speaking engagements).

104 Long, *ACHR: An Evaluation*, 57–58.

105 Long, *ACHR: An Evaluation*.

106 Long, *ACHR: An Evaluation*, 57–58 (listing locations of forums and workshops).

107 Long, *ACHR: An Evaluation*, 58.

108 Long, *ACHR: An Evaluation*.

109 Long, *ACHR: An Evaluation*, 59.

110 Long, *ACHR: An Evaluation* (remarking also that private organizations such as the ACHR have a large role in working to stimulate public understanding and guiding public and private action).

111 Long, *ACHR: An Evaluation*, 60.

112 Long, *ACHR: An Evaluation*, 61.

113 Long, *ACHR: An Evaluation*. The various organizations' histories recount this meeting: For example, in 1952, members of Delta Sigma Theta attended the American Council on Human Rights meeting in Cleveland, in which 3,000 delegates from various fraternities and sororities came to represent their organizations. Paula J. Giddings, *In Search of Sisterhood: Delta Sigma Theta and the Challenge of the Black Sorority Movement* (New York: William Morrow, 1988), 221.

114 Long, *ACHR: An Evaluation*, 61; see generally ACHR: Mobilization for Human Rights.

115 Long, *ACHR: An Evaluation*, 61.

116 Long, *ACHR: An Evaluation*, 62.

117 Long, *ACHR: An Evaluation*.

118 Long, *ACHR: An Evaluation*, 63.

119 Long, *ACHR: An Evaluation*, 63–64 (quoting the *Cleveland Press, Cleveland News, Pittsburgh Courier*, and describing coverage in *Color* magazine).

120 Long, *ACHR: An Evaluation*, 64 (listing approved resolutions, including cloture by majority vote, civil rights legislation, and the appointment of African Americans by the president).

121 Long, *ACHR: An Evaluation*.

122 Long, *ACHR: An Evaluation*, 64–65 ("the financial income exceeded expenditures").

123 "Resolutions Adopted at Joint Convention, Cleveland Ohio, December 27, 1952," *Congress and Equality* (Spring 1953): 3.

124 "Resolutions Adopted at Joint Convention," 3–4.

125 Long, *ACHR: An Evaluation*, 65–66 (listing topics of *Congress and Equality* publications between Summer 1949 and Spring 1953).

126 Long, *ACHR: An Evaluation*, 65.

127 Long, *ACHR: An Evaluation*, 67.

128 Long, *ACHR: An Evaluation* (also including curbing filibusters).

129 Long, *ACHR: An Evaluation* (listing the seven brochures and their topics).

130 Long, *ACHR: An Evaluation*, 67–68 (including a list of matters of particular interest, such as "action needed now to defeat pro-segregation aspects of the draft bill" and "letter to President Truman urging him to appoint a Negro administrative assistant").

131 Long, *ACHR: An Evaluation*, 68.

132 Long, *ACHR: An Evaluation*.

133 Long, *ACHR: An Evaluation*, 69.

134 Long, *ACHR: An Evaluation* (listing forty-two newspapers that use ACHR press releases).

135 Long, *ACHR: An Evaluation*, 70–71.

136 Long, *ACHR: An Evaluation*, 70 ("Mr. Henderson's ill advised and unwise attack on Senator Ives does not represent the thinking of the rank and file of the college men and women for whom he is spokesman").

137 Long, *ACHR: An Evaluation*, 71 ("As a lobbying organization, the council has played second fiddle to the NAACP and other organizations working in the field of civil rights").

138 Long, *ACHR: An Evaluation*, 71–76 (listing all eighty-five articles in chronological order).

139 Long, *ACHR: An Evaluation*, 76.

140 Long, *ACHR: An Evaluation*. This contest was won by Miss Willie Lee Martin of Benedict College, whose entry was "Human Rights—Democracy's Birthright."

141 Long, *ACHR: An Evaluation*, 76–77.

142 See Long, *ACHR: An Evaluation*, 77.

143 Long, *ACHR: An Evaluation*, 78; see ACHR: Mobilization for Human Rights, 10.

144 Long, *ACHR: An Evaluation*, 3; "Local Councils on Human Rights," 6; "Formation of Local Councils Moves Forward," *Congress and Equality* (Summer 1949): 6; Campbell, "American Council on Human Rights," 3.

145 Long, *ACHR: An Evaluation*, 6; "Local Councils on Human Rights," 1.

146 Long, *ACHR: An Evaluation*, 78–79.

147 Long, *ACHR: An Evaluation*, 79.

148 Long, *ACHR: An Evaluation*, 78–79.

149 Long, *ACHR: An Evaluation*, 79.

150 Long, *ACHR: An Evaluation*, 80–81.

151 Long, *ACHR: An Evaluation*, 80.

152 Long, *ACHR: An Evaluation*, 81.

153 Long, *ACHR: An Evaluation*.

154 Long, *ACHR: An Evaluation*, 82. For an example of a Local Council workshop, see "Local Council Activity," *Congress and Equality* (Summer 1950): 4.

155 Long, *ACHR: An Evaluation*, 81–82.

156 Long, *ACHR: An Evaluation*, 82.

157 Long, *ACHR: An Evaluation*.

158 Long, *ACHR: An Evaluation*, 83–84.

159 Long, *ACHR: An Evaluation*.

160 Long, *ACHR: An Evaluation*, 85.

161 Long, *ACHR: An Evaluation*, 86.

162 Long, *ACHR: An Evaluation*, 87.

163 Long, *ACHR: An Evaluation*, 88.

164 Long, *ACHR: An Evaluation*.

165 Long, *ACHR: An Evaluation*, 89.

166 Long, *ACHR: An Evaluation*.

167 Long, *ACHR: An Evaluation*.

168 Long, *ACHR: An Evaluation*.

169 Long, *ACHR: An Evaluation*.

170 Long, *ACHR: An Evaluation*, 88.

171 Long, *ACHR: An Evaluation*, 91.

172 Long, *ACHR: An Evaluation*.

173 Long, *ACHR: An Evaluation*.

174 Long, *ACHR: An Evaluation*.

175 Long, *ACHR: An Evaluation*, 92.

176 Long, *ACHR: An Evaluation*.

177 Long, *ACHR: An Evaluation*, 94.

178 Long, *ACHR: An Evaluation*, 94–95.

179 Long, *ACHR: An Evaluation*, 96.

180 Long, *ACHR: An Evaluation*, 97.

181 Long, *ACHR: An Evaluation*, 99–100.

182 Long, *ACHR: An Evaluation*, 101.

183 Long, *ACHR: An Evaluation*, 101–2.

184 Long, *ACHR: An Evaluation*, 103.

185 Long, *ACHR: An Evaluation*.

186 Long, *ACHR: An Evaluation*, 104.

187 *Sphinx*, December 1949, 4.

188 *Sphinx*, December 1949, 15.

189 *Sphinx*, December 1949, 10–11.

190 *Sphinx*, December 1949, 10–11.

191 *Sphinx*, December 1949, 10–11.

192 *Sphinx*, December 1949, 12, 29.

193 Charles H. Wesley, *The History of Alpha Phi Alpha: A Development in College Life, 1906–1979*, 16th ed. (Baltimore: Foundation Publishers, 1996), 319.

194 *Dorsey v. Stuyvesant Town Corp.*, 87 N.E.2d 541 (N.Y. 1949).

195 *Johnson v. Bd. of Trs.*, 83 F. Supp. 707, 710 (E.D. Ky. 1949); Wesley, *History of Alpha Phi Alpha*, 303.

196 Wesley, *History of Alpha Phi Alpha*, 321.

197 *Salvant v. Louisville & Nashville R.R. Co.*, 83 F. Supp. 391 (W.D. Ky. 1949).

198 *Monk v. City of Birmingham*, 87 F. Supp. 538 (N.D. Ala. 1949).

199 *Webb v. School Dist. No. 90, Johnson Cty.*, 206 P.2d 1066 (Kan. 1949).

200 *Morgan v. Commonwealth of Va.*, 328 U.S. 373 (1946).

201 *Whiteside v. S. Bus Lines, Inc.*, 177 F.2d 949 (6th Cir. 1949).

202 Wesley, *History of Alpha Phi Alpha*, 327.

203 Wesley, *History of Alpha Phi Alpha*, 327.

204 Brief for Petitioner, *Henderson v. United States*, 70 S. Ct. 843 (1950) (No. 25), 96.

205 Brief for Petitioner, *Henderson v. United States*, 99.

206 Brief for Petitioner, *Henderson v. United States*, 94–95.

207 See Brief for Petitioner, *Henderson v. United States*, 94–103.

208 Laura Lovelace, "Message of Supreme Basileus," *Ivy Leaf*, March 1951, 4.

209 Lovelace, "Message of Supreme Basileus," 4.

210 Lovelace, "Message of Supreme Basileus," 4. See also Scott, "Your ACHR News," *Ivy Leaf*, September–December 1950, 10 (stating that the Senate Wherry rule, which requires sixty-four votes to shut off debate, was a major reason behind the failed employment bill); Scott, "Your ACHR News," *Ivy Leaf*, March 1961, 8–9 (stating that it was the opinion of ACHR as well as of several senators that the Wherry Rule was one of the biggest obstacles for passing civil rights legislation like the FEPC bill, which was never allowed to come to a vote on the Senate floor).

211 Lovelace, "Message of Supreme Basileus."

212 Scott, "Your ACHR News," *Ivy Leaf*, March 1950, 6.

213 Scott, "Your ACHR News," *Ivy Leaf*, September 1951, 4.

214 Scott, "Your ACHR News," September 1951, 4 (noting that the appointment system in 1951 was a seniority system).

215 Scott, "Your ACHR News," *Ivy Leaf*, December 1951, 5.

216 *Henderson v. United States*, 339 U.S. 816 (1950); *D.C. v. John R. Thompson Co.*, 346 U.S. 100 (1953).

217 Scott, "Your ACHR News," *Ivy Leaf*, March 1952, 5.

218 Scott, "Your ACHR News," March 1952, 5.

219 Scott, "Your ACHR News," March 1952, 5.

220 Scott, "Your ACHR News," September–December 1952, 4–5.

221 Scott, "Your ACHR News," September–December 1952, 4–5.

222 Scott, "Your ACHR News," June 1952, 8–9.

223 Dorothy H. Davis, "ACHR Sends Proposal to President Eisenhower," *Ivy Leaf*, June 1953, 3.

224 *Bolling v. Sharpe*, 347 U.S. 497 (1954); *Brown v. Bd. of Educ.*, 347 U.S. 483 (1954); Parker, *Past Is Prologue*, 198.

225 *Brown v. Bd. of Educ.*, 483; The title of the pamphlet was "Integrating Our Schools," and it was available at the ACHR headquarters in D.C. Dorothy H. Davis, "ACHR Urges Steps to Integrate Our Schools," *Ivy Leaf*, September 1954, 25.

226 Davis, "ACHR Urges Steps to Integrate Our Schools."

227 William L. Crump, *The Story of Kappa Alpha Psi: A History of the Beginning and Development of a College Greek Letter Organization, 1911–1999* (Philadelphia: Kappa Alpha Psi, 2003), 85 (internal quotation marks omitted).

228 Crump, *Story of Kappa Alpha Psi*, 85.

229 "United for Human Rights . . . Kappa Adds Its Strength to Council Working for Fuller Civil Liberties," *Kappa Alpha Psi Journal*, May 1949, 43–44.

230 "United for Human Rights," 43–44.

231 Crump, *Story of Kappa Alpha Psi*, 97, 99. For information on Henderson's work with ACHR, see Gregory S. Parks, "'Lifting as We Climb': The American Council on Human Rights and the Quest for Civil Rights," *American University Journal of Gender, Social Policy & the Law* 25, no. 3 (2017).

232 "Always Against Segregation: Color, Straight Talk at Jenkins' Inaugural," *Kappa Alpha Psi Journal*, February 1949, 29.

233 "Always Against Segregation," 29 (internal quotation marks omitted).

234 "Always Against Segregation," 29 (internal quotation marks omitted).

235 "Always Against Segregation," 29 (internal quotation marks omitted).

236 "Always Against Segregation," 29–30.

237 *United States v. Sacher*, 182 F.2d 416, 417–18, 430 (2d Cir. 1950).

238 *Sweatt v. Painter*, 339 U.S. 629, 630–31 (1950). For further details about Heman Sweatt, see generally Gary M. Lavergne, *Before* Brown*: Heman Marion Sweatt, Thurgood Marshall, and the Long Road to Justice* (Austin: University of Texas Press, 2010).

239 *Sweatt*, 339 U.S. at 632–35, 636.

240 *Carter v. School Board*, 87 F. Supp. 745, 746, 747–50, 753 (E.D. Va. 1949), rev'd, 182 F.2d 531, 532 (4th Cir. 1950).

241 *Carter v. School Board*, 745, 746, 747–50, 753.

242 *Carr v. Corning*, 182 F.2d 14, 14–15 (D.C. Cir. 1950).

243 *Henderson v. United States*, 63 F. Supp. 906, 908 (D. Md. 1945).

244 *Henderson v. United States*, 63 F. Supp. 908.

245 *Henderson v. United States*, 63 F. Supp. 913 (citing *Plessy v. Ferguson*, 163 U.S. 537 [1896]), emphasis added.

246 *Henderson v. United States*, 63 F. Supp. 913.

247 *Henderson v. United States*, 63 F. Supp. 915–16.

248 *Henderson v. United States*, 63 F. Supp. 916.

249 *Henderson v. Interstate Commerce Comm'n*, 80 F. Supp. 32, 35–39 (D. Md. 1948).

250 *Henderson v. United States*, 339 U.S. 816, 817 (1950).

251 Brief for Elmer W. Henderson, *Henderson v. United States*, 339 U.S. 816 (No. 25), 1949 WL 50667.

252 Brief for Elmer W. Henderson, *Henderson v. United States*, 339 U.S. 816.

253 See Gregory S. Parks, "Belford Vance Lawson, Jr., Life of a Civil Rights Litigator," *University of Maryland Law Journal of Race, Religion, Gender & Class* 12 (2012): 320, 339–40.

254 Jack Greenberg, *Crusaders in the Courts: How A Dedicated Band of Lawyers Fought for the Civil Rights Revolution* (New York: Basic Books, 1994), 73.

255 Parks, "Belford Vance Lawson, Jr.," 339–40.

256 *Henderson v. United States*, 339 U.S. 823; see also *Mitchell v. United States*, 313 U.S. 80 (1941).

257 *Henderson v. United States*, 339 U.S. 823–24.

258 *Henderson v. United States*, 339 U.S. 824.

259 *Henderson v. United States*, 339 U.S. 824.

260 *Henderson v. United States*, 339 U.S. 824.

261 *Henderson v. United States*, 339 U.S. 824.

262 *Henderson v. United States*, 339 U.S. 824.

263 *Henderson v. United States*, 339 U.S. 824–25.

264 *Henderson v. United States*, 339 U.S. 825 (internal quotation marks omitted).

265 *Sweatt v. Painter*, 339 U.S. 629 (1950); *McLaurin v. Oklahoma State Regents*, 339 U.S. 637 (1950).

266 Derek Charles Catsam, *Freedom's Main Line: The Journey of Reconciliation and the Freedom Rides* (Lexington: University Press of Kentucky, 2009), 56.

267 Crump, *Story of Kappa Alpha Psi*, 103. A. M. Tinsley graduated from Temple University and then Meharry Medical College. He served as head of the NAACP in Richmond, Virginia, and was later elected head of the NAACP for the state of Virginia. For his work he was acknowledged by other African American fraternities, including Alpha Phi Alpha and Omega Psi Phi. Crump, *Story of Kappa Alpha Psi*, 103–4.

268 Crump, *Story of Kappa Alpha Psi*, 103–4.

269 Crump, *Story of Kappa Alpha Psi*, 104.

270 "Fraternity Leadership: A Pre-Conclave Message from the Grant Basileus," *Oracle*, December 1949, 3.

271 "Harold R. Boulware, Lawyer; Was a Pioneer in Civil Rights," *New York Times*, January 30, 1983, 26.

272 *Rice v. Elmore (Rice II)*, 165 F.2d 387, 388 (4th Cir. 1947); *Elmore v. Rice (Rice I)*, 72 F. Supp. 516, 517 (E.D.S.C. 1947).

273 *Rice I*, 528.
274 *Rice II*, 388.
275 *Rice II*, 389.
276 *Brown v. Baskin* (*Baskin I*), 80 F. Supp. 1017, 1018 (E.D.S.C. 1948).
277 *Baskin I*, 1019.
278 *Baskin I*, 1019.
279 *Baskin I*, 1021.
280 *Baskin v. Brown* (*Baskin II*), 174 F.2d 391, 394 (4th Cir. 1949).
281 Carl A. Blunt et al., *Distinguished Omegas in Civil Rights* (2008), 10. Hayzel B. Daniels was a lawyer, politician, major NAACP supporter, and activist in the civil rights movement. See Alton Hornsby Jr., ed., *Black America: A State-by-State Historical Encyclopedia, Volume 1: A–M* (Santa Barbara, Calif.: Greenwood, 2011), 49–50.
282 Blunt et al., *Distinguished Omegas in Civil Rights*.
283 Complaint at 7, *Phillips v. Phoenix Union High Schools*, No. 72909 (Ariz. Super. Ct. Feb. 9, 1953).
284 Blunt et al., *Distinguished Omegas in Civil Rights*, 10.
285 *Phillips v. Phoenix Union High Schools*, slip op. at 2 (Ariz. Super. Ct. Feb. 9, 1953).
286 *Heard v. Davis*, No. 77497, slip op. at 3, 5 (Ariz. Super. Ct. May 5, 1954).
287 Hornsby, *Black America*, 50.
288 Robert L. Gill, *A History of the Omega Psi Phi Fraternity* (Washington, D.C.: Omega Psi Phi Fraternity, 1963), 53.
289 Gill, *History of the Omega Psi Phi Fraternity*; *Kraemer v. Shelley*, 355 Mo. 814 (1946); *Sipes v. McGhee*, 316 Mich. 314 (1947).
290 Gill, *History of the Omega Psi Phi Fraternity*, 53.
291 *Shelley v. Kraemer*, 334 U.S. 1, 4 (1948).
292 *Shelley v. Kraemer*, 4–7, 10, 12–13, 15, 19, 20.
293 "Fraternity Leadership," 3, 53.
294 "Fraternity Leadership," 3, 53–54.
295 "Fraternity Leadership," 3, 54.
296 Gill, *History of the Omega Psi Phi Fraternity*, 54.
297 "Fraternity Leadership," 3, 54.
298 *Morgan v. Virginia*, 328 U.S. 373, 374 (1946).
299 *Morgan v. Virginia*, 374–75, 380, 386.
300 *Morgan v. Virginia*, 377 (citing *S. Pac. Co. v. Arizona*, 325 U.S. 761, 766–71 [1945]).
301 *Morgan v. Virginia*, 386.
302 *Morgan v. Virginia*, 389 (Burton, J., dissenting).
303 Eric Pace, "James M. Nabrit Jr. Dies at 97; Led Howard University," *New York Times*, December 30, 1997, B8.
304 *Sweatt v. Painter*, 339 U.S. 629, 631 (1950).
305 *Sweatt v. Painter*, 632.
306 *Sweatt v. Painter*, 632 (quoting *Sweatt v. Painter*, 210 S.W.2d 442, 446 [Tex. App. 1948]).
307 *Sweatt v. Painter*, 636.
308 *Sweatt v. Painter*, 636.
309 *Terry v. Adams*, 345 U.S. 461, 462, 470 (1953); see *Smith v. Allwright*, 321 U.S. 649, 666 (1944); *Grovey v. Townsend*, 295 U.S. 45, 55 (1935); *Nixon v. Condon*, 286 U.S. 73, 89 (1932); *Nixon v. Herndon* 273 U.S. 536, 541 (1927).
310 *Terry v. Adams*, 461, 463.
311 *Terry v. Adams*, 463.
312 *Terry v. Adams*, 463.
313 *Terry v. Adams*, 469–70.
314 *Terry v. Adams*, 468 (citing *Ex parte Siebold*, 100 U.S. 371, 393 [1879]).

315 "Fraternity Leadership," 3, 54–55.

316 Gill, *History of the Omega Psi Phi Fraternity*, 55.

317 Gill, *History of the Omega Psi Phi Fraternity*, 50.

318 Gill, *History of the Omega Psi Phi Fraternity*, 55.

319 Gill, *History of the Omega Psi Phi Fraternity*, 55.

320 Gill, *History of the Omega Psi Phi Fraternity*, 56.

321 See generally Gill, *History of the Omega Psi Phi Fraternity*, 51–64 (describing the social goals of the national fraternity and the social goals being pioneered by its individual members).

322 See generally Gill, *History of the Omega Psi Phi Fraternity* (illustrating the legal battles fought by chapters and individual members on the issues of racial discrimination and segregation).

323 *Davis v. Cty. Sch. Bd.*, 103 F. Supp. 337 (E.D. Va. 1952), *rev'd sub nom. Brown v. Bd. of Educ.*, 349 U.S. 294 (1955).

324 *Brown v. Bd. of Educ.*, 347 U.S. 483 (1954).

325 *Davis v. Cty. Sch. Bd.*, 337.

326 *Davis v. Cty. Sch. Bd.*, 340.

327 *Davis v. Cty. Sch. Bd.*, 340–41.

328 *Brown v. Bd. of Educ.*, 349 U.S. 294, 294 (1954).

329 *Bryce v. Byrd*, 201 F.2d 664, 665 (5th Cir. 1953). "Jesse N. Stone Jr. . . . [was] a Louisiana lawyer, educator, and activist who broke color barriers in state government." "Jesse N. Stone, Noted Louisiana Lawyer and Educator, Dies," *Jet*, June 4, 2001, 53.

330 *Byrd v. Brice*, 104 F. Supp. 442, 442 (W.D. La. 1952).

331 *Byrd v. Brice*, 442–43.

332 *Byrd v. Brice*, 443. "The applicant shall in all cases be able to establish that he is the identical person whom he represents himself to be when applying for registration. If the registrar has good reason to believe that he is not the same person, he may require the applicant to produce two credible registered voters of his precinct to make oath to that effect." *Byrd v. Brice*, 443.

333 *Byrd v. Brice*, 443.

334 *Brown v. Bd. of Educ.*, 347 U.S. 483 (1954). *Brown v. Board of Education* is a hallmark case in U.S. Supreme Court lore that declared unconstitutional state laws establishing separate public schools for black and white students. Alex McBride, "Landmark Cases: *Brown v. Board of Education* (1954)," *PBS*, December 2006, www.pbs.org. The decision overturned *Plessy v. Ferguson*, which allowed state-sponsored segregation in the forum of public education. McBride, "Landmark Cases."

In making its decision, the Supreme Court stated that segregation by itself was harmful to black students and unconstitutional. *Brown v. Bd. of Educ.*, 495. In addition, the Court found that a significant psychological and social disadvantage was given to black children from the nature of segregation. *Brown v. Bd. of Educ.*, 493–94. "Segregation of white and colored children in public schools has a detrimental effect upon the colored children. The impact is greater when it has the sanction of the law, for the policy of separating the races is usually interpreted as denoting the inferiority of the Negro group. A sense of inferiority affects the motivation of a child to learn. Segregation with the sanction of law, therefore, has a tendency to [retard] the educational and mental development of Negro children and to deprive them of some of the benefits they would receive in a racial[ly] integrated school system. We conclude that, in the field of public education, the doctrine of 'separate but equal' has no place. Separate educational facilities are inherently unequal." *Brown v. Bd. of Educ.*, 494–95.

335 *Brown v. Bd. of Educ.*, 495.

336 *Brown v. Bd. of Educ.*, 487–88, 493–95.

337 *Bolling v. Sharpe*, 497, 498.

338 *Bolling v. Sharpe*, 400–500.

339 Blunt et al., *Distinguished Omegas in Civil Rights*, 9.

340 Julian Williams, "Black Radio and Civil Rights: Birmingham, 1956–1963," *Journal of Radio Studies* 12 (2005), 47, 53.

341 Williams, "Black Radio and Civil Rights," 55–56.

342 Blunt et al., *Distinguished Omegas in Civil Rights*, 9.

343 Blunt et al., *Distinguished Omegas in Civil Rights*.

344 Williams, "Black Radio and Civil Rights," 56.

345 Henry and Curry, *Aaron Henry*, 69. Aaron Henry, civil rights activist, was born on July 2, 1922, to sharecroppers Ed and Mattie Henry in Coahoma County, Mississippi. Aaron Henry and Constance Curry, *Aaron Henry: The Fire Ever Burning* (Jackson: University Press of Mississippi, 2000), xiix. During this time of segregation, Henry worked in the cotton fields on plantations, but later facing more serious segregation after being drafted into the U.S. Army in 1943. Henry and Curry, *Aaron Henry*, 58. After serving in World War II as a staff sergeant in the Pacific Theater, he attended the Pharmacy School at Xavier University in New Orleans and graduated in 1950. Henry and Curry, *Aaron Henry*, 65. Henry served in the State House of Representatives from 1982 until 1996. Constance Curry, "Aaron Henry: A Civil Rights Leader of the 20th Century," *Mississippi History Now*, http://mshistorynow.mdah.state.ms.us. However, his retirement was cut short as he suffered from a stroke in 1996 and died on May 19, 1997, in Clarksdale, Mississippi. Curry, "Aaron Henry: A Civil Rights Leader of the 20th Century." See also Robert M. Thomas Jr., "Aaron Henry, Civil Rights Leader, Dies at 74," *New York Times*, May 21, 1997, www.nytimes.com. His memory and work for African American voters will never be forgotten.

346 Henry and Curry, *Aaron Henry*, 68.

347 Henry and Curry, *Aaron Henry*, 69.

348 Henry and Curry, *Aaron Henry*, 112.

349 Henry and Curry, *Aaron Henry*, 113.

350 Henry and Curry, *Aaron Henry*, 128.

351 Henry and Curry, *Aaron Henry*, 142.

352 Curry, "Aaron Henry."

353 Curry, "Aaron Henry."

354 Mary E. Vroman, *Shaped to Its Purpose: Delta Sigma Theta—The First Fifty Years* (New York: Random House, 1965), 99.

355 Giddings, *In Search of Sisterhood*, 221–22, 242.

356 Vroman, *Shaped to Its Purpose*, 241.

357 Giddings, *In Search of Sisterhood*, 223–24, 242.

358 "Delta Sigma Theta's Five Point Project Manual," 24 (on file with authors).

359 "Achievement and Potentiality," *Delta*, 1962, 32.

360 "Achievement and Potentiality," 32.

361 Dr. Geraldine P. Woods, "Decisive Action for Freedom through Education," *Delta*, March 1967, 18, 191.

362 Woods, "Decisive Action," 191.

363 *Delta*, 1979, 40.

364 Vroman, *Shaped to Its Purpose*, 127.

365 Ellen T. Law, "Overcoming Barriers to Intergroup Communications," *Delta: Communications* 46 (1960): 23.

366 Vroman, *Shaped to Its Purpose*, 89, 127, 244, 256.

367 See Vroman, *Shaped to Its Purpose*.

368 See Marybeth Gasman, "Passive Activism: Empirical Studies of Black Greek-Letter Organizations," in *Black Greek-Letter Organizations 2.0: New Directions in the Study of African*

American Fraternities and Sororities, ed. Matthew W. Hughey and Gregory S. Parks (Jackson: University Press of Mississippi, 2011).

369 Gasman, "Passive Activism, Empirical Studies of Black Greek-Letter Organizations."

370 Giddings, *In Search of Sisterhood*, 220–21.

371 Geraldine Woods, "Delta Meets the Challenge of Tomorrow's Opportunities for Minority Youth," *Delta*, 1963, 55.

372 W. Sherman Savage and L. D. Reddick, *Our Cause Speeds On: An Informal History of the Phi Beta Sigma Fraternity* (Atlanta: Fuller Press, 1957), 158.

373 "Conclave Highlights," *Crescent*, Spring 1950.

374 Savage and Reddick, *Our Cause Speeds On*, 171.

375 "Asia, now Africa," *Crescent*, Spring 1950, 13.

376 Savage and Reddick, *Our Cause Speeds On*, 182. Brown was president from 1951 to 1953 and a member of the Iota Sigma graduate service chapter. He was subjected to phone threats and vandalism after his fraternity bought a home in a white neighborhood.

377 Savage and Reddick, *Our Cause Speeds On*, 182.

378 Savage and Reddick, *Our Cause Speeds On*, 183.

379 "Sigmas Hold Successful Conclave," *Crescent*, Spring 1952, 34.

380 Savage and Reddick, *Our Cause Speeds On*, 183.

381 "Conclave Highlights," *Crescent*, Spring 1950.

382 "Conclave Highlights," *Crescent*, Spring 1950.

383 Savage and Reddick, *Our Cause Speeds On*, 185.

384 Savage and Reddick, *Our Cause Speeds On*, 188.

385 Savage and Reddick, *Our Cause Speeds On*, 197.

386 "Education, The Key to Freedom," *Crescent*, Spring 1955, 13.

387 "Sigmas in Gala Meet," *Pittsburg Courier*, January 9, 1954, www.fultonhistory.com.

388 Lullelia W. Harrison, *Torchbearers of a Legacy: A History of Zeta Phi Beta Sorority, Inc. 1920–1997* (Washington, D.C.: Zeta Phi Beta Sorority, 1998), 46.

389 Harrison, *Torchbearers of a Legacy*, 46–47.

390 "Twenty-Second Annual Boule Held in Jacksonville, Florida," *Archon* 10, no. 3 (1942).

391 "Dickson Recreational and Religious Education Project," *Archon* 10 no. 3 (1942): 7, 8.

392 "Rho Zeta Chapter and Iota Alpha," *Archon* 10, no. 3 (1942): 18.

393 "Twenty-Second Annual Boule."

394 "Iota Alpha Chapter," *Archon* 10, no. 3 (1942): 19; "Iota Zeta Chapter," *Archon* 10, no. 3 (1942): 18.

395 "Eta Zeta Establishes Memorial Scholarship Fund," *Archon* 11, no. 1 (1944): 20; "Psi Chapter Presents Annual Zeta Blue Revue," *Archon* 11, no. 1 (1944): 16.

396 Harrison, *Torchbearers of a Legacy*, 161.

397 "Kappa Zeta Strong in Dallas," *Archon* 24, no. 2 (1959).

398 "Shoe Bank Is Sponsored by Rho Zeta Chapter," *Archon* 22, no. 1 (1957): 23.

399 "A Fearless Spirit," *Archon* 10, no. 3 (1942): 3; Lullelia W. Harrison, "Echoes from the Southern Region," *Archon* 10, no. 3 (1942): 4.

400 Rubye G. Watts, "Highways of Sigma," *Aurora* 17, no. 1 (1947): 4.

401 Harrison, *Torchbearers of a Legacy*, 163.

402 Harrison, *Torchbearers of a Legacy*, 163; Pearl Schwartz White, *Behind These Doors—A Legacy: The History of Sigma Gamma Rho Sorority*, ed. Lillie Wilkes (Chicago: Sigma Gamma Rho Sorority, 1974), 68.

403 Harrison, *Torchbearers of a Legacy*, 204; White, *Behind These Doors*, 71.

404 White, *Behind These Doors*, 60.

405 Harrison, *Torchbearers of a Legacy*, 163.

406 "Grand Elected to ACHR Post," *Archon* 25, no. 1 (1960): 53.

407 Harrison, *Torchbearers of a Legacy*, 55–57.

408 Harrison, *Torchbearers of a Legacy*, 55–56.

409 Harrison, *Torchbearers of a Legacy*, 64.

410 Harrison, *Torchbearers of a Legacy*, 58.

411 Harrison, *Torchbearers of a Legacy*, 55–58.

412 "A First from George Peabody College in Nashville," *Archon* 21, no. 2 (1956): 27.

413 "Shoe Bank Is Sponsored By Rho Zeta Chapter," *Archon* 22, no. 1 (1957): 23.

414 "Tau Zeta, Only Greek Body in County, Reveals Calendar," *Archon* 22, no. 2 (1957): 33.

415 "Alpha Phi Zeta Awards Two Scholarships to Students," *Archon* 22, no. 2 (1957): 40; "Awards $300 Scholarships," *Archon* 22, no. 2 (1957): 41.

416 "Alpha Chi Zeta Awards $200 Scholarship to Miss Buckley," *Archon* 22, no. 2 (1957): 42; "Alpha Eta Zeta Lists 1956–'58 Scholarship Total—$1700," *Archon* 22, no. 2 (1957): 41.

417 "Midwestern Regional Scholarships to Misses Webb and Hall," *Archon* 22, no. 2 (1957): 40.

418 Stephanie J. Shaw, *What a Woman Ought to Be and to Do: Black Professional Women Workers during the Jim Crow Era* (Chicago: University of Chicago Press, 1996).

419 Mary Breaux Wright, "Finer Womanhood: It Never Goes Out of Style," Zeta Phi Beta Sorority, March 10, 2015, www.zphib1920.org.

420 White, *Behind These Doors*, 68.

421 White, *Behind These Doors*, 63; Harrison, *Torchbearers of a Legacy*, 54. The American Council on Human Rights consisted of Alpha Kappa Alpha sorority, Alpha Phi Alpha fraternity, Kappa Alpha Psi fraternity, Sigma Gamma Rho sorority, and Zeta Phi Beta sorority. For a more detailed history of the organization, see Gregory S. Parks et al., "Complex Civil Rights Organizations: Alpha Kappa Alpha Sorority, An Exemplar," *Alabama Civil Rights and Civil Liberties Law Review* 5, no.1 (2014).

422 Harrison, *Torchbearers of a Legacy*, 163.

423 Harrison, *Torchbearers of a Legacy*, 163; White, *Behind These Doors*, 68.

424 White, *Behind These Doors*, 56.

425 "Sigma Sorors at ACHR's Workshop on Planning for Integration," *Aurora* 24, no. 2 (1955): 6.

426 The Commission on Evaluation consisted of Howard Hale Long as chairman and members Enos S. Andrews, Vivian E. Cook, Patricia Roberts, James N. Saunders, Josephine C. Smith, and Lorraine A. Williams. Paul Cooke served as the researcher. Long, *ACHR: An Evaluation*, ii.

427 Long, *ACHR: An Evaluation*, iii.

428 Long, *ACHR: An Evaluation*, viii–x.

429 "A Chronicle of Alpha Kappa Alpha Sorority," *Ivy Leaf*, 32, no. 2 (June 1954): 4.

430 "7th District Pledges Aid in Segregation Battle," *Oracle*, 1954.

431 "7th District Pledges Aid in Segregation Battle," *Oracle*, 1954.

432 "Public Affairs," *Aurora*, no. 1 (1954).

433 "To Secure These Rights: A Statement Adopted by a Group of Southern Negro Educators, Hot Springs, Arkansas," *Aurora* 24, no. 1 (1954): 4–5; Edna Douglas, "An Open Letter from the Grand Basileus," *Aurora* 24, no. 2 (1955): 2–37.

434 "Zeta Sigma, St. Louis, Mo.," *Aurora* 24, no. 3 (1955): 24.

435 Harrison, *Torchbearers of a Legacy*, 58.

436 Harrison, *Torchbearers of a Legacy*, 73.

437 "A Scene at Camp Achievement," *Aurora* 24, no. 4 (1955): 7; "Sigma Gamma Rho Sorority Gives Second $1,000 Check to Camp Achievement," *Aurora* 26, no. 1 (1956): 5; White, *Behind These Doors*, 76.

438 "Kappa Sigma New York City," *Aurora* 27, no. 2 (1958): 21.

439 "A Chronicle of Alpha Kappa Alpha Sorority," *Ivy Leaf* 32, no. 1 (March 1954): 29.

440 *Bolling v. Sharpe*, 347 U.S. 497 (1954).

441 *Bolling*, 347 U.S. 499–500.

442 Crump, *Story of Kappa Alpha Psi*, 110.

443 Crump, *Story of Kappa Alpha Psi*, 110.
444 Friends Committee on National Legislation, *A Political Action Handbook* (Washington, D.C.: American Council on Human Rights, 1955).
445 "Conclave Resolutions," *Crescent*, Spring 1956, 6–8.
446 Vroman, *Shaped to Its Purpose*, 108, 121, 135.
447 Vroman, *Shaped to Its Purpose*, 111, 113, 116.
448 Vroman, *Shaped to Its Purpose*, 12, 126.
449 "Scholarships: Our Challenge . . . Our Responsibility," *Aurora* 35, no. 1 (1955): 3.
450 "Scholarships: Our Challenge . . . Our Responsibility," *Aurora* 35, no. 1 (1955): 5, 8.
451 Gill, *History of the Omega Psi Phi Fraternity*, 24.
452 Gill, *History of the Omega Psi Phi Fraternity*.
453 Nancy Bullock McGhee, "Report of the President Board of Directors," *Ivy Leaf*, December 1956, 34.
454 McGhee, "Report of the President Board of Directors," 34.
455 McGhee, "Report of the President Board of Directors," 34.
456 McGhee, "Report of the President Board of Directors," 34.
457 McGhee, "Report of the President Board of Directors," 35.
458 McGhee, "Report of the President Board of Directors," 35.
459 McGhee, "Report of the President Board of Directors," 35.
460 "ACHR Board Reaffirms Registration and Vote Campaign," *ACHR and Equality* 7 (Fall 1956): 1.
461 "ACHR Board Reaffirms Registration and Vote Campaign," 1.
462 "ACHR Board Reaffirms Registration and Vote Campaign," 2.
463 "ACHR Board Reaffirms Registration and Vote Campaign," 4.
464 "ACHR Board Appoints Blue Director," *ACHR and Equality* 7 (Fall 1956): 4.
465 "ACHR Board Appoints Blue Director."
466 "Three Means to Fight Racial Discrimination," *ACHR and Equality* 7 (Fall 1956): 3.
467 *ACHR and Equality* 7 (Fall 1956).
468 "ACHR Board Members and Staff Meet with Local Councils, Other Greeks," *ACHR and Equality* 7 (Fall 1956): 2.
469 "Civil Rights Measures 'Represent Substantial Gains," *ACHR and Equality* 7 (Fall 1956): 6.
470 McGhee, "Report of the President Board of Directors," 36.
471 McGhee, "Report of the President Board of Directors," 36.
472 McGhee, "Report of the President Board of Directors," 36.
473 Laura K. Campbell, "ACHR Holds National Workshop on Leadership Responsibilities and Techniques," *Ivy Leaf*, December 1957, 10.
474 *Thompson v. Cty. Sch. Board*, 144 F. Supp. 239 (E.D. Va. 1956), aff'd sub nom; *Sch. Bd. v. Allen*, 240 F.2d 59 (4th Cir. 1956), supplemented 159 F. Supp. 567 (E.D. Va. 1957), decree aff'd sub nom; *Cnty. Sch. Bd. v. Thompson*, 252 F.2d 929 (4th Cir. 1958).
475 *Thompson v. Cty. Sch. Board*, 239.
476 *Sch. Bd. v. Allen*, 64.
477 *Thompson*, 159 F. Supp. 567, 568.
478 *Thompson*.
479 *Thompson*, 571.
480 *Cty. Sch. Bd. v. Thompson*.
481 *NAACP v. Patty*, 159 F. Supp. 503, 506 (E.D. Va. 1958).
482 *NAACP v. Patty*, 506, 521, 524, 528.
483 *Harrison v. NAACP*, 360 U.S. 167, 172 (1959).
484 *Harrison v. NAACP*, 173.
485 *NAACP v. Patty*, 159 F. Supp. 503, 529 (E.D. Va. 1958).
486 *NAACP v. Patty*, 533–34.

487 *Harrison v. NAACP*, 170.

488 *Harrison v. NAACP*, 179.

489 "ACHR Board Maps . . . for 1957 and 1958," *ACHR and Equality* 7, no. 2 (January 1957): 1.

490 "ACHR Board Maps," 1.

491 "Greeks Use Their Potential to Get Citizens Registered," *ACHR and Equality* 7, no. 2 (January 1957): 3.

492 "How to Wreck Your ACHR Local Council," *ACHR and Equality* 7, no. 2 (January 1957): 4.

493 "ACHR Presses Ike's Administration on Pledges on Employment," *ACHR and Equality* 7, no. 2 (January 1957): 5.

494 *ACHR and Equality* 7, no. 2 (January 1957).

495 "Civil Rights: The Role of ACHR in Passage of the Civil Rights Legislation," *ACHR and Equality* 9 (December 1957): 1–2.

496 "Proposed Civil Rights Legislation," *ACHR and Equality* (Winter 1957): 2.

497 "The ACHR Legislative Agenda," *ACHR and Equality* 9 (December 1957): 3.

498 Campbell, "ACHR Holds National Workshop," 11.

499 Blunt et al., *Distinguished Omegas in Civil Rights*, 14.

500 Blunt et al., *Distinguished Omegas in Civil Rights*.

501 Bunthay Cheam, "Green, Ernest G. (1941–)," *BlackPast*, www.blackpast.org.

502 Cheam, "Green."

503 "Ernest G. Green, Co-Chairman/Partner, Madison Asset Management Group LLC," *Gideon's Promise*, http://gideonspromise.org.

504 "Ernest G. Green, Co-Chairman/Partner"; Cheam, "Green."

505 Laura K. Campbell, "Supreme Basileus Participates in ACHR Future Program," *Ivy Leaf*, September 1958, 3.

506 "On the Subject of Public Accommodation in Washington D.C.," *ACHR and Equality* (March 1958).

507 "On the Subject of Public Accommodation."

508 "Salvage Committee Aids Negro Students," *Archon* 24, no. 2 (1959).

509 "Salvage Committee Aids Negro Students."

510 "Sigma Gamma Rho Leader Elected President," *Aurora* 27, no. 2 (1958): 13.

511 White, *Behind These Doors*, 82.

512 White, *Behind These Doors*, 83.

513 "A.C.H.R. Urges Protest Aid," *Archon* 25, no. 1 (1960): 33.

514 *Cooper v. Aaron*, 358 U.S. 1, 3 (1958).

515 *Cooper v. Aaron*, 4, 8–10, 15, 18.

516 See *Cooper v. Aaron*, 4.

517 *Aaron v. McKinley*, 173 F. Supp. 944 (E.D. Ark. 1959), aff'd sub nom; *Faubus v. Aaron*, 361 U.S. 197 (1959).

518 *Aaron v. McKinley*, 945.

519 *Aaron v. McKinley*, 952.

520 *Aaron v. McKinley*. All of the high schools in the district were closed for the 1958–59 school year. *Aaron v. McKinley*.

521 *Aaron v. McKinley*, 947. In all, 19,000 electors voted against racial integration, while only 7,500 voted in favor. *Aaron v. McKinley*.

522 *Aaron v. McKinley*, 950.

523 *Aaron v. McKinley*, 951.

524 "A Chronicle of Alpha Kappa Alpha Sorority," *Ivy Leaf*, 1959, 6.

525 "ACHR Board Meets in Washington," *Ivy Leaf*, September 1959, 6.

526 "A Chronicle of Alpha Kappa Alpha Sorority," *Ivy Leaf*, February 1961, 7.

527 White, *Behind These Doors*, 82.

528 Harrison, *Torchbearers of a Legacy*, 58.

529 Louise Batson, "Director Seeks New Support," *Archon* 25, no. 1 (1960): 10.

530 "Gamma Xi Sigma's 1963 Calendar Girls," *Aurora* 32, no. 4 (1963).

531 "Eta Sigma Atlanta, Georgia," *Aurora* 35, no. 1 (1965): 46, 49.

532 *Gomillion v. Lightfoot* (*Gomillion I*), 167 F. Supp. 405 (M.D. Ala. 1958), aff'd, 270 F.2d 594 (5th Cir. 1959), rev'd, 364 U.S. 339 (1960).

533 *Gomillion v. Lightfoot* (*Gomillion III*), 364 U.S. 339, 340 (1960).

534 *Gomillion I*, 407.

535 *Gomillion I*, 410.

536 *Gomillion v. Lightfoot* (*Gomillion II*), 270 F.2d 594, 601 n.3 (5th Cir. 1959).

537 *Gomillion III*, 341.

538 *Gomillion III*, 346–48.

539 Mabel Bell Croos, ed., "Among Our National Programs: ACHR," *Ivy Leaf*, February 1961, 7.

540 Parker, *Past Is Prologue*, 199.

541 Parker, *Past Is Prologue*, 9.

542 Parker, *Past Is Prologue*, 199.

543 Parker, *Past Is Prologue*, 9.

544 "Sit-Ins," *Highlights from the American Council on Human Rights*, February 1961, 3.

545 "Conference of Leaders," *Highlights from the American Council on Human Rights*, February 1961, 1, 4.

546 *Highlights from the American Council on Human Rights*, February 1961, 1–3.

547 *Highlights from the American Council on Human Rights*, February 1961, 1–3.

548 "Sororities Asked to Sacrifice Dances, Fancy Clothes to Pursue Rights Fight," *Los Angeles Tribune* 2, no. 9 (April 8, 1960): 12.

549 *Highlights from the American Council on Human Rights*, 1, 4; "U.S.A. Could Lose Rights for All: ACHR Director Speaks to NBA," *Tri-State Defender*, July 23, 1960.

550 "ACHR Recommends Forty Outstanding Women to JFK," *New Pittsburgh Courier* 2, no. 9, 9 (1959–65).

551 "ACHR Contributes to Atlanta Women's Steering Committee," *New Pittsburgh Courier* 1, no. 44, 14 (1959–65).

552 Vroman, *Shaped to Its Purpose*, 90.

553 "The Story of the Friendship Trees," *Delta*, 1962, 47.

554 "International Understanding," *Delta*, March 1967, 56–57.

555 Vroman, *Shaped to Its Purpose*, 88.

556 Vroman, *Shaped to Its Purpose*, 91.

557 "Fact Sheet of Progress in Civil Rights of Particular Interest to Residents of the District of Columbia," *American Council on Human Rights*, 1962.

558 "American Council on Human Rights in 6th Leadership Confab," *New Pittsburgh Courier* 3, no. 33 (1959–65), 9.

559 Harrison, *Torchbearers of a Legacy*, 164.

560 Harrison, *Torchbearers of a Legacy*, 164. CARE was founded in 1945 by twenty-two American organizations that came together to send life-saving care packages to World War II survivors. See CARE, "History of CARE," October 15, 2013, www.care.org.

561 See "A Chronicle of Alpha Kappa Alpha Sorority," *Ivy Leaf*, March 1964, 9 (Phi Delta Kappa had sought membership in the ACHR early on, though there were some questions as to whether it had the financial wherewithal to do so). Note that the volume numbering of the AKA journal was not consistent over time, thereby making it difficult to find a particular article by volume. For this reason, we are omitting volume numbers hereinafter. See also Edna Over Gray, "Report of President at Annual Meeting" (Congress & Equal. Am. Council on Human Rights, Washington, D.C., Summer 1949), 4 (it is apparent that Phi Delta Kappa was an active ACHR member, at least by 1951). See also *Highlights from the American Council on Human Rights* 2 (February 1961).

562 Parker, *Past Is Prologue*, 9.
563 "A Chronicle of Alpha Kappa Alpha Sorority," *Ivy Leaf*, March 1964, 9, 13.
564 "A Chronicle of Alpha Kappa Alpha Sorority," 9, 13; Parker, *Past Is Prologue*, 199.
565 "A Chronicle of Alpha Kappa Alpha Sorority," 9.
566 "What They Say about ACHR," *About the American Council on Human Rights* (n.d.), 1.
567 Wendy M. Laybourn and Gregory S. Parks, "Brotherhood and the Quest for African American Social Equality: A Story of Phi Beta Sigma," *University of Maryland Law Journal of Race, Religion, Gender & Class* 16, no. 1 (2016); Wendy Marie Laybourn and Gregory S. Parks, "The Sons of Indiana: Kappa Alpha Psi and the Fight for Civil Rights," *Indiana Law Journal* 91, no. 4 (2016):1425–72; Gregory S. Parks and Caryn Neumann, "Lifting as They Climb: Race, Sorority, and African American Uplift in the 20th Century," *Hastings Women's Law Journal* 27, no. 1 (2016); Marcia Hernandez and Gregory S. Parks, "Fortitude in the Face of Adversity: Delta Sigma Theta's History of Racial Uplift," *Hastings Race and Poverty Law Journal* 13, no. 2 (2016); Wendy Marie Laybourn and Gregory S. Parks, "Omega Psi Phi Fraternity and the Fight for Civil Rights," *Wake Forest Journal of Law and Policy* 6, no. 1 (2015). Gregory S. Parks, Rashawn Ray, and Shawna M. Patterson, "Complex Civil Rights Organizations: Alpha Kappa Alpha Sorority, An Exemplar," *Alabama Civil Rights and Civil Liberties Law Review* 6 (2014).

CONCLUSION

1 Donatella della Porta and Mario Diani, *Social Movements: An Introduction* (New York: John Wiley, 2006), 150.
2 See generally Herbert G. Blumer, "Collective Behavior," in *Principles of Sociology*, ed. Alfred McClung Lee (New York: Barnes & Noble, 1969), 65–121.
3 Jo Freeman and Victoria Johnson, *Waves of Protest: Social Movements since the Sixties* (Lanham, Md.: Rowman & Littlefield, 1999), 302.
4 Shaun Harper and Frank Harris III, "The Role of Black Fraternities in the African American Male Undergraduate Experience," in *African American Men in College*, ed. M. J. Cuyjet (San Francisco: Jossey-Bass, 2016), 128–53.
5 Crystal Renee Chambers et al., "Academic Achievement of African American Fraternities and Sororities," in *African American Fraternities and Sororities: The Legacy and the Vision*, 2nd ed., ed. Tamara L. Brown, Gregory S. Parks, and Clarenda M. Phillips (Lexington: University Press of Kentucky, 2012), 189, 198–203.
6 Chambers et al., "Academic Achievement," 242.
7 Chambers et al., "Academic Achievement."
8 Chambers et al., "Academic Achievement," 201.
9 Chambers et al., "Academic Achievement."
10 Prudence L. Carter, *Keepin' It Real: School Success beyond Black and White* (Oxford: Oxford University Press, 2005), 137.
11 See Carter, *Keepin' It Real*, 50.
12 Carter, *Keepin' It Real*, 29; Stephen B. Knouse et al., "The Relation of College Internships, College Performance, and Subsequent Job Opportunity," *Journal of Employment Counseling* 36 (1999): 35; Cecil Douglas Johnson, "In Search of Traditional and Contemporary Career Success: What's an African American Male to Do?" (Ph.D. diss., University of Georgia, 2001).
13 Mark 3:25.
14 Michael J. Stern and Andrew S. Fullerton, "The Network Structure of Local and Extra-local Voluntary Participation: The Role of Core Social Networks," *Social Science Quarterly* 90 (2009): 553.
15 Reynaldo Anderson et al., "Black Greek-Letter Fraternities and Masculinities," in *Black Greek-Letter Organizations 2.0: New Directions in the Study of African American Fraternities*

and Sororities, ed. Matthew W. Hughey and Gregory S. Parks (Jackson: University Press of Mississippi, 2011), 114, 120–31; Rashawn Ray et al., "'Invictus' and 'If—': Meaning Making and the Shaping of a Collective Black Greek Identity," in Brown, Parks, and Phillips, *African American Fraternities and Sororities*, 445.

16 Anderson et al., "Black Greek-Letter Fraternities," 130; Lindsay H. Hoffman and Osei Appiah, "Assessing Cultural and Contextual Components of Social Capital: Is Civil Engagement in Peril?," 19 *Howard Journal of Communications* 19 (2008): 334.

17 Anderson et al., "Black Greek-Letter Fraternities," 130.

18 Cf. Matthew W. Hughey, "'Cuz I'm Black and My Hat's Real Low?' A Critique of Black Greeks as 'Educated Gangs,'" in *Black Greek-Letter Organizations in the Twenty-First Century: Our Fight Has Just Begun*, ed. Gregory S. Parks (Lexington: University Press of Kentucky, 2008), 385, 401–2.

19 Matthew W. Hughey, "'I Did It for the Brotherhood': Nonblack Members in Black Greek-Letter Organizations," in Parks, *Black Greek-Letter Organizations in the Twenty-First Century*, 313, 318–20.

20 Hughey, "'I Did It for the Brotherhood.'"

21 Cf. Kenneth I. Clarke Sr. and Tamara L. Brown, "Faith and Fraternalism: A Doctrinal and Empirical Analysis," in Hughey and Parks, *Black Greek-Letter Organizations 2.0*, 69, 70–71.

22 See Clarke and Brown, "Faith and Fraternalism."

23 See Brother P., "Ex-BGLO Union's Weblog," Wordpress, http://exbglounion.wordpress.com.

24 Rashawn Ray and Kevin W. Spragling, "Am I Not a Man and a Brother? Authenticating the Racial, Religious, and Masculine Dimensions of Brotherhood within Alpha," in *Alpha Phi Alpha and the Crisis of Organizational Identity: A Case Study within Black Greekdom*, ed. Gregory Parks and Stefan Bradley (Lexington: University Press of Kentucky, 2011), 207.

25 Ray and Spragling, "Am I Not a Man and a Brother?," 219.

26 Alan D. DeSantis and Marcus Coleman, "Not on My Line: Attitudes about Homosexuality in Black Fraternities," in Parks, *Black Greek-Letter Organizations in the Twenty-First Century*, 291.

27 Ray and Spragling, "Am I Not a Man and a Brother?," 225.

28 DeSantis and Coleman, "Not on My Line," 308.

29 Lynn A. Hampton and Ebony M. Duncan, "Identities and Inequalities: An Examination of the Role of Racial Identity in the Formation of Social Capital Inside a Voluntary Youth Organization," *Social Identities* 17 (2011): 477.

30 Hampton and Duncan, "Identities and Inequalities," 487.

31 See generally Hampton and Duncan, "Identities and Inequalities."

32 See generally Brian D. Christens et al., "Assessing Community Participation: Comparing Self-reported Participation Data with Organizational Attendance Records," *American Journal of Community Psychology* 57 (2016): 415–25.

33 Christens et al., "Assessing Community Participation."

34 See Christens et al., "Assessing Community Participation," 416.

35 Katie E. Corcoran et al., "Perceptions of Structural Injustice and Efficacy: Participation in Low/Moderate/High-Cost Forms of Collective Action," *Social Inquiry* 85 (2015): 429–61.

36 See Corcoran et al., "Perceptions of Structural Injustice and Efficacy."

37 See Corcoran et al., "Perceptions of Structural Injustice and Efficacy"; Jennifer M. Peach et al., "Recognizing Discrimination Explicitly while Denying It Implicitly: Implicit Social Identity Protection," *Journal of Experimental Social Psychology* 47 (2011): 283–92.

38 Corcoran et al., "Perceptions of Structural Injustice and Efficacy"; Peach et al., "Recognizing Discrimination Explicitly."

39 Jessica M. A. Vitak et al., "It's Complicated: Facebook Users' Political Participation in the 2008 Election," *Cyberpsychology, Behavior, and Social Networking* 14 (2011): 107–14.

40 Vitak et al., "It's Complicated," 107.

41 Vitak et al., "It's Complicated."
42 Donald R. Matthews and James Warren Prothro, *The Negroes and the New Southern Politics* (New York: Harcourt, Brace & World, 1966), 446.
43 Matthews and Prothro, *Negroes and the New Southern Politics.*
44 Paula D. McClain et al., "Group Membership, Group Identity, and Group Consciousness: Measures of Racial Identity Politics?," *Annual Review of Political Science* 12 (2009): 471, 474.
45 McClain et al., "Group Membership," 474.
46 McClain et al., "Group Membership," 475.
47 William E. Cross, *Shades of Black: Diversity in African American Identity* (Philadelphia: Temple University Press, 1991), 157.
48 Cross, *Shades of Black*, 158–59.
49 Cross, *Shades of Black*, 190–91.
50 Cross, *Shades of Black*, 159.
51 Cross, *Shades of Black*, 159.
52 Cross, *Shades of Black*, 207.
53 Cross, *Shades of Black*, 210.
54 Cross, *Shades of Black*, 212.
55 See Joe L. Lott II, "Racial Identity and Black Students' Perceptions of Community Outreach: Implications for Bonding and Social Capital," *Journal of Negro Education* 77 (2008): 3.
56 Jane Junn and Natalie Masuoka, "Identities in Context: Politicized Racial Group Consciousness among Asian American and Latino Youth," *Applied Developmental Science* 12 (2008): 93, 95.
57 McClain et al., "Group Membership," 476.
58 Junn and Masuoka, "Identities in Context," 95.
59 McClain et al., "Group Membership," 478 (citing sources); see also Arthur H. Miller et al., "Group Consciousness and Political Participation," *American Journal of Political Science* 25 (1981): 494, 503–4.
60 Shaun Harper, Lauretta F. Byars, and Thomas B. Jelke, "How Black Greek-Letter Organization Membership Affects College Adjustment and Undergraduate Outcomes," in *African American Fraternities and Sororities: The Legacy and the Vision*, ed. Tamara L. Brown, Gregory S. Parks, and Clarenda M. Phillips (Lexington: University Press of Kentucky, 2006), 135.
61 Harper, Byars, and Jelke, "How Black Greek-Letter Organization Membership Affects College Adjustment and Undergraduate Outcomes," 136.
62 Harper, Byars, and Jelke, "How Black Greek-Letter Organization Membership Affects College Adjustment and Undergraduate Outcomes," 137.
63 Shanette C. Porter and Gregory S. Parks, "The Realities and Consequences of Unconscious Anti-Black Bias among BGLO Members," in Hughey and Parks, *Black Greek-Letter Organizations 2.0*, 162, 165.
64 Porter and Parks, "Realities and Consequences," 163.
65 Porter and Parks, "Realities and Consequences," 165.
66 Porter and Parks, "Realities and Consequences," 168.
67 Porter and Parks, "Realities and Consequences."
68 Porter and Parks, "Realities and Consequences."
69 Harold L. Angle and James L. Perry, "An Empirical Assessment of Organizational Commitment and Organizational Effectiveness," *Administrative Science Quarterly* 26 (1981): 1, 2.
70 Angle and Perry, "Empirical Assessment of Organizational Commitment."
71 Angle and Perry, "Empirical Assessment of Organizational Commitment."
72 See generally Bernard M. Bass, "From Transactional to Transformational Leadership: Learning to Share the Vision," *Organizational Dynamics* 18 (1990): 19.

73   See generally Peter Y. T. Sun and Marc H. Anderson, "The Importance of Attributional Complexity for Transformational Leadership Studies," *Journal of Management Studies* 49 (2012): 1001.

74   See generally Voyce Li et al., "The Divergent Effects of Transformational Leadership on Individual and Team Innovation," *Group and Organization Management* 41 (2016): 66.

75   Philip Davies, "The Cassandra Complex: How to Avoid Generating a Corporate Vision That No One Buys Into," in *Success in Sight: Visioning*, ed. Andrew Kakabadse et al. (London: Thomson, 1998), 103–23.

76   See generally Pamela Jean Springer, "The Relationship between Learned Helplessness and Work Performance in Registered Nurses" (Ph.D. diss., University of Idaho, 1999).

77   See generally Laurence J. Peter and Raymond Hull, *The Peter Principle: Why Things Always Go Wrong* (New York: Harper, 2011).

78   See generally Gautam Mukunda, *Indispensable: When Leaders Really Matter* (Boston: Harvard Business Review Press, 2012).

79   Mukunda, *Indispensable*.

80   Mukunda, *Indispensable*; see also Gautam Mukunda, "Trump Is about to Test Our Theory of When Leaders Actually Matter," *Harvard Business Review*, November 9, 2016; Zira Kalan, "Are Barack Obama and Mitt Romney Good Leaders?," *U.S. News*, October 5, 2012.

81   William Shakespeare, *Macbeth*.

INDEX

ABOUT THE AUTHORS

Gregory S. Parks is Associate Dean of Research, Public Engagement, & Faculty Development and Professor of Law at Wake Forest University School of Law. He is a trained lawyer and social scientist, and his work focuses on race, law, social science, and popular culture.

Matthew W. Hughey is Associate Professor of Sociology at the University of Connecticut. He holds affiliate positions at Nelson Mandela University (South Africa), the University of Barcelona (Spain), and the University of Cambridge (England). His research and teaching concentrate on the formation and function of race and racism